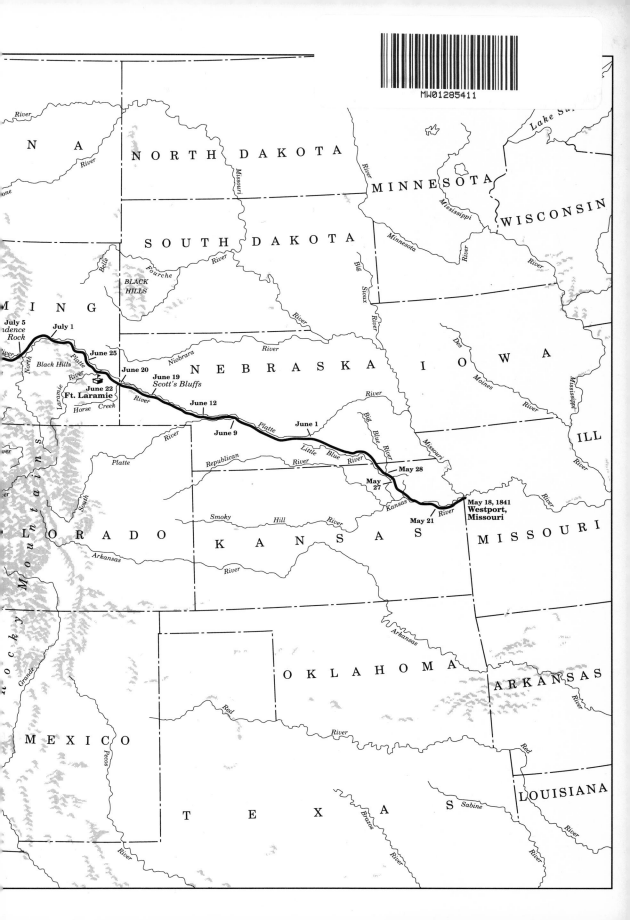

The Bidwell-Bartleson Party

The Bidwell-Bartleson Party

1841 California Emigrant Adventure

*The Documents and Memoirs
of the Overland Pioneers*

Edited and with an Introduction by

Doyce B. Nunis, Jr.

WESTERN TANAGER PRESS
Santa Cruz, California
1991

© 1991 by Doyce B. Nunis, Jr.

Maps by Eagle Eye Maps
Cover: *Platt River, Nebraska* by Albert Bierstadt, from the Manoogian Collection.
Cover design by Lynn Piquett
Typography by TypaGraphix

ISBN: 0-934136-32-7
Library of Congress Card Catalog Number: 88-51900

Printed in the United States America on acid-free paper.

Western Tanager Press
1111 Pacific Avenue
Santa Cruz, CA 95060

For my
MOTHER AND FATHER
who brought me and my brother
overland to the Golden State
by automobile in 1938

An event which will probably be regarded as of some importance in the future history of California, was the arrival in Nov. last year [1841] of an exploring party, from the United States. This consisted of thirty-one men, and one woman and child from Independence a town on the western frontier of Missouri . . . they came in carriages to within about 200 miles of this place and probably would have come in them, the whole distance, had they not been unfortunate in not being able to find the proper pass of the snowy mountains. This company arrived in good health, without accidents, and without much difficulty at the house in which I am writing, without any other guide than a letter I had sent them the year previous. . . . If any proof were wanting of the unprecedented energy and enterprise of the people of our western frontier I think this would be sufficient; their object was to see if California was indeed, the fine country it had been represented, and with the ulterior object of emigrating to it if it should meet their expectations. They were well received by the Governor, and particularly by the military commandant, and assured that all facilities will be afforded them for the acquirement of lands.

JOHN MARSH TO COMMODORE THOMAS AP CATESBY JONES
NOVEMBER 25, 1842
Manuscript in Bancroft Library,
University of California, Berkeley

Table of Contents

ILLUSTRATIONS

Acknowledgements

My interest in the history of the Bidwell-Bartleson party spans some thirty years. In 1960 I began my first research effort related to that pioneer overland band. Two years later the fruits of that endeavor were published in *Josiah Belden, 1841 Overland California Pioneer: His Memoir and Early Letters* by the Talisman Press, Georgetown, California, a work now long out of print. In the intervening years, I have continued to keep an eye on the subject, always with the hope of producing a more definitive study.

The latter opportunity came rather unexpectedly when I was approached by Hal Morris, the publisher and proprietor of Western Tanager Press in Santa Cruz, two years ago to undertake a new edition of the famed journal-letter written by John Bidwell that described the 1841 party's overland trip. Happily, I was able to persuade him to broaden the scope of the planned publication to include all known firsthand accounts of the 1841 California emigration, as well as select supporting documents. By coincidence, the Los Angeles Corral of Westerners joined in the enterprise, sponsoring a special edition of the work as their *Brand Book 18,* along with a trade edition for Western Tanager Press. The end result is this book. I am grateful to both parties for making this publication possible.

In bringing this manuscript to completion, many debts have been incurred over the past three decades from individuals who have been of immeasurable assistance in my research. Four of these valued friends and esteemed colleagues are deceased, but my debt to them remains: James de T. Abajian, former librarian, California Historical Society, San Francisco; Rev. John F. Bannon, S.J., professor emeritus, Saint Louis University; Rev. William L. Davis, S.J., archivist emeritus, Gonzaga University, Spokane, Washington; and Dale L. Morgan of the Bancroft Library, University of California, Berkeley.

For publication permissions, I am indebted to the following institutions: Bancroft Library, University of California, Berkeley; California State Library, Sacramento; Loyola University Press, Chicago; Oregon Historical Society, Portland; Rosenbach Museum and Library, Philadelphia; and Yale University Library, New Haven. For permission to reproduce photographic portraits from their collections, I am grateful to the Bancroft Library; Brigham Young University Library, Provo, Utah; California State Library; California Department of Parks and Recreation, Sutter's Fort, Sacramento; Colorado Historical Society, Denver; Jesuit Missouri Province Archives, St. Louis; Santa Clara University Archives;

and the Society of California Pioneers, San Francisco. The Jesuit Missouri Province Archives provided four drawings depicting scenes on the overland trail to Soda Springs by Father Nicholas Point, S.J., and the Department of Special Collections, University Library, Washington State University, Pullman, granted permission to reproduce ten additional Point drawings from the Pierre Jean De Smet Papers. The maps are the handiwork of Eagle Eye Maps.

I wish to add my deep appreciation for the research assistance so generously afforded me by Ms. Kris White, Manuscript Librarian, Oregon Historical Society. I am doubly grateful to Ms. Annegret Ogden, Reference Librarian, Bancroft Library, and Ms. Kathleen C. Eustis, California Section, California State Library, for their unfailing help. My longtime friend Gary Kurutz of the California State Library assisted me with one annoying bibliographical problem. Lastly, a special note of thanks is tendered to Ms. Nancy Merz, Associate Archivist, Jesuit Missouri Province Archives, St. Louis, and Ms. Tina A. Oswald, Manuscript Librarian, Washington State University, Pullman, for their help in obtaining copies and permissions for the use of the Nicholas Point drawings.

To those past and present, to each, my gratitude.

Introduction

In 1841 the Bidwell-Bartleson party made the first planned overland emigration west to California—with one contingent splitting off for Oregon. Nineteen ninety-one marks the 150th anniversary of that remarkable pioneering journey. This volume, which brings together for the first time all known memoirs and documents relating to that epic trip, is offered as a fitting memorial and tribute to those courageous and hardy emigrants who pointed the way for hundreds of thousands who followed them in the ensuing decades to the Golden State or to Oregon.

One does not need to look far for the obvious influence the Bidwell-Bartleson party exerted on overland emigration, mostly due to John Bidwell's published journal-letter (Chapter One). In 1842, 125 emigrants made the trek to Oregon; in 1843, 875 followed, while 38 headed for California. The following year, 1844, witnessed 1,475 Oregon-bound pioneers, with 53 opting for California. In 1845, some 2,500 emigrants settled in Oregon, and California received 260. The next year, 1,500 emigrated to California overland, with 1,200 going to Oregon.

Even during the two-year Mexican War, emigrants still flocked to California, 450 in 1847 and 400 in 1848. Oregon, after the 1846 boundary settlement with Britain, attracted 4,000 in 1847 and 1,300 in 1848. But the gold rush would radically change emigrant patterns. By 1860, California could enumerate 200,335 overland emigrants, but Oregon could only point to 53,062. Both figures, nevertheless, are impressive.[1]

The year 1840, on the eve of the Bidwell-Bartleson party's trek westward, was one of triumph and turmoil throughout the world. In the Pacific it witnessed the final surrender of the Maori chiefs and their acceptance of British sovereignty in New Zealand. In Europe the long-fought Carlist Wars in Spain came to an end, but trouble was rife in the Middle East. The Quadruple Alliance (Russia, Britain, Prussia, and Austria) threw their support to Turkey in an endeavor to solve the hereditary possession of Egypt, claimed by Mehemet Ali. By September the British launched a military offensive that forced Mehemet Ali to agree to what became known as the Treaty of London. At the same time, the prolonged Afghan War was also terminated when the Afghan forces tendered their surrender to the British. Indeed, British imperial power was triumphant for all the world to see.

On the other side of the Atlantic, the United States was gripped by a series

1

of growing crises. Foremost was the increasing fervor of the anti-slavery movement. This led to the formation of a new political movement, the Liberty Party,
which put forward its own presidential candidate, James G. Birney, in the 1840
presidential election. Although he garnered little more than 7,000 votes, it was
an ominous sign, for all of his votes were drawn from the free states. When
the ballots were counted on December 2, the incumbent Democrat, President
Martin Van Buren, was defeated by the Whig nominee, William Henry Harrison of Ohio, famed for his defeat and slaying of Tecumseh at the Battle of
Tippecanoe during the War of 1812. His campaign for election was the proto-
type of what became standard practices for those subsequently running for
the office of president: slogans, hoopla, and personal involvement. Not only
did the Whigs carry the presidency, they also, for the first time since 1800, earned
a Congressional majority. But the key point about the 1840 presidential election was the fact that anti-slavery sentiment now was a factor to be reckoned
with — it would be a recurring problem that would interject itself into national
politics until the Civil War.

On an equally distressing note, the nation, now composed of twenty-six
states, was trying to recoup from the Panic of 1837 — America's first great depression. The economic crisis had been brought about by reckless speculation. The
impact was swift and direct. The price of cotton fell by almost 50 percent; bank
after bank suspended specie payments. The sale of public lands, an essential
source of federal revenue, fell dramatically. The southern and western states
were hit the hardest.

In sharp contrast, the following year, 1841, was fairly placid and unmomen-
tous. It was marked, however, by one singular event in the United States. When
President Harrison gave his inaugural address on March 4, it proved the longest
one on record. That he gave it in a pouring rain proved fatal. Exactly thirty
days later, on April 4, he died of pneumonia, age sixty-eight. He was the first
president to die in office and to be succeeded by the vice president, in this
instance, John Tyler of Virginia. The transition of power was bitterly contested
and a number of important constitutional questions were eventually settled,
the most important being that a vice president becomes fully vested with all
the powers of the presidency by right of succession. That struggle, compounded
by Tyler's fiscal policies aimed at reviving the nation's faltering economy, still
reeling from the effects of the Panic of 1837, produced considerable political
turmoil. Indeed, all but one member of Tyler's cabinet, inherited from Harrison, abruptly resigned en masse on September 11, 1841, in open defiance.
For the ensuing three years, there was considerable flux in the cabinet due to
politics, especially from the invigorated Democratic Party, greatly influenced
by John C. Calhoun, the senior senator from South Carolina.

It was in this milieu that events began to unfold on the far frontier of the

United States during the years 1840–1841 that would lead to the ultimate acquisition of the Oregon Country in 1846 and the Mexican Cession in 1848, which included California and the Southwest. The key to this extraordinary westward expansion of the nation began with the formation of the Western Emigration Society in western Missouri in 1841. Prior to the formation of the society, only thirteen Americans had emigrated overland to Oregon, in 1840, and only a handful of missionaries previously; none to Mexican California. The society would irrevocably alter that; it would point the way to westward migration.

The Western Emigration Society was the result of three main factors, among others. Foremost was the debilitating effect the Panic of 1837 had on Missouri and its neighboring areas, the territories of Iowa and Arkansas. A second was the growing awareness among frontiersmen of the attractive prospect of settlement in the Oregon Territory. A third, one which was entirely new in 1841, was the high expectations one might realize in Mexican California. The idea of emigration to both, however, was the stimulus behind the formation of the Western Emigration Society, the object being a more economically secure life. In the realization of that goal, one man made a noteworthy contribution. He literally wrote, inadvertently, the first overland trail guide, one that would inspire others to emigrate to the Pacific slope. His name was John Bidwell.

John Bidwell has been hailed by his principal biographer as the "Prince of California Pioneers."[2] That appellation is well deserved, for it was earned by six decades of important contributions to the development of his adopted state. From the very outset of his arrival in Mexican California, November 4, 1841, he began to make his mark on the future thirty-first state in the Union. While clerking for John A. Sutter at Bodega Bay, his first job in California, Bidwell commenced a lengthy letter to a Missouri friend, Elam Brown. As he later wrote to historian Hubert H. Bancroft in 1884, "I promised items of our journey and of the country here &c." He categorically stated, "I never wrote it for publication . . . [but the letter] happened to get into the hands of a printer in Missouri."[3]

Dated March 30, 1842, Bidwell's long and detailed narrative subsequently found its way east. It has been thought in the past that it was carried back to Missouri by Joseph B. Chiles, who had been a fellow member in the overland trek westward. But that appears in doubt, for in Bidwell's account there is an entry for "August '42." Since Chiles departed in the spring of 1842, April to be exact, this would rule him out as the courier. The internal date of August 1842 would also imply that the long letter probably did not reach Missouri until early 1843 at best. But published it was, by some unknown printer either in Independence, Liberty, or Weston.

However, the internal date of "August '42" in Bidwell's letter is puzzling. Is it an error on the part of the writer, a typographical mistake, or an insertion supplied by the printer? It seems plausible that Bidwell could have taken from March 30 to August (or later) to complete his lengthy letter. Because he was extracting from his manuscript journal, he probably did take longer to complete the letter. If true, then he commenced his letter on March 30 and completed it some months later, the exact date unknown.

If the "August '42" is correct, then two additional questions arise. How did the letter reach Missouri? Certainly, the only known overland eastbound travelers in 1842 returning to Missouri were ten members of the Bidwell-Bartleson party who made the initial overland trip, among them Chiles and Charles Hopper. The latter were entrusted with a letter, dated April 5, 1842, from Dr. John Marsh to his parents living in Massachusetts. These returnees departed shortly after, taking the southern route to Santa Fe, then the Santa Fe Trail north to Independence, which they reached on September 9.[4] It has been accepted by some historians that this party's departure and arrival dates would have accommodated the conveyance of Bidwell's account written to his Missouri friend, Elam Brown. If such was the case, then a publication date for the journal in 1843 would have been quite feasible. However, if this was not the happenstance, then the year 1844 would appear more acceptable. That would mean Bidwell's letter was not received until well into the year 1843 or early 1844. Would Bidwell have entrusted it to a stranger, or would he send it by someone he knew, someone who was returning to Missouri?

A possible courier may have been Lansford W. Hastings, who led an overland party first to Oregon, then to California, in 1843. He decided to journey east in January 1844. Bidwell became "well acquainted with him," and on Hastings's return trip to Missouri, Bidwell might well have dispatched the letter by him.[5] This conjecture would imply that the journal was published in 1844. But the time gap and the silence of Bidwell, Chiles, Hopper, and Hastings on this matter are no help at all in sorting out the question of the transmittal of Bidwell's letter to a Missouri friend.

A major key to this perplexing puzzle is Bidwell's reference to the following in his letter:

> There is now a Bishop at Monteray [sic], lately come from Mexico, come to revive the missions—but the people all objected to his remaining in the country. The consequence would be perhaps the people would have to pay tithes. (August '42) the Bishop has not yet arrived on this side of the Bay [of San Francisco].[6]

This reference was to Francisco García Diego y Moreno, the first bishop of the Californias (Upper and Lower), who had served as a missionary in the territory, 1831–1835. The Mexican-born prelate was consecrated in Mexico City, October 4, 1840. He did not reach San Diego by ship until December 10, 1841, a year later. After a brief stay there, he decided to relocate to Santa Barbara, arriving January 11, 1842. This became his episcopal seat. The bishop remained at Mission Santa Barbara until 1844, except for a brief trip to nearby Mission Santa Inés in September 1842 and a trip south during March–April 1843 to visit the missions of San Gabriel, San Fernando, and San Buenaventura on a pastoral, confirmation tour.

It was not until early May 1844 that he commenced his first visit to northern California. His itinerary included calls at Missions Santa Inés, May 4; La Purísima, May 7; San Luis Obispo, May 13; and San Antonio, May 19, en route to Monterey, which his party reached on May 26. After a modest civic reception and confirmation there, he visited Missions Santa Cruz, June 15; San Juan Bautista, June 21; Santa Clara, June 30; and San José, July 11, as well as the pueblo church in that town. On July 16, 1844, the party reached Mission Dolores, near the Presidio of San Francisco. This was as far north as Bishop García Diego traveled. He did not attempt to visit Mission San Rafael and San Francisco Solano, because Mariano Guadalupe Vallejo had made it known that the bishop was not welcome in the region of the territory he dominated. Returning overland to Santa Barbara, the bishop confirmed again at two of the missions he had visited on the trek north. His longest pastoral visitation was completed on his return to Mission Santa Barbara, August 10, 1844.[7]

One important point needs to be made concerning the bishop's pastoral tour. Church canon law in the nineteenth century (still applicable today) required that when a bishop made an episcopal visit to any of the churches under his jurisdiction *he must inspect and sign the parochial registers*. This canonical requirement is referred to as the *Auto de Visíta* in Spanish. Thus, on June 10, 1844, Bishop García Diego examined the baptismal register at Mission San Carlos Borroméo near Monterey and duly signed his name. This is the only such autographed entry in the parochial records at that mission. He did likewise at Mission Dolores on July 16. Since the bishop's signature appears in all the mission registers from Santa Inés to Dolores during the period of May to July 1844, this is proof positive that he did not undertake a pastoral visit in 1842 to northern California; that visit was made in 1844.

These data cast serious doubts on Bidwell's journal entry cited above. Nevertheless, he was right about the prospect of tithes being levied on the Californians. On February 4, 1842, Bishop García Diego issued a pastoral letter outlining his plans for the Diocese of the Californias, plans which were to be financed by tithes. That prospect alienated Vallejo, and many others, and motivated him to warn the bishop not to venture north or east of San Francisco Bay on his 1844 pastoral junket. On the other hand, one thing should be obvious:

"August '42" does not correlate with the facts. Thus, Bidwell is mistaken in respect to the bishop's presence in Monterey in 1842. Nor had the bishop come to "revive the missions"; instead, his responsibility was to establish and implement a new diocese.

On the other hand, if Bidwell's entry is correct, then the date used in parentheses should read August '44. (The '42 may be a misreading of Bidwell's holographic manuscript, long lost, on the part of the printer.) Since the bishop had been at Mission Dolores in mid-July 1844, Bidwell was probably under the impression that he would travel on across the bay, not knowing that Vallejo had negated that prospect. If, then, this date is correct, the following conclusions can be drawn. First, Bidwell took over two years to write his letter to his friend, Elam Brown. Second, his narrative could not have been published until the late winter of 1844–45 at the earliest, more likely 1845.

In sum, the following puzzles remain unsolved in respect to Bidwell's letter. When did he write it; when was it completed? When and by whom was it dispatched east to Missouri? Who was the publisher; where was the place; and what was the year the long letter was printed?

Bidwell's original published account contains another puzzling clue as to the date when it was written. He carefully detailed the weather from November 4, 1841, to April 2, 1842, without missing a single day (pp. 23–24). He follows this with the comment: "From March, the rainy season gradually decreases, ceases entirely about the middle of May. During the summer months, heat is intense . . . " (p. 24). Then he confounds the reader in cataloguing the resources of the countryside with this statement: "Apple and peach trees beautifully arrayed, what time apples are ripe, I cannot say, but presume in June or July" (p. 25).

From these remarks, it would appear that references to the post-April 2, 1842, date had been gleaned from old-time residents who informed him about the weather pattern from May through July. Accepting that as such, it is quite probable that his letter was completed prior to May, mayhap as early as sometime in April, for he had not personally yet experienced a California summer or harvested an apple, since he only arrived in the previous early fall. But that supposition appears untenable because, once again, Bidwell confounds the situation by writing: "I have not seen a mosquito here this summer . . ." (p. 31). This remark clearly implies that the journal-letter was not completed until sometime during the summer of 1842.

Another facet to the puzzling circumstances surrounding the Bidwell narrative is that George McKinstry, Jr., an 1846 overland emigrant, carried with him that year a copy of the published Bidwell pamphlet. That very fact means that Bidwell's published letter became California's first overland guidebook. That copy, the only one surviving, is in the Bancroft Library, University of California, Berkeley. In that copy there is boldly inscribed on the preface page, which is the first page in this copy (it lacks its wrappers and title page), "Geo McKinstry Jr. En Route for California, 1846." There is also the marginal note for the Bidwell entry for "Saturday, [July] 3rd" (p. 7): "We camped at the spring Monday, July 6th, 1846." Again, at the bottom of another page (p. 13) of the pamphlet is this notation: "We cooked our supper & breakfast with fires made from the remains of these wagons. McKinstry, Jr." Thus it is abundantly clear that McKinstry was traveling with this copy in hand. The question arises, would that pamphlet be available in 1846 if it had been published in 1843 or 1844? Does it not indicate that the pamphlet was published later, say in 1845?

The last word in this matter belongs to Bidwell. In 1890 he wrote to a correspondent: "'. . . this journal—never written or intended for publication—was printed without my knowledge in pamphlet form, and found its way to California and came into the hands of Dr. Marsh as early as 1843 or 1844.'"[8] Was that recollection penned fifty-eight years after the supposed completion of his journal-letter correct? The reader must decide.

However, because of the publication of Bidwell's journal, the first planned overland emigrant party has been dubbed the Bidwell-Bartleson party, and rightly so. Bidwell provides us the best account of that overland trek, which was led by the train's captain, John Bartleson, the latter's only claim to fame.

Fortunately, one copy of that first printing has survived. As noted above, it belonged to George McKinstry, Jr., an 1846 overland emigrant, and found its way into H. H. Bancroft's historical materials now housed in the Bancroft Library. Unfortunately, the copy lacks its original wrappers and title page. Thus there is no way of ascertaining for certain the printer, place of publication, and year.

Unhappily for the cause of history, the travel journal which Bidwell maintained from the outset of the trip has never been discovered, if it still survives. It certainly existed, for at the beginning of his published account, he remarked: "I am compelled to abridge my Journal and likewise a description of the country so far as I have been able to travel." Happily, the loss of that original manuscript journal is compensated for in the printed text of Bidwell's March 30, 1842, narrative letter, which hereinafter will be referred to as his *Journal*. It is this version, based on the Bancroft Library copy, which comprises the main element in this book. It is the fulcrum on which all else is centered.

Bidwell's *Journal* is the chief documentary source which details the rigors of the first planned overland emigrant party determined on reaching California. Utilizing the central route to the Pacific Coast, in 1841 the Bidwell-Bartleson party blazed a trail that subsequently became the American highway to Eldorado.

Prior to 1841, other emigrants had made overland journeys to the Pacific slope. The first northern-route emigration across the plains was undertaken by Jason and Daniel Lee's small missionary band in 1834, and in 1836, by the

Whitman-Spaulding party. Their destination was Oregon. In the wake of these two missionary bands, in 1839 a fragment of the "Peoria party," including Thomas J. Farnham, of whom we will hear more, made the trip. But the emigrant number was small. Beginning in 1829, from Santa Fe, a number of trading caravans annually ventured to California via the southern route, using the Old Spanish Trail or variants thereof. Around this same time, fur-trade parties traveled these same trails. And a few of the men who made that journey became permanent California residents.[9]

The trail taken by the Bidwell-Bartleson company, after leaving what later became known as the Oregon Trail, was somewhat similar to that etched by two previous fur-trapper expeditions. Jedediah S. Smith had made the trip in 1826 and 1827, and Joseph R. Walker, employed by Captain Benjamin L. E. Bonneville, in 1833.[10] However, the Bidwell-Bartleson party was unique. As one historian declared, its significance lay in the fact that it "was the entering wedge for the new type of migration to California": determined pioneers bent on permanent settlement.[11]

Captivated by excited reports on the wonders and opportunities rife in Mexican California, in late winter of 1840 the Western Emigration Society was established in frontier Missouri. One of its earliest recruits was young John Bidwell. Chief propagandist in urging Americans to head for the "land of perennial spring and boundless fertility" was Antoine Robidoux, a longtime trapper and trader in the transmontane west. Having only recently returned from a trip to California over the southern route, he waxed eloquent on the country he had visited.[12] Robidoux's vivid portrait was soon seconded by Dr. John Marsh, a California resident, who had lived in Independence, Missouri, before heading south, first for Santa Fe in 1835, then California in 1836. He wrote several letters to Missouri friends from his rancho at the foot of Mt. Diablo in what today is Contra Costa County, east of Oakland.[13] Joseph B. Chiles, who joined the 1841 emigrant train, recalled that William Baldridge, a fellow party member, "had been corresponding with Dr. Marsh whose descriptive letters of Cal[ifornia] and its climate and resources, had awakened in him a great desire to see the country . . . "[14]

In addition to waxing on the benefits of the countryside, Marsh also suggested a plausible overland route. He based his suggestions on the prior experiences of the American fur man, Jedediah S. Smith; Hudson's Bay Company explorer and trader, Peter S. Ogden, who made a comparable journey in 1827; and Joseph R. Walker's 1833–1834 travels. From these he arrived at a pretty good idea of the country that stretched between the Missouri River and the Sierra Nevada. In essence, Marsh "figured out a route, which . . . was direct, with good pasturage and water all the way."[15] He dispatched copies of the route to three former Missouri friends, Baldridge, Michael C. Nye, and Samuel C. Owens, all of Independence. Marsh had operated a store in that Missouri frontier town from 1833 to 1835 before his departure for Santa Fe, later California. While keeping store there, he also became acquainted with John A. Sutter, who finally reached California in 1839; John Bartleson, destined to lead the overland party; and Elias Barnett.[16] All of this information, especially Marsh's letters, found printed exposition in the local Missouri press. Within a month, some 500 pledges to undertake the trek west were received by the newly formed society. Among that number were Baldridge, Barnett, Bartleson, Bidwell, and Nye.

One St. Louis newspaper, reporting early in 1841 on a subsequent meeting of 58 Jackson County residents gathered to make plans for the western journey, heralded the advantages and challenge awaiting the bold and adventuresome:

> The climate is salubrious and delightful — the soil rich — the natural productions various — and all the means of a pleasant and comfortable subsistence afforded in abundance. A glorious era is, no doubt, dawning in those regions so favored by nature; and they who first take possession have all before them to choose. To the young, the bouyant, and the enterprizing the field is full of promise. They may not only grow rich by skill, industry and perseverance; but may achieve the splendid fame of laying deep and broad the foundation of an empire![17]

But popular enthusiasm soon waned. Thomas J. Farnham, a member of the Peoria party that ventured to Oregon in 1839, returned east after first visiting Monterey and Santa Barbara. Disillusioned by that experience, particularly the harsh treatment meted out by the California authorities against a number of Americans and English arrested in April 1840 as suspected revolutionaries, the infamous "Graham Affair," Farnham made no bones about his disdain for the Mexican province. His views found ready exposition in 1841 by several disparaging letters that were dutifully, if not gleefully, reprinted in Missouri newspapers.[18] Bidwell later wrote: "Just at this time [1841], and it overthrew our project completely — was published the letters of Farnham in the New York papers and republished in all the papers of the frontier at the instigation of the Weston [Missouri] merchants and others." In calculating terms, the hostile press cautioned: ". . . fellow citizens, if you really wish to lead a quiet, industrious, useful life, if you wish to help on the country to which you owe your birth . . . stay at home."[19] The resolution of the pledged members in the newly formed emigrant society withered in the face of Farnham's bleak report and the severe admonition of the local press. But Bidwell was not dissuaded; he remained firm.

When the appointed May 9th rendezvous at Sapling Grove was at hand, only Bidwell appeared. Gradually, a little over a tenth of the original pledged number finally congregated. Among them were Marsh's friends, Baldridge, Barnett, Bartleson, and Nye, as well as Bidwell.[20]

Born at Ripley, in western New York state, August 5, 1819, John Bidwell was the descendant of English pioneers who emigrated to colonial Connecticut some time before 1640. The family name was derived from Biddulph Castle, one of the oldest castles in Norfolk County, England. Biddulph was a Saxon word that translates as War Wolf. From it are derived a variety of names in use today: Bidwell, Bidewell, and Bedwell. Thus Bidwell's ancestry can be traced to Norfolk County.

John's father, Abram Bidwell, was born in Stillwater, New York, in 1769. He married quite young, in 1786, a girl of his own age, Abigail Benedict. Subsequently, the couple moved to Canada, settling near Montreal. The War of 1812 forced a crisis. Abram and his eldest son, David, were conscripted into the British army. Determined on avoiding such service, Abram deserted and made his way back to the United States. In the meantime, he arranged what was thought to be safe return passage to obtain the release of David from army service. But the safe conduct proved false; Abram was arrested for desertion. His luck held: he was able to effect an escape and reach the safety once more of his family.

Not long after this harrowing experience, Abram became a widower with seven children. Fortunately, he met Clarissa Griggs (b. 1778), a well-educated woman who had been a teacher. After a proper courtship, they were married. Following a brief residence in Vermont, the family moved to Chautauqua County in western New York. Here the couple's children were born. John was the second born amongst their brood of five: in all, two daughters and three sons.

One characteristic which dominated Abram Bidwell's life was his restlessness. He could not stay put too long in one place. When John was ten, the family was transplanted to Erie, Pennsylvania; then in 1834 to western Ohio, near Greenville. No doubt his mother's educational background resulted in John receiving a solid education himself. Determined on learning, at the age of seventeen he enrolled in Kingsville Academy in Astabula County, Ohio. He saved his earnings to pay the tuition and, to avoid the cost of transportation, walked 300 miles from his home in Drake County to the academy. But his tenure was brief; his father's serious illness cut short his study. He returned home to help the financially strapped family. To earn a living, he stunned his neighbors by passing a very difficult teacher's examination which earned his appointment to the principalship of Kingsville Academy, near Greenville.[21]

From the age of eighteen, Bidwell supported himself either by farming or teaching school. And like his peripatetic father, he, too, had wanderlust. As he later recalled, in the spring of 1839, he "conceived a desire to see the great prairies of the West . . . " So he set out, making his way first to Cincinnati, down the Ohio by steamboat to St. Louis, and then overland to Burlington in Iowa Territory. There he took up some land in Platte County, which had recently been acquired by Missouri. His "means being all spent, [he] was obliged to accept the first thing that was offered and began teaching in the county about five miles from the town of Weston, which was on the north side of the Missouri

River and about four miles above Fort Leavenworth in Kansa Territory."[22] He became a country school teacher.

His arrival on the frontier was opportune. The prospects of a major emigrant party bound for California was in the air. The formation of the Western Emigration Society could not help but attract young Bidwell. That attraction was reinforced by his personal encounter with Antoine Robidoux. In later recollections he explained the results of that meeting:

> His description of California was in the superlative degree favorable, so much so that I resolved if possible to see that wonderful land, and with others helped to get up a meeting at Weston and invited him to make a statement before it in regard to this wonderful country. Roubideaux [sic] described it as one of perennial spring and boundless fertility, and laid stress on the countless thousands of wild horses and cattle . . . . He said that the Spanish [Mexican] authorities were most friendly, and that the people were the most hospitable on the globe; that you could travel all over California and it would cost you nothing for horses or food. Even the Indians were friendly. His description of the country made it seem like a Paradise.[23]

What more could a peripatetic youth want? Bidwell fell — hook, line, and sinker. He was California-bound from that moment on.

Because of the lack of response to previous plans for a much larger company of recruits, the emigrant company was not formally organized until May 18 near the banks of the Kansas River. There in a town hall–style meeting, the diehard would-be emigrants elected Talbot H. Green, president, and John Bidwell, secretary. After adopting rules and regulations for conduct on the trail, John Bartleson was elected captain. The choice was under duress: he threatened to pull out with his contingent if not elected party commander.[24]

All of the emigrants were green recruits; none had ever traveled west of the Missouri settled frontier. Bidwell remarked, somewhat inaccurately, "Our ignorance of the route was complete. We knew that California lay west, and that was the extent of our knowledge."[25]

Fortunately for the expedition, news was received that a party of Jesuit missionaries was preparing to travel west under the guidance of Thomas F. Fitzpatrick, an experienced trapper who knew the proper route to the Rockies.[26] Fortunately, the California-bound emigrants associated themselves under his leadership for that portion of the trip that took them across South Pass into present-day Idaho. Father Pierre Jean De Smet, the leader of the Jesuit missionaries, when the two groups split, one heading north, the other southwest, commented: "They who had started, purely with the design of seeking their fortune in California, and [who] were pursuing their enterprise with the constancy which is characteristic of Americans," broke away at Soda Springs.[27]

Up until Soda Springs, the Bidwell-Bartleson party followed in the wake of the Fitzpatrick-led Jesuit company. It traveled along what was destined to be christened the Oregon Trail. Bidwell described that passage succinctly in his *Journal*, mentioning the famous landmarks which made lasting impressions on all trail travelers: Courthouse Rock, Chimney Rock, Scott's Bluff, Fort Laramie, and Independence Rock. But the California emigrants were strictly on their own after leaving Soda Springs.

Having parted company with the missionaries and their experienced guide on August 11, the Bidwell-Bartleson party headed southwest.[28] Ignorant of the exact trail, the company was not without some knowledge of the terrain which lay ahead of them as various party members testify, including Josiah Belden, Bidwell, Chiles, Nicholas Dawson, and Nye. Certainly some information was supplied by Thomas Fitzpatrick, the Jesuits' guide. Although he had never undertaken the California journey, he was intimately acquainted with Jedediah Smith and Joseph Walker, companion mountain men who had previously made the trip.[29]

Antoine Robidoux, one of the chief inspirations for the formation of the overland party, undoubtedly supplied what information he had from his years of traversing the transmontane west. In 1837, accompanied by his brother, Louis, he had made the overland journey to California from Santa Fe and, like Fitzpatrick, had an acquaintance with trappers who had been with Smith and Walker on their far western travels.[30]

The exploits of the mountain men were not unknown to the company. Under date of July 5, while the travelers were at Independence Rock, Bidwell observed in his *Journal* that the landmark had been named by Captain William Sublette, who had once celebrated the 4th there. In a later recollection, Bidwell refers to William Sublette's taking the first wagon train across to South Pass in 1830. Jedediah Smith had been a longtime associate of Sublette prior to 1830, and as a partner in the Smith, Jackson, and Sublette fur company had undertaken his two California trips in 1826 and 1827, which have been alluded to. The activities of that famous fur-trade partnership were reported in detail in various newspaper accounts and in official reports to the federal government.[31]

Father De Smet in one of his letters mentions Bonneville's 1833 expedition in the transmontane region which was led by Joseph Walker. Nicholas Dawson, an emigrant member, later echoed this by referring to "Joe Walker's" California trip, a trip undertaken while in Bonneville's employ. Washington Irving popularized that venture in a book published in 1837.[32]

A map in the possession of Elam Brown, shown to Bidwell by his Missouri friend, cast some light on the terrain, even though it was inaccurate. Bidwell records, under entry of September 29 in his *Journal:* "Traveled about 20 miles, course of the stream was WNW. According to the map Mary's river ran WSW.

Strong doubts were entertained about this being Mary's river." Nicholas Dawson subsequently observed that the Bidwell-Bartleson party "had some old maps." The maps, however, only proved to be illusory.[33]

By far the best information of a practical route the company could follow came from the letters of Dr. John Marsh, already mentioned. In his letter to Nye, one which was published in the local Missouri press, Marsh described a plausible trail west, urging the recipient "to follow it over the Rockies and Sierras to California, and to come direct to his rancho," situated at the foot of Mt. Diablo. Chiles recalled that the company "had learned through Dr. Marsh's letters the latitude for San Francisco Bay, and they thought the sun sufficient to guide them." Furthermore, among the resolutions adopted at a February 1, 1841, meeting of the Western Emigration Society read: "That Marsh's route is believed to be the best by which to cross the mountains." That suggested route compares favorably with the one taken by the emigrant train southwest from Soda Springs.[34]

On August 11 the Bidwell-Bartleson party's wagons struck southwest from the established trail along the course of the Bear River. Pushing on through the fertile Cache Valley, they suffered greatly from the intense heat. Further on they entered Bear Canyon where the only water available was a salt creek. Reaching a rolling plain, they encamped, dispatching two men to reconnoiter, who later reported that the Great Salt Lake was only ten miles away.

Two days later the several men who had gone north to Fort Hall in search of a possible guide returned empty-handed.[35] However, they did bring back some advice. On reaching the lake, they had been warned to strike west immediately; otherwise they would surely perish in the waterless wasteland to the south. At the same time, if they wandered too far north, badlands would confront them, making travel exhaustive. Their best hope was to strike Mary's River (later renamed the Humboldt) and follow its course west to the mountains.

On August 24 the party headed their wagons west and north around the Great Salt Lake. Dust blinded the emigrants' eyes while the endless sea of sagebrush plagued the wagon wheels. The vista appeared unlimited. Finding good spring water at the foot of the Hansel Mountains, the travelers established a camp. Rather than continue to exhaust themselves and their animals, Bartleson and Charles Hopper headed west to try to ascertain the headwaters of the sought-after Mary's River. As the days passed, the grass to sustain the livestock in the camp's vicinity was depleted. In the bargain, the weather was turning colder, an ominous sign first alarmingly noticed one morning when the water froze in the buckets. Finally, on September 9, the scouts returned with the happy news that Mary's River was just five days' march west, or so they thought.

By early September the grueling travel began to take its toll on the animals. Benjamin Kelsey was forced to abandon his wagons on September 12. He packed his wife and baby daughter, along with what possessions he could manage, on to horses and mules. The monotony of the desertlike terrain was finally lifted by the sight of snow-capped Pilot Peak. At least it held the promise of much-needed water. Little did the company realize that they were still hundreds of miles from the Sierra Nevada.

There was little recourse. It became obvious that the wagons, with the diminishing number of animals to haul them, were liabilities hindering progress and speed, both so essential with the press of winter at hand. Taking what they would, the party abandoned wagons and possessions. Their inexperience in packing horses properly produced disaster when they tried to trail the loose animals. The oxen proved the most troublesome. But with foodstuffs running out, the oxen had to be tended, since they afforded the only ready supply of fresh meat.

Drudging doggedly on, the weary party continued to struggle south hoping to find a pass over the nearby mountains. Again, luck was with them. They found and stumbled through a pass in the Pequop Mountains. They then descended into a valley filled with numerous hot springs. From there they struck a small stream on September 24, hoping against all odds that it would lead them to Mary's River. To no avail. It ran dry. Still moving west, shortly they found another lively stream, and hope flared anew. But for two troublesome days, doubt reigned supreme. Why did the stream flow north, then northwest? Having no other recourse, they stuck to its banks. On the third day all was smiles. The stream turned and flowed to the southwest: Mary's River at last!

The valley through which the river flowed was hardly a paradise. There was a scarcity of forage for the livestock. Nervously, notice was taken of signs of Indian presence in the valley, a worrisome prospect and potential danger for man and beast. But the abundance of good water was a blessing long denied the emigrants after leaving Soda Springs.

Crossing Mary's River on October 9, the haggard travelers moved west to what was later renamed Humboldt Lake and Sink. To their west lay another lake and sink, named by John C. Frémont in 1845 in honor of Kit Carson, the famed scout. On leaving the latter, Bartleson led his train southwesterly into some low mountains where they came upon another river. Mistakenly, they concluded that this was the head of the San Joaquin. Since the banks of the river were covered with numerous cottonwoods, willows, and balm of Gilead trees, they called it the Balm River. Later the river would be named in honor of Joseph R. Walker, who was the first to stumble on to it in his 1833 trip to California. When the stream petered out in the high mountains, it became obvious this was not the much-sought San Joaquin.

On October 16 the party began their descent from the higher elevation. It was a hazardous enterprise, fraught with danger and accident. Gratefully, all came through the ordeal with only a few bruises. Gaunt and haggard, they slaughtered a horse that night to augment the diet of beef. Two more weeks were spent in the hopes of finding an escape from the rugged mountains that locked the hungry and worn travelers in their granite embrace. Was there no way out?

Again, fate smiled. On the morning of October 30, having worked their way through the tortuous Stanislaus River canyon, much to the utter amazement and abandoned delight of all, the company looked out upon a magnificent valley, rich in timber, which stretched between the mountains they were descending and another range further to the west. The latter had given the false appearance of a continuous mountainous chain from higher elevations. At last they had found what had been sought so long, the San Joaquin Valley with its flowing river.

The following day the starving men spent their time hunting. By day's end, numerous wildfowl, along with thirteen deer and antelope, refurbished the empty larder. The party dined in sumptuous fashion on the day's kill. On midmorning November 2, Thomas Jones, who along with Andrew Kelsey had become separated from the main body on October 23 in the passage from Mary's River, as had Bidwell for a period of time, rejoined his comrades. Like the rest, Jones and Kelsey had luckily stumbled their way into the San Joaquin Valley several days earlier. By happenstance, they came across an Indian on horseback who shouted to them, "Marsh, Marsh."[36]

Although unable to communicate with the Indian other than through gestures, the two followed his lead. He guided them straight to Marsh's rancho at the foot of Mt. Diablo. Warmly received, the two men were fed. When rested, Jones set out on horseback with some victuals for his fellow travelers, accompanied by one of Marsh's Indian *vaqueros*. Fortunately, Jones met the rest of the party and provided them with some additional foodstuffs. Now refreshed, all headed for Marsh's ranch.[37]

On November 4, 1841, Marsh greeted the forlorn new arrivals, offering them his hospitality. They were a pitiful lot, with no food, little money, and few possessions. But the Bidwell-Bartleson party had successfully made the first planned overland emigrant journey to California, bearing with courage and great fortitude the vicissitudes of their trail ordeal. These hardy pioneers were the harbingers of many thousands to come.

In the spring of 1842 when ten of the emigrants decided to return east on horseback, Chiles and Hopper among them, they carried a most prophetic letter from Marsh directed to his parents in Massachusetts. Dated April 3, 1842, Marsh wrote:

> A company of about thirty of my old neighbors in Missouri arrived here the first of November last, and some of them are about returning and are the bearers of this. They arrived here directly at my house with no other guide but a letter of

mine. From all the numerous letters I have received from the United States I am satisfied that an immense emigration will soon swarm to this country. I am now fully satisfied that the Anglo-Saxon race of men who inhabit the United States are destined very shortly to occupy this delightful country. A young woman with a little child in her arms came in the company last fall and was about a month in my house. After this, the men ought to be ashamed to think of difficulties. It is an object I much desire and have long labored for, to have this country inhabited by Americans. It will now soon be realized.[38]

A primary contributor to that prospect was the *Journal* of John Bidwell, even though that was never its intent or purpose. When published, it became the first guidebook for overland travel to California, a prototype of many others to come.[39]

Marsh fully understood the significance of the Bidwell-Bartleson party's overland trip. He wrote to Commodore Thomas Ap Catesby Jones, November 24, 1842:

An event which will probably be regarded as of some importance in the future history of California was the arrival in last November of 31 men and one woman and child from Independence. . . . This company arrived in good health and without incident . . . at the house in which I am writing, and without any other guide than a letter I had the year previous sent them. . . . While the Americans in California are looking forward . . . to the increase of our countrymen in this country, the English, here, are equally confident that the whole country will soon be an appendage of the British Empire.[40]

Thanks to overland pioneers who began to come in increasing numbers from 1843 on, the latter prospect completely vanished.

Bidwell's *A Journey to California, with Observations about the Country, Climate and the Route to this Country* . . . , after its initial appearance as a Missouri imprint in 1843, 1844, or 1845, has been previously reprinted three times. After Bidwell's death in 1900, C[harles] C. Royce prepared a tribute, *John Bidwell, Pioneer Statesman, Philanthropist, a Biographical Sketch* (Chico, 1906), which did not include the *Journal*. That publication was incorporated in a second memorial tribute, prepared at the instigation of Mrs. Annie E. K. Bidwell, the widow, entitled *Addresses, Reminiscences, etc., of General Bidwell* (Chico, 1907). The latter included a reprint of the *Journal* from the Bancroft Library copy. A second publication was designed and printed by John Henry Nash, *A Journey to California, with Observations about the Country, Climate and the Route to this Country by John Bidwell* (San Francisco, 1937), with an introduction supplied by Herbert I. Priestley. A third reprint was sponsored by The Friends of the Bancroft Library as a keepsake for its membership under the title, *A Journey to California, 1841. The first emigrant party to California by wagon train. The Journal of John Bidwell*

(Berkeley, 1964), with an introduction by Francis P. Farquhar. The latter printed for the first time a facsimile of the original Missouri imprint. This book reprints the *Journal* (based on the 1964 edition) for the fourth time with the difference that the text has been more critically annotated than any previous edition. In editing the *Journal,* reliance has been placed on the original edition. In addition, it should be pointed out that photostat copies of the original imprint can be found in the Research Library, University of California, Los Angeles; the Huntington Library; and the Missouri Historical Society.

In 1877 Bidwell dictated his recollections to S. S. Boynton at the request of H. H. Bancroft. Twelve years later, in 1889, he prepared another version of his recollections, which appeared serially in three articles in *The Century Illustrated Monthly Magazine* in 1890. The Chico *Advertiser* later reissued them in a posthumous pamphlet, adding a section from a later version to complete the textual narrative under the title *Echoes of the Past* (Chico, c. 1914).

About 1891 Bidwell prepared another version of his memoirs for Bancroft. In that manuscript he makes references to the *Century* article in describing the trip west, which is dismissed in a single page. He has nothing new to add to his previous dictation in that respect. C. C. Royce in his memorial volume, *John Bidwell . . . ,* published yet another recollection by the pioneer, "Early California Reminiscences." This was first published in the magazine *Out West* and appeared serially in eight installments, January–August 1904, four years after Bidwell's death. Royce also included the first *Century* article in his 1906 volume and all three in the 1907 volume.

Milo M. Quaife edited the three installments of the 1889 Bidwell recollections, which appeared in the *Century* series. These appeared in the *Lakeside Classics,* sponsored by R. R. Donnelley & Sons, as *Bidwell's Echoes of the Past* (Chicago, 1928), coupled with Rev. John Steele's *In Camp and Cabin.* The former was reprinted as a paperback by the Citadel Press as *Echoes of the Past* (New York, 1962), but without proper attribution. This edition uses a facsimile of the Chico *Advertiser* edition title page; however, the reproduced text is a photocopy of the *Lakeside Classics'* 1928 printing. Lindley Bynum included the three *Century* articles in his *In California Before the Gold Rush* (Los Angeles, 1948). Last, two handsomely designed and printed books have also reprinted the *Century* articles. Oscar Lewis provided an introduction and a few annotations to both. The Penlitho Press designed and reprinted the first *Century* article, *The First Emigrant Train to California* (Menlo Park, Calif., 1966), while Lewis Osborne designed and executed *Life in California Before the Gold Discovery* (Palo Alto, Calif., 1966), which reprinted the second and third articles in that series. The text for Chapter Three is based on Bynum's edition and checked against the *Century* articles. Some of Bynum's parenthetical material has been deleted and new annotations added.

In summary, Bidwell prepared four different recollections. Although they vary in phraseology, the information presented is substantively the same in three of them. The original 1877 dictation, as well as the 1891 version, have not been published before. The latter, however, has nothing of import in respect to the 1841 overland journey and is not included in this volume.

Other members of the Bartleson party contributed their memoirs to H. H. Bancroft. These included Joseph B. Chiles, "A Visit to California in Early Times" (1871); Charles Hopper, "Narrative of Charles Hopper a California Pioneer of 1841 written by R. T. Montgomery at Napa 1871"; and Josiah Belden, "Statement of Historical Facts of California by Josiah Belden of Santa Clara Co.," which appeared in three installments in *Touring Topics* in 1930, but unedited, and later in *Josiah Belden, 1841 California Overland Pioneer: His Memoir and Early Letters*, edited by Doyce B. Nunis, Jr. (Georgetown, Calif., 1962).[41] Robert H. Thomes' memoir of the trip west was dictated to Albert G. Toomes and published in the San Francisco *Evening Bulletin*, June 27, 1868, and reprinted in Oscar T. Shuck, comp., *California Scrap-Book . . .* (San Francisco, 1868), pp. 181–184.

Three other 1841 pioneers provided accounts of the epic overland journey. Mrs. Benjamin (Nancy A.) Kelsey, the only woman who accompanied the Bidwell-Bartleson party into California, gave her brief recollection in an interview published in the San Francisco *Examiner*, February 5, 1893 (p. 19, cls. 6–7); later reprinted in "A California Heroine," *The Grizzly Bear*, XXXVIII (February 1915): 6–7, and in the same magazine in Minnie B. Heath, "Nancy Kelsey— The First Pioneer Woman to Cross [the] Plains," LX (February 1937): 3, 7. It was also reprinted in the Oakland *Tribune*, September 27, 1925 (p. 5, cl. 5).

A second party member who offered his brief recollections of the 1841 overland journey many years later was James P. Springer. He gave his short account in a letter to the editor of the San Jose *Tribune*, dated July 15, 1856. A copy of this clipping found its way into Alexander S. Taylor's compilation of data, his "Discoverers and Founders of California," a manuscript in the Bancroft Library. The clipping was later interpolated to imply that Springer gave his recollections to Taylor. A search of the manuscript mentioned proves that this was not the case.

The last party member to record his account was Nicholas Dawson. On completing his memoirs, they were published in 1901, probably in Austin, Texas. This work was republished under the title *Narrative of Nicholas "Cheyenne" Dawson . . .* (San Francisco, 1933), with an introduction by Charles L. Camp. It should be noted that Dawson wrote his dated recollections after reading Bidwell's *Century* articles. Dawson also read Mrs. Kelsey's newspaper interview. Later, he entered into correspondence with Bidwell, discussing the 1841 journey prior to penning his own version.[42]

A small body of contemporary documents survive that shed considerable information on the Bidwell-Bartleson party. First among these are the diaries of James John. The first diary, which abruptly ends under entry of August 20, 1841, is housed in the Oregon Historical Society. George H. Himes prepared it for publication under the title, "The Diary of James St. Johns," which was printed in the St. Johns [Oregon] *Review* in six installments in March–April 1906.[43] The second diary is held by the Rosenbach Museum and Library, Philadelphia. That copy is a curious item. The Philadelphia manuscript is a condensed version of the Oregon Historical Society diary. My good friend, the late Dale L. Morgan, was of enormous help years ago in searching out this item. He wrote, under cover of a personal letter, January 17, 1961:

> I suppose it [the Philadelphia manuscript] is a condensation of the original diary the rest of the way to California too, but there is no way of telling. Down to September 5, [1841], the Philadelphia MS. is in a different hand; from September 6 to the arrival at Sutter's, it is in John's own hand. Appended to his diary are "Extracts from Bidwells journal from 20th of Oct. to the 4th of Nov.," covering the period after John separated from the company in the Sierra. These extracts are considerably more terse than the published Bidwell diary, and perhaps closer to the original.

James P. Springer, who went back to Missouri in 1842, but returned permanently in 1852, also kept a diary. It seems that he made several round trips from Missouri to California prior to his last move. During his several trips, he wrote a number of articles and pamphlets extolling the virtues of California. His diary, however, has yet to come to light. If found, it should prove to be of intrinsic worth, for writing in 1856, he listed with amazing accuracy that portion of the Bidwell-Bartleson company that came to California.[44]

The Reverend Joseph Williams, a trail companion to Soda Springs, Idaho, published his travel account in *Narrative of a Tour from the State of Indiana to the Oregon Territory in the Years 1841–42* (Cincinnati, 1843).[45] A reprint of this rarity was published in New York in 1921 with an introduction by James C. Bell, Jr., and an edited version was included in LeRoy R. Hafen and Ann W. Hafen, eds., *To the Rockies and Oregon, 1830–1842* (Glendale, Calif., 1955), Part III.

The last extant documentary material relating to the Bidwell-Bartleson 1841 overland party is found in the writings of the three Jesuit priests who accompanied them to Soda Springs. Father Nicholas Point described his missionary travels in a number of letters, a portion of which touch on the months of May through August when the California emigrants were associated with his missionary band. Those manuscripts are housed in the Collège Sainte-Marie, Montréal, Canada.[46] He also sketched contemporary scenes of his travels in the West, several of which portray events on the route west to Soda Springs. A number of these sketches are housed in the Jesuit Archives of the Missouri Province, St. Louis.[47] The Department of Special Collections, Washington State University, Pullman, holds additional Point drawings in the De Smet

Collection. Fortunately, a large body of Point's writings and work have been translated and edited by Joseph P. Donnelly, *Wilderness Kingdom: Indian Life in the Rocky Mountains: 1840–1847. The Journals & Paintings of Nicolas Point, S.J.* (New York, 1967).[48]

Father Gregory Mengarini's accounts are rather dispersed. A number of his early letters detailing his impressions of the West were published in the *Woodstock Letters*.[49] Another portion of his letters are housed in the National Library, Rome, Italy. As to whether or not those manuscripts reveal any additional information pertinent to the Bidwell-Bartleson party, I am uninformed. The Jesuit Missouri Province Archives in St. Louis also contain a few additional letters that touch on the year 1841. Lastly, in 1884, while serving on the faculty at Santa Clara College (now University) in California, Father Mengarini dictated his recollections at the request of several Jesuit colleagues. A few copies of that narrative were printed as a memorial for private circulation after his death. Albert J. Partoll has edited that dictation, "Mengarini's Narrative of the Rockies," published in *Frontier and Midland*, XVIII (1938): 193–202, 258–266; reprinted in *Sources of Northwest History No. 25* (Missoula, Montana, n.d.), and in *Frontier Omnibus,* ed. by John W. Hakola (Missoula and Helena, Montana, 1962), pp. 139–160.

Father De Smet, leader of the Jesuit missionaries, wrote rather extensively on his 1841 exiences. His writings dealing with that fruitful period of his life saw publication first in the United States under the title *Letters and Sketches: With a Narrative of a Year's Residence Among the Indian Tribes of the Rocky Mountains* (Philadelphia, 1843). That work has seen many subsequent republications, the more recent being found in Reuben G. Thwaites, ed., *Early Western Travels, 1748–1846* (32 vols., Cleveland, 1904–1907; reprint ed., New York, 1966). And a number of this pioneer priest's 1841 letters have been published in Hiram M. Chittenden and Alfred D. Richardson, eds., *Life, Letters and Travels of Father Pierre-Jean De Smet, S.J., 1801–1872* (4 vols., New York, 1905).

It should be noted, however, that these published sources of Father De Smet's letters and travels are far from complete. It is to be hoped that one day this body of unpublished writings will see definitive publication since there exists a large quantity of untouched material housed in widely diffused Jesuit and Church archival depositories both here and in the United States and especially abroad.

However, there is no question: the principal chronicler and historian of the 1841 California overland party was John Bidwell. His *Journal,* coupled with his 1877 dictation for Bancroft and his 1890 *Century Magazine* article, "The First Emigrant Train," are the best and most complete narratives of that overland trip. Bidwell's 1891 dictation for Bancroft only references the latter in recalling the 1841 journey and another recollection offers nothing of import and thus have been omitted. The first three documents are reprinted herein with only slight editorial intrusion and with annotations supplied to amplify and correct the respective texts where needed.

Following the Bidwell narratives, arranged in alphabetical order, are all known documents and recollections which have come down to us from members of the Bidwell-Bartleson party. Several contributions are very valuable and add data to Bidwell's accounts; on the other hand, several are very slight and thin in their content. That caveat aside, all are reprinted, again with only very minimal editorial intrusion in respect to occasional sentence structure, punctuation, and paragraphing. Annotations have been provided for clarity and correction where required.

In addition to these sources authored by 1841 California overland pioneers, four other participants' accounts, at least as far as Soda Springs, are also included as the concluding chapters, again arranged in alphabetical order. These include extracts from three letters written on the overland journey by Father Pierre Jean De Smet to his superior, the brief recollection of Father Gregory Mengarini, and the narratives of Father Nicholas Point and Rev. Joseph Williams, the Protestant minister who was en route to Oregon. These primary sources have also been treated in a similar mannger as those mentioned above.

To round out this volume, fourteen sketches by Father Nicholas Point depicting scenes on the journey from Westport, Missouri, to Soda Springs, Idaho, have been included as illustrations.[50] Where possible, all known photographs of the 1841 California emigrants that have been located are included, along with a few other likenesses of important individuals germane to the Bidwell-Bartleson party story. In addition, a lengthy discussion of the roster of the 1841 overland party is included in Appendix A, while Appendix B presents basic biographical sketches of the California-bound contingent. Appendix C contains miscellaneous documents, among them two items relating to the formation of the Western Emigration Company; John Marsh's report of the arrival of the newcomers to the California authorities; and Nicholas Dawson's chronology of the trek west.

Notes

1 John D. Unruh, Jr., *The Plains Across: The Overland Emigrants and the Trans-Mississippi West, 1840–1860* (Urbana, Ill., 1979), pp. 119–120. I have omitted enumerating the overland emigration to Utah, which for the period 1840–1860 totals 42,862, since there were other factors involved in that emigration. However, the effect of Bidwell's journal-letter must not be discounted even in that case.

2 Rockwell D. Hunt, *John Bidwell, Prince of California Pioneers* (Caldwell, Idaho, 1942).

3 Henry R. Wagner and Charles L. Camp, comps., *The Plains & the Rockies, A Bibliography . . .*, ed. by Robert H. Becker (4th ed., San Francisco, 1982), pp. 203–204, which quotes the letter from Bidwell to Bancroft, May 23, 1884.

4 George D. Lyman, *John Marsh, Pioneer* (New York, 1930), p. 249; Helen S. Giffen,

Trail-Blazing Pioneer, Colonel Joseph Ballinger Chiles (San Francisco, 1959), pp. 32–34. Giffen holds the view that Chiles took Bidwell's letter east, but belies Bidwell's own testimony that he never intended it for publication, least of all in the Missouri frontier newspapers.

5 J. R. McBride in his recollections, published in *Tullidge's Quarterly Magazine,* 3 (1884): 311–320, unequivocally declared that Bidwell's journal was published at Weston in 1844. Cited in Becker, ed., *The Plains & the Rockies,* p. 204, based on a letter from the late Dale L. Morgan. That being the case, then Lansford W. Hastings becomes the more likely courier. Hubert H. Bancroft, *History of California* (7 vols., San Francisco, 1884–1890), IV: 306, attests to the Bidwell friendship with Hastings.

6 Bidwell, *Journal,* p. 27 (1st ed.).

7 Zephyrin Engelhardt, *Missions and Missionaries of California* (4 vols., Santa Barbara, 1908–1915), IV: 259–267; Maynard Geiger, *Franciscan Missionaries in Hispanic California, 1769–1848* (San Marino, Calif. 1969), pp. 100–101.

8 Bidwell to Alice M. Cameron, December 7, 1890, quoted in Becker, ed., *The Plains & the Rockies,* p. 204. Becker himself concludes, ". . . the journal was published some time between the winter of 1842–43 and the summer of 1844, at a town in western Missouri . . ."

9 Oscar O. Winther, *The Great Northwest* (2nd ed., New York, 1950), pp. 115–118, 121–124; Eleanor Lawrence, "Mexican Trade Between Santa Fe and Los Angeles," *California Historical Society Quarterly,* X (1931): 27–39; Robert G. Cleland, *This Reckless Breed of Men: The Trappers and Fur Traders of the Southwest* (New York, 1950), *passim.*

10 Cleland's book, just cited, compactly covers these men's exploits, but greater coverage is rendered in Dale L. Morgan, *Jedediah Smith and the Opening of the West* (Indianapolis, 1953), pp. 193–255, and Washington Irving, *The Adventures of Captain Bonneville, U.S.A. . . . ,* ed. by Edgeley W. Todd (Norman, 1961), pp. 162 *et seq.*

11 John W. Caughey, *California* (Rev. ed., Englewood Cliffs, N.J., 1959), p. 213.

12 William S. Wallace, "Antoine Robidoux," in LeRoy R. Hafen, ed., *The Mountain Men and the Fur Trade in the Far West* (10 vols., Glendale, Calif., 1965–1972), IV: 261–273.

13 Lyman, *John Marsh,* pp. 195–207.

14 Joseph B. Chiles, "A Visit to California in Early Times," pp. 2–3. Dictation for H. H. Bancroft, 1878, MS, Bancroft Library. (Hereinafter cited Chiles, "Early Times.")

15 Charles Wilkes, *Narrative of U.S. Exploring Expedition* (5 vols., Philadelphia, 1844), V: 181; Lyman, *John Marsh,* p. 237. It would appear that Marsh knew very little about Ogden's journey, since his journal was lost in a boating accident. Perhaps at best he had some hearsay from the annual Hudson's Bay Company California Brigade which passed his way en route to their traditional camping grounds near the present city of Stockton.

16 Lyman, *John Marsh,* pp. 191–192, 237–238.

17 *The Western Atlas, and Saturday Evening Gazette,* March 6, 1841. Dale L. Morgan, [Newspaper Transcripts] *The Mormons and the Far West,* Henry E. Huntington Library, San Marino. (Hereinafter cited *DLM Transcripts.*)

18 Farnham reached California by ship. He took passage from Oregon to Honolulu, then on the *Don Quixote,* Captain John Paty, visited Monterey from April 18 to 28, then on to Santa Barbara, May 1–5, before sailing south to Mazatlán, where he made an overland passage across Mexico to the Gulf, and then shipped north from there. Adele Ogden, "Trading Vessels on the California Coast, 1786–1848," p. 906, typescript MS, Bancroft Library. Farnham published his *Travels in the Great Western Prairies . . . and the Oregon Territory* (Poughkeepsie, N.Y., 1841) on his return. However, his *Travels in the Californias and Scenes in the Pacific Ocean* was not published in New York until

1844; later reprinted under the title *Travels in California* (Oakland, 1947). Farnham's disdain for the governmental officials is patently obvious. (See pp. 59 *et seq.* in the latter edition, for example.) One of Farnham's letters appeared in the St. Louis *Missouri Argus,* June 26, 1840. *DLM Transcripts.* This made it easy to copy in other local Missouri papers, a common habit of the day.

19 *The Western Atlas . . . ,* May 1, 1841. *DLM Transcripts.*

20 The *Daily Missouri Republican,* May 19, 1841, reported the rendezvous at Sapling Grove as of May 10.

21 Biographical data has been drawn from Hunt, *John Bidwell,* pp. 1–29, and Bidwell's c. 1891 dictation, pp. 1–9, Bancroft Library.

22 John Bidwell, *Echoes of the Past,* ed. by Milo M. Quaife (Chicago, 1928), pp. 1–2.

23 *Ibid.,* p. 14

24 *Ibid.,* pp. 21–22. The company arrived at the Kansas (actually two miles west of the River) on May 16, striking out on the trail, May 19. *A Journal to California, 1841. The first emigrant party to California by wagon train. The Journal of John Bidwell,* introduction by Francis P. Farquhar (Berkeley, 1964), p. 2. This publication reproduces a facsimile of the only known copy of Bidwell's long narrative letter describing the trip, which was published in one of the Missouri frontier towns. (Hereinafter cited Bidwell, *Journal.* Page references will be to the facsimile copy.) Green was using an alias; his real name was Paul Geddes. He was absconding with funds from a bank he had embezzled. For a fuller explanation, consult Bancroft, *California,* III: 756–766, and John A. Hussey, "New Light Upon Talbot H. Green as Revealed by His Own Letters and Other Sources," *California Historical Society Quarterly,* XVIII (1939): 26–63.

25 Bidwell, *Echoes,* pp. 15–16.

26 The *Daily Missouri Republican,* April 20, 1841, reported the projected Jesuit missionary trek west under "Father De Smait" [Smet].

27 Letter, August 16, 1841, Pierre Jean De Smet, S. J., *Letters and Sketches . . .* (Philadelphia, 1843), reprinted in Reuben G. Thwaites, ed., *Early Western Travels, 1748–1846* (32 vols., Reprint ed.; New York, 1966), XXVII: 236. (Hereinafter cited De Smet, *Letters and Sketches.*)

28 Bidwell, *Echoes,* pp. 39–65, describes the trip from a later perspective.

29 Morgan, *Jedediah Smith,* Chs. 10, 12; *Adventures of Zenas Leonard, Fur Trapper,* ed. by John C. Ewer (Norman, 1959), pp. 63–132, for a firsthand report on the 1833–1834 Walker trip.

30 William S. Wallace, *Antoine Robidoux* (Los Angeles, 1953), *passim,* and Joseph J. Hill, "Antoine Robidoux, Kingpin in the Colorado River Fur Trade, 1824–1844," *Colorado Magazine,* VII (1930): 125–132.

31 Doyce B. Nunis, Jr., "The Fur Men: Key to Westward Expansion, 1822–1830," *The Historian,* XXIII (1961): 167–190.

32 Hiram M. Chittenden and Alfred D. Richardson, eds., *Life, Letters, and Travels of Father Pierre-Jean De Smet* (4 vols., New York, 1905), I: 300 (hereinafter cited *De Smet Letters*); *Narrative of Nicholas "Cheyenne" Dawson . . .* (San Francisco, 1933), pp. 14–15 (hereinafter cited *Dawson Narrative*).

33 Bidwell, *Echoes,* p. 16; *Dawson Narrative,* p. 16.

34 Chiles, "Early Times," p. 3; Lyman, *John Marsh,* p. 237; "California and Oregon," *Colonial Magazine,* V (1841): 220–230, and *Chamber's Journal* X (August 21, 1841): 245, published a number of resolutions adopted. Bancroft, *California,* IV: 267, suggests the date of February 1, 1841.

35 The number of men who went to Fort Hall is unclear. In his *Journal,* p. 10, Bidwell refers to "several." Later, p. 12, he names one, Broloski, and records the other "men"

rejoined the party. In his "Emigrant Train," p. 24, reprinted in Quaife edition, Bidwell states four men went to the fort. *Dawson Narrative,* p. 16, gives the figure as two. Father De Smet mentions only the party's leader (Bartleson) as going on to Fort Hall. *Letters and Sketches,* p. 236.

36 Two of the best descriptions of the Bidwell-Bartleson party's overland route are presented in Dale L. Morgan, *The Humboldt, Highway of the West* (New York, 1943), pp. 62–78, and George R. Stewart, *The California Trail* (New York, 1962), pp. 7–29. Also useful, especially for its maps, is Ralph Moody, *The Old Trails West* (N.p., 1963), pp. 249–284.

37 Bidwell, *Journal,* p. 19. *Dawson Narrative,* p. 28, says only Jones and an Indian directed the company to Marsh's rancho.

38 Printed in Lyman, *John Marsh,* 349. The letter was posted to Danvers, Massachusetts, from Independence, September 12, 1842, by Charles Hopper, who returned to Missouri with Chiles. "Narrative of Charles Hopper . . . ," p. 9, MS, Bancroft Library.

39 For a survey of these guidebooks, see Thomas F. Andrews, "The Controversial Hastings Overland Guide: A Reassessment," *Pacific Historical Review,* XXXVII (1968): 21–34.

40 MS, Bancroft Library.

41 The three installments appeared as Josiah Belden, "The First Overland Emigrant Train to New California," *Touring Topics,* 22 (June 1930): 14–18, 56; "Pastoral California Through Gringo Eyes," *ibid.,* 22 (July 1930): 44–47, 71; 22 (August 1930): 40–47, 53–54. The Nunis edited version also includes a letter from Belden to his sister, December 21, 1841, that describes some of the overland trip (pp. 115–118), which is reprinted in this volume.

42 Dawson in his preface states he began writing his narrative on March 1, 1894, and finished it sometime after January 1, 1901, as he mentions on page 101 of the first edition. This would seem to indicate that the date of 1894 given in *A Bibliography of the History of California,* comp. by Robert E. Cowan and Robert G. Cowan (Reprint ed., Los Angeles, 1933), p. 161, is in error.

Few copies of the original edition are known to exist: one is in the library of the University of Texas; University of California, Los Angeles; Bancroft Library; and California State Library. The latter library accessioned the book in July 1901. (Letter from Allen R. Ottley, at the time California Section Librarian, to this writer, January 24, 1962.)

Another copy of this rarity was in the collection of Thomas W. Streeter. It was sold at auction by Parke-Bernet Galleries, October 23, 1968, for $375, to an known bidder. *The Celebrated Collection of Americana formed by the late Thomas Winthrop Streeter* (7 vols., New York, 1966–1969), 5: 2104, Lot 3089, which gives the publication date as [N.p., 1894?], no doubt relying on the Cowans' bibliography.

43 Copy in Oregon Historical Society, Portland.

44 San Francisco *Chronicle,* June 12, 1856; San Jose *Tribune,* July 23, 1856; J. P. Munro-Fraser, *History of Santa Clara County . . .* (San Francisco, 1881), p. 471.

45 There are four other known copies: Huntington Library, New York Historical Society, University of Chicago, and Yale University.

46 Personal letter from Rev. Paul Desjardins, S.J., then archivist for the Collège Sainte-Marie, June 30, 1962.

47 John F. McDermott, "De Smet's Illustrator: Father Nicolas Point," *Nebraska History,* XXXIII (1952): 34–40.

48 Point wrote "Recollection of the Rocky Mountains," which appeared originally in the *Woodstock Letters,* XI (1883): 298–321. This is reprinted in the Donnelly book on pp. 11–18, which also includes Point's "Historical Notes," pp. 19–35. These two recollections add little to the Bidwell-Bartleson party story, other than Point's description of Captain Bartleson as "calm in temperament but enterprising in character . . . ." (p. 26).

49 Citations are given in Carlos Sommervogel, ed., *Biblioteque de la Compagnie de Jesus* (11 vols., Brussels and Paris, 1890–1919), V: 946; references to Father Point, VI: 921. Mengarini's "The Rocky Mountains . . ." was published posthumously in the *Woodstock Letters,* 17 (1888): 298–313; 18 (1889): 25–43, 142–152.

50 The Pierre Jean De Smet Papers, Department of Special Collections, Washington State University Library, Pullman, contain an additional ten drawings depicting scenes on the overland trail from Westport, Missouri, to Soda Springs, Idaho. Regrettably, publication permission to use these was denied, but the Library did approve reproduction of ten of the twenty pertinent Point drawings in the De Smet Papers.

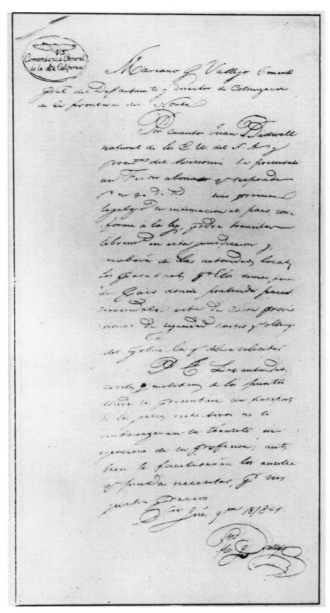

Translation of original passport from Gen. M. G. Vallejo to John Bidwell:
Mariano G. Vallejo, General Ambassador of the Department and Director of Colonization of the Northern Frontier. / For as much as John Bidwell of the United States of North America and State of Missouri, has presented a certificate of good conduct and seeks to obtain legal residence in this country as required by law: he shall be allowed to travel freely in this jurisdiction and he shall be accorded by the local authorities, pass-ports for the various places where he may wish to stay. This will serve him as a provisional letter of security until he obtain from the Government a permanent one, which he will have to demand. / Consequently the Civil and Military authorities of the Districts where he will present himself with pass-ports of the representative judges, will not obstruct his transit nor the exercise of his profession. / They will also render him the assistance he may need according to value. / San Jose, 9 bre 18, 1841. /
M. G. Vallejo (*Courtesy California State Library*)

CHAPTER ONE

A Journey to California, 1841: The Journal Account

by John Bidwell

Preface

The publisher of this Journal, being aware, that a great many persons, in Missouri and of the other Western States, are at this time anxious to get *correct information* relative to Oregon and California, hopes in part to gratify them by giving publicity to these sheets through the press; having been solicited to do so, by men of information who have perused them in manuscript.

The author, Mr. John Bidwell a young man of good acquirements and unexceptionable moral character, came to Missouri from the Buckeye State about 4 years ago, and resided in Platte County two years, during which time he made many staunch friends, and was prosperous in business.

But the many inducements held forth to enterprising young men to go to California, caused him to adopt the motto "Westward ho," shoulder his rifle and join one of the California companies which leave the rendezvous near Independence annually. Prior to his going, he promised his friends to keep a Journal, noticing the incidents of the trip, and also give his observations of the country after his arrival *there* — this promise he has redeemed, by forwarding the publisher this copy of his Journal, &c.

A Journey to California, 1841

Bodega, Port of the Russians
Upper California, March 30th 1842![1]
Most Esteemed, Sir: — Owing to circumstances I am compelled to abridge my Journal and likewise a description of the country so far as I have been able to travel. By perusing the following pages you will learn most of the particulars

of all my travels since I left the United States.

I will now begin with my daily Journal, from the time the Company arrived at Kanzas river, till they arrived at Marsh's in Upper California.

The Missionary Company consisted of 11 persons viz — Capt. [Thomas] Fitzpatric[k], the Pilot; Father [Pierre Jean] De Smet, Pont [Nicholas Point] and Mengarine [Gregory Mengarini], missionaries; John Grey [Gray], hunter, — Romaine [English traveler], and 5 teamsters.[2]

Our company was composed of the following individuals; T[albot] H. Green [Paul Geddes], G. Hinshaw [George Henshaw], Charles Hopper, J[ames] P. Springer, A[ndrew] G[winn] Patton, J[ohn] Bartleson, N[icholas] Dawson, Josiah Belden, J. M. Jones, J. [David] W. Chandler, John De Swart [John L. Swart or Schwart or Schwartz], H. S. Brolaske [Henry L. Brolaski], M[ichael] C. Nye, Elias Barnet[t], Major Walton, A[mbrose] Walton, Green McMahan [Samuel Green McMahan], J[ohn] McDowel[l], R. H. Thomas [Robert H. Thomes], Elisha Stone, Isaiah [or Isaac or Zedekiah] Kelsey, Saml. Kelsey and family, William Towler [Fowler], Richard Williams and family, E. [Charles] W[illiam] Flügge, W[illiam] P. Overton, Geo. Simpson, V. W. Dawson, Andrew Kelsey, Benj. Kelsey and family, Ewd. [Edward] Rogers, D[avid] F. Hill, A. [Grove C.] Cook, Jones, Carroll, Jas. Ross, Henry Huber, John Roland, Wm. Belty, Thos. Jones, Augustus Fifer [or Pfeiffer], Jas. John, R[obert] Rickman, H[enry] Peyton, [Joseph B.] Chiles, Charles Weaver [Charles María Weber] and James [George?] Shotwell; the last six did not overtake us at Kanzas river.[3]

The trappers for the mountains are the following — Jas. Baker, Piga (a French-man), and Wm. Mast [or Mest].

A[mos] E. Frye and Rogers on a pleasure excursion — [Joseph] Williams, a preacher on a visit to Oregon.

May. Tuesday 18th 1841. Having waited at this place (2 miles W. of Kanzas river) 2 days, and all the Company being arrived, except those heretofore mentioned, the Company was convened for the purpose of electing a Captain and adopting rules for the government of the Company; when T[albot] H. Green was chosen President — and J. Bidwell, Secretary.

After the rules were read and adopted, J[ohn] Bartleson was elected Captain; it will be understood that Fitzpatrick was Capt. of the Missionary Company and pilot of the whole. Orders were given for the company to start in the morning, and the meeting broke up.

Wednesday, 19th. This morning, the wagons started off in single file; first the 4 carts and 1 small wagon of the missionaries, next 8 wagons drawn by mules and horses and lastly, 5 wagons drawn by 17 yoke of oxen. It was the calculation of the company to move on slowly till the wagon of [Joseph B.] Chiles overtook us.[4] Our course was west, leaving the Kanzas no great distance to our left, we traveled in the valley of the river which was prairie excepting near the margin of the stream. The day was very warm and we stopped about noon, having traveled about 12 miles.

This afternoon we had a heavy shower of rain and hail. Several Kanzas Indians came to our camp; they were well armed with bows and arrows, and some had guns. They were daily expecting an attack by the Pawnees, whom they but a short time ago had made inroads upon, and had massacred at one of their villages a large number of old men, women and children, while the warriors were hunting buffalo.

Thursday, 20. The day was tolerably pleasant. Our road was interrupted by small streams which crossed our course in every 2 or 3 miles during the day. The land was prairie, except the narrow groves which accompanied every stream—timber principally, bur-oak, black walnut, elm and white hickory. Travelled this day about sixteen miles and encamped in a beautiful grove of timber through which meandered a small stream.

Friday, 21st. Our oxen left us last night, and it was 9 o'clock before we were all ready to start, passed a considerable stream called Vermillion, a branch of the Kanzas. On its banks was finer timber than we had heretofore seen, hickory, walnut &c. &c. The country was prairie, hilly and strong; we passed in the forenoon a Kanzas village, entirely deserted on account of the Pawnees, encamped by a scattering grove, having come about 15 miles.

Saturday, 22nd. Started at six o'clock this morning, travelled about 18 miles, high rolling prairie, encamped on a small stream, shaded by a few willows.

Sunday, 23rd. All the oxen were gone this morning excepting nine. There was considerable complaint among the company, some saying at this slow rate of traveling we would have to winter among the Black Hills, and eat our mules &c. We, however, made a start about 9 in the morning, proceeded about 9 miles and stopped to wait for Chiles' waggon which overtook us about 5 P.M.; 14 Pawnees were seen by the wagon, well armed with spears &c. It was supposed they were on an expedition against the Kanzas.

Monday, 24th. Travelled about 13 miles today over rolling prairies and arrived at the Big Vermillion, a branch of the Kanzas. Here we were obliged stop, the water being so high as to render it impossible to cross with the waggons.[5]

Tuesday, 25th. Passed the stream without much trouble and made a stretch of about 20 miles when we encamped on the border of a beautiful forest where we found plenty of grass and water. The country, over which we passed, was similar to that of yesterday.

Wednesday, 26th. Two waggons were broke today; about a dozen Pawnees came to our camp, stopped to repair the waggons, having come about 15 miles. A deer was brought in by C. Hopper. A man by the name of Williams, a Methodist preacher overtook the company this evening on his way to visit the Oregon Territory.[6] He had not arrived in time to start with the company from the settlements, and had travelled entirely alone, without any gun or other weapon of defence, depending wholy on Providence for protection and support.

Thursday, 27th. Started late, being detained at repairing the waggons. The day was warm, but the evening mild and pleasant. Encamped in a commodious valley, well watered by a beautiful little stream which glided smoothly through the scattering grove, come about 15 miles.

Friday, 28th. Started about sunrise, travelled about 5 miles and stopped to take breakfast. The heat was oppressive and we were compelled to go 20 miles farther before we came to either wood or water. The stream on which we encamped is a fork of the Kanzas and is well known to all the mountaineers, by the name of the Big Blue; an antelope was killed.

Saturday, 29th. We again started about sunrise and travelled not less than 2 miles. One antelope was killed — saw several elk.

Sunday, 30th. Nothing of importance occurred — distance about 15 miles — grass mingled with rushes afforded our animals plenty of food of the best quality. Game appeared to increase, though but one deer and one antelope were brought in.

Monday, 31st. This morning about 10 o'clock we met six waggons with 18 men, with fur and robes on their way from Ft. Larimie to St. Louis. Ft. Larimie is situated on Larimie's fork near its junction with the N. fork of Platte, and is about 800 miles from Independence. The waggons were drawn by oxen and mules — the former looked as though they received a thousand lashes every day of their existence! The rusty mountaineers looked as though they never had seen razor, water, soap, or brush. It was very warm, and we travelled till dark before we were able to reach water, and then it was not fit to drink, and then we could not procure any wood, grass scarce.

June. Tuesday, 1st. This morning we hastened to leave our miserable encampment and proceeding directly north, we reached Big Platte river about 12 o'clock. The heat was uncommonly oppressive. I here discovered the ground was in many places hoary with Glauber Salts, or at least I was unable to distinguish them by taste. This afternoon we had a soaking shower, which was succeeded by a heavy hailstorm. Wonderful! This evening a new family was created! Isaac Kelsey was married to Miss Williams, daughter of R. Williams. The marriage ceremony was performed by the Rev. Pr. Williams, so we now have five families if we include a widow and child.

Wednesday, 2nd. This morning the company was convened for the purpose of taking a vote upon the question whether the companies should continue to travel together; that some were complaining that the missionaries went too fast; but the very thought of leaving Mr. Fitzpatrick who was so well acquainted with the Indians, &c. &c., met, as it ought to have done, the disapprobation of all. We now proceeded directly up the river, making this day about twelve miles.

Thursday, 3rd. Still continued up the river, travelled about 16 miles, rained in the afternoon.

Friday, 4th. Half past six this morning saw us on the march. The valley of the river was here about 4 miles wide. Antelope were seen in abundance. A young man (Dawson) was out hunting, when suddenly a band of Chienne [Cheyenne] Indians about 40 in number came upon him; they were pleased to strip him of his mule, gun and pistol, and let him go. He had no sooner reached the camp and related the news than the whole band came in sight. We hastened to form a carral (yard) with our waggons, but it was done in great haste. To show you how it affected the *green ones,* I will give the answer I received from a stout, young man (and he perhaps was but one of 30 in the same situation), when I asked him how many Indians there were. He answered with a trembling voice, half scared out of his wits, there are lots, gaubs, fields and swarms of them!!! I do really believe he thought there were some thousands. Lo! there were but 40, perfectly friendly, delivered up every article taken, but the pistol.

Saturday, 5th. Started early to get clear of our red visitors. Descried a large herd of buffalo on the opposite side of the river — saw several boats descending the river, laden with fur, robes, &c. They belonged the American Fur Company — one of our Company, E. Stone, returned with them.[7] The latter part of the day was very inclement, high winds, dark clouds rushed in wild confusion around and above us. Soon with amazement we saw a lofty water spout, towering like a huge column to support the arch of the sky; and while we were moving with all haste lest it should pass over us and dash our wagons to pieces, it moved off with the swiftness of the wind and was soon lost among the clouds. Rain & hail succeeded, the largest hailstones I ever saw. Several were found, an hour after the sun came out bright & warm, larger than a turkey egg; 9 of the Indians that left us this morning, returned this evening.

Sunday, 6th. This morning was extremely cool for the season; 25 more of the same Indians came up with us.

Monday, 7th. Three Indians continued with us. The wind blew very hard towards evening; 3 buffaloes were killed and part of their meat was brought to the camp.

Tuesday, 8th. There were 8 or 10 buffalo killed today, but not one-tenth of the meat was used; the rest was left to waste upon the prairie. In the afternoon we passed the confluence of the N. & S. forks of Platte river & encamped, having come about 18 miles; many hundred of buffaloes were seen at this place. The scenery of the country on the Platte is rather dull and monotonous, but there are some objects which must ever attract the attention of the observant traveler; I mean the immense quantity of buffalo bones, which are everywhere strewed with great profusion, so that the valley, throughout its whole length and breadth, is nothing but one complete slaughter yard, where the noble animals used to graze, ruminate and multiply in uncounted thousands — but they are fast diminishing. If they continue to decrease in the same ratio that they have for the past 15 or 20 years, they will ere long become totally extinct. It has been but a few years since they left the frontiers of Missouri, and are now fast retreating towards the Rocky Mountains.

The Indians are anxious to preserve them, and it is said of them that they never kill as long as they have any meat remaining, but behold with indignation the shameful and outrageous prodigality of the whites, who slaughter thousands merely for their robes and leave the meat, which is far more delicious than that of tame cattle, to waste, or be eaten by wolves & vultures.

Wednesday, 9th. Spent the day in crossing the S. fork of Platte — a buffalo was killed from a herd that came within 300 yards of the camp. We crossed the river by fording, the water being sufficiently shallow — width of river here about ⅔ of a mile — its waters are muddy like those of the Missouri.

Thursday, 10th. This morning the most of the oxen were again at large, owing to the neglect of the owners to the great danger of losing them by the Indians and by their mingling with buffalo, or by their straying so far that it would be impossible to track them on account of the innumerable tracks of the buffalo. Making therefore rather a late start, we continued to ascend the river on the N. side. We traveled about 14 miles and encamped on the river. Buffalo were seen in countless thousands on the opposite side of the river; from the time we began to journey this morning till we ceased to travel at night, the whole south side of the stream was completely clouded by these huge animals, grazing in the valley and on the hills, ruminating upon the margin of the river, or crowding down its banks for water.

Through the remissness of the sentinels, the guard last night was nearly vacant; and as this was considered dangerous ground on account of the warlike Pawnees, Chiennes, &c., a court martial was called to force those to their duty on guard, who were so negligent & remiss.

Friday, 11th. The oxen had wandered about ½ mile from the camp this morning, when a man was sent to bring them in; he soon came running back in great haste, crying "the Indians are driving the oxen off"!! In less than half an hour the oxen were at camp and not an Indian seen — all this is easily accounted for when we consider how timidity and fear will make every bush, or stone, or stump an Indian, and 40 Indians, thousands. Vast herds of buffalo continued to be seen on the opposite side of the river. Distance today about 20 miles.

Saturday, 12th. Left the S. fork, and after a march of 12 miles found ourselves on the N. fork. In the afternoon passed a small ash grove of about 25 trees — timber is so scarce that such a grove is worthy of notice. We encamped on the N. fork having come about 18 miles; on leaving the S. fork we left the buffalo also.

Sunday, 13th. A mournful accident occurred in the camp this morning—a young man by the name of Shotwell while in the act of taking a gun out of the wagon, drew it, with the muzzle towards him in such a manner that it went off and shot him near the heart. He lived about an hour and died in the full possession of his senses. His good behavior had secured him the respect and good will of all the company; he had resided some 8 or 9 months on or near the Nodaway river, Platte purchase, Missouri, prior to his starting on this expedition; but he said his mother lived in Laurel County, Kentucky, and was much opposed to his coming into the West. He was buried in the most decent manner our circumstances would admit of, after which a funeral sermon was preached by Mr. Williams. In the afternoon we passed on about 5 miles, making an inland circuit over the hills which approached boldly to the river and compelled us to leave its banks. We, however, reached it again by descending the dry channel of Ash creek on which was considerable timber—ash, cedar &c.

Monday, 14th. The day was so cool and rainy we did not travel.

Tuesday, 15th. There was so sudden a change from cool to cold that we were not comfortable in our best apparel. I do not remember that I ever have experienced weather so cold at this season of the year—traveled about 16 miles.

Wednesday, 16th. Several wild horses were seen on the opposite side of the river. Advanced about 20 miles; encamped on the river, opposite to high and uneven bluffs, bearing considerable forests of pine.

Thursday, 17th. Continued to coast along up the river—encamped on its banks nearly opposite to a huge isolated bluff bearing some resemblance to an immense castle in ruins. Its distance from us no one supposed more than 1½ miles, and yet it was at least 7. This deception was owing to the pure atmosphere through which it was viewed, and the want of objects, by which only, accurate ideas of distance can be acquired without measure.

Friday, 18th. About 12 o'clock today we passed another object, still more singular and interesting. It is called by the mountaineers, the Chimney [Rock], from its resemblance to that object, and is composed of clay and sand so completely compact as to possess the hardness of a rock.[8] It stands near the high bluffs that bound the valley on the south, and has been formed from a high isolated mound which, being washed on every side by the rains and snows of ages, has been worn down till nothing is left but the centre which stands upon an obtuse cone, and is seen towering like a huge column at the distance of 30 miles. The column is 150 feet above the top of the come and the whole, 250 feet above the level of the plain. Distance made today about 20 miles.

Saturday, 19th. We gradually receded from the river in order to pass through a gap in a range of high hills called Scott's Bluffs.[9] As we advanced towards these hills, the scenery of the surrounding country became beautifully grand and picturesque—they were worn in such a manner by the storms of unnumbered seasons that they really counterfeited the lofty spires, towering edifices, spacious domes and in fine all the beautiful mansions of cities. We encamped among these envious objects having come about 20 miles.

Here were first found the mountain sheep; two were killed and brought to camp. These animals are so often described in almost every little School Book that it is unnecessary for me to describe them here.

Sunday, 20th. Passed through the Gap—came into an extensive plain, the beautiful scenery gradually receded from view—came to a creek called Horse—passed it, reached the river again—cool and windy—having come about 23 miles.[10]

Monday, 21st. We had an uncommonly good road today—an abundance of cottonwood timber—traveled late, having taken a stride of 27 miles.

Tuesday, 22nd. Eight miles this morning took us to Fort Larimie, which is on Larimie's fork of Platte about 800 miles from the frontiers of Missouri. It is owned by the American Fur Company.[11] There is another fort within a mile and a half of this place, belonging to an individual by the name of Lupton.[12] The Black Hills were now in view; a very noted peak, called the Black Hill mountain, was seen like a dark cloud in the western horizon. [*Remark.*] The country along Platte river is far from being fertile and is uncommonly destitute of timber. The earth continues, as we ascend, to become more strongly impregnated with Glauber Salts.

Wednesday, 23d. Remained at the Fort; the things of Mr. Shotwell were sold at auction.

Thursday, 24th. Left the Fort this morning and soon began to wind among the Black Hills. Two of our men stopped at the Fort (Simpson and Mast), but two other men with an Indian and his family joined us to travel to Green river. Encamped, having made about seventeen miles—hills here sandy—many wild pears, likewise an abundance of peas, wild—though the bush was dissimilar to ours, yet the pods bore an exact similarity, taste, the same.

Friday, 25th. Journeyed over hills and dales—encamped on a stream affording plenty of grass, bitter cottonwood timber. It resembles the sweet cottonwood of Missouri, except the leaves are like those of the willow—distance 18 miles.

Saturday, 26th. Travelled about 18 miles, and missing our road, encamped on the North fork. At noon we passed the best grass I had seen since I left the frontier of Missouri; it was like a meadow, kind of blue grass—found buffalo, killed three.

Sunday, 27th. Day was warm, road hilly, found no water for 20 miles, encamped on a stream affording grass and timber in abundance, cottonwood,

&c. Found no hard timber.

Monday, 28th. Passed an immense quarry of beautiful white alabaster; 3 buffalo killed, distance travelled 18 miles; encamped on a little rivulet affording as good water as ever run.

Tuesday, 29th. Arrived at the N. fork this evening, road good, distance travelled 15 miles.

Wednesday, 30th. Ascended the N. fork about 16 miles and encamped on it. Buffalo in abundance, killed six.

July. Thursday, 1st. Spent the day in passing over the river to the north side of it. The water ran very rapidly, and it was with considerable difficulty that we forded it. One mule was drowned, and one waggon upset in the river. The water in the N. fork is not so muddy as the South fork.

Friday, 2nd. Continued to coast up the N. fork; the bottoms of the river were in many places completely covered with Glauber Salts, so much so that even handfuls could be taken up perfectly white. A man (Mr. Belden) was hunting a short distance from the company, and left his horse tied while he crept in pursuit of a buffalo, but he was not able to find the same place again and consequently lost his horse. Though the country is perfectly free from timber, excepting near the river, yet there is so great a similarity in the hills that experienced hunters are frequently bewildered in a clear day, when attempting to find a certain place a second time.

Saturday, 3rd. Left the N. fork; a distance of 12 miles took us to a spring of cool, though unpleasantly tasted water. The day was intensely warm, and road mountainous; killed four buffalo and two deer.

Sunday, 4th. Pursued our way over hills and dales, scorched with heat; came to a small copse of red willows, from which issued excellent springs of water. Three buffalo killed, distance travelled 22 miles.

Monday, 5th. The hills continued to increase in height. After travelling 16 miles we encamped at a noted place called Independence Rock. This is a huge isolated rock covering an area, perhaps of half a square mile, and rising in shape of an irregular obtuse mound to the height of 100 feet. It took its name from the celebration of the 4th of July at this place by Capt. Wm. Sublette, and it now bears many names of the early travellers to these regions.[13] Immediately at the base of these rocks flows a small stream called Sweet Water and is a branch of the N. fork; six buffalo killed today.

Tuesday, 6th. This morning John Gray and Romaine were sent on to Green river to see if there were any trappers at the rendezvous, and then return to the company with the intelligence. All hands were anxious to have their names inscribed on this memorable landmark, so that we did not start until near noon; went up stream about 8 miles and encamped on Sweet Water.

Wednesday, 7th. As we journeyed, the mountains were high and naked;

passed a pond that was nearly dried up, perfectly white with Glauber Salts, and in many places two or three inches deep, so that large lumps weighing several pounds were taken up. Buffalo increased in number; 10 were killed. Travelled today about 14 miles.

Thursday, 8th. This morning we came in sight of Wind River mountains; their snow-enveloped summits were dimly seen through the misty clouds that obscured the western horizon. Made about 15 miles today and encamped on Sweet Water in full view of thousands of buffalo; 20 were killed. We now began to lay in meat to last us over the mountains to California.

Friday, 9th. Travelled about 18 miles, killed ten buffalo.

Saturday, 10th. Travelled about 14 miles and stopped to kill and dry meat. Buffalo began to grow scarce.

Sunday, 11th. More than half the company sallied forth to kill meat, but the whole killed but 6 or 7 buffalo. Remained hunting and drying meat; killed today but 4 or 5 buffalo.

Tuesday, 13th. Left our hunting encampment and met John Gray and Romaine returning from Green river. They found no person at the rendezvous on Green river, nor any game ahead; it was therefore thought best to lay in more meat, while we were in the vicinity of the buffalo. We therefore came to a halt, having travelled about 15 miles.

Wednesday, 14th. Company engaged in hunting and curing meat.

Thursday, 15th. As many of the company had articles of traffic which they wished to dispose of at Green river, a subscription was raised to recompense any who would go and find the trappers. John Gray started in pursuit of them, while the company marched on slowly, waiting his return. Travelled about 6 miles today.

Friday, 16th. Traveled about 10 miles and encamped opposite the Wind River mountains where we were in full view of many lofty peaks glittering with eternal snow and frost under the blaze of a July sun.

Saturday, 17th. Traveled about 5 miles—still on Sweet Water.

Sunday, 18th. Left Sweet Water this morning, course S.W. Crossed the divide which separates the water of the Atlantic and Pacific oceans, and after a travel of 20 miles reached Little Sandy, a branch of Green river—1 buffalo was killed.

Monday, 19th. 15 miles took us on to Big Sandy, which is likewise a branch of Green river—2 buffalo were killed.

Tuesday, 20th. Traveled about 18 miles in a circuitous direction, first west and then south. Country was extremely dry and dusty—no game seen but a few antelope—encamped on Big Sandy, having come about 18 miles.

Wednesday, 21st. Descended Big Sandy about 15 miles and again encamped upon it—no grass, had a little rain this evening but not enough to lay the dust.

Thursday, 22d. Descended Big Sandy about 12 miles and stopped where we found plenty of grass—this was very acceptable as our teams were already much jaded for the want of grass. The oxen, however, stood travel, &c., as well as the horses and mules. Gray returned this evening having found Trapp's [Fraeb's] company, which consisted of about 20 men. They had returned to meet our company, though on their way to hunt buffalo, and were now encamped on Green river about 8 miles distant.[14] Gray had suffered much in overtaking the trappers; his mule gave out, there being no water for a great distance, and he himself was so much reduced by hunger and thirst that he was unable to walk. He was therefore compelled to crawl upon his hands and feet, and at last came up with the company in the most forlorn situation imaginable—if they had been another half mile farther, he never could have reached them.

Friday, 23d. Went to Green river—distance 8 miles—spent the remainder of the day trading with the hunters.

Saturday, 24th. Remained at this encampment and continued our traffic with the hunters. Chiles sold his oxen, 2 yoke, and wagon, another also was left.

Sunday, 25th. Left the rendezvous this morning, 6 of the company, viz., John Gray, Peyton, Frye, Rogers, Jones and Romaine, started to return to the United States. Baker stopped in the mountains to trap, crossed Greene river and descended it about 8 miles. Trapp and his company likewise left in pursuit of buffalo.

[*Remark.*] I will not omit to state the prices of several kinds of mountain goods. Powder which is sold by the cupful (pint) is worth $1 per cup. Lead 1.50 per lb., good Mackanaw blankets 8 to 15 dollars; sugar $1 per cupful; pepper $1 also; cotton and calico shirts from 3 to 5$; rifles from 30 to 60. In return, you will receive dressed deerskins at $3, pants made of deerskins $10, beaver skins $10, moccasins $1; flour sold in the Mts. at 50 cents per cupful, tobacco at $2 per lb., butcher knives from 1 to 3$. A good gun is worth as much as a horse; a cap lock is preferred, caps worth $1 per box. We crossed Green river, went about 8 miles down stream and encamped.

Monday, 26th. Left Green river—moved off in a W. direction—distance 12 miles—encamped on a branch of Green river called Ham's fork. Land high, dry and barren, except upon the streams, which afford grass in abundance; also black currants, which though not delicious are acceptable.[15]

Tuesday, 27th.   Advanced upstream about 12 miles.
Wednesday, 28th. do [ditto].   do.   12 do.
Thursday, 29th.   do.   do.   12 do.

Friday, 30th. Traveled about 5 miles and encamped. Guess what took place; another family was created! Widow Gray, who was a sister to Mrs. Kelsey, was married to a man who joined our Company at Fort Larimie. His right name I forget; but his everywhere name, in the mountains, was Cocrum. He had but one eye—marriage ceremony performed by Father De Smet.[16]

Saturday, 31st. Left Ham's fork this morning. A distance of 14 miles, over an uncommonly hilly road, took us to Black's fork of Green river, on which we encamped. Here we found a little grass and no wood. The hills, which everywhere rose to view, were thinly clad with shrubby cedars. The fruit found in this lonesome part of creation — serviceberries on the mts. and currants on the streams. In the afternoon we descried a large smoke rising from beyond the intervening chain of hills. From this and other signs we were assured that there were plenty of Indians in the country. It was necessary therefore to keep a vigilant look-out, lest the Blackfeet should leave us minus a few horses.

Sunday, August 1st. Ascended Black's fork about 12 miles.

Monday, 2nd. Retraced about 2 miles of yesterday's travel, and went up another defile, in order to find a practicable route across the divide between the waters of Green and Bear rivers; plenty of grass, good spring water, distance 11 miles.

Tuesday, 3rd. Ascended a high divide and passed down by a most difficult route into the valley of Bear river. The course of this stream was marked out as it wound its way through the vale by the willows that skirted its banks. Reached the river, where we found abundance of grass, having come about 20 miles.

Wednesday, 4th. Did not travel.

Thursday, 5th. Proceeded down stream about 18 miles.

Friday, 5th [6th]. Had a fine road down the valley of Bear river and made about 25 miles during the day. Found many kinds of wild currants, red, black, yellow, &c., some of which were of an excellent quality.

Saturday, 7th. This morning we were obliged to make an inland circuit from the river, the bluffs approaching so near the river as to render it impossible to continue along its banks. We, however, reached it again by a most beautiful defile, and beautifully watered by a small rivulet proceeding from a spring. In the afternoon we again left the river on account of the hills, and did not reach it again until dark. The bluffs were exceedingly high, and no person could ever believe that wagons ever passed these huge eminences of nature, did he not witness it with his own eyes. But the pleasing view we had from their top, just as the sun was going to sleep behind the western mountains, paid us for all our trouble. A most beautiful landscape presented itself to view — the rugged summits of almost every shape were fantastically pictured upon the sky bounding the western horizon. A beautiful little lake was seen to the south, whose surface was fancifully mottled with numerous islands, while the river meandered proudly through the valley among willows and scattering cottonwoods till it disappeared among the hills in the shades of the evening. Distance traveled today 16 miles.

Sunday, 8th. Started about noon and went ten miles; scenery of the country was grand.

Monday, 9th. Distance 18 miles.

Tuesday, 10th. The day was fine and pleasant; a soft and cheerful breeze and the sky bedimmed by smoke brought to mind the tranquil season of autumn. A distance of 10 miles took us to the Soda Fountain, where we stopped the remainder of the day. This is a noted place in the mountains and is considered a great curiosity—within the circumference of 3 or 4 miles there are included no less than 100 springs, some bursting out on top of the ground, others along the banks of the river which are very low at this place, and some, even in the bottom of the river. The water is strongly impregnated with soda, and wherever it gushes out of the ground, a sediment is deposited, of a redish color, which petrifies and forms around the springs large mounds of porus rock; some of which are no less than fifty feet high. Some of these fountains have become entirely dry, in consequence of the column of water which they contained becoming so high as to create sufficient power by its pressure to force the water to the surface in another place. In several of the springs the water was lukewarm—but none were very cold. The ground was very dry at this time, and made a noise as we passed over it with horses, as though it was hollow underneath. Cedar grows here in abundance, and the scenery of the country is romantic. Father De Smet, with 2 or 3 Flathead Indians, started about dark this evening to go to Fort Hall, which was about 50 miles distant.[17]

Wednesday, 11th. Having traveled about 6 miles this morning the Company came to a halt—the Oregon Company were now going to leave Bear river for Ft. Hall, which is situated on Lewis river, a branch of the Columbia. Many who purposed in setting out to go immediately through to the California, here concluded to go into Oregon so that the California company now consisted of only 32 men and one woman and child, there being but one family.[18] The two companies, after bidding each other a parting farewell, started and were soon out of sight. Several of our Company, however, went to Ft. Hall to procure provision, and to hire if possible a pilot to conduct us to the Gap in the California mountains, or at least to the head of Mary's river. We were therefore to move slowly 'till their return. Encamped on Bear river, having come about 12 miles.[19]

I, in company with another man (J. John), went some distance below the camp to fish in the river; fished sometime without success—concluded we could spend the afternoon more agreeably. The day was uncomfortably warm, could find no place to shelter us from the burning sun, except the thick copses of willows—these we did not like to enter on account of the danger of falling in with bears. We concluded to ascend the mountain, where were two spots of snow in full view, in order to enjoy the contrast between a scorching valley and a snowy mountain. Supposed the snow not more than 4 miles distant; set out without our guns knowing they would be a hindrance in ascending the mountain. Our march was unremitted for at least 4 miles, had only gained the side of a hill which we at first supposed not more than a mile off; here we lingered to observe several kinds of trees which we had not before observed, among which were a kind of rock maple, choke cherry &c. But conscious of being defeated in our object, if we lost much time, we ran up the eminence with renewed vigor, till at last gained the summit. But, being determined not to be outdone, we continued on under all the strength we could command. Crossed a valley ¾ of a mile wide, ascended craggy steeps and passed through thickets of the densest kind; night obscured the valley below us, lost sight of the snow above us, afraid to return lest we might fall in with bears, as their signs were plenty and fresh; continued to ascend the mountain till midnight, could not find the snow—we were cold, not having our coats. Clouds drifted against the mountain and made us wet—slept under a pine tree which afforded us a good shelter. Morning came, it found us about half a mile below the snow, took as much as we could conveniently carry; took another route down the mountain, running and jumping as fast as our strength would permit, arrived at the camp about noon. They supposed, without doubt, that the Blackfeet had got us, had been up all night on guard, every fire had been put out, they had been out twice in search of us and were about to start again when we arrived. We were received with a mixture of joy and reprehension. The company was soon under way and traveled about 4 miles.

Friday, 13th. Traveled about 10 miles in a southerly direction. It was the intention of the company to stop and hunt in Cash valley, which is on Bear river 3 or 4 days' travel from its mouth.

Saturday, 14th. Left the river on account of the hills which obstructed our way on it; found an abundance of choke cherries, many of which were ripe. Road uncommonly broken, did not reach the river; distance about 14 miles.

Sunday, 15th. Continued our journey over hills and ravines, going to almost every point of the compass in order to pass them. The day was very warm— the grass had been very good, but it was now very much parched up. Having come about 15 miles, we encamped on a small stream proceeding out of the mountains at no great distance from us. But we were surprised to see it become perfectly dry in the course of an hour; some of the guard said there was plenty of water in it about midnight.

Monday, 16th. This morning there was abundance of water in the little stream and it was running briskly when we left it. If the water was not supplied by the melting of the snow in the mountains, it was really an interesting spring; found an abundance of choke cherries, very large and exquisitely delicious, better than any I ever eat before. Distance traveled, 12 miles.

Tuesday, 17th. Traveled about 16 miles; saw a large smoke rising out of the mountains before us. It had probably been raised by the Indians, as a telegraph, to warn the tribe that their land was visited by strangers. We were unable to procure any fuel this evening; we therefore slept without fire. The Indians found in this region are Shoshonees; they are friendly.

Wednesday, 18th. Traveled but a short distance when we discovered that a deep salt creek prevented our continuing near the river. In ascending this stream in search of a place to cross it, we found on its margin a hot spring, very deep and clear. The day was very warm and we were unable to reach the river; encamped on this salt creek and suffered much for water, the water being so salt we could not drink it. Distance 15 miles.

Thursday, 19th. Started early, hoping soon to find fresh water, when we could refresh ourselves and animals, but alas! The sun beamed heavy on our heads as the day advanced, and we could see nothing before us but extensive arid plains, glimmering with heat and salt. At length the plains became so impregnated with salt that vegetation entirely ceased; the ground was in many places white as snow with salt & perfectly smooth — the mid-day sun, beaming with uncommon splendor upon these shining plains, made us fancy we could see timber upon the plains, and wherever timber is found there is water always. We marched forward with unremitted pace till we discovered it was an illusion, and lest our teams should give out we returned from S. to E. and hastened to the river which we reached in about 5 miles.

A high mountain overlooked us on the east and the river was thickly bordered with willows — grass plenty but so salt our animals could scarcely eat it; salt glitters upon its blades like frost. Distance 20 miles.

Friday, 20th. Company remained here while two men went to explore the country. They returned bringing the intelligence that we were within ten miles of where the river disembogued itself into the Great Salt Lake. This was the fruit of having no pilot — we had passed through Cash valley, where we intended to have stopped and did not know it.

Saturday, 21st. Marched off in a N.W. direction, and intersected our trail of Thursday last, having made a complete triangle in the plain. At this intersection of the trails, we left a paper elevated by a pole, that the men returning from Fort Hall might shun the tedious rounds we had taken. Found grass and water which answered our purpose very well, though both were salt. Distance ten miles.

Sunday, 22nd. This morning a man (Mr. Brolaski) returned from the Fort, and said the reason why he came alone was the other men had left him, because he was unable to keep up with them; he having a pack horse laden with provision. He had seen the paper at the intersection of the trails, and was guided by it to the camp; the others were undoubtedly going the rounds of the triangle. Sure enough, they came up in the afternoon, having gone to the river and back; no pilot could be got at the Fort. The families that went into Oregon had disposed of their oxen at the fort and were going to descend the Columbia river with pack horses — they in exchange received one horse for every ox. Their waggons they could not sell. They procured flour at 50 cents a pint, sugar same price and other things in proportion. Near where we were encamped here were a few hackberry trees.[20]

Monday, 23rd. Started, bearing our course west, in order to pass the Salt Lake — passed many salt plains and springs in the forenoon. The day was hot — the hills and land bordering on the plains were covered with wild sage. In passing the declivity of a hill, we observed this sage had been plucked up and arranged in long minows [windrows], extending near a mile in length. It had been done by the Indians, but for what purpose we could not imagine, unless it was to decoy game. At evening we arrived in full view of the Salt Lake; water was very scarce. Cedar grows here both on the hills and in the valleys. Distance 20 miles.

Tuesday, 24th. Cattle strayed this morning to seek water — late start — day was warm — traveled about 10 miles in a W. direction, encamped where we found numerous springs, deep, clear and somewhat impregnated with salt. The plains were snowy white with salt. Here we procured salt of the best quality. The grass that grew in small spots on the plains was laden with salt which had formed itself on the stalks and blades in lumps, from the size of a pea to that of a hen's egg. This was the kind we procured, it being very white, strong and pure.

Wednesday, 25th. Remained here all day.

Thursday, 26th. Traveled all day over dry, barren plains, producing nothing but sage, or rather it ought to be called, wormwood, and which I believe will grow without water or soil. Two men were sent ahead in search of water, but returned a little while before dark, unsuccessful.

Our course intersected an Indian trail, which we followed directly north towards the mountains, knowing that in these dry countries the Indian trails always lead to the nearest water. Having traveled till about 10 o'clock P.M. made a halt, and waited till morning. Distance about 30 miles.

Friday, 27th. Daylight discovered to us a spot of green grass on the declivity of the mountain towards which we were advancing. 5 miles took us to this place, where we found, to our great joy, an excellent spring of water and an abundance of grass. Here we determined to continue 'till the route was explored to the head of Mary's river and run no more risks of perishing for want of water in this desolate region.

Saturday, 28th. Company remained here. A Shoshonee Indian came to our camp; from him we learned that there were more Indians not far off who had horses. Several men and myself went in search of them. Having gone about 5 miles, up hills and down hills covered with thick groves of cedar (red), we unexpectedly came to an Indian, who was in the act of taking care of some meat — venison — which he had just killed; about half of which we readily purchased for 12 cartridges of powder & ball. With him as a pilot we went in pursuit of other Indians; he led us far up in the mountains by a difficult path, where we found two or three families, hid as it were from all the world, by the roughness of nature. The only provision which they seemed to have was a few elder berries and a few seeds; under a temporary covert of bushes, I observed the aged Patriarch, whose head looked as though it had been whitened by the frosts of at least 90 winters. The scars on his arms and legs were almost countless—a higher forehead I never saw upon man's head. But here in the solitude of the mountains and with the utmost contentment, he was willing to spend the last days of his life among the hoary rocks and craggy cliffs, where perhaps he, in his youthful gayety, used to sport along crystal streams which run purling from the mountains. Not succeeding in finding horses, we returned to the camp.

Sunday, 29th. Capt. Bartleson with C. Hopper started to explore the route to the head of Mary's river, expecting to be absent about 8 or 9 days—the Company to await here his return.

Monday, 30th. Nothing of importance occurred.

Tuesday, 31st. No success hunting.

September. Wednesday, 1st. An ox killed for beef.

Thursday, 2d. Idle in camp.

Friday, 3d. Four or 5 Indians came to camp—bought three horses of them.

Saturday, 4th. Bought a few serviceberries of the Indians.

Sunday, 5th. Grass having become scarce, we concluded to move on a little every day to meet Capt. B. & H. Traveled about 6 miles and encamped by a beautiful cedar grove.

Monday, 6th. Traveled about 7 miles.

Tuesday, 7th. Traveled about 7 miles; antelope appeared to be plenty.

Wednesday, 8th. Exceedingly cold; ice in our water buckets. Part of the Company remained on account of the cold—2 wagons with owners being contrary, went on.

Thursday, 9th. The part of the Company that remained yesterday went on and overtook the 2 wagons. Capt. Bartleson & Hopper returned, bringing intelligence that they had found the head of Mary's river—distant about 5 days' travel. Distance traveled today about 12 miles S.W. direction. The Indians stole a horse—day cool.

Friday, 10th. Traveled about 15 miles and encamped without water.

Saturday, 11th. Traveled about 15 miles and came to water, course W.

Sunday, 12th. Mr. Kelsey left his wagons and took his family and goods on pack horses, his oxen not being able to keep up. Distance today about 12 miles.

Monday, 13th. Traveled about 15 miles south, between salt plains on the E. and high mts. on the W.

Tuesday, 14th. Traveled about 25 miles and stopped about 9 o'clock at night, in the middle of a dry plain, destitute of water.

Wednesday, 15th. Started very early, day was exceedingly warm, passed through a gap in a ridge of mountains, came into a high dry plain, traveled some distance into it, saw the form of a high mountain through the smoky atmosphere — reached it, having come about 15 miles — found plenty of water — our animals were nearly given out. We were obliged to go so much further in order to get along with the wagons. We concluded to leave them, and pack as many things as we could.

Thursday, 16th. All hands were busy making pack saddles and getting ready to pack. While thus engaged, an Indian, well advanced in years, came down out of the mountains to our camp. He told us by signs that the Great Spirit had spoken to him to go down upon the plains in the morning, and on the E. side of the mts. he would find some strange people, who would give him a great many things. Accordingly he had come. We gave him all such things as we had intended to throw away; whenever he received anything which he thought useful to him, he paused and looking steadfastly at the sun, addressed him in a loud voice, marking out his course in the sky, as he advanced in his invocation, which took him about 2 minutes to perform. As he received quite a number of articles, it took him a considerable part of the day to repeat his blessings. No Persian, in appearance, could be more sincere.

Friday, 17th. About 11 A.M. all were ready to start; horses, mules, and 4 oxen, packed. Proceeded south along the mts. seeking a place to pass through. At length an Indian trail took us across into a dry plain, perfectly destitute of grass and water. Traveled 'till about midnight, having come about 17 miles. This plain was white in many places with salt, and the cool evening contrasting with the color of the salt on the ground gave a striking similarity to winter. Two of the oxen that were carrying packs got lost from the Company in the night, about 8 miles from where we encamped, but it was supposed they would follow on.

Saturday, 18th. Morning found us on the east side of a mountain not far from its base but there were no signs of water; the lost oxen not having come up, I, in company with another young man, went in search of them, while the company went on, promising to stop as soon as they found water. I went back about 10 miles, but found nothing of their trail — the sun was in a melting mood — the young man became discouraged and in spite of all my entreaties returned to the company. About an hour after I found the trail of the oxen which bore directly north (the Comp. were traveling S.W.). After pursuing it some distance, I discovered fresh mocasin tracks upon the trail, and there began to be high grass which made me mistrust the Indians had got the oxen. But my horse was good and my rifle ready, and I knew the Indians in these parts to be very timid, for they were generally seen in the attitude of flight. But what made me most anxious to find the oxen was prospect of our wanting them for beef. We had already killed 4 oxen and there were but 13 remaining, including the lost ones, and the Co. was now killing an ox every two or three days. Having followed the trail about 10 miles directly north, to my great delight I found the oxen. I was soon in motion for the Company, but not being able to overtake them, was obliged to stop about dark. I passed the night rather uncomfortably, having neither fire nor blanket. I knew Indians to be plenty from numerous signs, and even where I slept, the ground had been dug up that very day for roots. The plains here were almost barren, the hills were covered with cedar.

Sunday, 19th. This morning, I met 3 men who were coming to bring me water, &c. Arrived at camp; they journeyed yesterday about 17 miles, did not travel today.

Monday, 20th. Passed along one of the highest mountains we had seen in our whole journey, seeking a place to scale it, as we wished to travel W. instead of S. being convinced, that we were already far enough south. At length passed through and descended into a beautiful valley, inclining towards the W. All now felt confident that we were close on the headwaters of Mary's river—distance 25 miles. Two hunters slept out last night, the Company taking a different direction from that which they expected.

Tuesday, 21st. Hunters returned; many antelope were seen and 2 or 3 killed. About 10 o'clock A.M. as we were coasting along the mountain in a W. direction, we came to some hot springs, which were to me a great curiosity. Within the circumference of a mile there were perhaps 20 springs, the most of which were extremely beautiful, the water being so transparent we could see the smallest thing 20 or 30 feet deep. The rocks which walled the springs, and the beautifully white sediment lodged among them, reflected the sun's rays in such a manner as to exhibit the most splendid combination of colors, blue, green, red, &c., I ever witnessed. The water in most of them was boiling hot. There was one, however, more beautiful than the rest; it really appeared more like the work of art than of nature. It was about 4 feet in diameter, round as a circle, and deeper than we could see—the cavity looked like a well cut in a solid rock, its walls being smooth and perpendicular. Just as I was viewing this curiosity, some hunters came up with some meat. We all partook, putting it into the spring, where it cooked perfectly done in 10 minutes—this is no fish story![21]

The earth around the Springs was white with a substance which tasted strongly of potash, and the water in the springs was of this quality. Traveled about 15 miles. Several Indians came to our camp, several of whom had guns. From signs, the valley contained thousands.

Wednesday, 22d. This morning 80 or 90 Indians were seen coming full speed from the W. Many had horses—one was sent about half a mile in advance of the rest—so we ought also to have done, but Capt. B. was perfectly ignorant of Indian customs, and the whole band of savages were suffered to come directly up to us, and almost surround our camp, when Mr B. Kelsey showed by forcible gestures they would be allowed to proceed no farther. The Indians were well armed with guns and bows and arrows. The only words I recollect of hearing Capt. Bartleson say were "let them gratify their curiosity!!" The Indians were Sheshonees, but like other savages always take the advantage where they can. Besides, they were not a little acquainted with warfare, for they undoubtedly visited the Buffalo Country (having many robes) which requires much bravery to contend with the Blackfeet and Chiennes, who continually guard the buffalo in the region of the Rocky mountains. They traveled as near us as they were allowed, till about noon, when they began to drop off, one by one, and at night there were but 8 or 10 remaining. Distance about 12 miles.

Thursday, 23d. We could see no termination of the valley, nor any signs of Mary's river. We therefore concluded that we were too far south, and passed over the mountains to the north, where we struck a small stream running towards the N.W. On this we encamped and found plenty of grass; a few fish were caught, some of which were trout, which led us to the conclusion that this was a branch of Mary's river. Distance 18 miles.

Friday, 24th. As we descended the stream, it rapidly increased in size, and proved to be a branch of a larger stream. The country was desolate and barren, excepting immediately on the streams, where grew a few willows and cottonwoods; the hills in some places produced a few shrubby cedars. Traveled today about 20 miles.

Saturday, 25th. The creek became perfectly dry and its banks rose to high perpendicular precipices, so that there was no other road than the dry bed of the stream. Having come about 15 miles, we encamped in a place affording a little grass and water, where we could see nothing but the sky. But the men who ascended the precipice to see what was the prospect ahead said that in about a mile we would come to a valley—this was delightful news.

Sunday, 26th. The valley, seen yesterday evening, was but 4 or 5 miles in length and led into another difficult defile, though not so long as the one of yesterday, for we passed it into another valley. Distance 18 miles—the stream continued to increase in size.

Monday, 27th. Road was very difficult all day, course of the stream W. Traveled about 20 miles.

Tuesday, 28th. Traveled about 70 miles. Several Indians came to our camp this evening—no timber excepting willows, grass plenty.

Wednesday, 29th. Traveled about 20 miles, course of the stream was W.N.W. According to the map Mary's river ran W.S.W. Strong doubts were entertained about this being Mary's river. The men who got directions at Fort Hall were cautioned that if we got too far south, we would get into the Great Sandy Desert—if too far north, we would wander and starve to death on the waters of the

Columbia, there being no possibility of getting through that way. We had now been 6 days on this stream, and our course had averaged considerably north of west.

Thursday, 30th. Our course today was about due north, 18 miles.

October 1st. The stream had already attained the size of which we supposed Mary's river to be, and yet its course was due N.W. Distance 20 miles.

Saturday, 2d. Having traveled about 5 miles, we all beheld with delight the course of the river change to S.W. Here was excellent grass — it was 3 or 4 feet high, and stood thick like a meadow, it was a kind of bluegrass. The whole valley seemed to be swarming with Indians, but they were very timid. Their sable heads were seen in groups of 15 or 20, just above the tops of the grass to catch a view of us passing by. Whenever we approached their huts, they beckoned us to go on — they are extremely filthy in their habits. Game was scarce, tho' the Indians looked fat and fine. They were Shashonees.

Sunday, 3d. Traveled about 12 miles today west.

Monday, 4th. Distance 25 miles S.W. Country dry, barren, sandy except on the river.

Tuesday, 5th. Today was very warm, and the oxen were not able to keep up with the horses. Traveled about 30 miles and stopped on the river about dark — grass plenty, willows — this going so fast was the fault of Capt. B., nothing kept him from going as fast as his mules could possibly travel. But his dependence was on the oxen for beef — for it was now all we had to live upon.

Wednesday, 6th. Company was out of meat and remained till the oxen came up; several Indians came to camp, one of whom we hired to pilot us on.

Thursday, 7th. Capt. Bartleson, having got enough meat yesterday to last him a day or two, and supposing he would be able to reach the mountains of California in 2 or 3 days, rushed forward with his own mess, consisting of 8 persons at a rate entirely too fast for the oxen, leaving the rest to keep up if they could, and if they could not it was all the same to him. The day was very warm. The Indian pilot remained with us — the river spread into a high, wide swamp, covered with high cane grass — Indians were numerous. Encamped by the swamp about dark, having come about 25 miles — water bad — no fuel, excepting weeds and dry cane grass which the Indians had cut in large heaps to procure sugar from the honey dew with which it was covered.

Friday, 8th. The swamp was clouded with wild geese, ducks &c., which rose from its surface at the report of our guns. We traveled about 6 miles and stopped to kill a couple of oxen that were unable to travel.

Saturday, 9th. Crossed Mary's river where it led from the swamp into a lake beyond; our pilot led us south on the trail of Capt. B. Crossed a plain which is covered with water the greater part of the year — then came into sand hills, among which traveling was very laborious. Saw to the W. of us a lake, presenting a sheet of water 20 or 30 miles in extent. Encamped by another swamp, in which the water was very nauseous. Distance 28 miles. Large numbers of Indians lived about this place, but few (50 or 60) visited our camp. Crossed Mary's river — it was here running E. leading from the lake which we saw to the W. of us yesterday, into the swamp by which we staid last night. Our course today was S.W. Distance 15 miles — encamped upon the lake.

Monday, 11th. Left the lake this morning, going into the mountains on a S. W. course. Today we left the trail of Capt. B. and having traveled 19 miles, arrived on a stream which flowed rapidly, and afforded more water than Mary's river. We thought now, without doubt, that we were safe on the waters of the St. Joaquin (pronounced St. Wawkeen) according to Marsh's letter.[22] Here grew willows, balm Gilead, and a few cottonwoods.[23] The course of the stream as far as we could see was S. — but knew not how soon it might take a turn here in the mountains.

Tuesday, 12th. Traveled about 4 miles upstream, and encamped, understanding our Indian (having hired another pilot) that it would be a long day's travel to water, after leaving the creek.

Wednesday, 13th. Traveled about 13 miles and only crossed a bend of the river; at this place it run due north. Day was hot, the creek had dwindled to half its first size.

Thursday, 14th. This morning we saw at a distance Capt. B. with his 7 men, coming in a direction towards us, but we made no halt, ascended the stream about 20 miles. The mountains continued to increase in height.

Friday, 15th. Advanced upstream about 12 miles and arrived at the base of very high mountains. The creek had become a small spring branch, and took its rise at no great distance in the mountains. But we saw plainly that it was impossible to progress farther without scaling the mts., and our Indian guides said they knew no further.

Saturday, 16th. This morning 4 or 5 men started to ascend several of the high peaks to ascertain if it was possible to pass the mountains. Just as they were going to start Capt. B. came up. He was in rather a hungry condition, and had been travelling several days without provision, excepting a few nuts which they had purchased from the Indians and which they had eaten on a very small allowance. We killed yesterday the best ox we had. This we shared freely with them. There were now but 3 oxen left and they were very poor. But there was no time to loose. The explorers returned & reported that they thought it almost an impracticability to scale the mountains, which continued to increase in height as far as they could see. This evening the Company was convened for the purpose of deciding by vote whether we should go back to the lake and take a path which we saw leading to the N.W., or undertake to climb the mountains. We had no more provision than would last us to the lake — nearly all were unanimous against turning back. I should have mentioned that our Indian pilots last night absconded. This stream I shall call Balm river, there being many balm Gilead trees upon it. (It is not laid down on any map.)[24]

Sunday, 17th. This morning we set forth into the rolling mountains; in many places it was so steep that all were obliged to take it on foot. Part of the day we travelled through vallies between peaks, where the way was quite level — passed down and up thro' forests of pine, fir, cedar, &c.; many of the pines were 12 ft. in diameter and no less than 200 ft. high. Encamped on the side of the mountain, so elevated that the ice remained all day in the streams — but we had not yet arrived at the summit. Killed another ox this evening — made 12 miles.

Monday, 18th. Having ascended about half a mile, a frightful prospect opened before us — naked mountains whose summits still retained the snows perhaps of a thousand years, for it had withstood the heat of a long dry summer, and ceased to melt for the season. The winds roared — but in the deep dark gulfs which yawned on every side, profound solitude seemed to reign. We wound along among the peaks in such a manner as to avoid most of the mountains which we had expected to climb — struck a small stream descending towards the W., on which we encamped, having come 15 miles.

The rivulet descended with great rapidity and it was the opinion of all that we were at least 1 mile perpendicular below the place where we began to descend. The stream had widened into a small valley. Cedars of uncommon size, pines, the most thrifty, clothed the mountains. (One pine, as it was near our camp, was measured. Though it was far from being the tallest, it was 206 ft. high.) All were pleased to think that we were crossing the mountains so fast.

Tuesday, 19th. Descending along the stream, we found several oak shrubs which confirmed us in the hope that we were on the waters of the Pacific. But the route became exceedingly difficult — the stream had swelled to a river — could not approach it — could only hear it roaring among the rocks. Having come about 12 miles a horrid precipice bid us stop — we obeyed and encamped. Those who went to explore the route had not time to come to any conclusion where we could pass. We had descended rapidly all day; the mts. were still mantled with forests of towering pines. The roaring winds and the hollow murmuring of the dashing waters conveyed in the darkness of the night the most solemn and impressive ideas of solitude. To a person fond of a retired life, this, thought I, would be a perfect terrestrial Paradise, but it was not so to us, when we knew that winter was at hand, and that Capt. Walker (the mountaineer) had been lost in these very mountains 22 days before he could extricate himself.[25]

Wednesday, 20th. Men went in different directions to see if there was any possibility of extracting ourselves from this place without going back. They returned and reported it was utterly impossible to go down the creek. One young man was so confident that he could pass along the creek with his horse that he started alone, in spite of many persuasions to the contrary. Capt. B. also being tired of waiting for the explorers to return, started down the stream, which so jaded his animals that he was obliged to wait all day to rest them before he was able to retrace his steps. In the meantime the rest of the Company, suffering for water, were obliged to travel. We proceeded directly N. up the mountains about 4 miles, found a little grass and water — here we killed one of the 2 oxen.

Wednesday, 21st. Our route today was much better than expected, though in any other place than the mountains it would be considered horrible. Capt. B. with his 7 or 8 overtook us, but we heard nothing of J. John's. Distance about 10 miles; could see no prospect of a termination to the mts., mts., mountains!

Thursday, 22d. Descended towards the river about 15 miles — had a tolerable road — arrived within about a mile of the river — could not approach nearer. Here was considerable oak, some of which was evergreen, and thought to be live oak. 3 Indians came to camp; killed the last ox — let this speak for our situation and future prospects!

Friday, 23d. Having no more meat than would last us 3 days, it was necessary to use all possible exertions to kill game, which was exceedingly scarce. For this purpose I started alone, very early in the morning, to keep some distance before the Company, who had concluded to continue as near as possible to the creek on the N. side. I went about 4 miles — met the Indian who came to us last night — obtained a little provisions made of acorns — got an Indian boy to pilot me to his house. He took me down the most rugged path in all nature — arrived on the banks of a river at least ¾ of a mile perpendicular from where I started with him — found no more provision, continued down the river — oak in abundance, buckeye, and a kind of maple. The mountains, which walled in the stream, were so steep that it was with great difficulty I scaled them — having in one place come within an inch of falling from a craggy cliff down a precipice nearly a fourth of a mile perpendicular. 4 long hours I labored before I reached the summit — proceeded directly to intersect the trail of the Company. Mts. covered with the largest and tallest pines, firs, &c., thick copses of hazel &c. — travelled till dark over hills, dales, crags, rocks, &c., found no trail — lay down and slept.

Saturday, 24th. Concluded the Co. had gone north. I travelled E., found no trail — traveled S. — came to the place where I left the Company yesterday morning, having made a long quadrangle in the mts., 8 by 10 miles — took the trail of the Company. They had with great difficulty descended to the river, saw where they staid last night. Distance about 6 miles. Ascended on the S. side of the creek a high precipice. I overtook them; they had traveled today 10 miles. They had hired an Indian pilot who had led them into the worst place he could find and absconded. 5 horses and mules had given out; they were left. I learned likewise that two hunters (A. Kelsey & Jones) started shortly after I did, and had not returned; part of a horse was saved to eat.

Monday, 25th. Went about 6 miles & found it impossible to proceed. Went back about two miles and encamped—dug holes in the ground to deposite such things as we could dispense with. Did not do it, discovering the Indians were watching us; among them was the old, rascally pilot. White oak in abundance.

Tuesday, 26th. Went S. about 3 miles and encamped in a deep ravine. It was urged by some that we should kill our horses and mules—dry what meat we could carry and start on foot to find the way out of the mountains.

Wednesday, 27th. It commenced raining about one o'clock this morning and continued till noon—threw away all our old clothes to lighten our packs, fearing the rain would make the mts. so slippery as to render it impossible to travel. I have since learned that the Indians in the mountains, here, prefer the meat of horses to cattle, and here in these gloomy corners of the mts. they had been accustomed to bring stolen horses and eat them. Here and there were strewed the bones of horses, so the design of the veteran Indian pilot is apparent in leading us into this rugged part of Creation.

As we left this place one of the men, G. Cook, remained concealed to see if the old pilot was among the Indians, who always rushed in as soon as we left our encampments to pick up such things as were left. The old gentleman was at the head of this band, and as *he had undoubtedly led us into this place to perish,* his crime merited death—*a rifle ball laid him dead in his tracks.* We proceeded S. about 6 miles. As we ascended out of the ravine, we discovered the high mountains we had passed were covered with new snow for more than a half mile down their summits.

Thursday, 28th. Surely no horses nor mules with less experience than ours could have descended the difficult steeps and defiles which we encountered in this day's journey. Even as it was, several horses and mules fell from the mountain's side and rolling like huge stones, landed at the foot of the precipices. The mountains began to grow obtuse, but we could see no prospect of their termination. We eat the last of our beef this evening and killed a mule to finish our supper. Distance 6 miles.

Friday, 29th. Last night, the Indians stole a couple of our horses. About noon we passed along by several huts, but they were deserted as soon as we came in sight, the Indians running in great consternation into the woods. At one place the bones of a horse were roasting on a fire; they were undoubtedly the bones of the horses we had lost. Travelled no less than 9 miles today; the night was very cool and had a heavy frost. Although our road was tolerably level today, yet we could see no termination to the mountains—and one much higher than the others terminated our view. Mr. Hopper, our best and most experienced hunter, observed that "If California lies beyond those mountains we shall never be able to reach it." Most of the Company were on foot, in consequence of the horses giving out, and being stolen by the Indians, but many were much fatigued and weak for the want of sufficient provision; others, however, stood it very well. Some had appetites so craving that they eat the meat of most of the mule raw, as soon as it was killed; some eat it half roasted, dripping with blood.

Saturday, 30th. We had gone about 3 miles this morning, when lo! to our great delight, we beheld a wide valley! This we had entirely overlooked between us and the high mountain which terminated our view yesterday. Rivers evidently meandered through it, for timber was seen in long extended lines as far as the eye could reach. But we were unable to reach it today, and encamped in the plains. Here grew a few white oaks. Travelled today about 20 miles. Saw many tracks of elk. The valley was wonderfully parched with heat, and had been stripped of its vegetation by fire. Wild fowls, geese, etc., were flying in multitudes.

Sunday, 31st. Bore off in a N.W. direction to the nearest timber; day was warm, plain dry and dusty, reached timber which was white oak (very low & shrubby) and finally, the river which we had left in the mts., joyful sight to us poor famished wretches!!! Hundreds of antelope in view! Elk tracks thousands! Killed two antelopes and some wild fowls; the valley of the river was very fertile and the young tender grass covered it, like a field of wheat in May. Not a weed was to be seen, and the land was as mellow and free from weeds as land could be made by plowing it 20 times in the U.S. Distance today 20 miles.

November. Monday, 1st. The Company tarried to kill game; an abundance of wild fowl and 13 deer and antelopes were bro't in. My breakfast, this morning, formed a striking contrast with that of yesterday which was the lights of a wolf.

Tuesday, 2d. Capt. B. with his 7 remained to take care of the meat he had killed—while the rest of the Company went on. We passed some beautiful grapes, sweet and pleasant. The land decreased in fertility as we descended the stream. Behold! This morning, Jones, who left the camp to hunt on the 23rd ult. came to the camp. They (he and Kelsey) had arrived in the plains several days before us, and found an Indian, who conducted them to Marsh's house, but he brought bad news; he said there had been no rain in California for 18 months, and that the consequence was, there was little breadstuff in the country. Beef, however, was abundant and of the best quality. Travelled today 16 miles.

Wednesday, 3d. We waited till Capt. B. came up, and all started for Marsh's about noon; arrived at the St. Joaquin and crossed it—distance 13 miles—found an abundance of grass here. The timber was white oak, several kinds of evergreen oaks, and willow — the river about 100 yds. in width.

Thursday, 4th. Left the river in good season and departing gradually from its timber came into large marshes of bulrushes. We saw large herds of elk and wild horses grazing upon the plain. The earth was in many places strongly impregnated with salt — came into hills. Here were a few scattering oaks — land appeared various, in some places black, some light clay color, and in other mulatto (between black and white) sometimes inclining to a red soil, but it was all parched with heat. Finally we arrived at Marsh's house, which is built of unburnt bricks, small and has no fireplace — wanting a floor and covered with bulrushes. In fact it was not what I expected to find; a hog was killed for the company. We had nothing else but beef; the latter was used as bread, the former as meat. Therefore I will say we had bread and meat for dinner. Several of our company were old acquaintances of Marsh in Missouri, and therefore much time was passed in talking about old times, the incidents of our late Journey, and our future prospects. All encamped about the house — tolerably well pleased with the appearance of Dr. Marsh, but much disappointed in regard to his situation, for among all his shrubby white oaks, there was not one tall enough to make a rail-cut. No other timber in sight, excepting a few cotton-woods and willows.[26]

Friday, 5th. Company remained at Marsh's getting information respecting the country.

Saturday, 6th. Fifteen of the Company started for a Spanish town, called the Pueblo of St. Joseph [which is situated about (40?) miles from Marsh's], to seek employment.[27]

Observations about the Country

You will, undoubtedly, expect me to come out in plain language, either for or against the country; but this I cannot do, not having been able to see as much of it as I intended before I wrote to you. I have, however, been diligent in making inquiries of men who are residents in the country. This will, in some measure, answer the place of experience. The whole of my travels in California, I will now briefly relate; and then make a recapitulation, describing the country, &c.

Wednesday, 10th. I went to R. Livermore's, which is about 20 miles from Marsh's, nearly W.; he has a Spanish wife and is surrounded by 5 or 6 Spanish families.[28]

On the 11th I returned to Marsh's. This evening M. Nye, of Weston, Mo., returned from the Mission of St. Joseph, bringing the intelligence that part of those who started down to the Pueblo were detained at the Mission, and that the others were sent for, in consequence of not bringing passports from the States. He likewise brought a letter from the Spanish Commander in Chief of Upper California to Marsh, requesting him to come, in all possible haste, and answer or rather explain the intention of the company in coming to California.[29] News had just arrived by the papers of the United States, via Mexico; it was the remark of some foolish editor that the United States would have California, and if they could not get it on peaceable terms, they would take it by force. This created considerable excitement among the suspicious Spaniards. All, however, obtained passports from the General, till they should be able to procure them from the Governor at Monterry.[30] On the 15th I started for the Mission of St. Joseph, and arrived there on the 16th, returned to Marsh's on the 18th.

Started for Capt. Sutter's on the 21st and arrived there on the 28th. This place is situated nearly due N. of Marsh's, on the Sacramento river, and about 75 miles.[31] We were received by Capt. Sutter with great kindness, and found here J. John, who had left us in the mountains on the 10th of last month, Oct. He arrived 1 day sooner at this place than we did at Marsh's. Capt. Sutter, on hearing of the Company, immediately sent in search of us, loading 2 mules with flour and sugar for our comfort. I remained with Capt. S. about 5 weeks; during which time, I was principally employed in studying the Spanish language. I made no travel here, except about 15 miles up the American fork, a considerable branch of the Sacramento river. On the 27th of Dec. Mr. Flugge, one of our Company who went into Oregon, arrived at Capt. Sutter's—he came with the trapping company from Ft. Vancouver on the Columbia; and brought the intelligence that the families had safely landed in the Columbia, and were well pleased with the country—that an express came bringing the news from Green river, that Trapp and 1 of his men were killed by the Chienne Indians, 2 or 3 days after we had left that place.[32]

The Journey from Oregon to this place by land cannot be performed in less than 6 or 8 weeks with horse. [Remark.] Capt. Sutter has bought out the whole Russian settlement, consisting of about 2000 head of cattle, 600 horses, and 1000 sheep, besides dry property. All the Russians, owing to their dissatisfaction of some proceedings of this Government, relative to themselves, have left the country; they consisted of about 300 men, besides women and children.[33]

On the 8th of January '42, I left Capt. S's, in his employ for the Russian settlement. I descended the Sacramento in a launch, of 30 tons, into the Bay of St. Francisco. I landed at Sousalita [Sausalito] pronounced Sow sa le ta, on the N. side of the Bay, in full view of the vessels lying at anchor at port St. Francisco. I here took it by land and in 3 days arrived at this place which is about 6 miles from Bodaga, the Russian port, and 60 miles north of Port St. Francisco.

Since my arrival here, I have made two trips to Ross, which is about 30 miles N. of this place on the Pacific; most of the Russians resided at this place. And once I have been to Sousalita, through the Mission of San Rafael. These are all my travels in California.[34]

It will be necessary for me to describe Marsh's house, as I have made it rather a starting place. It is about 50 miles from Port St. Francisco, 6 or 7 miles S. of the Sacramento river, 15 miles from the Bay, St. F., & 15 or 20 miles below the mouth of S. Joaquin river and is among a few scattering oaks overlooked by a high mountain peak on the W. which is a termination of that chain of mountains which terminated our view on the 29th of October last. The high California mountains are in full view, and the country which intervenes between them and the Ocean is on an average 100 miles wide; most of the land in these parts is unfit for cultivation, but well adapted to grazing. The reason of this is because it is too wet in winter and too dry in summer. In many places the soil is black and has every appearance of being as fertile as any land I ever saw, but I am informed this is never sown or planted in consequence of its drying too much in summer and cracking open; it may be considered a prairie country, for the plains are destitute of timber — streams are frequent and always skirted by timber. Every kind of timber which I have seen you will see in the following list: oak, cottonwood, willow, ash, black walnut, box elder, alder, buckeye, redwood, pine, fir, sicamore, madrone [Spanish name], laurel, cedar, maple, hazel bushes and whortle berries [huckle-berries]; here are many other shrubs but I don't know their names.

Oak — here are many kinds of oak, but the only kind which I remember to have seen in the U.S. resembling the oak of this is the white oak; this grows on almost every stream, frequently among the mountains, sometimes in the middle of plains; the other kinds of oak are principally evergreen, as they retain their leaves all the year. I have been told by many that it answers every purpose that the oak does in the U.S. excepting for rails and building, it being generally too shrubby. It grows very large in places. I have seen trees 10 or 12 feet in diameter.

Cottonwood — this grows neither large nor tall, and only on streams or in low places. On the Sacramento and its branches are more or less of it.

Willows — these grow on every stream, both great and small, and are often so densely interwoven along banks of rivers that a bird can't fly through them.

Ash — this is very scarce, it is the kind called white ash, but it is so low that it is not valuable for building; it is an excellent substitute for hickory, making axe helves, gun sticks, &c.

Black Walnut — I am not aware that this grows in any other place than on the Sacramento river; even here, confined to a few miles, grows shrubby.

Box Elder — an abundance on every stream.

Alder—this is an excellent substitute for hickory; it is also found in abundance.

Buckeye—this grows very small, always branching from the ground; it bears a larger nut than the buckeye of the United States.

Redwood—this is abundant in almost every mountain; it is a kind of hemlock or cedar, found on both sides of the St. Francisco Bay, sometimes grows in valleys. It is the most important timber in California, generally 150 feet high; but I have seen many 200 feet high and not less than 15 feet in diameter. It splits the easiest of any timber I ever saw; it is very durable, houses, doors, &c., are made of it.

Fir—this generally grows with the redwood, but not so useful.

Sicamore—grows in plenty along the Sacramento river, principally used for canoes, not hollow, as in the U.S.

Pine—this is abundant in the mountains, but is difficult to obtain; what kind it is I am unable to say.

Madrone—grows as abundant as the oak. It is one of the most beautiful trees I have ever seen—is an evergreen, retaining a bright green foliage, but that which renders it so pleasing is the color of the bark of all its branches. It is smooth like the sicamore, and of a lively scarlet color, is a most excellent firewood, and I have been informed by creditable gentlemen that it is an ellegant substitute for mahogany.

Laurel—another beautiful evergreen, and on the N. side of the Bay abundant; the largest are two feet in diameter, tough wood. I have not learned its uses.

Cedar—scarce here, but abundant in the mountains.

Maple—plenty in some places, different from any I have heretofore seen, but curly sometimes; will answer every purpose maple does in the United States, but for sugar, too warm here.

Hazle bushes grow on almost every stream, and in the mountains, among the redwood, produce nuts as in Missouri, and being tough, make excellent withs.

Whortle berries abundant on the hills.

I will here observe that there is no [oak except?] live oak in California, but presume that there is timber to answer all purposes for shipbuilding.

Grass. The grass is not like that of the prairies of the United States. It is of a finer and better quality. It ceases to grow about the first of July in consequence of the heat, and dries; the cattle, however, eat it, and become remarkably fat. It begins to grow again in October or November, when the rainy season sets in, and continues to grow all winter. When I went to Ross, the Russian establishment, the grass all along the Pacific (on the 3rd Feb.), was at least a foot high; green and growing finely.

Mustard grows in abundance.

Here on this side of the Bay is an abundance of red and white clover growing with the grass.

Here are also innumerable quantities of wild oats, which I am told grow nearly all over California, and grow as thick as they can stand, producing oats of an excellent quality; but as neither cattle nor horses are ever fed here, they are never harvested.

Wheat — on the south side of the Bay of St. Francisco, the soil, climate, &c., are as well adapted to raising wheat as in any part of the world. I have been credibly informed that it yields from 70 to 115 fold — wheat will always come up the second year and produce more than half as much as it did the first. This is because of its scattering on the ground while harvesting. Wheat is sown in December, January and February, harvested in June and first of July. North side of the Bay will not yield more than 15 or 20 fold.

Corn does not grow well in any part of California; it, however, thrives far better on the north side of the Bay than on the south. It will not yield more than 15 or 20 bushels to the acre — when you read my description of the climate you will not wonder. The corn is of a small kind planted in April and May.

Potatoes — Irish potatoes grow well and are of a good quality — should be planted in April.

Sweet potatoes have never been tried.

Beans are produced abundantly, likewise peas; peas are planted in gardens about the 10th of March and are ripe about the last of May.

Barley yields well, and is sown at the time of wheat.

Onions, cabbages, parsnips, beets, turnips grow well.

Climate

First, I will commence with the rainy season, as it was about the beginning of this part of the year that I arrived in California; October is said to be a doubtful month in regard to the commencement of the rainy season. It, however, sets in about the 10th of November. The rains are never very cold, and there are many warm and beautiful showers, like those of summer in the U.S. Judge from the following diary of the weather, which I have regularly attended to since coming here.

NOVEMBER 4th. 1841. Day warm	8th.	"	do	do	do
and pleasant. Evening cool.	9th.	"	do	do	do
5th. Day warm	10th.	"	do	do	do
6th. " Bright and clear, warm	11th.	"	do	do	do
7th. " do [ditto] do do	12th.	"	do	do	do

13th.   "   do   do   do
14th.   "   mild and pleasant
15th.   "   pleasant, warm and rainy.
16th.   Rain today. Evening cool.
17th.   Warm and rainy.
18th.   Showery today, morning clear.
19th.   Cloudy all day.
20th.   Pleasant day. Evening cool.
21st.   Morning cool, day cool with
        N.W. breeze, rainy evening.
22nd.   Warm showers.
23rd.   A few showers.
24th.   Cloudy, evening cool with
        frost.
25th.   do   without frost.
26th.   Warm and clear.
27th.   do   cloudy.
28th.   Clear though somewhat cool.
29th.   Day cloudy and moderate.
30th.   do   do

DECEMBER 1st. Clear and warm.
 2nd.   Mild and warm.
 3rd.   Mild but somewhat hazy.
 4th.   A little rain.
 5th.   Rained nearly all day.
 6th.   Inclined to be fair.
 7th.   Fair and mild.
 8th.   Drizzling rain.
 9th.   Rained half the day.
10th.   do   do
11th.   Fine day.
12th.   Rained and blew all day.
13th.   Tolerably fair.
14th.   Same.
15th.   Drizzly all day.
16th.   Forenoon rainy, aftern'n
        cloudy.
17th.   Fair sun shone bright.
18th.   Light showers.
19th.   Fine day, mild evening.

20th.   do   do
21st.   Pleasant day.
22nd.   Pleasant weather.
23rd.   Same.
24th.   Same.
25th.   Light showers of rain.
26th.   Fair and pleasant.
27th.   Same.
28th.   Same.
29th.   Inclined to be cool.
30th.   Rainy.
31st.   Fair day.

JANUARY 1st. Same.
 2nd.   Same.
 3rd.   Same.
 4th.   Same.
 5th.   Fair clear weather.
 6th.   Light showers.
 7th.   Cloudy, no rain, warm.
 8th.   Clear and warm.
 9th.   do   do
10th.   do   do
11th.   Cloudy, heavy frost in
        morning.
12th.   Inclined to be fair.
13th.   Rainy, warm showers.
14th.   Pleasant weather.
15th.   do   do
16th.   Rain half the day.
17th.   Fine weather.
18th.   do   do
19th.   do   do
20th.   Cool.
21st.   Cloudy.
22nd.   Fine and clear.
23rd.   do   do
24th.   do   do
25th.   do   do
26th.   Variable and rainy.
27th.   Fine weather.

28th. Cloudy weather.
29th. Variable and rainy.
30th. Cloudy and cool.
31st. Rainy and warm.

FEBRUARY 1st. Fine weather.
 2nd. Same.
 3rd. Same.
 4th. Rainy.
 5th. Bright & clear.
 6th. Same.
 7th. Same.
 8th. Same.
 9th. Same.
10th. Same.
11th. Rainy.
12th. Fine and warm.
13th. Same.
14th. Same.
15th. Same.
16th. Rainy.
17th. Fair and pleasant.
18th. Same.
19th. Same.
20th. Same.
21st. Light showers.
22nd. Rained nearly all day.
23rd. Fair weather.
24th. Same.
25th. Same.
26th. Rainy.
27th. Cloudy and cool.
28th. Fine and pleasant.

MARCH 1st. Fair.

2nd. Same.
3rd. Cool and cloudy.
4th. Same.
5th. Bright, clear and warm.
6th. Same.
7th. Rainy.
8th. This morning snowed
     5 minutes.
9th. Cool.
10th. Fine and warm.
11th. Same.
12th. Same.
13th. Same.
14th. Same.
15th. Same.
16th. Cloudy.
17th. Inclined to rain.
18th. Fine.
19th. Showery.
20th. Rainy.
21st.   do and cool.
22nd. Rainy and cool.
23rd. Morning rain, evening fair.
24th. Cloudy.
25th. Fine.
26th. Rainy in afternoon.
27th. Cloudy and rainy.
28th. Fair.
29th. Same.
30th. Same.
31st. Rainy.

APRIL 1st. Fine.
 2nd. Very fine, strawberries will
     be ripe in a few days.

[*Remark.*] — When it is rainy the wind is always from the south. And when fair from the W.N.W. Here are many very bright frosty mornings which freeze the ground sometimes an inch deep. I have seen the ice half an inch thick. But seldom thicker than a pane of glass. There are but few mornings that we have frost; it, however, freezes in daytime.

Summer

From March, the rainy season gradually decreases, ceases entirely about the last of May. During the summer months, heat is intense, so that it is customary for laborers to be unimployed from ten A.M. till four P.M.

Certain situations are much protected from heat by N.W. breezes which always prevaile in summer.

When the wind from the sea is blowing in the morning, it continues till ten o'clock A.M. Heat then becomes intense, but it generally begins about 3 or 4 in the afternoon. The mountains frequently preclude the sea breeze from many situations, so there is a great difference in places but a few miles apart. It seldom thunders or lightnings here. I will here remark that there is more rain on the N. side of St. Francisco bay than on the south; why it is so I am unable to explain. It is in California as it is in the Rocky Mountains and, I believe, in all mountains or mountainous countries, very warm during the day and cool at night—so cool that there are frosts sometimes even as late as July. The nights are not proportionably cold in winter; in fact, many of them are quite warm.

The cool nights, together with the dryness of the summer, are undoubtedly the reason why corn, and many other things, do not come to so great perfection here as in many other parts of the world. Watermelons and pumpkins are produced here in abundance, though I fear not so well as in Missouri. They are said not to be so sweet as in the U. States but they last longer, frequently to December, up in June. Strawberries are found in many places in abundance, large and delicious, and are ripe about the middle of April.

Falling of the Leaves

This is very different in California from what it is in the U.S.; there, they become yellow by frosts, &c., and hasten down in showers, so that in a week or two the whole vegetable world is stript of its foliage. But here, most of the trees are evergreens, and those that are not, gradually resign their verdure till they are quite naked about the first of January.

Resources of the Country

All concur in pronouncing the country good for fruit, apples, &c. I presume it is so; I went to Ross (this is the most northern settlement in California) on the 25th of January—I saw here a small but thrifty orchard, consisting of apple, peach, pear, cherry and quince trees—the peach trees had not shed their leaves and several were in blossom, the quince and more than half the apple trees were as green as in summer. There were roses, marygolds and several kinds of garden flowers in full bloom. I again visited this place on the 3rd Feb., saw wild plants in bloom—such as violet, &c. Apple and peach trees beautifully arrayed in blossoms; what time apples are ripe, I cannot say, but presume in June or July.

Pear trees, I am informed, come to great perfection. Fig trees likewise are found in almost every orchard and grow well.

The wine grape is cultivated and grows to great perfection.

You have undoubtedly heard that here are English and American settlements in California; but it is not the case. There are from 3 to 600 foreigners here, principally English and American, but they do not live in settlements by themselves; they are scattered throughout the whole Spanish population, and most of them have Spanish wives, and in fine they live in every respect like the Spaniards.[35] I know of but two American families here—one, the family of Mr. Kelsey who came with us, and the other, Mr. Walker, who came here from Jackson County, Mo., by way of Oregon.

He is brother to Capt. Walker, the mountaineer; he likes California better than Oregon—there are many English and American traders on the coast.[36]

The population of the Spaniards probably will not exceed 5000.[37]

It is a proverb here (and I find a pretty true one) that a Spaniard will not do anything which he cannot do on horseback—he does not work perhaps on an average one month in the year—he labors about a week, when he sows his wheat, and another week, when he harvests it. The rest of the time is spent riding about.

I know a few Spaniards who are industrious and enterprising. They have become immensely rich. This likewise is the case with the foreigners, who have used the least industry. Wealth here principally consists in horses, cattle, and mules.

Fences are in many places made with little trouble. Capt. Sutter has about 300 acres under fence; his fences are made of small round sticks, inserted end-wise into the ground and lashed with cowhide. But where the redwood grows, fences are made of rails, the same as in the States.

Wheat, corn and potatoes are seldom surrounded by a fence. They grow out in the plains and are guarded from the cattle and horses by the Indians, who are stationed in their huts near the fields.

You can employ any number of Indians by giving them a lump of beef every week, and paying them about one dollar for same time. Cattle are so wild, however, as to keep some distance from houses. Since my residence in the country I have become sick of the manner of fencing or protecting grain, etc., from cattle as done by the Spaniards. To farm well, you must make fences as in the U. States.

The land on the north side of the Bay is beautifully diversified with hills and valleys. The farms are chosen according to circumstances among the hills, and are very scattering. Some hills are timbered, some are not, affording excellent pasturage for cattle, horses, etc. The timber grows generally on creeks and ravines on the sides of mountains south and southeast of the Bay.

The Sacramento spreads into a wide valley or plain through which run most of its tributaries, the St. Joaquin, etc. These plains are now the province of thousands of elk, antelope, deer, wildhorses, etc. They might easily be changed to raising of thousands of fine cattle.

Tule marshes. Tule is a name given by Spaniards to a kind of bulrush. They grow very large, sometimes an inch in diameter, and occupy large portions of the valley of the Sacramento; they are called marshes, because they grow on the lowest ground and are covered in the rainy season with water, which continues till evaporated by heat of summer. These are the haunts of incalculable thousands of wild geese, ducks, brants, cranes, pelicans, etc., etc.

Situations on the coast are not so pleasant as I expected on account of the stiff N.W. breezes of summer, and the fogs that rize from the Ocean in the morning, obscuring everything till sometimes near 12 o'clock—the trees along the coast are governed by the northwesters, and lean to the southeast.

One Spanish league (this is about 6½ sections or square miles) is considered a farm.[38] This I believe is the smallest grant which the Spanish [Mexican] Government gives and 11 leagues the largest; the grantee is allowed to take it in the shape of the valley or tillable land, and not include mountains which bound the valleys.

To obtain a grant you must become a citizen, which requires a year's residence, and to become a member of the Catholic Church—(see another remark relative to this).[39]

Houses are most universally built of unburnt bricks. This is the Spanish mode—they could just as well make and burn brick here as well as anywhere, and build good houses.

Sheep—in some places there are a great many; on the farm of Livermore, I saw 6000. Capt. Sutter has 1,000. They are small and the wool rather coarse.

Hogs—there are a few hogs here, but they can be raised here as well as in the U.S. The few I have seen looked fine. A hog weighing 200 lbs. is worth four or five dollars.

Cattle—of all places in the world, it appears to me, that none can be better adapted to the raising of cattle than California. The cattle here are very large, and a person who has not a thousand is scarcely noticed as regards stock.

R. Livermore and the Spaniard adjoining have about 9,000 head; I. Reed (an Irishman) has 2,000; Valleo (pronounced Vag-ya-ho) is the most wealthy Spaniard in the country, and has 12,000 head![40] Capt. Sutter has 2,000 head. There is no regular price for cattle, but it is about $4 dollars per head. I have been assured any quantity might be bought for $2 per head—yet such opportunities I do not think common—a few years ago, cattle could be bought for $1 per head; times have changed. Hides are worth anywhere on the coast $2—tallow $6 per hundred lbs.—many persons own from 1,000 to 6,000 but it is unnecessary to insert names here.

Horses—these are next in number to cattle. They are not in general large, but they answer every purpose; the price is various. I have known good horses to sell from 8 to 30$—mares are never worked or rode; they are worth from 3 to 5$. Capt. Sutter has about 600 head of horses; Valleo has from 2,000 to 3,000. A hundred persons might be mentioned who have from 300 to 800. Horses here are not subject to diseases.

Mules—these are large and fine, and are worth before they can be rode about $10 per head; after being broke to the saddle $15. Jacks worth from 100 to 200$.

Oxen—the Spaniards work oxen by lashing a straight stick to the horns. Good tame working oxen worth about $25. It is actually more work to haul the clumsy, awkward, large, unhandy carts of the Spaniards, than an American wagon with a cord of wood.

Butter and cheese—but little butter and cheese made in this country; pains not being taken to milk the cows; butter is worth 50 cents per lb. What a chance there is in this line of business for industrious Americans. No doubt sale for any quantity could be made to ships, but the price would become somewhat less.

Missions—missions are nearly all broken up; but few pretend to preach or teach, and those that still remain are fast declining—whether the missions have ever been the means of doing the Indians much good, I cannot say, but I do not like this manner of civilizing the Indians, who still live in filth and dirt, in mud houses without floors or fireplaces. Whenever an offence is committed, like stealing, they are plunged into the prison houses, laden with irons and made to toll a bell every minute in the night. This was the case at St. Joseph when I was there on the 16th of November last.

Missions that have ceased their labors have distributed the cattle and horses among the Indians, after reserving a large share for the priests, etc. And artful men have taken advantage of the times and purchased the cattle and horses from the Indians for a small quantity of ardent spirits or some trifling articles, leaving them destitute. All the missions were once very rich in cattle, etc., but they are now very much reduced; there are about 22 missions in Upper California.[41] The mission of San Gubler [San Gabriel] had 100,000 head of cattle, that of St. Joseph 18,000, that of St. Clara 30,000, many other had intermediate numbers—these missions likewise had horses, sheep, etc., in proportion.[42] There is now a Bishop in Monterey, lately arrived from Mexico, come to revive the missions—but the people all objected to his remaining in the country. The consequence would be, perhaps, that the people would have to pay tithes. August, '42 — the Bishop has not yet arrived on this side of the Bay.[43]

Honeybee — I have been informed that there is a kind of honeybee in this country which makes honey; but they are not like the honeybee of the States, and are neither plenty nor common. If bees were brought to this country I think they would do well.

Health — the country is acknowledged by all to be extremely healthy; there is no disease common to the country; the fever and ague are seldom known. I knew a man to have several chills, but he had been intoxicated several days in succession. The Indians who did so several years ago were (it is the opinion of all of whom I inquired) afflicted with the smallpox. They use on all occasions, both in health and in sickness, excessive sweatings. The manner of doing it is by heating a large house, which they build and cover like a cockpit, very hot, and lie in it until they are so weak they can hardly stand, and then coming out entirely naked throw themselves upon the cold damp ground, or into the water. This occurs daily under my own observation.

Water — there are abundance of springs here; the water, I believe, is universally freestone water. Every family is supplied with either a spring or a running stream. There is limestone in the country, but not to say plenty; there is enough, I presume, including the shells of the seashore to supply every want.

Trees begin to unfold their leaves about the 1st. March, but do not all entirely unfold their leaves till the middle of May. Strawberries ripe about the 1st June.

Mills — mills go by horse power; in fact, I know of but 1 grist and 1 saw mill in California.[44] The streams, I believe, in general are not very suitable for mills, there not being sufficient, near the sea, and in winter the waters rise so high that the dams would be swept away. But good mill writes [millwrights] no doubt would succeed in establishing mills on most of the streams. The Sacramento river is the most beautiful river I ever saw for steamboat navigation. It has several streams which would be navigable in high water.

Dews on the coast are very heavy, but they extend but a few miles back into the country. Since I wrote relative to the fog on the seashore, I have been told that from St. Francisco south there is but little fog.

Lumber is generally sawed by hand; it is worth from $40 to 50 per thousand ft. redwood.

Fish — there is a great abundance of salmon in every stream, particularly in the spring of the year, when they are very fat. The Sacramento and its branches contain an abundance.

Whales likewise I see almost daily spouting along the coast. There are other fish which come up from the ocean.

There are few snakes here, the rattlesnake and corral, the others are common.

Bears are plenty — they are of the grizzly kind, but are not so tenacious of life as those of the Rocky Mountains; they are very large.

The animals along the coast are the sea lion, sea elephant, seals, etc. There are an abundance of prairie wolves, wolves of another kind also, very large. An animal is found here called by the Spaniards the lion, but I think it is the real panther. It frequently kills horses; it latterly killed two on the place I have charge of.

Crows — buzzards and vultures are large and numerous.

Musquitoes are not troublesome, excepting on the Bay of St. Francisco, and in the neighborhood of marshes. Horse flies are not numerous or bad.

Here grows a root in great abundance which answers every purpose of soap to wash with.

The wages of white men are about $25 per month; mechanics get $3 per day. Indians hired from 4 to 6$ per month but are very indolent.

Goods are very high, owing to the high duty on them; factory cloth is 50 cts. per yard, blankets from $5 to 10, shirts are worth $3, sugar from 15 to 30 cts., tea $2, coffee 50 cts. Goods are cheaper in Oregon than in the Western states, so they would be here but for cause above mentioned. Shoes worth from $3 to 5, boots $10, other things in proportion.

Wheat worth $1 per bushel; corn, I cant say.

The ploughs with which the Spaniards work are rude and awkward.

Guns are very high; a good first rate rifle is worth from 75 to 100 dol. — one of our Company sold a rifle for 30 head of cattle. Guns worth $15 in the States are worth $50 here.

It is seldom a Spaniard makes a charge against travelers for his hospitality. They are kind in this respect; but I cant say how much they p——r [sic].

The number of civilized Indians in California are about 15,000.[45]

I have learned but little concerning the mines of the country; there is a silver mine near Monterey but it has not been worked. How extensive it is, I cannot say.

The dexterity with which the Spaniards use the lasso is surprising; in fact, I doubt if their horsemanship is surpassed by the Cossacks of Tartary. It is a common thing for them to take up things from the ground going upon a full run with their horses; they will pick up a dollar in this way. They frequently encounter the bear on the plain in this way with their losas [lassos], and two holding him in opposite directions with ropes fastened to the pomels of their saddles. I was informed that two young boys encountered a large buck elk in the plains, & having no saddles fastened the ropes round the horses' necks, and actually dragged the huge animal into the settlements alive.

I will here remark that all who would come to this country must bring passports from the Governors of their resident States.

Whether persons of any other denomination than Catholic would when piously disposed be interrupted by the law, I can't say but think not.

The best part of California, I am told, lies high upon the Sacramento; the country S. and E. of Marsh's is unoccupied; likewise north, excepting Capt. Sutter's grant of 11 leagues.[46] As Capt. Sutter in order to fulfill his contract with the Government is obliged to have a certain number of settlers. Perhaps a person could not do better than to join him — it would at any rate be a good place to come to on arriving in the country, on account of the Sacramento river, which can be descended every week or two in launches to this place.

Capt. Sutter would give any information to emigrants, and I believe render any assistance in his power. The Pueblo of St. Joseph would be another good place to arrive at; it is situated near the S.E. extremity of the Bay of St. Francisco. There is a number of Americans and English in the place. Mr. Gullnack is noted for his kindness to strangers and would undoubtedly give the best advice in his power. Mr. Forbes likewise who lives near the place is capable of giving any information.[47]

So long as the Spanish Government holds this country, neighborhoods and settlements will be thin; it will therefore be sometime before districts can be organized, schools established, etc, etc.; people coming to this country want all the land the law will allow them. Wealth is as yet the sole object of all — consequently houses are generally from 3 to 10 miles distant from each other; but it is my opinion a Spanish boy would not think it so hard to go 10 miles on horseback to school as children generally do half a mile.

I have endeavored to state facts with impartiality as well as I could. I will here remark that at least half of the Company with whom I came are going to return this spring to the U. States; many of them well pleased with the country; and others so sick they cannot look at it. People generally look on it as the garden of the world, or the most desolate place of Creation. Although the country is not what I expected, yet if it were not under the Mexican Government, I should be as willing here to spend the uncertain days of my life as elsewhere. It may be I shall, as it is, but I intend to visit the United States as soon as I can, if possible the coming fall.

Let me here remark that those of the Company who came here for their health were all successful. A young man by name of Walton, who when he set out was of a death-like appearance — having been afflicted with dropsy or consumption, landed in perfect health.[48]

In upper California there are no large towns. Monterry is the principal, and contains about 500 or 600 inhabitants; the Pueblo of St. Joseph about 300 — Port St. Francisco 50.[49]

People say there has been already 3 times as much rain this winter (of '41 and '42) as they ever knew in one season before. Notwithstanding this, I do not think the rains and snows here are disagreeable as those of the United States. Where the land has not been pastured by cattle and horses, the rains make it very soft and miry, so that it is extremely bad travelling in some places.

If I were to come to this country again, I would not come with wagons, but would pack animals, either mules or horses — mules are rather better than horses generally for packing, but the latter for riding. As I have come but one route to this country, I cannot recommend any other. This journey with packed animals could be performed in three months, provided the company have a pilot (and surely no other company than ours ever started without one).

Allowing a person to be 3 months on the route, he will need in the provision line 100 lbs. of flour, 50 lbs. bacon, and if a coffee drinker 20 lbs. of sugar and coffee to his taste — a few other things, dried fruit, rice &c. would not come amiss. With all these he would have to be prudent, and before passing the mountains or buffalo range, it will be necessary to lay in 150 lbs. of dried buffalo meat. A person will need one animal to pack his provision, one to carry his clothing and one to ride. It would be well to bring some kinds of mountain goods in order to traffick in the mountains, provided one was so unlucky as to have a horse stolen by the Indians or loose one otherwise. A person if fond of sporting or intends to hunt, will require 5 lbs. powder and 10 lbs. of lead; if the gun is a cap lock one, he should be provided with fire works — flint, steel, lint, &c. If a few extra boxes of caps, they will sell well — should bring a good supply of clothing (a hunter should wear nothing but buckskin), clothes being very dear here. Persons coming here with the intention of settling will do well to bring an extra animal laden with guns or dry goods, as they are more current than money. If, however, any large quantity were brought into the country, duties would be required which would overrun the profit.

The Route to this Country

I now will describe the route to this country as well as I can, knowing that if we had had directions as follow, we could have found our way much better. You have [leave] Westport following the Santa Fe road, till you arrive at Elm Grove, which is 25 miles from Westport; going about 6 miles you leave the Santa Fe road to the left and take a west course and arrive at the Kansas river. Here you start in the road of the mountain traders and which you follow all the way to the mountains. Its course till you strike Platte river is considerably N. of W. You ascend Platte river 6 or 8 days travel till you arrive at the confluence of the N. and S. forks. About 6 miles above this place is where we forded the S. fork; this place is easily known by the bluffs coming in upon the banks, leaving no valley on the river. If you cannot ford here, two day's upstream travel will take you to a place where, being passed over, you take the road to the N. fork, which you will ascend, all the time in the road, till you reach Ft. Larimie. The Black Hills here set in, and the route could not be described intelligibly—a pilot must be along. It will not perhaps be difficult at any time to procure a pilot at this place to go to the rendezvous on Green river—you will here get directions to Bear river—you descend this stream, passing the Soda Fountain, about 8 miles, beyond which the river turns to the south. You will, perhaps, have to make several inland circuits from the river. Here is no road, and the way will have to be explored as you advance.

Thus continue till you arrive at Salt Creek, which you will see mentioned on the 18th August, when you will seek the first opportunity to take a W. direction through the hills. About 30 miles will bring you in view of the Great Salt Lake. You will have to keep near the high mts. to the N. to procure water—continue about 2 days along these mts. in a W. course—then turn directly S.W. In order to do this, your travelling will be perhaps sometimes S. and then W. on account of the hills—keep out of the smooth, white salt plains, and 5 days travel will take you to the head of Mary's, Ogden's or Buanaventura river. It will be necessary to compare this with the Journal. Descend this stream until on the N. side you come to where it spreads into a swamp of cane grass. Keeping as near the swamp as you can, cross a small outlet and take a S. direction about 30 miles; now 15 miles S. or S.W. will take you to the S. side of the Lake. You now continue S. bearing very little to the west, pass a long narrow Lake of beautiful water, and 4 days will take you to the great Gap in the mountains. The mountains become low so gradual that you are at them before you are aware of it. One day will take you into the plains of the St. Joaquin. You will undoubtedly see Indians here who can tell you the way to Capt. Sutter's, if you can speak this much Spanish—*por donda esta el rancho de Capitan Sutter?* It will be about 5 day's travel, perhaps west of north.

There would be many advantages in coming to this country by water—so many useful things could be brought, such as ploughs, wagons, &c. Surely no American could reconcile himself to the awkward utensils of the Spaniards. I am not prepared to say what would be the value of a good American wagon, not less than $200 or 300. I will say plainly that I do not know that you can live any better here than in Missouri—but your prudence and economy would not fail to make you a vast fortune, provided you come in time to get a farm in a suitable place and conform to the Spanish laws. . . . Persons wanting any information by letter will direct their letters to New Helvetia, Rio Sacramento, Upper California, to myself or Capt. Sutter.

I will here speak of the climate on the seashore and can say that with the exception of a few frosty mornings in the winter, the summer is nearly as cold as the winter. In fact I believe the cold of the summer is as disagreeable as that of the winter. There have been, speaking of the seashore, but few warmer days here than those I have experienced in Missouri—but in other parts of the country it is excessively hot a few hours in the middle of the day.

Although fruit trees along the seashore are in blossom in Jan., Feb. and March, yet the cold of summer coming on retards their growth so that no apples are ripe until the first of September — I speak particularly of the seashore. A small distance from it there is a difference of 1½ months. Never did I expect to see the earth so beautifully arrayed in flowers as it is here, and from the variety of the humble bees, I certainly think that if bees could only once be brought here, they would do exceedingly well.

Wild oats in some places ripen the last of May. I have not seen a musquito here this summer; but as I was going into the Bay, a small party attacked me and succeeded in taking a little blood! This country is surely a healthy one — I have known but one person to die, and it was the opinion generally the cause of his death was intemperance and the want of exercise. I asked a respectable physician what disease prevailed most in California. He answered "the knife," having reference to the treacherous Spaniards.[50] I have not seen one without a knife since I have been here, but I cannot say that I fear them — I too carry a knife and pistol.

It is now preached in all the missions that people will have to pay tithes this year. The Bishop has found a letter which lately has fallen from Heaven (so the priests say who read copies of it in all the churches). The contents of said letter I have not been told. The sheet is very large and written in a hand different from any in the world.[51]

A General is expected every day from Mexico with 500 or 600 men — he is to be both Military and Civil Governor.[52]

To my friends and others I must speak candidly of Dr. Marsh here. What he was in Missouri I can't say — I speak for the emigrant, that he may be on his guard, and not be gulled, as some have been on coming to this country, by him. He is perhaps the meanest man in California. After the Company had encamped near his house about 2 days, and there had been killed for them a small hog and a bullock, he began to complain of his poverty, saying "the Company had already been more than $100 expense to him — God knew whether he would ever get a rial of it or not." But poor as the Company was, he had already got from them 5 times the value of his pig and bullock in different kinds of articles — powder, lead, knives, &c. He charged the Company $3 apiece to go and get their passports — a good price for his services. There is not an individual in California who does not dislike the man. He is seldom admitted into a house to sleep. If rightly informed, he had to sleep under his cart in a Spanish town to which he had taken some hides. No other foreigner would be obliged to do so. He came to this country pretending to be a physician. He has, however, gained by it — he has charged and received $25 for 2 doses of salts — he has refused his assistance to a female in labour and not expected to live, without immediate relief, unless the husband promised him for his pay 50 cows. When he first came to this country, he hired in the family of an obliging American, during which time he laid out 50 cents for some fresh fish. After having a whole year clear of charges, he dunned the man for his 50 cents. I might write 50 pages detailing similar incidents, but it is unnecessary to mention but one more. A child being afflicted with the headache, Dr. Marsh was called, administered 2 or 3 doses of medicine — made a charge of 50 cows. The family was a poor one, not having more than 150 and in order to reduce the price, charged the Dr. 25 cows for washing a couple of shirts; so he went off grumbling with 25. Enough of him.[53]

It is the report now that the Mexican Government will allow a person to hold property in this country without his becoming a Catholic, &c.

To all of my acquaintances and friends who may be in bad health I would recommend a trip to California. All whom I have heard speak of the climate as regarded their health say its effects have been salutary.

Notes

1 Bidwell writes from Bodega Bay, which is in Sonoma County. It was named for the captain of the *Sonora,* Juan Francisco de la Bodega, who first discovered it on October 3, 1775. Between 1812 and 1841 it was used by the Russians as a harbor, which they called Romanzov. In March 1842, Bidwell was posted there as a clerk in the employ of John A. Sutter, who had only recently purchased Fort Ross and related Russian interests in the area. Erwin C. Gudde, *California Place Names* (Rev. ed., Berkeley and Los Angeles, 1969), p. 33; Hunt, *John Bidwell,* pp. 96–100.

2 Bidwell fails to list the three Jesuit brothers who were members of the missionary band: William Claessens, Charles Huet, and Joseph Specht. Perhaps he included them in the teamsters' count. *Please note: all bracketed inserts have been provided by the editor. However, bracketed words in italics appear in the original text as such.*

3 See Appendix A for a full discussion of the membership of the company. In his roster, Bidwell omits Nelson McMahan and Mrs. Gray and child.

4 Joseph B. Chiles (1810–1885), a Kentucky native, made the 1841 overland trek as part of the "Chiles mess," which included his friends and Missouri neighbors, John Bartleson, Charles Hopper, Michael Nye, and Robert Rickman.

5 The company was camped on the Big Blue, since they had reached the Big Vermillion, which is a branch of the Blue rather than the Kansas, on May 23. By May 27 they reached the Little Blue, which Bidwell mistakenly calls the Big Blue on May 28. Irene D. Paden, *The Wake of the Prairie Schooner* (New York, 1943), pp. 47–49, 65–66.

6 Williams, *Narrative of a Tour,* pp. 29–45 (reprint ed.).

7 The American Fur Company was founded by John Jacob Astor in 1808, centering its activities south of the Great Lakes. In 1822 it formed the Western Department, which was charged with the opening up of the Missouri River trade. Gradually it was able to buy out or take over its competitors. In 1834 Astor disposed of his interest in the company. It continued to function with trading posts on the Great Plains until 1864, when it was acquired by the Northwest Fur Company. Howard R. Lamar, ed., *The Reader's Encyclopedia of the American West* (New York, 1977), p. 28.

8 A vivid description of Chimney Rock, or "Nose Mountain," is found in Warren A. Ferris,

John Bidwell (*Courtesy California State Library*)

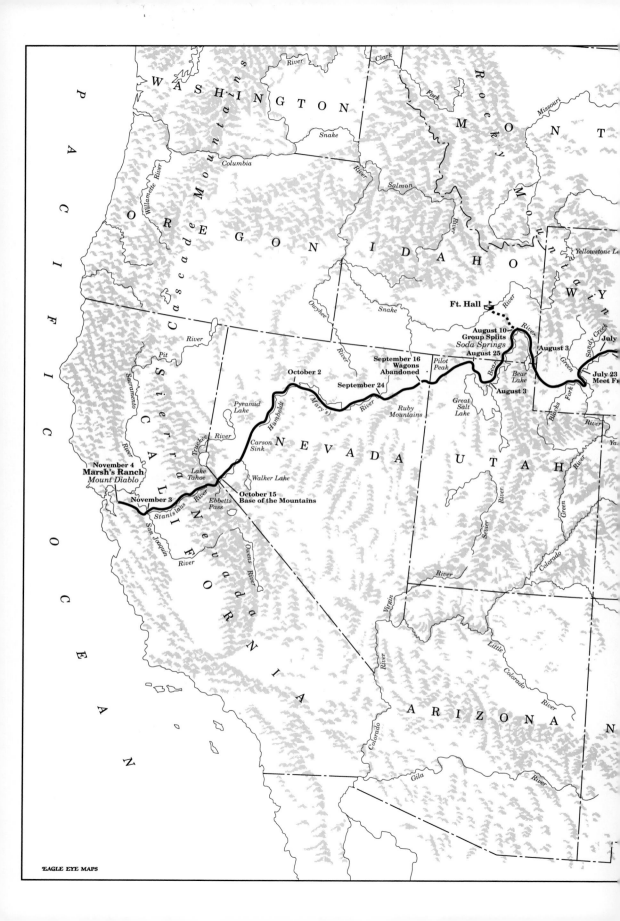

WASHINGTON

Clark
River

Fork

ROCKY MOUNTAINS

Missouri

River

Snake

Columbia

River

Salmon

River

OREGON

Willamette River

Cascade Mountains

IDAHO

Owyhee

River

Snake

MONT

WY

Yellowstone L

Ft. Hall

**August 10
Group Splits**
Soda Springs
August 25

August 3

July

River

Green

River

Sandy Creek

**July 23
Meet Fr**

July

August 3

**September 16
Wagons
Abandoned**

*Pilot
Peak*

August 3

*Bear
Lake*

Bear

River

Blacks Fork

October 2

Pit

River

Sierra

*Pyramid
Lake*

September 24

Mary's

Humboldt

River

*Ruby
Mountains*

*Great
Salt
Lake*

UTAH

Ya

River

Sevier

River

Green

River

NEVADA

*Carson
Sink*

Truckee

River

*Lake
Tahoe*

**November 4
Marsh's Ranch**
Mount Diablo

Sacramento

River

River

November 3

Stanislaus

River

*Ebbetts
Pass*

Walker Lake

**October 15
Base of the Mountains**

San Joaquin

River

Owens River

CALIFORNIA

Virgin

River

Colorado

River

ARIZONA

River

*Little
Colorado*

Colorado

River

N

Colorado

River

Gila

River

PACIFIC OCEAN

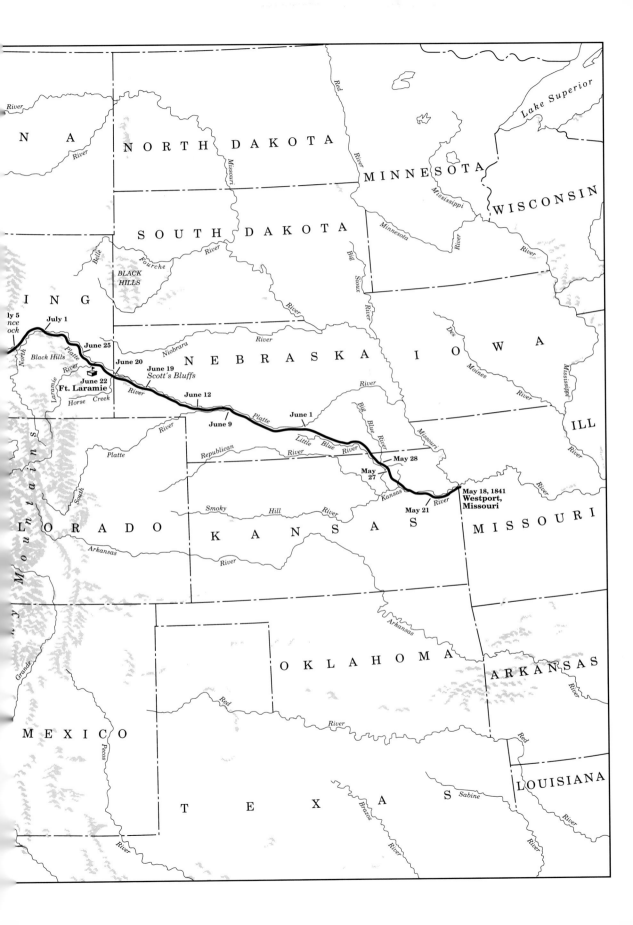

Josiah Belden (*Courtesy California Pioneer Society, San Francisco*)

Joseph B. Chiles (*Courtesy California State Library*)

Nicholas "Cheyenne" Dawson
(*Courtesy Bancroft Library*)

Antoine Robidoux, 1843
(*Courtesy Museum of New Mexico, Santa Fe*)

James Baker, who was with the Jesuit missionary party (*Courtesy Brigham Young University Library, Provo*)

Nancy A. Kelsey (*Courtesy California State Library*)

Benjamin Kelsey (*Courtesy California State Library*)

Robert H. Thomes (*Courtesy California State Library*)

Thomas F. Fitzpatrick portrait painted by Waldo Love, 1936 (*Courtesy Colorado Historical Society, Denver*)

Father Pierre Jean De Smet, S.J. (*Courtesy Jesuit Missouri Province Archives*)

Father Gregory Mengarini, S.J. (*Courtesy University of Santa Clara Archives*)

Charles M. Weber *(Courtesy California State Library)*

Samuel McMahan (*Courtesy California Department of Parks and Recreation, Sutter's Fort, Sacramento*)

Dr. John Marsh *(Courtesy California State Library, Sacramento)*

Life in the Rocky Mountains, ed. by LeRoy R. Hafen (Rev. ed., Denver, 1983), pp. 103, 117n.

9 Scott's Bluff, today Scotts Bluff in western Nebraska, was named for Hiram Scott, a young man who entered the fur trade in 1823. In 1828, due to a severe illness, his company of trappers left him behind in the care of two companions. As the main party pushed on, Scott and his caretakers finally were able to construct a bullhide boat to take them downriver to the appointed rendezvous. However, when they reached the designated bluffs, they found the main party had already left for St. Louis. Scott, unable to ride or walk, was abandoned by his traveling companions. His remains were discovered the following spring. A full description is found in *ibid.,* pp. 30–31. For a good summary of Scott's short life and death, see LeRoy R. Hafen, "Hiram Scott," in LeRoy R. Hafen, ed., *The Mountain Men and the Fur Trade of the Far West* (10 vols., Glendale, Calif., 1965–1972), I: 355–366.

10 Horse Creek in southeastern Wyoming is located several miles southeast of the present-day town of Torrington. Paden, *In the Wake of the Prairie Schooner,* p. 158 (map).

11 Fort Laramie was founded by the fur-trade partnership of William Sublette and Robert Campbell in 1834. Originally christened Fort William, later Fort John, it was sold in 1835 to another fur-trade partnership, which in turn merged with the American Fur Company in 1836. In 1849 it was purchased by the U.S. government as a military post, serving as such until 1890, when it was abandoned. Today a historic monument, it is situated on the left bank of the Laramie River, about a mile below its junction with the North Platte. Robert W. Frazer, *Forts of the West* (Norman, 1965), p. 182.

12 Lancaster P. Lupton (1807–1885), a graduate of West Point, entered the fur trade after resigning his commission in 1836. He built a trading post on the South Platte shortly thereafter. In 1840 or 1841, he relocated on the right bank of the North Platte, about three-fourths of a mile above the mouth of Laramie Fork; subsequently it was called Fort Lupton. However, Lupton sold out in the spring of 1842 to a rival fur concern that continued to operate the fort until abandoned in 1845. Ann W. Hafen, "Lancaster P. Lupton," in Hafen, ed., *The Mountain Men,* II: 209–216.

13 William L. Sublette (1799–1845) began his fur-trade career in 1823. His name looms large in the annals of the trade, especially his partnership with Jedediah S. Smith and David W. Jackson, 1826–1830. The name given to this impressive Oregon Trail landmark arose from the fact that on July 4, 1830, Sublette encamped there with a company of eighty-one men, outbound for the annual fur-trade rendezvous on the Green River, which duly celebrated Independence Day. It should also be noted that Sublette's party was the first one to utilize wagons, thus blazing what was to become the Oregon Trail. John E. Sunder, *Bill Sublette, Mountain Man* (Norman, 1959), *passim;* Dale L. Morgan and Eleanor T. Harris, *The Rocky Mountain Journals of William Marshall Anderson* (San Marino, Calif., 1967), p. 118.

14 A German from St. Louis, Henry Fraeb entered the far-western fur trade early on, for by 1829 he was a seasoned veteran whom his men usually called "Frapp." He was slain in 1841 not long after his party's encounter with the overland travelers. LeRoy R. Hafen, "Henry Fraeb," in Hafen, ed., *The Mountain Men,* III: 131–139.

15 Bidwell has confused several place name identifications here. Blacks Fork should read Hams Fork; shortly he refers to Blacks Fork, which is today called the Little Muddy. The company pioneered the way across the Bear River divide in blazing this wagon trail.

16 The Rev. Williams gives the man's name as Richard Fillan. Actually, his name was Richard Phelan. The Rev. Williams calls him Fillan (*Narrative* p. 42), while James John in his diary calls him Cockrel. This is confirmed by a drawing of Father Nicholas Point (published herein, Drawing No. 9) for he carved his name on Independence Rock on July 5, along with the three Jesuit priests, brothers, and their teamsters. It would

appear that he spotted the widow Gray and took a fancy to her. Perhaps that is the reason he joined the Bidwell-Bartleson party at Fort Laramie. This would afford him an opportunity to court the lady, a courtship which proved successful. Since Phelan is an Irish name, he was no doubt Catholic, thus Father De Smet performed the nuptials. Phelan had been a fur trapper for some time, but opted for farm life in Oregon with his new bride.

17 The first permanent U.S. Army post west of the Continental Divide, Fort Hall was established by would-be fur trader Nathaniel Wyeth in 1834. It was built on the Snake River above the mouth of the Portneuf in present-day Idaho. Pressed by competition from the Hudson's Bay Company's Columbia Department, it was sold to that rival in 1837. The HBC abandoned it in the winter of 1855–1856. In 1849 a like-named fort was established by the U.S. Army on August 5, 1849, about three miles above the HBC Fort Hall. This in turn was reestablished on May 27, 1870, to the east of the old HBC post, about eight miles south of the town of Blackfoot. Lamar, ed., *Encyclopedia of the American West,* p. 389; Frazer, *Forts of the West,* pp. 44–45.

18 For the Oregon-bound party, see Tobie, "From the Missouri to the Columbia, 1841," pp. 135–159. Also, consult Appendix A for roster and discussion.

19 Mary's River was first named the Ogden River for Peter Skene Ogden, famed Hudson's Bay Company explorer and fur man. Later it was renamed Mary's River for his Indian wife. In 1845 Lieutenant John C. Frémont dubbed it the Humboldt in honor of the great German naturalist. It rises a hundred miles west of the Great Salt Lake, and its course takes it almost three hundred miles west and southwest to where it flows into Humboldt Lake and Sink. Thwaites, ed., *Early Western Travels,* XXVIII: 113, *note* 53.

20 The hackberry tree (*Celtis occidentalis*) resembles the elm. It bears small, sweet, edible fruit resembling the cherry.

21 Stewart, *The California Trail,* p. 27, writes: "One sure point is marked by the hot springs which they passed on September 21 and which Bidwell described in some detail. These beautiful springs still bubble out near the base of the Ruby Mountains, just as they did when Bidwell saw them."

22 As noted in the Introduction, Dr. John Marsh wrote to several friends in Westport, Missouri, detailing a route to California. However, Bidwell was mistaken. The party had not stumbled on to the San Joaquin River. They had not yet crossed the Sierras.

23 The balm of Gilead is a small evergreen tree of the myrrh family usually called the American balsam fir.

24 This stream was first discovered by Joseph R. Walker in 1833 and later named in his honor.

25 Joseph R. Walker (1798–1872) was one of fur trade's most intrepid mountain men, who first entered the Santa Fe Trail trade in 1820 or 1821. In 1832 he joined Captain Benjamin L. E. Bonneville's fur brigade as the captain's chief lieutenant. After a year in the field, in late July 1833, acting on Bonneville's instructions, Walker and a party of forty men set out for California. By early September the party reached Humboldt Lake. From there they moved on to Carson Lake. Pushing on, for three grueling weeks, starved and frozen, they battled against granite bluffs and endless snow banks, finally making their way across the Sierra. Sustained by "famine-blue flesh of famished horses — seventeen of them — they worked their way between the Merced and Tuolumne rivers after ascending a southerly tributary of the East Walker River." They had reached California the hard way. The year following, most of the Walker party returned east to report to Bonneville. It fell to Walker and two of his men to behold the marvels of Yosemite and the giant sequoias, a happenstance that was duly reported to their leader. Ardis M. Walker, "Joseph R. Walker," in Hafen, ed., *The Mountain Men,* V: 361–380.

26 Marsh's rancho was originally called the Meganos. First granted to José Noriega in

1835, Marsh received the grant in 1837. Situated in Contra Costa County, the ranch, comprised of four leagues, stretched between Mt. Diablo and Brentwood. Marsh's claim was patented for 13,316 acres on August 19, 1867. Marsh renamed his rancho Pulpunes. Robert G. Cowan, *Ranchos of California* (Fresno, 1956), p. 47, No. 246.

27 Fifteen of the party started for San Jose. Marsh provided them travel directions. Among those departing were Josiah Belden, Henry L. Brolaski, Grove Cook, Michael Nye, James Springer, and Charles Weber. Bidwell, *Echoes*, p. 71; Frederic Hall, *The History of San Jose and Surroundings . . .* (San Francisco, 1871), p. 135; Oscar T. Shuck, *Sketches of Leading and Representative Men of San Francisco* (San Francisco, 1875), p. 921. However, they were arrested two miles from the pueblo (a fallout from the Graham Affair of 1840) and confined for six days before they were released. Bancroft, *California*, IV: 274–275.

28 Robert Livermore (1790–1858), a native of London, England, came to California in 1822. On April 8, 1839, via Salvio Pacheco as a surrogate title holder (Livermore was not a Mexican citizen, thus the ruse), was granted two leagues in Alameda County, the Rancho Pozitas. The title was patented to him and José Noriega, a total of 8,880 acres, on May 25, 1872. Bancroft records that Livermore had a reputation as "a hospitable and honest man, a good representative of his class." *Ibid.*, pp. 715–716; Cowan, *Ranchos of California*, p. 63, No. 356.

29 The request was from Mariano Guadalupe Vallejo. Marsh had informed Vallejo on September 19, 1841: "A strong body of American farmers are coming here, a young man of the party got lost since 10 Days, nearly starved to death and on foot [James John]; he don't know which Direction the party took. I believe they will come about the Direction of the Pueblo [San Jose]." *Vallejo Collection*, X: 282. Vallejo, already alerted to the prospect of the Americans' arrival both from Marsh as well as from Mexico City itself, was at Mission San Jose at the time. It was there that he arrested those trying to reach San Jose. One of those arrested, the name is unknown, produced Marsh's Missouri letter and gave it to the general, who read it with anger. He immediately wrote to Marsh to come to the mission "with the greatest possible promptness." He then dispatched Nye with the letter. Within a day and night Nye returned with Marsh, who placated the irate official by signing a "surety for 15 individuals of the expedition from Missouri." Passports then were issued to the new arrivals. Vallejo to Marsh, November 11; Marsh's surety statement, November 13, 1841, *Vallejo Collection*, X: 335, 340; John Bidwell, "Life in California Before the Gold Rush," *The Century Illustrated Monthly Magazine*, XLI (December 1890): p. 165; Lyman, *John Marsh*, pp. 246–247.

30 The governor at this time was a native son, Juan Bautista Alvarado (1809–1882), who served from 1836 to 1842. James D. Hart, *A Companion to California* (Rev. ed., Berkeley and Los Angeles, 1987), p. 12.

31 John Augustus Sutter (1803–1880) was a German-born, Swiss-reared immigrant who came to the U.S. in 1834. Subsequently, he traveled to St. Louis, then overland to Oregon. From there he took ship to Honolulu and arrived in San Francisco (then called Yerba Buena) in 1839. In 1841 he was granted eleven leagues of land at present-day Sacramento, which stretched from present-day Nicolaus to Marysville on both sides of the Feather River, which he dubbed Nueva Helvetia (New Switzerland). He built a fort, now an historic monument, as headquarters for his operations. Marguerite E. Wilbur, *John Sutter, Rascal and Adventurer* (New York, 1949), pp. 1–132; Cowan, *Ranchos of California*, p. 53, No. 284.

32 Charles W. Flügge reached California overland by joining the annual Hudson's Bay Company fur brigade to the Sacramento River area under the command of Michel Laframboise. Doyce B. Nunis, Jr., "Michel Laframboise," in Hafen, *The Mountain Men*, V; 164–167. Fur trader Henry Fraeb's death has been well described in several accounts.

However, there is a disagreement as to the date of his unfortunate demise at the hand of a large party of Indians on a branch of the Yampa River in the valley of the Little Snake. Flügge's report would indicate the date was July 24 or 25, two or three days after Fraeb's party's meeting with the overland party on July 22, 1841. However, LeRoy R. Hafen, "Henry Fraeb," in *ibid.,* III: 131–139, asserts that Fraeb and four of his men perished at the hands of the Indian party in late August 1841.

Flügge, German born, subsequently worked for Sutter for several years, then went into business as a storekeeper in Los Angeles. After a trip to Germany, he returned to Los Angeles, acting in an erratic manner, which suggests he was insane. In 1852 he wandered off by himself into the nearby country and was found dead some twelve miles from the city. Bancroft, *California,* III: 741–742.

33 The Russian settlement at Fort Ross was effected in 1811, the fort in 1812. It became the main base for exploiting the sea otter trade along the coast as well as supplying foodstuffs to Russian Alaska. The colonists were withdrawn in 1833, and in 1841 Sutter purchased all Russian interests in the area, including Port Bodega to the south. Clarence J. Du Four, "The Russian Withdrawal from California," *California Historical Society Quarterly,* XII (1933): 240–276.

34 Mission San Rafael Arcangel was founded originally as an *asistencia* for Mission Dolores' ailing neophytes who needed a better climate than that afforded in the San Francisco Bay area. The site was selected by Gabriel Moraga "in the lee of Mount Tamalpais . . . between a line of rolling, tawny hills, crowned here and there with live oaks." It was dedicated on December 14, 1817. Friar Luis Gil proceeded to build a combination chapel, hospital, and monastery. In 1823 it was elevated to a mission and thus became the twenty-first and last of the Franciscan missions established in California. Secularized in 1834, by 1841 it was mostly in ruins, as described by the French visitor, Eugene Duflot de Mofras. Francis J. Weber, comp. and ed., *The Penultimate Mission: A Documentary History of San Rafael Arcangel* (Los Angeles, 1983), pp. vii–viii.

35 Bancroft opines: "The total population of foreign adults . . . in 1840, not including roving trappers and horse-thieves in the interior, was in round numbers 380 souls, of which number 120 had come before 1830, and 240 before 1835." *California,* IV: 117.

36 Joel P. Walker, brother of Joseph R. Walker, brought his family from Oregon late in 1841, traveling with the land contingent of the Charles Wilkes' U.S. Exploring Expedition under the command of Lieutenant George F. Emmons, U.S.N. Walker was accompanied by his wife, Mary Young of Missouri, "the 1st white woman to arrive in Cal. by land or to settle north of the [San Francisco] bay," as well as three sons and two daughters: John, Joseph, Newton, Isabella, and new-born baby Louisa, as well as Walker's sister. Bidwell fails to mention that two other American families were with the Emmons party, Burrows, wife and child, and Warfields, wife and child. *Ibid.,* V: 765; Charles Wilkes, *Columbia River to the Sacramento* (Oakland, 1948), p. 24.

37 Bancroft estimates California's population in 1845 at 6,900 *Californios* and 3,180 "civilized" Indians. The foreign population he gives as 680. *California,* IV: 649.

38 A Spanish square league equals 6.935 square miles or about 4,438 acres. Cowan, *Ranchos of California,* p. 148.

39 This is not accurate. One could obtain a land grant from the governor if one of the following conditions was met: naturalization, marriage to a *Californio,* or location of a land title at least twenty-five miles inland from the ocean, based on the 1824 land act of the Mexican Congress. Bancroft, *California,* II: 515–516 and *note.* Conversion to the Catholic Church was not a requirement even in marriage. However, a Catholic marriage required the children to be raised in the faith.

40 Bidwell alludes to Robert Livermore (already identified), his neighbor was Salvio Pacheco,

who owned the Rancho Monte del Diablo, granted in 1834, which spread between present-day Pacheco and Suisun Bay. The grant was patented in 1859 for 17,922 acres. John Read, an Irish-born sailor, may have arrived in California around 1826. In 1834 he became a naturalized citizen and received the Rancho Corte de Madera del Presidio in Marin County centered around Point Tiburon. He died in 1843. His heirs received a patent for 7,845 acres in 1885. Mariano Guadalupe Vallejo was, indeed, one of the richest men in Mexican California. In 1834 he was granted the fifteen-league Rancho Petaluma in and around the present town of Sonoma. In 1874 he received a patent for 66,622 acres, one of the largest rancho grants made in Mexican California. Cowan, *Ranchos of California,* p. 32, No. 146; p. 30, No. 128; p. 60, No. 327. Bancroft, *California,* V: 689.

41 There were only twenty-one missions founded in California.

42 The missions mentioned were San Gabriel, San Jose, and Santa Clara. There is no question, in its heyday, San Gabriel had the largest cattle herd. However, with secularization these mission herds were quickly decimated by their civilian administrators. Bancroft, *California,* IV: 63.

43 Bidwell alludes to Francisco García Diego y Moreno (1785–1846), the first bishop of the Californias (including Upper and Lower California). Mexican born, he was a Franciscan missionary who was posted to California in 1831 as president of the missions from Soledad north to Sonoma (1831–1835). In 1840 he was made bishop and took up his residence at Mission Santa Barbara. Geiger, *Franciscan Missionaries in Hispanic California,* pp. 98–103. See the Introduction, pp. 4–5, *ante,* for a discussion of the bishop's visitation and questionable date of August '42.

44 The first gristmills in California date to 1798. A major one was built near Mission San Gabriel between 1810–1812. In 1821 it was remodeled by Joseph Chapman, an early American settler. By 1841–1842 there were gristmills in operation at Mission Santa Barbara, Santa Inés, San Luis Obispo, Santa Clara, Santa Cruz, and Dolores. Bancroft, *California,* I: 618, 718; II: 374, 497, 568, 579, 690, 725. As for sawmills, the first was erected at Mission San Gabriel in 1805, but apparently it did not last long. Danish-born Peter Lassen (1800–1893), who reached California in 1840 via St. Louis, overland to Oregon, then ship to San Francisco, built the territory's first sawmill in 1841. It was constructed on a site on the Rancho Zayante on or near the present village of Mt. Hermon. Isaac Graham purchased it later that year. It was demolished in 1906. Lumbering in California prior to that time was done through whipsawing, a method which was introduced by Anglos in 1816. Ruby J. Swartzlow, "Peter Lassen, Northern California Trail Blazer," *California Historical Quarterly,* XVIII (1939): 292–295; Sherwood D. Burgess, "Lumbering in California," *ibid.,* XLI (1962): 237–248.

45 Bancroft offers this appraisal of the Indian population: "The neophyte [Indians living at the missions] declined from 15,000 in 1834 to 6,000 in 1840; though the latter number would probably be reduced to 5,000 if restricted to the Indians absolutely living in community, and increased to 8,000 or 9,000 if extended to all on the [mission] registers whose whereabouts as vagrants or servants was somewhat definitely known." *California,* IV: 62–63.

46 Sutter's initial land grant, approved in 1841, was for eleven leagues centered in and around the present city of Sacramento, which he christened Neuva Helvetia. Cowan, *Ranchos of California,* p. 53, No. 284.

47 William Gulnac, a native of New York state, reached California in 1833 with his family from Honolulu. They arrived at Monterey on the 226-ton bark *Volunteer* (Captain Shaw) on May 13. In 1834 he became a naturalized citizen and took up his residence in San Jose. There he served as a minor official and was employed to survey the town's land.

In an 1841 census his age is given as forty, and he is recorded as having a wife, Isabel Ceseña, and six children. He received a rancho grant in 1844 for the eleven-league Campo de los Franceses in what was later San Joaquin County, in and around present-day Stockton, which he later sold to Charles M. Weber. Death claimed him in 1851. Bancroft, *California,* III: pp. 771–772.

James A. Forbes (1804–1881), a native of Scotland, lived in either Chile or Peru before taking up residence in California in 1831. He reached San Francisco in October on the whale ship *Fanny.* Naturalized in April 1834, he married a local woman and settled in the vicinity of San Jose. He served the town in a number of official capacities and from 1836 was the local agent for the Hudson's Bay Company. He joined Marsh in providing surety for the Bidwell-Bartleson party in November 1841 and was appointed the British vice-counsel in October 1843. *Ibid.,* p. 743.

48 Ambrose Walton apparently returned east in 1842. *Ibid,* V: 766.

49 Bancroft fixes the population of Monterey at 700 in 1840; 750 in and around San Jose; and 280 for the San Francisco area, excluding Indians in or nearby the areas. *Ibid.,* III: pp. 667, 698.

50 Bidwell displays here the long-held view of Anglos at the time that the Spanish were "treacherous." This idea was a hangover from the European religious wars, perpetuated as the "Black Legend," a concept which has been discredited by Philip W. Powell in his book, *Tree of Hate* (New York, 1971). Certainly, this was not true of Mexican California at the time. There are few records of internal violence between citizens.

51 On February 4, 1842, Bishop García Diego issued his first pastoral letter outlining his intention of introducing tithes and a religious defense of same. This was sent out under cover of a "Circular" to the resident clergy in the territory on February 11. All pastoral letters must be read from the pulpit. This is what Bidwell is referring to in this statement. Engelhardt, *Missions and Missionaries of California,* IV: 239–250. The two original documents are in the Santa Barbara Mission Archive Library.

52 General Manuel Micheltorena (c. 1833–1852) served as the thirteenth governor of California, 1842–1845. He arrived to take up his post with 300 soldiers, most of them ex-convicts. Their conduct pushed the *Californios* to rebellion, which ended in the forced expulsion of the governor and his motley army back to Mexico. Hart, *A Companion to California,* p. 317.

53 Marsh's reputation continued to decline as the years passed. After his wife's death, he "became a more lonely, cantankerous, and greedy man." The latter two characteristics lead to his murder by three of his *vaqueros* in 1856. *Ibid.,* p. 306; Lyman, *John Marsh,* pp. 314–322.

CHAPTER TWO

California 1841:
An Immigrant's Recollections
of a Trip Across the Plains

By John Bidwell

Written at the author's dictation by S. S. Boyton, 1877

In the summer of 1840, the weather being excessively hot, and needing some books and other things that could only be obtained in St. Louis, I set out for the latter place expecting to be gone a week. I went on the steamer *Shawnee* down to St. Louis, but as the navigation was bad owing to low water and snags, I was gone four weeks instead of one. On my return I found a man had jumped my ranch.[1]

The law at the time was such that I had to be twenty-one years of age or a man of family in order to hold the land. I was neither. The man who had my ranch was a sort of desperado, having killed at least one man, and I had no means of making him give up the land.

He said he wanted that quarter section and was bound to have it. I had some idea for a time of going to Texas, but there was much trouble there at the time so [I] didn't go. About this time a man came to the settlement by the name of Rowbadeaux [Robidoux].[2] He was an Indian trader and brother to the famous Joseph Roubadeaux [Robidoux] of St. Joseph, Missouri, whose trading post I was at in 1839.

Rowbadeaux [Robidoux] described California to us in glowing colors. He had gone to Santa Fe, thence to Arizona, thence to California and up to Monterey. He said it was a perfect paradise, a perpetual spring. He was a calm, considerate man and his stories had all the appearance of truth. He said the hospitality of the people was unbounded. Cattle and horses ranged there in the greatest abundance. The matter was talked over among us and a public meeting called. To hear more about this wonderful country on [the] Pacific Coast. Roubadeaux

77

[Robidoux] answered all our interrogations in a satisfactory manner. Every question in fact was favorably answered. One question that a Missourian always asks about a new country was answered in a humorous way. Question, "Is there any chills there?" "There never was but one man in California who had the chills. He was from Missouri and carried the disease in his system. It was such a curiosity to see a man shake with the chills that the people of Monterey went eighteen miles into the country to see him." The account given of the Pacific Coast was so inviting that many resolved to visit it. Immediately an organization was proposed and in due time effected.

At this meeting two committees were appointed, one on Rules and Regulations for the government of the company while crossing the plains; another committee for the organization of the company. Both in due time reported. The last-named committee, however, reported simply a pledge to be signed binding each one to dispose of his property, purchase a suitable outfit and rendezvous at Sapling Grove in Kansas Territory on the ninth day of the following May, ready for crossing plains. To that pledge during the winter some five hundred names were subscribed; in fact it had the appearance of the whole population preparing to emigrate. However, the merchants of the town of Weston, the principal town in Platte County, believing that so great an exodus from that recently settled locality would check, if not destroy, its prosperity and have a depressing effect upon the business of the whole region, set themselves to work to defeat the movement. They used all possible means fair and unfair to accomplish that end. They argued against it, denounced it, and ridiculed it. Everything they would hear unfavorable to California they reported against it and published their statements in all the nearest papers.

At a meeting of ours, a committee was appointed on correspondence to collect information in regard to California, and to correspond with other persons in all parts of the state who might have information or wish to join the expedition contemplated. Among other items of interest obtained was a letter from D. Marsh, an American living in California, to a friend in Jackson County, Missouri.[3] That letter gave a glowing account of California. We were led to believe that there would be an almost general emigration from all parts of Missouri as well as some from Illinois and other Western states.

During that winter I made two trips to Jackson County to see parties who had promised to join our company as well as to gather information respecting California and the route leading to it. But the skies began to be overcast. The exertions of our enemies begain to have its effect. The first great excitement had cooled down. Just at this time, and it overthrew our project completely, was published the letters of Farnham in the New York papers and republished in all the papers of the frontier, at the instigation of the Weston merchants and others.[4] Our company soon fell to pieces notwithstanding our pledge was as binding as language could make it. Well do I remember the concluding clause, which was to the effect, if not in the exact language, "That we pledged to each other our lives, our fortunes, and our sacred honor."

When May came, I was the only man that [was] ready to go of all who signed the pledge. In Weston, however, there was a man who had never signed the pledge but who had said from the beginning that he would go to California when May came. This was Robert. H. Thomes, a wagon maker at that time. As the time approached, I became very anxious about the expedition but supposed a few would go with me. Finally I could not find a single member of the company who was sure to go. I went forward with my preparations, however, and to the extend I could, I purchased an outfit which consisted of a wagon and some provisions, a rifle, and ammunition.

At almost the last moment, everyone abandoned the idea of crossing the plains. I cast about, however, and found in Platte County a man by the name of [George] Henshaw who was willing to go. He was old, quite an invalid, and nearly helpless. He had a fine black horse that he allowed me to dispose of. I sold him for a yoke of young cattle and a one-eyed mule for Henshaw to ride. With that much of an outfit we drove into Weston. To complete the outfit, we here purchased what we could and then joined R. H. Thomes, who was about ready to start. A merchant by the name of Nye, seeing our determination to go to California, said if we would wait a week he would let his son Mike [*sic*] go with us.[5] At the end of that time, we started. The people of Weston, notwithstanding their failure to make good their pledge and in spite of the breaking up of the company, evinced their good feeling toward us by following us out in great numbers and bidding us goodbye two miles from the town. Some even went four and the last six miles ere they said goodbye and turned back.

To reach Sapling Grove in Kansas Territory we had to travel down the Missouri River some fifty miles and then cross at the place known as Independence Landing. Then to go west about ten miles to the Missouri line and across into Indian Territory. On reaching Sapling Grove no one was there but we saw fresh wagon tracks and followed them to the Kansas River. They belonged to parties who had come, some from Arkansas, and some from different parts of Missouri to cross the plains. We camped here and waited to see if others would come. Every day for a week or more, wagons arrived with the same object in view. At last we took steps to see how many had arrived and found our numbers to be sixty-nine. Among these were about fifteen women and children. All were anxious for a start. We effected an organization and elected "Colonel" John Bartleson captain of the company.

No one of the party knew anything about mountaineering and scarcely anyone had ever been into the Indian Territory, yet a large majority felt that we were fully competent to go anywhere no matter what the difficulties might be or how numerous and warlike the Indians. We heard before starting, however, that a party of Catholic missionaries from St. Louis going to the Flathead Indians under the auspices of Father De Smet were soon expected and that they had for their guide the experienced Captain Fitzpatrick.

The more prudent advised waiting for the missionary party and finally with much persuasion they prevailed on the others to wait. But we did not have to wait long and we continued with them until we parted company on Bear River, emptying into Salt Lake, where their route diverged to the north past Fort Hall. Well it was that we did go with them and have the benefit of Captain Fitzpatrick's experience, not only to find the way but to avoid the dangers from hostile Indians. One incident I will mention to show how men unaccustomed to crossing the plains and seeing Indians will act. One of our men while hunting in close proximity to some Indians was surrounded by them. They demanded his gun and in his excitement he gave it up, also his horse. As soon as he could, he got away from them and started for the camp. He came in almost frightened to death. In his run he had lost his pistol. He cried, "Indians! Indians!" and said they were close upon us. I asked him where they were. "Don't you see them?" he exclaimed. "The plains are alive with them, there are thousands of them." He attempted to seize a gun but broke the stock. Then commenced a general stampede for the Platte River, distant about three miles. The women and children were crying and screaming. Oxen and mules were put to the gallop and away we all went pell-mell for the river. In this race for life, as we thought, no heed was taken for the hindmost; it was each for himself.

Captain Fitzpatrick did all that he could to stop the party. He [said] we were cowards, that if the Indians were hostile and should see us running, they would be sure to kill us. They ought to, he said, if we were such fools as to run. Up to this time, no one except [Nicholas] Dawson, the scared man, had seen any Indians. On reaching the river, Captain Fitzpatrick had all the wagons formed into a circle with the animals securely staked inside. In the course of half an hour the Indians came in sight. They proved to be a friendly party of Cheyenne Indians and readily gave up the gun and horse they had taken from Dawson. The man went by the name of "Cheyenne" Dawson on the remainder of the trip. These Indians were all mounted on horseback and gaily dressed in their beaded buckskin costume, fancifully painted with vermillion and all, except one squaw or medicine woman, as Captain Fitzpatrick said she was, had guns. The missionaries had their things loaded upon carts and drove from three to five mules in line to each cart. These carts were easily upset but aside from that were much more convenient about traveling than our wagons.[6] In the employ of the missionaries, as hunters and drivers were several excellent Rocky Mountain hunters. In their company was also an English gentleman traveling for pleasure, and he had in his employ a noted hunter and trapper by the name of John Gray.

Route

Let me give you now the route we took. We crossed the Big Blue bearing a little northerly so as to strike [the] Platte River, which we followed up on the south side above the junction of the North and South forks. Ascending the South Fork either one or two days' journey, we found a ford where we crossed with our wagons. The ford was deep and it was only by putting our efforts on the top of the wagon beds that we managed to keep them dry. As there was only certain teams and wagon that could cross and recross, it took us an entire day to get all our things across the river.

We experienced a great danger at this point from the innumerable heads of buffalo. All the plains were literally black with them crowding to the river for water. The ground literally thundered with the vast herds that came rush[ing] down to the river. We sat up all night shooting at them to keep them from running over us. The numbers on the south side, however, were vastly greater than on the north side. For a whole day, I think even for two days as we ascended the S[outh] Fork after we crossed over, there was no time when there were not countless thousands of buffalo in sight.

Just where we struck the Platte for the first time, we had a wedding in the company between a young man by the name of Kelsey and a Miss Williams.[7] The event was signalized by a most terrific hailstorm covering the ground to the depth of four inches. This happened on the evening of the hottest day we had experienced. The hailstones were so large and heavy that we thought they would kill our animals. Some of the stones measured two and a half inches in diameter. Some were found yet unmelted on our next day's travel.

Leaving the South Fork, we crossed over to the North Fork at a place called Ash Hollow. here one of our party by the name of Shotwell, accidentally in taking a gun out of a wagon from behind, shot and killed himself. No one in the party was seemingly more cautious and exemplary than he. He was tall, young and of fine presence, and was uniformly liked by all. No one had so frequently cautioned others about handling guns carelessly. His loss produced a sadness which lasted many days.

From Ash Hollow we continued up the north side of the North Fork, passing by those remarkable natural objects which time and seasons have worn into such fanciful shapes known as the Court House Rock, Chimney Rock and Scott's Bluff. These were of hard clay worn and cut into various shapes. The air was so clear that they stood out in bold relief and while seeming near at hand were several miles away.

Some of our party tried to reach Court House Rock but gave up after going nearly half a day. We all visited Chimney Rock and nearly all put their names on the rock or had them put on by others. Painted them [on] with tar and grease.

On arriving at Fort Laramie, our route continued west up the North Fork of the Platte for more than a hundred miles. At one place not far from Fort Laramie, we found extensive quarries of pure white translucent rock which we pronounced alabaster. This was on the banks of a small stream putting into the Platte. Crossing the North Fork of the Platte, we came to the Sweetwater River. Camped one night near Independence Rock, which already bore the names of some travelers and many mountaineers. Most of our company [did likewise].

Ascending the Sweetwater to its source and crossing the divide which forms the watershed at that point between the waters of the Mississippi and the Pacific, we struck and descended the Big Sandy River to Green River.

John Gray had been sent some days previously to find if possible some party of trappers in order to leave letters with them to go east whenever a party might do so that year or the next, as the case might be. We also wished to dispose of to [the] trappers such extra goods and provisions as we felt obliged to part with in order to lighten our wagons. We also wanted to trade for some fresh animals. Fortunately, a party of trappers was found under command of Captain Frapp [Fraeb].[8] They were trappers but at the time were just setting out for a trip further east in search of buffalos. There were no buffalos at this time so far west as Green River. Once in a while we passed an old skull, but the buffalo had decreased as we came up the Platte and had disappeared on the Sweetwater. Possibly at rare intervals and in small numbers the buffalo went as far west as Green River in this latitude. We met in that trapping party men who had tasted nothing but meat for ten years. Our flour was getting scarce and supposing that they would want bread, we at once said, "We can't spare you any flour or bread." Their answer was, "We don't want any bread, but if you have any, we want some good *old bacon* once more." As we had killed plenty of fresh meat, we were willing for them to have the bacon. After stopping one day we set forward crossing by way of Black and Ham's Forks of Green River to Bear River, which empties into Salt Lake. While on Green River we were close to hostile Indians without being aware of it, for Frapp's [Fraeb's] party — as we learned long afterwards — was shortly after we left them attacked by the Indians and Frapp [Fraeb] and several of his men killed.

In our camp was a man by the name of Bill Overton. One evening Overton said he had never been surprised in his life and didn't think anything would ever surprise him. "Why boys," he said, "I wouldn't be surprised if I should see a steamboat coming right along here." In 1872 while coming down Echo Canyon on the train of cars dashing in and out along the mountains, I thought of what Bill Overton had said more than thirty years before that. To be sure, it was not a steamboat but was just as great a wonder in reality.

Bear River ran a long ways to the north, thence west, passing Soda Fountain, the most remarkable soda springs I have ever seen in my life. Then the river turns and runs a hundred miles or more into Salt Lake.

Here I want to mention how little was known in 1841 of the true geography of that vast region lying west of Salt Lake. Previous to setting out I consulted maps so as to learn as much as possible about the country. None of that region was correctly laid down on the maps. As for Salt Lake, there was a large lake marked in that region but it was several hundred miles long from north to south with two large rivers running from either end and diverging as they ran west and entered the Pacific Ocean.

My friends in Missouri advised me to bring tools, and in case we could not get through with our wagons, to build canoes and go down one of the rivers. While our company proceeded slowly down Bear River toward Salt Lake, four men were sent to Fort Hall on Snake River to gain information in regard to the country to the west. It was thought that Captain Grant, then in charge of the fort, or trappers who might be there would give knowledge of that almost unknown region.[9] Our first camp was about twelve miles from Soda Fountain. The day had been very hot, and as we went very slowly, two of us thought we would go fishing. While along the stream a certain mountain peak appeared in sight covered with snow. We set out to go to it but did not return to the camp to tell the others we were going. It lay off to the west and appeared two or three miles only. Traveling hard till sundown, we found ourselves on a ridge with the snow on a still higher ridge beyond us. Between the two lay a narrow valley. My companion's name was James John. I said, "Jimmy, hold on, we can't never reach that snow tonight." He cast a most disdainful look at me but did not answer a word and continued on down toward the valley. I then resolved not to say return under any circumstances and soon overtook him. It was then almost sundown, and we must have been fifteen miles at least from the train. His manner toward me on the mountain had implied that he thought I was [as] determined to keep on as long as he would. We entered the valley and saw many Indian fires. Before it was entirely dark, we had selected a ridge we intended to ascend. The density of the thickets, sharpness of the rocks and craggy nature of the country, with deep chasms on either side which we could not see but only knew of by the gurgling of the waters in the canyons, made the ascent most difficult. Neither intimated to the other any purpose of return. Our moccasins became worn out and our feet were bleeding, but on we went till morning. At last we came to such rocks that we could hardly get around or over them. The skies were at the same time so overcast with clouds that it became difficult to see anything. We crawled under a stunted tree and shivered there without fire, coats, blankets, or anything to eat the remainder of the night. This scrubby pine was almost on the line of the very highest timber on the mountain. When daylight came, we discovered we had lain in the nest of a grizzly bear. The hair was rubbed off the brush, and there were all the signs of the grizzly's lair. Neither of us yet said go back. We went on as soon as day dawned and in about two hours found the snow. The snow was hard and compact, in fact, almost like ice. I cut some out with my knife and filled my handkerchief with it. The question now was how to get back again, for we both agreed that to return the way we came would be impossible on account of the condition of our feet. We, therefore, selected what seemed to be a shorter but at the same time steeper route. At first the way was smooth and easy but soon we were sliding down in the snow and mud with our buckskin suits wet and bedraggled. This way soon led into a most rugged canyon and thickets so dense that it became impossible to pass through them except in the trails of the grizzly bears. The stream was swift and cold, but the rocks were so tremendous and the thickets so bad that we had to cross and recross this stream many times. Some of these crossings had so recently been passed by bears that the leaves and bushes were still wet where they had passed. We carried our sheath knives in our hands at every step, for we knew not at what instant we would meet a bear face to face. We eventually emerged into the open valley we had crossed the evening before. The Indian signs were so plain that we dared not stop or look around but hurried cautiously across the opposite mountain as soon as possible. Many Indians must have camped in the valley the night before but had evidently left that very morning.

About one o'clock in the afternoon we came in sight of the company. They were on the march, but as soon as they saw us, they all ran to meet us, glad to see us alive again.

The evening previous, on our failure to return to camp, all became alarmed and feared the Indians had killed us. We had told no one we were going away, and our company had been cautioned by Captain Fitzpatrick to be on their guard against the Blackfeet Indians who infested this neighborhood. To guard against an attack in the night, a corral had been formed of the wagons, all of the animals staked inside of it, and every man stood guard all night to guard against the danger. When daylight came half of the company mounted animals and went in search of us. They saw our tracks but mistook them for Indian tracks and returned and reported that we must certainly be dead, that is, killed by the Indians. Still another party was sent out to make search in another direction but no tidings could be found of us. Under the impression that we were beyond doubt killed by the Indians, our company started on. On meeting them, they were wholly surprised yet really rejoiced to see us. A few, however, were angry to think we had only been up to bask in the snow, and one man even suggested that we ought to be horsewhipped. We laid hold of our rifles at once and told him neither he nor anyone else should apply such language to us. Our four men sent to Fort Hall overtook us in Cache Valley. They were able to learn very little of the region lying west of Salt Lake. Their information was to the effect that there was a great and almost impassable desert which we were liable to become involved in if [we] went too far to the south. That there was a stream running west which had been visited by one of the trappers belonging to the Hudson Bay Company, among whom it was known by the name of Mary's or Ogden's River. That we must try to strike that stream, for to the south of it we would find no feed for animals. That we must be careful not to go too far to the north, for if we did, we would become involved in a maze of canyons and streams with precipitous cliffs which led off into the Columbia River and where we should be sure to wander and starve to death. The fact was no one knew but little about the country. No one had been through to California by that route so far as we could learn. As we approached Salt Lake, we were misled quite often by the mirage. The country, too, was obscured by smoke.[10]

The water in the Bear River become too salty for use. The sagebrush on the small hillock of the almost level plain became so magnified as to look like trees. Hoping to find water and supposing these imaginary trees to be growing upon some stream and knowing nothing about the distance to Salt Lake, we kept pushing ahead mile after mile. Our animals almost perished for want of water while we were traveling over this salt plain which grew softer and softer till our wagons cut into the ground five or six inches and it become impossible to haul them. We still thought we saw timber but a short distance ahead when the fact really was there was no timber and we were driving straight for the Great Salt Lake. In our desperation we turned north of east a little and struck Bear River a few miles from its mouth. The water here was too salty to quench thirst; our animals would scarcely taste it, yet we had no other. The blades of the grass looked luxuriant but were shining with salt. We were all worn down and jaded out so much, however, that we had to remain here two nights and one day. Without knowing where to find water, we struck out to the west. The first night we camped we found the water very brackish, but still we had to use it. This water was in deep holes. Here I saw the last of the hackberry timber. It had been growing smaller and smaller ever since we left Missouri. The next day we found no water at all and were obliged to camp that night without any. Ourselves and the stock were almost famished with thirst. In our trouble we turned directly north toward some high mountains and in the afternoon of the next day found springs of good water and plenty of grass.

Notwithstanding the information obtained at Fort Hall, it was deemed necessary to send men out to explore the country. While this party was gone, our animals were turned out to recruit. The party was gone eight days but obtained no definite idea regarding the country. On their return we started again, but at the end of three days it became évident to all that our wagons would have to be left. The whole region was so obscured by smoke that we could make but little progress. Mountain ranges seemed to lie before us no matter in which direction we traveled. On the third day with our wagons we did not become aware of our approach to them till we saw the crags looming up ahead of us in the smoky sky almost over our heads. It was painfully evident that we must make greater progress or winter would set in long before we could reach the Pacific Coast. That night we determined to leave our wagons, so early the next morning we set to work making pack-saddles for our animals. We had to pack mules, horses, and oxen. On the afternoon of the second day, we were ready to start. No one of us had seen horses packed or helped to pack any, and our first day's experience is almost painful to recall to mind. We had to throw many things away and there appeared just one native to receive our bounty. This was an old Indian who came down from the high mountains ahead of us. He approached our camp in a somewhat cautious yet not timid manner. The first thing given him was a pair of pantaloons. He immediately turned toward the sun and commenced a long and eloquent harangue. As he was perfectly naked, he was shown how to wear the pants. As article after article was given him during the day, he turned toward the sun and gave thank in a long speech. As the day wore on and he had many things given him, his talks grew shorter, but for each he made something of a speech. The first two addresses must each have been fully half an hour long. We called him the Persian from his evident sun worship. I never saw anything like it before nor have I since that time.

Our trials in packing would have been very ludicrous if they had not been so painful. The packs would turn and get down in the dirt. Old mules that were almost skeletons would run and kick at the packs. The work oxen would jump and bellow and try to throw off their loads. We did not get started until late and then undertook to cross the mountain range ahead of us. We continued on till midnight but found no water. The company became scattered, and part of the animals were lost, among them my yoke of oxen. I had to go in search of them, and "Cheyenne" Dawson started with me. The company was to wait at the first water they reached. Dawson and I went back nearly ten miles ere we found the trail the oxen had taken, and then Dawson refused to go further and returned to overtake the company again. I continued on till about three P.M. I found the trail leading due north. After following this for four or five miles, I discovered Indian tracks following the cattle. The country became grassy, an indication of water, and the oxen were evidently trying to find it. Finally the grass became coarse and tall, and I found the oxen were following a regular Indian path. In fact I feared the Indians were driving the oxen.

Expecting soon to meet Indians, I examined my arms, which consisted of a flintlock rifle and a pair of dragoon pistols also flintlocked. All our company had these guns and pistols. Old hunters in Missouri whom I asked what kind of guns to bring said, "Don't have anything to do with those new-fangled things called caps; if you do, you will lose by it. If they once get wet, you are gone, but if you lose your flint, you can easily pick up a stone that will take its place." Having examined and reprimed my arms, expecting any moment to see Indians, I continued on till I came suddenly upon the oxen lying side by side near the trail. It was then nearly sundown. Fortunately, both had their packs on. I immediately shifted the heaviest pack to the back of the one that had borne the lightest one and started back to overtake the company again. I continued on past the place where the oxen had turned off the main trail, past also where I had started back with Dawson, and kept on until I found water, but the company had not waited for me as they had agreed to do. Not being able to find the trail any further and fearing to go to any of the numerous fires I saw to the west lest I might come in contact with Indians, I had to remain till daylight. The company, I had expected, would pursue a westerly course, but no trails led in that direction. To the north lay mountains and to the south a plain of indurated clay so hard as to leave no impressions of animal's hoofs. I prosecuted my searching, making circles, and had made several of these, gradually enlarging them until I must have been two miles from my oxen, which I had left tied to a willow bush for want of trees. All at once I saw horsemen approaching me from the south. Supposing them to be Indians, I made my way as rapidly as possible to where the oxen were so as to have them as a breastwork in case I was attacked. In attempting to cross a small spring branch about a quarter of a mile from where the oxen were, my horse mired down in the mud. I threw my gun and jumped off and pulled my horse out. He was covered with mud from ears to tail, his ears and eyes were full. While I was wiping off my gun and looking to the priming, the supposed Indians came galloping up to where I stood. They proved to be my friend R. H. Thomes and Grove C. Cook. They were coming with water and provisions to meet me. They agreed with me that the company had treated me badly in not waiting at the first water as they had agreed to do. They said, however, that Captain B[artleson] had insisted on the company's keeping right on. They had found good grass and water and that night we were once more together again.

In a few days, our course being somewhat south of west following the base of the mountain ranges, we came to a dry desert region without grass or water and with few or no hills to the south. Being obliged to camp without water, it was the opinion of all that we had come to the borders of that desert spoken of at Fort Hall. The only remedy was to go north and cross a mountain chain which was in sight. The first camp after crossing the divide was on a small spring branch which had trout in it. Some days previous to this while we were packing up one morning, about ninety Indians appeared in sight and rode towards us. Several of us said to Captain Bartleson, "You ought to send some men out to stop those Indians or they will surround us." He said we must be very careful how we treated the Indians, that it wouldn't do to make them angry or they would hurt us. As they still continued to come up and commenced to surround us, several of us seized out guns and ran toward them making signs that they must keep off to one side, which they did. During that day I said to one of the men who messed with Captain Bartleson, "Our captain don't appear to understand Indian character. If we don't make those fellows afraid of us, they will certainly attack us. Captain Bartleson is too timid and cautious with them." This must have been repeated to Captain Bartleson. We inferred that this must be a war party, as they had horses and guns while the Indians of the vicinity had neither; we thought it must be a party from some other quarter. We could not tell what their intentions might be but thought it best to regard them with suspicion. After leaving the camp last mentioned, the traveling was good for nearly half a day. We followed down the stream, but it soon ceased to have any water. This dry streambed we had to cross many times, but at last the banks became so steep that we were confined to the bed of the stream itself. Our animals became very foot-sore, so much so that they could scarcely stand, yet it was too rocky for them to lie down and the hills were too steep to attempt to get out of the canyon. We all agreed that it would be impossible for the animals to retrace their steps, as they were much worn down and jaded. Then came the discussion of the Fort Hall information that if we went too far north we would get into the canyons that led into the Columbia River and that we would find it impossible to escape from them. As this canyon had led us in an almost northerly direction for nearly a day, many became greatly alarmed, believing that we had gotten into one of these canyons and would perish there. At an early hour the next morning some of our men gained an elevation and reported that the country looked much more favorable two or three miles ahead. A desperate effort was made, and in a few hours we came out on what is now known as the Humboldt River. Believing it to be the stream which had been described to our men as Mary's or Ogden's River and that we had not become involved in any of the before mentioned intricate canyons, every heart was filled with joy.

We descended the Humboldt River seeing more or less Indians who did not appear to be hostile, yet they did not appraoch us. The country was almost destitute of game. We saw scarcely any deer or antelope. The whole region had been recently burned over. Almost our only dependence for provisions therefore was on our oxen, which we were still driving to meet any emergency, although they had become so poor that they could carry no loads. Some of our men had used up their tobacco and would do most anything to obtain more of it. I remember that some men cut out their pockets and chewed them. One man by the name of William Belty had a riding mule that kept in pretty good condition. He offered to let one of the men ride the mule each for a small piece of tobacco enough for him to chew during the day. One morning Belty lost his daily allowance of the weed, and though he looked closely, he could not find it. During the forenoon an Indian overtook us. He struck himself and said, "Shoshonie! Shoshonie!" We knew these Indians to be friendly. He at the same time held out in his hand the piece of tobacco, which he must have found after we left camp, for no Indians were around at that time. Belty was so unreasonable that he said the Indian was a thief and ought to be shot. I have no doubt he would have shot the Indian if I had not been with him.

As we followed down the Humboldt River, the driving of the oxen devolved first upon one and then on the another. One day before we reached the Humboldt Range of mountains, it became my turn to drive the loose cattle. For some reason, Captain Bartleson traveled so fast with the company that I could not keep up. At dark I must have been at least ten miles behind the train. Failing to overtake them, I was obliged to camp without blankets or provisions. Indians I knew to be numerous and for ought I knew were hostile. My idea was to be cautious and always prepared when going through an Indian country. I do confess that I didn't like to be left alone and to go off into the deep, gloomy bends of the Humboldt River among the willows and camp without blankets or supper.

The next morning, starting at daylight, I reached the company waiting for me to arrive because they had nothing for breakfast until they killed one of the oxen I was driving. As soon as I met Captain Bartleson, I complained in the strongest language I could command of his treatment in traveling so fast that I could not keep up. He said nothing at the time, on the contrary, appeared quite affable, but made no excuses. The captain's mess consisted of seven or eight men, and when the ox had been killed and divided, his mess asked for a double share of the meat, saying their horses were better able than the others to carry it and that they would repay it when we killed the next ox. We were all mounted and ready to travel about two in the afternoon, and then Captain Bartleson answered me and said he had been found fault with enough and wasn't going to stand it any longer. That he was going to California and all who could keep up might go with him and the rest could go to H[ell]. Having better animals than the rest, he could outtravel us and were soon out of sight.

Up to this time Charles Hopper, one of the their party, was considered our best mountaineer. All had confidence in his ability to find the best route through the mountains. As long as we could—about one day—we therefore followed their tracks. The Humboldt River was extremely dry that year, and as we approached the sink, it ceased to run, and we were enabled to cross dry shod in several places as we descended it. The seceding party having passed what is now known as the Humboldt Range of mountains and followed down the east side of the Humboldt River, we traversed the tracks of the party who had left us. Thrown entirely upon our own resources to find our way as best we could through this region and into California, Benjamin Kelsey proved to be our best leader. As soon as we reached what we supposed to be the furthest sink of the Humboldt, but which I am now inclined to think must have been what Frémont afterwards called Carson Lake, we endeavored to make our course more westerly, for we knew that the Pacific Ocean lay to the west.

At the sink of the Humboldt and on the lakes we had met many Indians, all of whom were friendly to us. We found among these Indians a solitary horse. In the edges of the water the tule was covered with honeydew to an extent that enabled the Indians to gather it in large quantities. They made it into balls about the size of one's fist and we bought and ate considerable of it. When we afterwards saw them gathering it, we saw that the Indians collected the insects that covered the honeydew as well as the dew itself and formed the whole into the ball.

The first stream we crossed was that now known as Walker's River, so called by Frémont in 1844 I think. This river we ascended to the foot of the high mountains whence it came. Here we deemed it best to give our animals a rest, for men and animals were much in need of it. In the meantime, men were sent to scale the mountains to the west to discover a pass. They were gone a day and a night and reported that the mountains were barely passable. At this time we had but two oxen left, and we had just killed the best of these and were drying meat preparatory to scaling the mountains the next day. The meat was dried to make our load as light as possible because neither men nor animals were able to carry heavy burdens over the mountains. A little before sundown, looking to the east, something was discovered moving in the distance. At first we supposed it to be Indians but our curiosity grew as we noticed their slow advance. Finally we discoverd horses, but still we could not account for the continued halting of the party when it was seen plainly that they were men with animals, and every now and then one of the men would sit down as if to rest.

To cut the story short, they proved to be the party who had left us nine days before in such haste to get to California. We learned from them that they had continued further south after passing the sink of the Humboldt River and had come to a considerable lake, probably what is now known as Walker Lake.

Having obtained from the Indians quantities of pine nuts and fresh fish, they had started west for the mountains. Fresh fish had given them all the dysentery, and they were so weak they could hardly stand. I well remember Captain Bartleson's exclamation as he sat eating what we had cooked for him. "Boys! If ever I get back to Missouri, I will never leave there again. Why I would be glad to eat from the same trough with my dogs there."

Ascending the mountains and crossing the divide or watershed, the second day we struck the sources of what proved to be the Stanislaus River. For one whole day or more the traveling was easy and delightful. At last the stream went into a canyon, and we were obliged to leave its margin and keep up to the north.

About the night of the third day we found ourselves checked by a deep and precipitous ravine and obliged to camp upon the high rocky point without grass or water for our animals. Some of the men descended into the canyon and reached water but were unable to bring any with them and reached camp about midnight more thirsty than ever. Early in the morning two parties were sent in different directions to explore the way. One went back to see how far before a crossing over the ravine could be found. Another went over the point to see if it were possible to pass over or down the canyon. This last party consisted of James John and myself. It was understood that we were not to fire a gun unless the route proved practicable, in which case the camp would move down the canyon. Here as on the expedition to reach snow on Bear River among the mountains, my comrade proved unmanageable. Believing it would be impossible to proceed in that direction with animals, I so stated. But James John said no, he said we can go here, and before I had time to expostulate further, he drew out his dragoon pistol and fired. I made all haste to return to camp but failed to reach there in time to stop Captain Bartleson and his mess. They were already descending. I told them it would be impossible to proceed. "Why did you fire your gun then?" said they. Having explained, they concluded to go on. However, J[ames] John was never more seen by any of us till we found him afterwards in California. His experience after he left us was of the severest character. He was repeatedly chased by the Indians and was without anything to eat till he was nearly starved yet managed to get through to Sutter's Fort and told S[utter] of our being on the route.

Bartleson and his men after the greatest difficulty were able to go about as far as I had gone. Finding it impossible to go ahead and from the weakened condition of the animals impossible to return that day, they were obliged to rest until the next day, carrying water in cups, boots, and hats for their animals, in order to keep them alive. At this place, too, there was little or no grass as the mountains had recently been burned over. The main camp by going back about four miles crossed over the ravine and took a westerly course. Camping for the night, one of Captain Bartleson's men overtook us and asked us to remain till they could come up, which we did. They had gone probably not over half a mile, but such was the nature of the ground, they were all day in retracing their steps. At one place it took all of the men either pushing or pulling to help each mule back up again, and for the whole distance the loads had to be carried on the backs of the men.

Pursuing a westerly course for a few days, we found ourselves obliged to keep on top of the ridges away from the stream. On one of these ridges we killed our last ox, who was so poor, as nearly all had been for weeks, that he had no marrow in his bones, he was literally only skin and bones.

In our straitened condition it was customary for one or more to go ahead of the party in order if possible to kill some kind of game, of which there was scarcely anything. There was nothing for game to live upon because fires had destroyed everything that would burn, and the country was literally desolated. The year had been extremely dry, and as we afterwards learned, everything in the way of crops had failed in California. The only thing in the shape of game killed by our whole party during our passage of the Sierra Nevada Mountains from Walker River till we reached the San Joaquin Valley consisted, so far as I can now remember, of a wild cat, a crow, and a few squirrels.

The next morning after the killing of our ox, I started ahead of the company to hunt for game. It was especially understood that the route would be west and on the north side of the stream. With that understanding, I gave myself time to reach the pond where they would probably camp for the night. Except the banks and bluffs of the Stanislaus River, the country consisted of open hills which were no longer rocky and precipitous. Indians were numerous, and many had visited our camp ere I left in the morning. Following an Indian trail, I descended to the river and down its bank for some ten miles. In the canyon I met many Indians or rather passed several villages of them. I saw, however, no young men, all were old men, women or children. I think the news of our coming had reached them, and the men had either gone toward our camp or to give the news to Indians farther ahead. I lost no time, however, in stopping at these villages. They made no attempt to interfere with me. None had any weapons or clothing that would indicate they had ever come in contact with civilization. At one place I obtained and ate some acorn bread not knowing what it was. The very last flour we had was used on Walker River when Captain Bartleson's men overtook us. Anything that would sustain life was now most acceptable. The large timber consisting of the firs, pines, including that mammouth of all pines, the sugar pine, and the cedar, were all new and most interesting to us. But we had no time, when nearly starved, to give attention to such objects. Our aim was to make distance on our way to the Pacific.

Ascending the precipitous bluffs on the north side of the stream in order to intersect the trail of the company going west, I traveled till nearly dark and began to look down with greater and greater care lest I should pass the trail without seeing it. At last I came on one of the fallen *Sequoia gigantea* in the Calaveras grove. This tree I afterwards described to Frémont and Sutter while at Sutter's Fort in 1844. I passed this tree and went on a short distance and then camped for the night. I selected a secluded place where the Indians would not be likely to see my fire and then lay down without food or blankets. It was not late in October, and the ice froze an inch thick during the night. The next morning, believing the company had borne to the north, my course was eastward to reach their trail. Not finding it, I turned to the south and struck the place of the camp which I had left on the morning of the previous day. Following this trail,

I found the company had not traveled west according to the understanding but had descended into the canyon on the very trail that I had followed and had ascended on the opposite side. I wondered at the attempt to perform so difficult a feat with the jaded animals. Many gave out and had to be left, the men carrying on their backs what they could of the burdens and leaving the rest. And here I witnessed a most horrible sight. For many miles the Indians were cutting the animals to pieces and carrying away the meat, poor as it was, for food. Late in the night I overtook the company.

As we advanced on our way next day, oak trees began to be abundant and we used acorns for food. Some of them we roasted and others boiled. The bitter acid contained in them soon made us sick. So much so we could not bear to see an acorn, and weak as we were, as far as possible avoided passing under oak trees. Some of the meat of one of the mules had been saved in case of an emergency for it was evident the meat of the last ox would soon be consumed. When it was gone, most if not all of us refused to touch the mule meat for some time. I was always so fond of bread that I could not imagine how any one could live without it. How the people in the Rocky Mountains had been able to live on meat alone was to me a mystery. When our flour began to give out, the idea of doing without bread was painful to me, and by greatest economy my mess managed to eke out their flour a short time longer than the others. It was bad enough to have poor beef, but when brought to it we longed for fat beef and thought with it we might possibly live without bread. But when poor mule meat stared us in the face, we said if we could only have beef, no matter how poor, we could live.

As we ascended the mountains to the south side of the Stanislaus River, Indians became more numerous, but their attitude towards us did not seem altogether that of friendship. They had evidently some of the implements of civilization, for we saw where trees had been hacked, showing they had axes. The Indians, too, which had cut the horses to pieces had something in the shape of knives or knife blades. But these Indians now betrayed a shyness or an unwillingness to come near us in a friendly manner. Though often seen, they were generally skulking or in flight, and our suspicions were aroused. Some thought best, others not, to stand guard over our horses at night. After a fatiguing day's travel, standing guard during a cold night was anything but a luxury. Still many of us did it. When the horses of the unwilling ones strayed beyond the line, we were not always careful to turn them back. The result was two of them one morning were missing. A search till nearly noon failed to discover them, and we began our march. In a few miles, coming in sight of an Indian village, all the Indians, men, women and children, were in rapid flight up the steep mountains to the south. On a fire close by the village and scattered around it were parts of the missing horses. The Indians had killed them and were preparing to have a grand feast.

It had rained for a day or two, and during the rain where we camped one night, one of our men, unknown to the others, remained behind in the bushes to see if any Indians approached our camping place. One Indian had been to our camp a number of times and had received presents of clothing; he had promised to show us the way out of the mountains. He had acted very oddly and had failed to return as he had promised, and it was believed by many that he intended to lead us in a wrong direction or in some way betray us. The man who remained was Grove Cook. We had gone only about half a mile when he heard his gun. Overtaking us, he said that same Indian came, and as he was picking up the things we had left, for we had to throw away something at every camp, he shot him. We never knew whether the Indian was killed or not. We had seen among the Indians bones of horses which we could not account for then, but the reason afterwards became very plain. The Catholic missionaries in California had induced, perhaps taken by force, many Indians inhabiting the region of country lying to the east of the San Joaquin River into the missions near the coast. Some of these Indians, after they had become expert horsemen and learned many of the ways of the Spanish race, had deserted to their native haunts. Precisely how or when they became fond of horseflesh I know not. Certain it was they were known before our coming to have subsisted for long years almost entirely upon horseflesh. For this purpose they were in the habit of making raids and sweeping whole ranches of bands of horses. In fact they were the terror of all the ranches between the San Joaquin Valley and the sea coast. Driving away their horses by hundreds, and that continually up to the time or nearly so that California came under the Americans, they were known everywhere as the Horse Thief Indians. Their most notable chiefs were Polo and José Jesús. Among these Indians we saw no firearms.

As we approached the San Joaquin Valley, the Coast Range Mountains or that portion of which Mt. Diablo is the northern terminus rose to view in the blue distance, but we had no knowledge of any intervening valley. Our traveling had been so circuitous, so irregular and indirect, that it was impossible for any one to say where we were or how far we had yet to travel. It was the opinion of most if not all that we were not yet within five hundred miles of the Pacific Ocean. That the blue range bounding the western horizon was simply the beginning of other and perhaps great ranges beyond. Then came a time of great discouragement, some saying if California lay beyond other ranges of mountains, that we could never live to get there. The line of our route passed through what is now known as Tuolumne County, probably very near the present town of Sonora. For some reason we had no glimpse of the great valley we were approaching till about noon of the day we reached it. All began then to quicken their pace; those who had the most strength and the best animals traveled the fastest. Night found us scattered on a line for miles in length. Every one traveled as long as he could see and then lay down to sleep. There was absolutely nothing for the horses to eat. Fire had left the valley black and desolate. We had killed a second mule and the meat still held out. At night we would unsaddle our animals and turn them loose. There was nothing for them to eat and not even a bush to tie them to.

When morning came the foremost of the party waited for the others to come up. They had found water in a stagnant pond, but what was better, they had killed a fat coyote, and with us it was anything but mule meat. As for myself, I was unfortunate being among those in the rear and not aware of the feast in the advance. I did not reach it in time to get any of the coyote except the lights and the windpipe. Longing for fat meat and willing to eat anything but poor mule meat and seeing a little fat on the windpipe of the coyote, I threw it on the coals to warm it and greedily devoured it.[11]

But halcyon days were at hand. We turned directly to the north to reach what seemed the nearest timber. This was at a distance of ten miles or so, which in our weakened condition it took us nearly all day to travel. It brought us to the Stanislaus River at a point not far from the foothills. Here the rich alluvial bottom was more than a mile wide; it had been burned over, but the new grass was starting up and growing luxuriantly though sparsely like thinly sown grain. But what gladdened our eyes most was the abundance of game in sight, principally antelope. Before dark we had killed two of them and two sandhill cranes, and besides there was an abundance of ripe and luscious wild grapes. Still we had no idea that we were yet in California, but supposed we had to cross the range of mountains to the west. It was determined to stay one day to hunt game and to rest for a new start.

The eve of the next day found us surrounded by abundance; thirteen deer and antelope had been killed. It was about the first of November, and there was no time to delay if we were going to reach California that fall. Most of the party were ready and anxious to press forward. Captain Bartleson and his men thought otherwise. They said we hadn't yet reached California, we probably still had a long distance to travel, that such a place as we were in could not be found everywhere and they were going to stop and lay in meat for the balance of the journey. Leaving them in camp and crossing the Stanislaus River, we proceeded down the north side of the same and camped. Early the next day the news came that the Indians in the night had attacked them and stolen all their horses. We remained till they came up, carrying on their backs such things as they were able. On the day we had stopped to hunt, two men had been sent ahead to see if signs of settlements could be found. They were gone two days and returned bringing news that they had fallen in with an Indian who conducted them across the valley to the foot of Mount D[iablo] to the ranch of Dr. Marsh.[12] This settled the question that we had actually arrived in California and were not far from San Francisco Bay. It was an occasion of great joy and gladness. We were not only near our journey's end but the men knew just where to go, instead of uncertainty. Dr. Marsh knew that we were coming, but it would take us two or three days yet to reach his place, which we did on the evening of the 4th of November 1841. He seemed delighted to see us and was very communicative and even enthusiastic. Some of our party had known his acquaintance in Missouri and all had a great deal to say. We camped near his house under the large spreading oaks. The country was nearly destitute of grass and the cause of it we learned to be the unprecedented dry season. He killed a hog for us, which was very acceptable. Although no grain had been raised and was consequently scarce, yet he managed to have a few tortillas made and distributed among us.

In return for the kindness extended to us, we opened our treasures consisting of cans of powder, butcher knives, lead, and various other useful articles and made the doctor what we considered liberal presents in return. I remember one of the party presented him with a case of surgical instruments. As for money, we had little or none. . . .

Editorial Comment. This dictation to S. S. Boyton in 1877 is in the form of a typescript, double-spaced manuscript in the Bancroft Library. However, in order to present it in readable form, in addition to providing paragraphing, punctuation, and correct spelling, all abbreviations, and these are used quite frequently in the typescript, have been spelled out.

Notes

1 Bidwell had taken up a claim in the Platte Purchase, but as he points out, he was underage so his claim was not enforceable.
2 This was Antoine Robidoux; his brother was Joseph Robidoux, the founder of St. Joseph, Missouri.
3 This might well be William Baldridge. See Chiles's "Early Times."
4 These were the highly critical letters of Thomas Jefferson Farnham which are discussed in the Introduction.
5 The reference here would be to Michael C. Nye.
6 The Jesuit party had five of the two-wheeled, or "Red River," carts.
7 This was the marriage of Isaac Kelsey to the Richard Williams's daughter, performed by Rev. Joseph Williams, who went to Oregon.
8 This was Henry Fraeb's trapping party.
9 Richard Grant (1794–1862), Canadian born, entered the employ of the Hudson's Bay Company in 1821. The scion of well-to-do family, he rose rapidly in the company's ranks. He had an extensive career in the Canadian fur trade before being appointed a chief trader. He was posted in that rank to Fort Hall in 1842, in charge of the Snake country trade until the fort was closed in 1856, due to Indian troubles. In the meantime, he became a friend to the many Oregon-bound emigrant trains in those years.

Merle Wells, "Richard Grant," in Hafen, ed., *The Mountain Men,* IX: 165–186.
10 Desert haze has the strong appearance of smoke due to dust kicked up by winds.
11 It is a well-known fact that when men have been on a stringent lean diet, they crave fat. This explains Bidwell's delight on this occasion.
12 The two men were Andrew Kelsey and Thomas Jones.

CHAPTER THREE

The First Emigrant Train to California

By John Bidwell

I n the spring of 1839—living at the time in the western part of Ohio—being then in my twentieth year, I conceived a desire to see the great prairies of the West, especially those most frequently spoken of, in Illinois, Iowa, and Missouri. Emigration from the East was tending westward, and settlers had already begun to invade those rich fields.[1]

Starting on foot to Cincinnati, ninety miles distant, I fortunately got a chance to ride most of the way on a wagon loaded with farm produce. My outfit consisted of about $75, the clothes I wore, and a few others in a knapsack which I carried in the usual way strapped upon my shoulders, for in those days travelers did not have valises or trunks. Though traveling was considered dangerous, I had no weapon more formidable than a pocket-knife. From Cincinnati I went down the Ohio River by steamboat to the Mississippi, up the Mississippi to St. Louis, and thence to Burlington, in what was then the Territory of Iowa.[2] Those were bustling days on the western rivers, which were then the chief highways of travel. The scenes at the wood landings I recall as particularly lively and picturesque. Many passengers would save a little by helping to "wood the boat," i.e., by carrying wood down the bank and throwing it on the boat, a special ticket being issued on that condition. It was very interesting to see the long lines of passengers coming up the gang-plank, each with two or three sticks of wood on his shoulders. An anecdote is told of an Irishman who boarded a western steamer and wanted to know the fare to St. Louis, and, being told, asked, "What do you charge for 150 pounds of freight?" Upon learning the price, a small amount, he announced that he would go as freight. "All right," said the captain; "put him down in the hold and lay some flour barrels on him to keep him down."

In 1839 Burlington had perhaps not over two hundred inhabitants, though it was the capital of Iowa Territory. After consultation with the governor, Robert Lucas of Ohio, I concluded to go into the interior and select a tract of land on the Iowa River.[3] In those days one was permitted to take up 160 acres, and where practicable it was usual to take part timber and part prairie. After working awhile at putting up a log house — until all the people in the neighborhood became ill with fever and ague — I concluded to move on and strike out to the south and southwest into Missouri. I traveled across country, sometimes by the sun, without road or trail. There were houses and settlements, but they were scattered; sometimes one would have to go twenty miles to find a place to stay at night. The principal game seen was the prairie hen; the prairie wolf also abounded.[4] Continuing southwest and passing through Huntsville I struck the Missouri River near Keytesville in Chariton County. Thence I continued up the north side of the river till the westernmost settlement in Missouri was reached; this was in Platte County. The Platte Purchase, as it was called, had been recently bought from the Indians, and was newly but thickly settled, on account of its proximity to navigation, its fine timber, good water, and unsurpassed fertility.

On the route I traveled I cannot recall seeing an emigrant wagon in Missouri. The western movement, which subsequently filled Missouri and other Western States and overflowed into the adjoining Territories, had then hardly begun, except as to Platte County. The contest in Congress over the Platte Purchase, which by increasing the area of Missouri gave more territory to slavery, called wide attention to that charming region.[5] The anti-slavery sentiment even at that date ran quite high. This was, I believe, the first addition to slave territory after the Missouri Compromise.[6] But slavery won. The rush that followed in the space of one or two years filled the most desirable part of the purchase to overflowing. The imagination could not conceive a finer country — lovely, rolling, fertile, wonderfully productive, beautifully arranged for settlement, part prairie and part timber. The land was unsurveyed. Every settler had aimed to locate a half-mile from his neighbor, and there was as yet no conflict. Peace and contentment reigned. Nearly every place seemed to have a beautiful spring of clear cold water. The hills and prairies and the level places were alike covered with a black and fertile soil. I cannot recall seeing an acre of poor land in Platte County. Of course there was intense longing on the part of the people of Missouri to have the Indians removed, and a corresponding desire, as soon as the purchase was consummated, to get possession of the beautiful land. It was in some sense perhaps a kind of Oklahoma movement. Another feature was the abundance of wild honeybees. Every tree that had a hollow in it seemed to be a bee-tree, and every hollow was full of rich golden honey. A singular fact which I learned from old hunters was that the honey-bee was never found more than seventy or eighty miles in advance of the white settlements on the frontier. On this attractive land I set my affections, intending to make it my home.

On my arrival, my money being all spent, I was obliged to accept the first thing that offered, and began teaching school in the country about five miles from the town of Weston, which was located on the north side of the Missouri River and about four miles above Fort Leavenworth in Kansas Territory. Possibly some may suppose it did not take much education to teach a country school at that period in Missouri. The rapid settlement of that new region had brought together people of all classes and conditions, and had thrown into juxtaposition almost every phase of intelligence as well as of illiteracy. But there was no lack of self-reliance or native shrewdness in any class, and I must say that I learned to have a high esteem for the people, among whom I found warm and lifelong friends.

But even in Missouri there were drawbacks. Rattlesnakes and copperheads were abundant. One man, it was said, found a place to suit him, but on alighting from his horse heard so many snakes that he concluded to go farther. At his second attempt, finding more snakes instead of fewer, he left the country altogether. I taught school there in all about a year. My arrival was in June, 1839, and in the fall of that year the surveyors came on to lay out the country; the lines ran every way, sometimes through a man's house, sometimes through his barn, so that there was much confusion and trouble about boundaries, etc. By the favor of certain men, and by paying a small amount for a little piece of fence here and a small clearing there, I got a claim, and purposed to make it my home, and to have my father remove there from Ohio.

In the following summer, 1840, the weather was very hot, so that during the vacation I could do but little work on my place, and needing some supplies — books, clothes, etc. — I concluded to take a trip to St. Louis, which I did by way of the Missouri River. The distance was six hundred miles by water; the down trip occupied two days, and was one of the most delightful experiences of my life. But returning, the river being low and full of snags, and the steamboat heavily laden — the boats were generally light going down — we were continually getting on sand bars, and were delayed nearly a month. This trip proved to be the turning-point in my life, for while I was gone a man had jumped my land. Generally in such cases public sentiment was against the jumper, and It was decidedly so in my case. But the scoundrel held on. He was a bully — had killed a man in Callaway County — and everybody seemed afraid of him. Influential friends of mine tried to persuade him to let me have eighty acres, half of the claim. But he was stubborn, and said that all he wanted was just what the law allowed him. Unfortunately for me, he had the legal advantage. I had worked some now and then on the place, but had not actually lived on it. The law required a certain residence, and that the pre-emptor should be twenty-one years of age or a man of family. I was neither, and could do nothing. Nearly all I had earned had been spent upon the land, and when that was taken I lost about everything I had. There being no possibility of getting another claim to suit me, I resolved to go elsewhere when spring should open.

In November or December of 1840, while still teaching school in Platte County, I came across a Frenchman named Roubideaux, who said he had been to California.[7] He had been a trader in New Mexico, and had followed the road traveled by traders from the frontier of Missouri to Santa Fé. He had probably gone through what is now New Mexico and Arizona into California by the Gila River trail used by the Mexicans. His description of California was in the superlative degree favorable, so much so that I resolved if possible to see that wonderful land, and with others helped to get up a meeting at Weston and invited him to make a statement before it in regard to the country. At that time when a man moved out West, as soon as he was fairly settled he wanted to move again, and naturally every question imaginable was asked in regard to this wonderful country. Roubideaux described it as one of perennial spring and boundless fertility, and laid stress on the countless thousands of wild horses and cattle. He told about oranges, and hence must have been at Los Angeles, or the mission of San Gabriel, a few miles from it. Every conceivable question that we could ask him was answered favorably. Generally the first question which a Missourian asked about a country was whether there was any fever and ague. I remember his answer distinctly. He said there was but one man in California that had ever had a chill there, and it was a matter of so much wonderment to the people of Monterey that they went eighteen miles into the country to see him shake. Nothing could have been more satisfactory on the score of health. He said that the Spanish authorities were most friendly, and that the people were the most hospitable on the globe; that you could travel all over California and it would cost you nothing for horses or food. Even the Indians were friendly. His description of the country made it seem like a Paradise.

The result was that we appointed a corresponding secretary, and a committee to report a plan of organization. A pledge was drawn up in which every signer agreed to purchase a suitable outfit, and to rendezvous at Sapling Grove in what is now the State of Kansas, on the 9th of the following May, armed and equipped to cross the Rocky Mountains to California. We called ourselves the Western Emigration Society, and as soon as the pledge was drawn every one who agreed to come signed his name to it, and it took like wildfire. In a short time, I think within a month, we had about five hundred names; we also had correspondence on the subject with people all over Missouri, and even as far east as Illinois and Kentucky, and as far south as Arkansas. As soon as the movement was announced in the papers we had many letters of inquiry, and we expected people in considerable numbers to join us. About that time

we heard of a man living in Jackson County, Missouri, who had received a letter from a person in California named Dr. Marsh, speaking favorably of the
country, and a copy of this letter was published.[8]

Our ignorance of the route was complete. We knew that California lay west,
and that was the extent of our knowledge. Some of the maps consulted, supposed of course to be correct, showed a lake in the vicinity of where Salt Lake
now is; it was represented as a long lake, three or four hundred miles in extent,
narrow and with two outlets, both running into the Pacific Ocean, either
apparently larger than the Mississippi River. An intelligent man with whom
I boarded — Elam Brown, who till recently lived in California, dying when over
ninety years of age — possessed a map that showed these rivers to be large, and
he advised me to take tools along to make canoes, so that if we found the country
so rough that we could not get along with our wagons we could descend one
of those rivers to the Pacific.[9] Even Frémont knew nothing about Salt Lake until
1843, when for the first time he explored it and mapped it correctly, his report
being first printed, I think, in 1845.[10]

This being the first movement to cross the Rocky Mountains to California,
it is not surprising that it suffered reverses before we were fairly started. One
of these was the publication of a letter in a New York newspaper giving a
depressing view of the country for which we were all so confidently longing.
It seems that in 1837 or 1838 a man by the name of Farnham, a lawyer, went
from New York City into the Rocky Mountains for his health. He was an invalid,
hopelessly gone with consumption it was thought, and as a last resort he went
into the mountains, traveled with the trappers, lived in the open air as the trappers lived, eating only meat as they did, and in two or three years he entirely
regained his health; but instead of returning east by way of St. Louis, as he had
gone, he went down the Columbia River and took a vessel to Monterey and
thence to San Blas, making his way through Mexico to New York.[11] Upon his
return — in February or March, 1841, he published the letter mentioned. His
bad opinion of California was based wholly on his unfortunate experience in
Monterey, which I will recount.

In 1840 there lived in California an old Rocky Mountaineer by the name
of Isaac Graham. He was injudicious in his talk, and by boasting that the United
States or Texas would some day take California, he excited the hostility and
jealousy of the people. In those days Americans were held in disfavor by the
native Californians on account of the war made by Americans in Texas to wrest
Texas from Mexico. The number of Americans in California at this time was
very small. When I went to California in 1841 all the foreigners — and all were
foreigners except Indians and Mexicans — did not, I think, exceed one hundred; nor was the character of all of them the most prepossessing. Some had
been trappers in the Rocky Mountains who had not seen civilization for a quarter

of a century; others were men who had found their way into California, as Roubideaux had done, by way of Mexico; others still had gone down the Columbia River to Oregon and joined trapping parties in the service of the Hudson Bay Company going from Oregon to California—men who would let their beards grow down to their knees, and wear buckskin garments made and fringed like those of the Indians, and who considered it a compliment to be told "I took ye for an Injin." Another class of men from the Rocky Mountains were in the habit of making their way by the Mohave Desert south of the Sierra Nevada into California to steal horses, sometimes driving off four or five hundred at a time.[12] The other Americans, most numerous perhaps, were sailors who had run away from vessels and remained in the country. With few exceptions this was the character of the American population when I came to California, and they were not generally a class calculated to gain much favor with the people. Farnham happened to come into the bay of Monterey when this fellow Graham and his confederates, and all others whom the Californians suspected, were under arrest in irons on board a vessel, ready for transportation to San Blas in Mexico, whither indeed they were taken, and where some of them died in irons. I am not sure that at this time the English had a consul in California; but the United States had none, and there was no one there to take the part of the Americans. Farnham, being a lawyer, doubtless knew that the proceeding was illegal. He went ashore and protested against it, but without effect, as he was only a private individual. Probably he was there on a burning hot day and saw only the dreary sandhills to the east of the old town of Monterey.[13] On arriving in New York he published the letter referred to, describing how Americans were oppressed by the native Californians, and how dangerous it was for Americans to go there. The merchants of Platte County had all along protested against our going, and had tried from the beginning to discourage and break up the movement, saying it was the most unheard-of, foolish, wild-goose chase that ever entered into the brain of man for five hundred people to pull up stakes, leave that beautiful country, and go away out to a region that we knew nothing of. But they made little headway until this letter of Farnham's appeared. They republished it in a paper in the town of Liberty in Clay County —there being no paper published in Platte County—and sent it broadcast all over the surrounding region.[14] The result was that as the people began to think more seriously about the scheme the membership of the society began dropping off, and so it happened at last that of all the five hundred that signed the pledge I was the only one that got ready; and even I had hard work to do so, for I had barely means to buy a wagon, a gun, and provisions. Indeed, the man who was going with me, and who was to furnish the horses, backed out, and there I was with my wagon!

During the winter, to keep the project alive, I had made two or three trips into Jackson County, Missouri, crossing the Missouri River, always dangerous in winter when ice was running, by the ferry at Westport Landing, now Kansas City. Sometimes I had to go ten miles farther down — sixty miles from Weston — to a safer ferry at Independence Landing in order to get into Jackson County, to see men who were talking of going to California, and to get information.

At the last moment before the time to start for the rendezvous at Sapling Grove — it seemed almost providential — along came a man named George Henshaw, an invalid, from Illinois, I think.[15] He was pretty well dressed, was riding a fine black horse, and had ten or fifteen dollars. I persuaded him to let me take his horse and trade him for a yoke of steers to pull the wagon and a sorry-looking, one-eyed mule for him to ride. We went via Weston to lay in some supplies. One wagon and four or five persons here joined us. On leaving Weston, where there had been so much opposition, we were six or seven in number, and nearly half the town followed us for a mile, and some for five or six miles, to bid us goodby, showing the deep interest felt in our journey. All expressed good wishes and desired to hear from us. When we reached Sapling Grove, the place of rendezvous, in May, 1841, there was but one wagon ahead of us. For the next few days one or two wagons would come each day, and among the recruits were three families from Arkansas. We organized by electing as captain of the company a man named Bartleson from Jackson County, Missouri. He was not the best man for the position, but we were given to understand that if he was not elected captain he would not go; and as he had seven or eight men with him, and we did not want the party diminished, he was chosen. Every one furnished his own supplies. The party consisted of sixty-nine, including men, women, and children.[16] Our teams were of oxen, mules, and horses. We had no cows, as the later emigrants usually had, and the lack of milk was a great deprivation to the children. It was understood that every one should have not less than a barrel of flour with sugar and so forth to suit; but I laid in one hundred pounds of flour more than the usual quantity, besides other things. This I did because we were told that when we got into the mountains we probably would get out of bread and have to live on meat alone, which I thought would kill me even if it did not others. My gun was an old flint-lock rifle, but a good one. Old hunters told me to have nothing to do with cap or percussion locks, that they were unreliable, and that if I got my caps or percussion wet I could not shoot, while if I lost my flint I could pick up another on the plains. I doubt whether there was one hundred dollars in money in the whole party, but all were enthusiastic and anxious to go.

In five days after my arrival we were ready to start, but no one knew where to go, not even the captain. Finally a man came up, one of the last to arrive, and announced that a company of Catholic missionaries were on their way from St. Louis to the Flathead nation of Indians with an old Rocky Mountaineer for a guide, and that if we would wait another day they would be up with us. At first we were independent, and thought we could not afford to wait for a slow missionary party. But when we found that no one knew which way to go, we sobered down and waited for them to come up; and it was well we did, for otherwise probably not one of us would ever have reached California, because of our inexperience. Afterwards when we came in contact with Indians our people were so easily excited that if we had not had with us an old mountaineer the result would certainly have been disastrous. The name of the guide was Captain Fitzpatrick; he had been at the head of trapping parties in the Rocky Mountains for many years.[17] He and the missionary party went with us as far as Soda Springs, now in Idaho Territory, whence they turned north to the Flathead nation. The party consisted of three Roman Catholic priests— Father De Smet, Father Pont, Father Mengarini[18]—and ten or eleven French Canadians, and accompanying them were an old mountaineer named John Gray and a young Englishman named Romaine, and also a man named Baker.[19] They seemed glad to have us with them, and we certainly were glad to have their company. Father De Smet had been to the Flathead nation before. He had gone out with a trapping party, and on his return had traveled with only a guide by another route, farther to the north and through hostile tribes. He was genial, of fine presence, and one of the saintliest men I have ever known, and I cannot wonder that the Indians were made to believe him divinely protected. He was a man of great kindness and great affability under all circumstances; nothing seemed to disturb his temper. The Canadians had mules and Red River carts, instead of wagons and horses—two mules to each cart, five or six of them— and in case of steep hills they would hitch three or four of the animals to one cart, always working them tandem. Sometimes a cart would go over, breaking everything in it to pieces; and at such times Father De Smet would be just the same—beaming with good humor.[20]

In general our route lay from near Westport, where Kansas City now is, northwesterly over the prairie, crossing several streams, till we struck the Platte River. Then we followed along the south side of the Platte to and a day's journey or so along the South Fork. Here the features of the country became more bold and interesting. Then crossing the South Fork of the Platte, and following up the north side for a day or so, we went over to the North Fork and camped at Ash Hollow; thence up the north side of that fork, passing those noted landmarks known as the Court House Rocks, Chimney Rock, Scott's Bluffs, etc., till we came to Fort Laramie, a trading post of the American Fur Company, near which was Lupton's Fort, belonging, as I understood, to some rival company. Thence after several days we came to another noted landmark called Independence Rock, on a branch of the North Platte called the Sweetwater, which we followed up to the head, soon after striking the Little Sandy, and then the

Big Sandy, which empties into Green River. Next we crossed Green River to Black Fork, which we followed up till we came to Ham's Fork, at the head of which we crossed the divide between Green and Bear rivers. Then we followed Bear River down to Soda Springs. The waters of Bear Lake discharged through that river, which we continued to follow down on the west side till we came to Salt Lake. Then we went around the north end of the lake and struck out to the west and southwest.

For a time, until we reached the Platte River, one day was much like another. We set forth every morning and camped every night, detailing men to stand guard. Captain Fitzpatrick and the missionary party would generally take the lead and we would follow. Fitzpatrick knew all about the Indian tribes, and when there was any danger we kept in a more compact body, to protect one another. At other times we would be scattered along, sometimes for half a mile or more. We were generally together, because there was often work to be done to avoid delay. We had to make the road, frequently digging down steep banks, filling gulches, removing stones, etc. In such cases everybody would take a spade or do something to help make the road passable. When we camped at night we usually drew the wagons and carts together in a hollow square and picketed our animals inside in the corral.[21] The wagons were common ones and of no special pattern, and some of them were covered. The tongue of one would be fastened to the back of another. To lessen the danger from Indians, we usually had no fires at night and did our cooking in the daytime.

The first incident was a scare that we had from a party of Cheyenne Indians just before we reached the Platte River, about two weeks after we set out. One of our men who chanced to be out hunting, some distance from the company and behind us, suddenly appeared without mule, gun, or pistol, and lacking most of his clothes, and in great excitement reported that he had been surrounded by thousands of Indians. The company, too, became excited, and Captain Fitzpatrick tried, but with little effect, to control and pacify them. Every man started his team into a run, till the oxen, like the mules and horses, were in a full gallop. Captain Fitzpatrick went ahead and directed them to follow, and as fast as they came to the bank of the river he put the wagons in the form of a hollow square and had all the animals securely picketed within. After a while the Indians came in sight. There were only forty of them, but they were well mounted on horses, and were evidently a war party, for they had no women except one, a medicine woman. They came up and camped within a hundred yards of us on the river below. Fitzpatrick told us that they would not have come in that way if they were hostile. Our hunter in his excitement said that there were thousands of them, and that they had robbed him of his gun, mule, and pistol. When the Indians had put up their lodges Fitzpatrick and John Gray, the old hunter mentioned, went out to them and by signs were made to understand that the Indians did not intend to hurt the man or to take his mule or gun, but that he was so excited when he saw them that they had to disarm him to keep him from shooting them; they did not know what had become of his pistol or of his clothes, which he said they had torn off. They surrendered the mule and the gun, thus showing that they were friendly. They proved to be Cheyenne Indians. Ever afterwards that man went by the name of Cheyenne Dawson.[22]

As soon as we struck the buffalo country we found a new source of interest. Before reaching the Platte we had seen an abundance of antelope and elk, prairie wolves and villages of prairie dogs, but only an occasional buffalo. We now began to kill buffaloes for food, and at the suggestion of John Gray, and following the practice of Rocky Mountain white hunters, our people began to kill them just to get the tongues and the marrow bones, leaving all the rest of the meat on the plains for the wolves to eat. But the Cheyennes, who traveled ahead of us for two or three days, set us a better example. At their camps we noticed that when they killed buffaloes they took all the meat, everything but the bones. Indians were never wasteful of the buffalo except in winter for the sake of the robes, and then only in order to get the whisky which traders offered them in exchange.[23] There is no better beef in the world than that of the buffalo; it is also very good jerked, i.e., cut into strings and thoroughly dried. It was an easy matter to kill buffaloes after we got to where they were numerous, by keeping out of sight and to the leeward of them. I think I can truly say that I saw in that region in one day more buffaloes than I have seen of cattle in all my life. I have seen the plain black with them for several days' journey as far as the eye could reach. They seemed to be coming northward continually from the distant plains to the Platte to get water, and would plunge in and swim across by thousands—so numerous were they that they changed not only the color of the water, but its taste, until it was unfit to drink; but we had to use it. One night when we were encamped on the South Fork of the Platte they came in such droves that we had to sit up and fire guns and make what fires we could to keep them from running over us and trampling us into the dust. We were obliged to go out some distance from camp to turn them: Captain Fitzpatrick told us that if we did not do this the buffaloes in front could not turn aside for the pressure of those behind. We could hear them thundering all night long; the ground fairly trembled with vast approaching bands; and if they had not been diverted, wagons, animals, and emigrants would have been trodden under their feet. One cannot nowadays describe the rush and wildness of the thing. A strange feature was that when old oxen, tired and foot-sore, got among a buffalo herd, as they sometimes would in the night, they would soon become as wild as the wildest buffalo; and if ever recovered it was because they could not run so fast as the buffaloes or one's horse. The ground over which the herds trampled was left rather barren, but buffalo-grass being short and curling, in traveling over it they did not cut it up as much as they would other kinds.

On the Platte River, on the afternoon of one of the hottest days we experienced on the plains, we had a taste of a cyclone: first came a terrific shower, followed by a fall of hail to the depth of four inches, some of the stones being as large as turkeys' eggs; and the next day a waterspout — an angry, huge, whirling cloud column, which seemed to draw its water from the Platte River — passed within a quarter of a mile behind us. We stopped and braced ourselves against our wagons to keep them from being overturned. Had it struck us it doubtless would have demolished us.

Above the junction of the forks of the Platte we continued to pass notable natural formations — first O'Fallon's Bluffs, then Court House Rocks, a group of fantastic shapes to which some of our party started to go.[24] After they had gone what seemed fifteen or twenty miles the huge pile looked just as far off as when they started, and so they turned and came back — so deceptive are distances in the clear atmosphere of the Rocky Mountains. A noted landmark on the North Fork, which we sighted fifty miles away, was Chimney Rock. It was then nearly square, and I think it must have been fifty feet higher than now, though after we passed it a portion of it fell off. Scott's Bluffs are known to emigrants for their picturesqueness. These formations, like those first mentioned, are composed of indurated yellow clay or soft sand rock; they are washed and broken into all sorts of fantastic forms by the rains and storms of ages, and have the appearance of an immense city of towers and castles. They are quite difficult to explore, as I learned by experience in an effort to pursue and kill mountain sheep or bighorn. These were seen in great numbers, but we failed to kill any, as they inhabit places almost inaccessible and are exceedingly wild.

As we ascended the Platte buffaloes became scarcer, and on the Sweetwater none were to be seen. Now appeared in the distance to the north of west, gleaming under its mantle of perpetual snow, that lofty range known as the Wind River Mountains. It was the first time I had seen snow in summer; some of the peaks were very precipitous, and the view was altogether most impressive. Guided by Fitzpatrick, we crossed the Rockies at or near the South Pass, where the mountains were apparently low.[25] Some years before a man named William Subletts, an Indian fur trader, went to the Rocky Mountains with goods in wagons, and those were the only wagons that had ever been there before us; sometimes we came across the tracks, but generally they were obliterated, and thus were of no service.[26] Approaching Green River in the Rocky Mountains, it was found that some of the wagons, including Captain Bartleson's, had alcohol on board, and that the owners wanted to find trappers in the Rocky Mountains to whom they might sell it. This was a surprise to many of us, as there had been no drinking on the way. John Gray was sent ahead to see if he could find a trapping party, and he was instructed, if successful, to have them come to a certain place on Green River. He struck a trail, and overtook a party on their way to the buffalo region to lay in provisions, i.e., buffalo meat, and they returned, and came and camped on Green River very soon after our arrival, buying the greater part, if not all, of the alcohol, it first having been diluted so as to make what they called whisky — three or four gallons of water to a gallon of alcohol. Years afterwards we heard of the fate of that party: they were attacked by Indians the very first night after they left us and several of them killed, including the captain of the trapping party, whose name was Frapp.[27] The whisky was probably the cause.

Several years ago when I was going down Weber Cañon, approaching Salt Lake, swiftly borne along on an observation car amid cliffs and over rushing streams, something said that night at the camp-fire on Green River was forcibly recalled to mind. We had in our party an illiterate fellow named Bill Overton, who in the evening at one of the camp-fires loudly declared that nothing in his life had ever surprised him. Of course that raised a dispute. "Never surprised in your life?" "No, I never was surprised." And, moreover, he swore that nothing ever *could* surprise him. "I should not be surprised," said he, "if I were to see a steamboat come plowing over these mountains this minute." In rattling down the cañon of Weber River it occurred to me that the reality was almost equal to Bill Overton's extravaganza, and I could but wonder what he would have said had he suddenly come upon this modern scene.

As I have said, at Soda Springs — at the northernmost bend of Bear River — our party separated. It was a bright and lovely place. The abundance of soda water, including the intermittent gushing so-called Steamboat Spring; the beautiful fir and cedar covered hills; the huge piles of red or brown sinter, the result of fountains once active but then dry — all these, together with the river, lent a charm to its wild beauty and made the spot a notable one. Here the missionary party were to turn north and go into the Flathead nation. Fort Hall, about forty miles distant on Snake River, lay on their route.[28] There was no road; but something like a trail, doubtless used by the trappers, led in that direction. From Fort Hall there was also a trail down Snake River, by which trapping parties reached the Columbia River and Fort Vancouver, the headquarters of the Hudson Bay Company.[29]

Our party, originally sixty-nine, including women and children, had become lessened to sixty-four in number. One had accidentally shot and killed himself at the forks of the Platte. Another of our party, named Simpson, had left us at Fort Laramie. Three had turned back from Green River, intending to make their way to Fort Bridger and await an opportunity to return home. Their names were Peyton, Rodgers, and Amos E. Frye. Thirty-two of our party, becoming discouraged, decided not to venture without path or guide into the unknown and trackless region towards California, but concluded to go with the missionary party to Fort Hall and thence find their way down Snake and Columbia rivers into Oregon.[30] The rest of us—also thirty-two in number, including Benjamin Kelsey, his wife and little daughter—remained firm, refusing to be diverted from our original purpose of going direct to California. After getting all the information we could from Captain Fitzpatrick, we regretfully bade good-by to our fellow emigrants and to Father De Smet and his party.

We were now thrown entirely upon our own resources. All the country beyond was to us a veritable *terra incognita,* and we only knew that California lay to the west. Captain Fitzpatrick was not much better informed, but he had heard that parties had penetrated the country to the southwest and west of Salt Lake to trap for beaver; and by his advice four of our men went with the parties to Fort Hall to consult Captain Grant, who was in charge there, and to gain information.[31] Meanwhile our depleted party slowly made its way down the west side of Bear River.

Our separation at Soda Springs recalls an incident. The days were usually very hot, the nights almost freezing. The first day our little company went only about ten miles and camped on Bear River. In company with a man named James John—always called "Jimmy John"—I wandered a mile or two down the river fishing. Seeing snow on a high mountain to the west, we longed to reach it, for the heat where we were was intense. So, without losing time to get our guns or coats or to give notice at the camp, we started direct for the snow, with the impression that we could go and return by sundown. But there intervened a range of lower mountains, a certain peak of which seemed almost to touch the snow. Both of us were fleet of foot and made haste, but we only gained the summit of the peak about sundown. The distance must have been twelve or fifteen miles. A valley intervened, and the snow lay on a higher mountain beyond. I proposed to camp. But Jimmy gave me a disdainful look, as much as to say, "You are afraid to go," and quickened his gait into a run down the mountain towards the snow. I called him to stop, but he would not even look back. A firm resolve seized me—to overtake him, but not again to ask him to return. We crossed the valley in the night, saw many Indian campfires, and gained a sharp ridge leading up to the snow. This was first brushy and then rough and rocky. The brush had no paths except those made by wild animals; the rocks were sharp, and soon cut through our moccasins and made our feet bleed. But up and up we went until long after midnight, and until a cloud covered the mountain. We were above the timber line, excepting a few stunted fir trees, under one of which we crawled to wait for day, for it was too dark to see. Day soon dawned, but we were almost frozen. Our fir-tree nest had been the lair of grizzly bears that had wallowed there and shed quantities of shaggy hair. The snow was still beyond, and we had lost both sight and direction. But in an hour or two we reached it. It was nearly as hard as ice. Filling a large handkerchief, without taking time to admire the scenery we started towards the camp by a new route, for our feet were too sore to go by way of the rocky ridge by which we had come. But the new way led into trouble. There were thickets so dense as to exclude the sun, and roaring little streams in deep, dark chasms; we had to crawl through paths which looked untrodden except by grizzlies; in one place a large bear had passed evidently only a few minutes before, crossing the deep gorge, plunging through the wild, dashing water, and wetting the steep bank as he went up. We carried our drawn butcher knives in our hands, for they were our only weapons. At last we emerged into the valley. Apparently numerous Indians had left that very morning, as shown by the tracks of lodge-poles drawn on the ground. Making haste, we soon gained the hills, and at about 2 P.M. sighted our wagons, already two or three miles on the march. When our friends saw us they stopped, and all who could ran to welcome us. They had given us up for lost, supposing that we had been killed by the hostile Blackfeet, who, as Captain Fitzpatrick had warned us, sometimes roamed through that region. The company had barricaded the camp at night as best they could, and every man had spent a sleepless night on guard. Next morning they passed several hours in scouring the country. Their first questions were: "Where have you been?" I was able to answer triumphantly, "*We have been up to the snow!*" and to demonstrate the fact by showing all the snow I had left, which was now reduced to a ball about the size of my fist.

In about ten days our four men returned from Fort Hall, during which time we had advanced something over one hundred miles toward Salt Lake. They brought the information that we must strike out west of Salt Lake—as it was even then called by the trappers—being careful not to go too far south, lest we should get into a waterless country without grass. They also said we must be careful not to go too far north, lest we should get into a broken country and steep cañons, and wander about, as trapping parties had been known to do, and become bewildered and perish.

September had come before we reached Salt Lake, which we struck at its northern extremity. Part of the time we had purposely traveled slowly to enable the men from Fort Hall the sooner to overtake us. But unavoidable delays were frequent: daily, often hourly, the road had to be made passable for our wagons by digging down steep banks, filling gulches, etc. Indian fires obscured mountains and valleys in a dense, smoky atmosphere, so that we could not see any considerable distance in order to avoid obstacles. The principal growth, on plain and hill alike, was the interminable sagebrush,[32] and often it was difficult, for miles at a time, to break a road through it, and sometimes a lightly laden wagon would be overturned. Its monotonous dull color and scraggy appearance gave a most dreary aspect to the landscape. But it was not wholly useless: where large enough it made excellent fuel, and it was the home and shelter of the hare—generally known as the "jack rabbit"—and of the sage-hen. Trees were almost a sure sign of water in that region. But the mirage was most deceptive, magnifying stunted sagebrush on diminutive hillocks into trees and groves. Thus misled, we traveled all day without water, and at midnight found ourselves in a plain, level as a floor, incrusted with salt, and as white as snow. Crusts of salt broken up by our wagons, and driven by the chilly night wind like ice on the surface of a frozen pond, was to me a most striking counterfeit of a winter scene. This plain became softer and softer until our poor, almost famished, animals could not pull our wagons. In fact, we were going direct to Salt Lake and did not know it. So, in search of water, we turned from a southerly to an easterly course, and went about ten miles, and soon after daylight arrived at Bear River. So near to Salt Lake were we that the water in the river was too salt for us or our animals to use, but we had to use it; it would not quench thirst, but it did save life. The grass looked most luxuriant, and sparkled as if covered with frost. But it was salt; our hungry, jaded animals refused to eat it, and we had to lie by a whole day to rest them before we could travel.

Leaving this camp and bearing northwest we crossed our tracks on the salt plain, having thus described a triangle of several miles in dimensions. One of the most serious of our troubles was to find water where we could camp at night. So soon came another hot day, and hard travel all day and all night without water! From a westerly course we turned directly north, and, guided by antelope trails, came in a few miles to an abundance of grass and good water. The condition of our animals compelled us to rest here nearly a week. Meanwhile two of the men who had been to Fort Hall went ahead to explore. Provisions were becoming scarce, and we saw that we must avoid unnecessary delay. The two men were gone about five days. Under their lead we set forth, bearing west, then southwest, around Salt Lake, then again west. After two or three fatiguing days—one day and a night without water—the first notice we had of approach to any considerable mountain was the sight of crags, dimly seen through the smoke, many hundred feet above our heads. Here was plenty of good grass and water. Nearly all now said, "Let us leave our wagons, otherwise the snows will overtake us before we get to California." So we stopped one day and threw away everything we could not carry, made pack-saddles and packed the oxen, mules, and horses, and started.

On Green River we had seen the style of pack-saddles used by the trapping party, and had learned a little about how to make them. Packing is an art, and something that only an experienced mountaineer can do well so as to save his animal and keep his pack from falling off. We were unaccustomed to it, and the difficulties we had at first were simply indescribable. It is much more difficult to fasten a pack on an ox than on a mule or a horse. The trouble began the very first day. But we started—most of us on foot, for nearly all the animals, including several of the oxen, had to carry packs. It was but a few minutes before the packs began to turn; horses became scared, mules kicked, oxen jumped and bellowed, and articles were scattered in all directions. We took pains, fixed things, made a new start, and did better, though packs continued occasionally to fall off and delay us.

Those that had better pack-saddles and had tied their loads securely were ahead, while the others were obliged to lag behind, because they had to re-pack, and sometimes things would be strewn all along the route. The first night I happened to be among those that kept pretty well back, because the horses out-traveled the oxen. The foremost came to a place and stopped where there was no water or grass, and built a fire so that we could see it and come up to them. We got there about midnight, but some of our oxen that had packs on had not come up, and among them were my two. So I had to return the next morning and find them, Cheyenne Dawson alone volunteering to go with me. One man had brought along about a quart of water, which he carefully doled out before we started, each receiving a little canister-cover full—less than half a gill; but as Dawson and I had to go for the oxen, we were given a double portion. This was all the water I had until the next day. It was a burning hot day. We could not find the trail of the oxen for a long time, and Dawson refused to go any farther, saying that there were plenty of cattle in California; but I had to do it, for the oxen were carrying our provisions and other things. Afterwards I struck the trail, and found that the oxen instead of going west had gone north, and I followed them until nearly sundown. They had got into a grassy country, which showed that they were nearing water. Seeing Indian tracks on their trail following them, I felt there was imminent danger, and at once examined my gun and pistols to see that they were primed and ready. But soon I found my oxen lying down in tall grass by the side of the trail. Seeing no Indians, I hastened to fasten the packs and make my way to overtake the company. They had promised to stop when they came to water and wait for me. I traveled all night, and at early dawn came to where there was plenty of water and where the company had taken their dinner the day before, but they had failed to stop for me according to promise. I was much perplexed, because I had seen many fires in the night, which I took to be Indian fires, so I fastened my oxen to a scraggy willow and began to make circles around to see which way the company had gone. The ground was so hard that the animals had made no impression, which bewildered me. Finally, while making a circle of about three miles away off to the south, I saw two men coming on horseback. In the glare of the mirage, which distorted everything, I could not tell whether they were Indians or white men, but I supposed them to be Indians, feeling sure our party would go west and not south. In a mirage a man on horseback looks as tall as a tree, and I could only tell by the motion that they were mounted. I made a beeline to my oxen, to make breastworks of them. In doing this I came to a small stream resembling running water, into which I urged my horse, whereupon he went down into a quagmire, over head and ears, out of sight. My gun also went under the mire. I got hold of something on the bank, threw out my gun, which was full of mud and water, and holding to the rope attached to my horse, by dint of hard pulling I succeeded in getting him out — a sorry sight, his ears and eyes full of mud, and his body covered with it. At last, just in time, I was able to move and get behind the oxen. My gun was in no condition to shoot. However, putting dry powder in the pan I determined to do my best in case the supposed Indians should come up; but lo! they were two of our party coming to meet me, bringing water and provisions. It was a great relief. I felt indignant that the party had not stopped for me — not the less so when I learned that Captain Bartleson had said, when they started back to find me, that they "would be in better business to go ahead and look for a road." He had not forgotten certain comments of mine on his qualities as a student of Indian character. An instance of this I will relate.

One morning, just as we were packing up, a party of about ninety Indians, on horseback, a regular war party, were descried coming up. Some of us begged the captain to send men out to prevent them from coming to us while we were in the confusion of packing. But he said, "Boys, you must not show any sign of hostility; if you go out there with guns the Indians will think us hostile, and may get mad and hurt us." However, five or six of us took our guns and went out, and by signs made them halt. They did not prove to be hostile, but they had carbines, and if we had been careless and had let them come near they might, and probably would, have killed us. At last we got packed up and started, and the Indians traveled along three or four hundred yards one side or the other of us or behind us all day. They appeared anxious to trade, and offered a buckskin, well dressed, worth two or three dollars, for three or four charges of powder and three or four balls. This showed that they were in want of ammunition. The carbines indicated that they had had communication with some trading-post belonging to the Hudson's Bay Company. They had buffalo-robes also, which showed that they were a roving hunting party, as there were no buffaloes within three or four hundred miles. At this time I had spoken my mind pretty freely concerning Captain Bartleson's lack of judgment, as one could scarcely help doing under the circumstances.

We now got into a country where there was no grass nor water, and then we began to catechize the men who had gone to Fort Hall. They repeated, "If you go too far south you will get into a desert country and your animals will perish; there will be no water nor grass." We were evidently too far south. We could not go west, and the formation of the country was such that we had to turn and go north across a range of mountains. Having struck a small stream we camped upon it all night, and next day continued down its banks, crossing from side to side, most of the time following Indian paths or paths made by antelope and deer. In the afternoon we entered a cañon the walls of which were precipitous and several hundred feet high. Finally the pleasant bermy banks gave out entirely, and we could travel only in the dry bed of what in the wet season was a raging river. It became a solid mass of stones and huge boulders, and the animals became tender-footed and sore so that they could hardly stand up, and as we continued the way became worse and worse. There was no place for us to lie down and sleep, nor could our animals lie down; the water had given out, and the prospect was indeed gloomy—the cañon had been leading us directly north. All agreed that the animals were too jaded and worn to go back. Then we called the men: "What did they tell you at Fort Hall about the northern region?" They repeated, "You must not go too for north; if you do you will get into difficult cañons that lead towards the Columbia River, where you may become bewildered and wander about and perish." This cañon was going nearly north; in fact it seemed a little east of north. We sent some men to see if they could reach the top of the mountain by scaling the precipice somewhere and get a view, and they came back about ten or eleven o'clock, saying the country looked better three or four miles farther ahead. So we were encouraged. Even the animals seemed to take courage, and we got along much better than had been thought possible, and by one o'clock that day came out on what is now known as the Humboldt River. It was not until four years later (1845) that General Frémont first saw this river and named it Humboldt.[33]

Our course was first westward and then southward, following this river for many days, till we came to its Sink, near which we saw a solitary horse, an indication that trappers had sometimes been in that vicinity. We tried to catch him but failed; he had been there long enough to become very wild. We saw many Indians on the Humboldt, especially towards the Sink. There were many tule marshes. The tule is a rush, large, but here not very tall. It was generally completely covered with honeydew, and this in turn was wholly covered with a pediculous-looking insect which fed upon it. The Indians gathered quantities of the honey and pressed it into balls about the size of one's fist, having the appearance of wet bran. At first we greatly relished this Indian food, but when we saw what it was made of—that the insects pressed into the mass were the main ingredient—we lost our appetites and bought no more of it.

From the time we left our wagons many had to walk, and more and more as we advanced. Going down the Humboldt at least half were on foot.

Provisions had given out; except a little coarse green grass among the willows along the river the country was dry, bare and desolate; we saw no game except antelope, and they were scarce and hard to kill; and walking was very fatiguing. Tobacco lovers would surrender their animals for anyone to ride who would furnish them with an ounce or two to chew during the day. One day one of these devotees lost his tobacco and went back for it, but failed to find it. An Indian in a friendly manner overtook us, bringing the piece of tobacco, which he had found on our trail or at our latest camp, and surrendered it. The owner, instead of being thankful, accused the Indian of having stolen it—an impossibility, as we had seen no Indians or Indian signs for some days. Perhaps the Indian did not know what it was, else he might have kept it for smoking. But I think otherwise, for, patting his breast, he said, "Shoshone, Shoshone," which was the Indian way of showing he was friendly. The Shoshones were known as always friendly to the whites, and it is not difficult to see how other and distant tribes might claim to be Shoshones as a passport to favor.

On the Humboldt we had a further division of our ranks. In going down the river we went sometimes on one side and sometimes on the other, but mostly on the north side, till we were nearing what are now known as the Humboldt Mountains. We were getting tired, and some were in favor of leaving the oxen, of which we then had only about seven or eight, and rushing on into California. They said there was plenty of beef in California. But some of us said: "No; our oxen are now our only supply of food. We are doing well, making eighteen or twenty miles a day." One morning when it was my turn at driving the oxen, the captain traveled so fast that I could not keep up, and was left far behind. When night came I had to leave the trail and go over a rocky declivity for a mile and a half into a gloomy, damp bottom, and unpack the oxen and turn them out to eat, sleeping myself without blankets. I got up the next morning, hunted the oxen out of the willow thicket, and re-packed them. Not having had supper or breakfast, and having to travel nine miles before I overtook the party, perhaps I was not in the best humor. They were waiting, and for the very good reason that they could have nothing to eat till I came up with the oxen and one could be killed. I felt badly treated, and let the captain know it plainly; but, much to my surprise, he made no reply, and none of his men said a word. We killed an ox, ate our breakfast, and got ready to start about one or two o'clock in the afternoon. When nearly ready to go, the Captain and one or two of his mess came to us and said: "Boys, our animals are better than yours, and we always get out of meat before any of the rest of you. Let us have the most of the meat this time, and we will pay you back the next ox we kill." We gladly let them have all they wished. But as soon as they had taken it, and were mounted ready to start, the captain in a loud voice exclaimed: "Now we have been found fault with long enough, and we are going to California. If you can keep up with us, all right; if you cannot, you may go to — — — "; and away they started, the captain and eight men. One of the men would not go with the captain; he said, "The captain is wrong, and I will stay with you, boys."

In a short time they were out of sight. We followed their trail for two or three days, but after they had crossed over to the south side of the Humboldt and turned south we came into a sandy waste where the wind had entirely obliterated their tracks. We were then thrown entirely upon our own resources. It was our desire to make as great speed as possible westward, deviating only when obstacles interposed, and in such case bearing south instead of north, so as to be found in a lower latitude in the event that winter should overtake us in the mountains. But, diverted by following our fugitive captain and party across the Humboldt, we thereby missed the luxuriant Truckee meadows lying but a short distance to the west, a resting-place well and favorably known to later emigrants. So, perforce, we followed down to the Sink of the Humboldt and were obliged to drink its water, which in the fall of the year becomes stagnant and of the color of lye, and not fit to drink or use unless boiled. Here we camped. Leaving the Sink of the Humboldt, we crossed a considerable stream which must have been Carson River, and came to another stream which must have been Walker River, and followed it up to where it came out of the mountains, which proved to be the Sierra Nevada. We did not know the name of the mountains. Neither had these rivers then been named; nor had they been seen by Kit Carson or Joe Walker, for whom they were named, nor were they seen until 1845 by Frémont, who named them.[34]

We were now camped on Walker River, at the very eastern base of the Sierra Nevada, and had only two oxen left. We sent men ahead to see if it would be possible to scale the mountains, while we killed the better of the two oxen and dried the meat in preparation for the ascent. The men returned towards evening and reported that they thought it would be possible to ascend the mountains, though very difficult. We had eaten our supper, and were ready for the climb in the morning. Looking back on the plains we saw something coming, which we decided to be Indians. They traveled very slowly, and it was difficult to understand their movements. To make a long story short, it was the eight men that had left us nine days before. They had gone farther south than we and had come to a lake, probably Carson Lake, and there had found Indians who supplied them plentifully with fish and pine nuts. Fish caught in such water are not fit to eat at any time, much less in the fall of the year. The men had all eaten heartily of fish and pine nuts, and had got something akin to cholera morbus. We were glad to see them although they had deserted us. We ran out to meet them and shook hands, and put our frying-pans on and gave them the best supper we could. Captain Bartleson, who when we started from Missouri was a portly man, was reduced to half his former girth. He said: "Boys, if ever I get back to Missouri I will never leave that country. I would gladly eat out of the troughs with my dogs." He seemed to be heartily sick of his late experience, but that did not prevent him from leaving us twice after that.

We were now in what is at present Nevada, and probably within forty miles of the present boundary of California. We ascended the mountains on the north side of Walker River to the summit, and then struck a stream running west which proved to be the extreme source of the Stanislaus River. We followed it down for several days and finally came to where a branch ran into it, each forming a cañon. The main river flowed in a precipitous gorge in places apparently a mile deep, and the gorge that came into it was but little less formidable. At night we found ourselves on the extreme point of the promontory between the two, very tired, and with neither grass nor water. We had to stay there that night. Early the next morning two men went down to see if it would be possible to get through down the smaller cañon. I was one of them, Jimmy John the other. Benjamin Kelsey, who had shown himself expert in finding the way, was now, without any election, still recognized as leader, as he had been during the absence of Bartleson. A party also went back to see how far we should have to go around before we could pass over the tributary cañon. The understanding was, that when we went down the cañon if it was practicable to get through we were to fire a gun so that all could follow; but if not, we were not to fire, even if we saw game. When Jimmy and I got down about three-quarters of a mile I came to the conclusion that it was impossible to get through, and said to him, "Jimmy, we might as well go back; we can't go here." "Yes, we can," said he; and insisting that we could, he pulled out a pistol and fired. It was an old dragoon pistol, and reverberated like a cannon. I hurried back to tell the company not to come down, but before I reached them the captain and his party had started. I explained, and warned them that they could not get down; but they went on as far as they could go, and then were obliged to stay all day and night to rest the animals, and had to go about among the rocks and pick a little grass for them, and go down to the stream through a terrible place in the cañon to bring water up in cups and camp-kettles, and some of the men in their boots, to pour down the animals' throats in order to keep them from perishing. Finally, four of them pulling and four of them pushing a mule, they managed to get them up one by one, and then carried all the things up again on their backs—not an easy job for exhausted men.

In some way, nobody knows how, Jimmy got through that cañon and into the Sacramento Valley. He had a horse with him—an Indian horse that was bought in the Rocky Mountains, and which could come as near climbing a tree as any horse I ever knew. Jimmy was a character. Of all men I have ever known I think he was the most fearless; he had the bravery of a bulldog. He was not seen for two months—until he was found at Sutter's, afterwards known as Sutter's Fort, now Sacramento City.

We went on, traveling west as near as we could. When we killed our last ox we shot and ate crows or anything we could kill, and one man shot a wildcat. We could eat anything. One day in the morning I went ahead, on foot of course, to see if I could kill something, it being understood that the company would keep on as near west as possible and find a practicable road. I followed an Indian trail down into the cañon, meeting many Indians on the way up. They did not molest me, but I did not quite like their looks. I went about ten miles down the cañon, and then began to think it time to strike north to intersect the trail of the company going west. A most difficult time I had scaling the precipice. Once I threw my gun up ahead of me, being unable to hold it and climb, and then was in despair lest I could not get up where it was, but finally I did barely manage to do so, and made my way north. As the darkness came on I was obliged to look down and feel with my feet lest I should pass over the trail of the party without seeing it. Just at dark I came to an enormous fallen tree and tried to go around the top, but the place was too brushy, so I went around the butt, which seemed to me to be about twenty or twenty-five feet above my head. This I suppose to have been one of the fallen trees in the Calaveras Grove of *Sequoia gigantea* or mammoth trees, as I have since been there, and to my own satisfaction identified the lay of the land and the tree. Hence I concluded that I must have been the first white man who ever saw the *Sequoia gigantea,* of which I told Frémont when he came to California in 1844.[35] Of course, sleep was impossible, for I had neither blanket nor coat, and burned or froze alternately as I turned from one side to the other before the small fire which I had built, until morning, when I started eastward to intersect the trail, thinking the company had turned north. But I traveled until noon and found no trail; then striking south, I came to the camp which I had left the previous morning. The party had gone, but not where they had said they would go; for they had taken the same trail I had followed, into the cañon, and had gone up the south side, which they had found so steep that many of the poor animals could not climb it and had to be left. When I arrived the Indians were there cutting the horses to pieces and carrying off the meat. My situation, alone among strange Indians killing our poor horses, was by no means comfortable. Afterward we found that these Indians were always at war with the Californians. They were known as the Horse Thief Indians, and lived chiefly on horse flesh; they had been in the habit of raiding the ranches even to the very coast, driving away horses by the hundreds into the mountains to eat.[36] That night after dark I overtook the party in camp.

A day or two later we came to a place where there was a great quantity of horse bones, and we did not know what it meant; we thought that an army must have perished there. They were of course horses that the Indians had driven in there and slaughtered. A few nights later, fearing depredations, we concluded to stand guard—all but one man, who would not. So we let his two horses roam where they pleased. In the morning they could not be found. A few miles away we came to a village; the Indians had fled, but we found the horses killed and some of the meat roasting on a fire.

We were now on the edge of the San Joaquin Valley, but we did not even know that we were in California. We could see a range of mountains lying to the west—the Coast Range, but we could see no valley. The evening of the day we started down into the valley we were very tired, and when night came our party was strung along for three or four miles, and every man slept right where darkness overtook him. He would take off his saddle for a pillow and turn his horse or mule loose, if he had one. His animal would be too poor to walk away, and in the morning he would find him, usually within fifty feet. The jaded horses nearly perished with hunger and fatigue. When we overtook the foremost of the party the next morning we found they had come to a pond of water, and one of them had killed a fat coyote; when I came up it was all eaten except the lights and the windpipe, on which I made my breakfast. From that camp we saw timber to the north of us, evidently bordering a stream running west. It turned out to be the stream that we had followed down in the mountains—the Stanislaus River. As soon as we came in sight of the bottom land of the stream we saw an abundance of antelopes and sandhill cranes. We killed two of each the first evening. Wild grapes also abounded. The next day we killed thirteen deer and antelopes, jerked the meat and got ready to go on, all except the captain's mess of seven or eight, who decided to stay there and lay in meat enough to last them into California! We were really almost down to tidewater, but did not know it. Some thought it was five hundred miles yet to California. But all thought we had to cross at least that range of mountains in sight to the west before entering the promised land, and how many more beyond no one could tell. Nearly all thought it best to press on lest the snows might overtake us in the mountains before us, as they had already nearly done on the mountains behind us (the Sierra Nevada). It was now about the first of November. Our party set forth bearing northwest, aiming for a seeming gap north of a high mountain in the chain to the west of us. That mountain we found to be Mount Diablo. At night the Indians attacked the captain's camp and stole all their animals, which were the best in the company, and the next day the men had to overtake us with just what they could carry in their hands.

The next day, judging by the timber we saw, we concluded there was a river to the west. So two men went ahead to see if they could find a trail or a crossing. The timber seen proved to be along what is now known as the San Joaquin River. We sent two men on ahead to spy out the country. At night one of them returned, saying they had come across an Indian on horseback without a saddle who wore a cloth jacket but no other clothing. From what they could understand the Indian knew Dr. Marsh and had offered to guide them to his place. He plainly said "Marsh," and of course we supposed it was the Dr. Marsh before referred to who had written the letter to a friend in Jackson County, Missouri, and so it proved. One man went with the Indian to Marsh's ranch and the other came back to tell us what he had done, with the suggestion that we should go on and cross the river (San Joaquin) at the place to which the trail was leading. In that way we found ourselves two days later at Dr. Marsh's ranch, and there we learned that we were really in California and our journey at an end. After six months we had now arrived at the first settlement in California, November 4, 1841.

Notes

1 At the time, Bidwell was principal of Kingsville Academy, near Greenville, Ohio. Hunt, *John Bidwell*, p. 27.

2 The Iowa Territory, carved out of the Wisconsin Territory, was created by Congress on June 12, 1838.

3 Robert Lucas (1781–1853), Virginia born, was a farmer and surveyor. He served in the Ohio legislature before moving on to become governor, 1832–1836. In 1838 he was appointed the first Iowa territorial governor and superintendent of Indian affairs, holding those posts until 1841. His last public office was as a delegate to the Iowa constitutional convention in 1844. Burlington served as the first capital, but was replaced by newly founded Iowa City in 1841. *Concise Dictionary of American Biography* (New York, 1946), p. 592.

4 *Tetraonidae cupido* and *Canis latrans,* respectively.

5 When Missouri was admitted to the Union via the Compromise of 1820, the state's northwest boundary was a north-south line which passed through present-day Kansas City, a boundary fashioned to preserve the Sauk and Fox Indians' reservation. Later, Missouri coveted the triangular section which is called the Platte Purchase. In 1836 the federal government purchased the land from the Indians for $7,500 in addition to a quantity of merchandise. The purchase was annexed to Missouri on March 28, 1837, thus extending its boundary to the Missouri River. The state subsequently divided the annexed land into six counties. James T. Adams, ed., *Dictionary of American History* (Rev. ed., 5 vols.; New York, 1942), IV: 286.

6 Bidwell is quite correct. The Missouri Compromise had prohibited, with the exception of Missouri, slavery north of the 36° 30′ (Missouri's southern boundary). By annexing the Platte Purchase with congressional approval, Missouri and the Congress actually violated the 1820 law.

7 There were six Robidoux brothers who had long careers in the fur and overland trade. My guess is that Bidwell met either Antoine (1794–1860) or Louis Robidoux (1796–1868). Both had traveled overland to California from Santa Fe, New Mexico, in 1837. Both of these fur men, along with their eldest brother, Joseph (1783–1868), had picked up additional information from fellow trappers and traders who began infrequent visits to California as early as 1826. In the bargain, beginning in 1829, an annual trading caravan went from Santa Fe to southern California. Wallace, "Antoine Robidoux," in Hafen, ed., *The Mountain Men*, VIII: 287–314; David J. Weber, "Louis Robidoux," *ibid.,* pp. 315–329.

8 Dr. John Marsh (1799–1856) came to California from Santa Fe in 1836. He settled in northern California in 1837. From contacts in his newly adopted homeland, he obtained a fairly good idea of the country stretching between Missouri and the Sierras and figured out a plausible route. He shared that description in letters to at least one of the Bidwell party, Michael C. Nye, as well as William Baldridge, who later dropped out from those planning to go west. Marsh also wrote to Samuel C. Owens, another Independence, Missouri, friend. Lyman, *John Marsh,* pp. 237–239.

9 Elam Brown (1797–c.1887–9), a native of New York, came overland to California in 1846 with his children in a party which he served as captain. He became a wealthy Contra Costa County farmer, "a rich man and respected citizen." He served as a delegate to the 1849 state constitutional convention and in the first two state legislatures. Bancroft, *California,* II: 732.

10 The description is found in John C. Frémont, *Report of the Exploring Expedition to the Rocky Mountains in the Year 1842, and to Oregon and North California in the Years 1843–'44* (Washington, D.C., 1845).

11 Thomas Jefferson Farnham's (1804–1848) interest in the West Coast was stirred by the Oregon missionary Jason Lee, who toured the western states in 1838 lecturing and raising money for the cause. Farnham, Vermont born, was at the time a young Peoria, Illinois, lawyer who had gone west for his health. He was smitten along with eighteen others to march to Oregon and seize it for the American government. He was also anxious to travel for the sake of his precarious health. His band set out in 1839, an adventure detailed in his *Travels in the Great Western Prairies* (Poughkeepsie, N.Y., 1841). For biographical data, see Thwaites, ed., *Early Western Travels,* XXIII: 10 (reprint ed.).

12 Bidwell's assessment of the number of former fur traders in California is exaggerated. That such men continued to dress in the fashion of mountain men is true. However, the horse thieves who periodically raided California ranchos were a mixture of Indians, Mexicans, and a few Americans.

13 Farnham was describing the "Graham Affair," a complex event which has been summarized in Doyce B. Nunis, Jr., *The Trials of Isaac Graham* (Los Angeles, 1967), pp. 21–31. Suffice it to say that the government feared the prospect of its overthrow by "foreigners"—both Americans and English. To preclude that prospect, it arrested, beginning on midnight April 6–7, 1840, those under suspicion. Farnham arrived at Monterey on the *Don Quixote* (under Captain John Paty) on April 18 and witnessed the severity with which the Monterey-area prisoners were being treated. Those arrested were shipped to Tepic for trial. On reaching Tepic, the English consul, Eustace Barron, along with the U.S. minister in Mexico City, took up the prisoners' cause since neither country had a consul in California. That intervention lead to their acquittal, release, and return to California for those who desired to do so.

14 *Missouri Argus,* June 26, 1840, *DLM Transcripts.*

15 George Henshaw joined the overland party but returned to the east in 1842. Bancroft, *California,* III: 781.

16 See Appendix A for a discussion of the number in the party.

17 Thomas Fitzpatrick (1799–1854) was a highly experienced fur trapper and mountain man, subsequently a guide and Indian agent. He entered the fur trade in 1823, was later associated with the Rocky Mountain Fur Company, followed by a like partnership in 1834, one that lasted until 1837. With the decline of the fur trade, he offered his serves as a trail guide beginning in 1836. Thereafter his services were sought out, for few men knew the trails west and the Indians better than Fitzpatrick. LeRoy R. and Ann W. Hafen, "Thomas Fitzpatrick," in Hafen, ed., *Mountain Men,* VII: 87–102. A

definitive biography is LeRoy R. Hafen, *Broken Hand: The Life Story of Thomas Fitzpatrick, Chief of the Mountain Men* (Reprint ed., Denver, 1973).

18 Pierre Jean De Smet (1801–1873), a Belgium-born Jesuit priest, was leading the first band of Catholic missionaries into the transmontane West. Accompanying him were Father Nicholas Point (1799–1868), French born, who maintained a journal of the overland trip as well as being the artist of the party, and Father Gregory Mengarini (1811–1886), Italian born. These three missionaries would found St. Mary's Mission in the Bitterroot Valley of western Montana, among the Flathead Indians. Point departed for a return to Canada in 1847, while Mengarini went in 1850 to Oregon for two years, then in 1852 was appointed one of the founders of today's Santa Clara University in California. De Smet spent many fruitful years in the Far West and served as a peace emissary on more than one occasion. He died in St. Louis after his retirement from active field work. Also in their missionary band were three Jesuit Brothers. The three priests' lives are treated in John U. Terrell, *Black Robe: The Life of Pierre-Jean De Smet* (Garden City, N.Y., 1964); Gregory Mengarini, *Recollections of the Flathead Mission . . .*, trans. and ed. by Gloria R. Lothrop (Glendale, Calif., 1977); and *Wilderness Kingdom: Indian Life in the Rocky Mountains: 1840–1847. The Journals & Paintings of Nicolas Point, S.J.*, trans. by Joseph P. Donnelly (New York, 1967). De Smet had paid a personal visit to the Bitterroot Valley in 1840, April to December, at the behest of the Flathead Indians, two of whom came to St. Louis in search of the "black robes," Jesuits, to come to missionize amongst them. That exploratory trip lead to the missionary band of 1841.

19 James Baker (1818–1898) entered the fur trade in 1836 as an employee of the American Fur Company. After spending several years in the mountains among various Indian tribes, notably the Shoshones, he became a professional guide. Nolie Mumey, "James Baker," in Hafen, ed., *The Mountain Men*, III: 39–53. John Grey (sometimes Gray) was an Iroquois whose real name was Ignace Hatchiorauquasha. He entered the Canadian fur trade as early as 1818 and spent all of his life in the trade until he retired to his home in Kansas City in September 1841, having completed his contract with the Jesuit missionaries to serve as their hunter as far as the Green River, where he turned back for the east. Merle Wells, "Ignace Hatchiorauquasha (John Grey)," in *ibid.*, VII: 161–175. There is little or no information on the Englishman named Romaine. It appears he was of a good family and was well traveled. He joined the trek west for the sheer adventure of it and a fascination with geography.

20 The Jesuit missionary band had four two-wheeled carts, called Red River carts, and one four-wheeled wagon, all drawn by mules, harnessed mainly in tandem pairs. The three priests rode saddled horses, while the three brothers tended the carts and wagon with the assistance of two teamsters.

21 This method of defense against possible Indian attack on the trail originated with the fur-trade firm of Smith, Jackson and Sublette. In taking the first wagons west on what was to become the Oregon Trail, parting St. Louis, April 10, 1830, William Sublette guided "a caravan of the wagons, drawn by five mules each, and two dearborns, drawn by one mule each," accompanied by twelve head of cattle and a milch cow. They headed west for the annual fur trade rendezvous on the Wind River, reaching their destination on July 16. The return trip was as uneventful as the outbound journey. But, as one newspaper reported, "in the event of an attack from the savages in the open plain, the wagons may be formed into a breastwork against which all their assaults will be unavailing." *Missouri Intelligencer,* October 9, 1830; *Missouri Republican,* October 19, 1830; *Niles' Register,* November 6, 1830. The background and reasons for this first wagon trip across the plains is discussed in Nunis, Jr., "The Fur Men: Key to Westward Expansion, 1822–1830," pp. 167–190.

22 Bidwell does not give Fitzpatrick the credit he deserves for defusing this potential crisis. He was able to retrieve Nicholas Dawson's clothes, rifle, pistol and mule. Hafen, *Broken Hand,* pp. 176–77.

23 Milo M. Quaife, in his edition of Bidwell's *Echoes of the Past,* p. 30, *note* 12, opines: "Whilst this statement may represent correctly what Bidwell observed, it is far from possessing general validity." I concur in that opinion.

24 O'Fallon Bluffs were named in honor of the longtime N.D. Indian agent, Benjamin O'Fallon (1793–1842). John W. Steiger, "Benjamin O'Fallon," in Hafen, ed., *The Mountain Men,* V: 255–281. Courthouse Rock was "named by an early party of immigrants from St. Louis who thought it looked like their own new courthouse with its rounded dome." Paden, *The Wake of the Prairie Schooner,* p. 140.

25 South Pass, on the Continental Divide in the Central Rockies, is situated in Fremont County, Wyoming. It became the famed gateway to the Far West. It was first discovered in October 1812 by Robert Stuart and his party, employees of the American Fur Company founded by John Jacob Astor. But the discovery remained unknown. In the spring of 1824 friendly Crow Indians told Jedediah Smith and his trapper party, which included Thomas Fitzpatrick, about an easy route across the southern end of the Wind River Mountains. Thus, Smith made the first effective discovery, quickly recognizing its enormous potential for easy access to the transmontane west. Larmar, ed., *Encyclopedia of the American West,* p. 1132.

26 William L. Sublette (1799–1845) entered the fur trade as an employee of General William H. Ashley and his partner Andrew Henry in 1823. Others in that year's party were Jedediah Smith and Thomas Fitzpatrick. With another partner, David Jackson, Sublette and Smith purchased the Ashley-Henry interests in 1826 and dominated the Far West fur trade until the partnership was dissolved in 1830. By 1834 he left the fur frontier and went into to business in St. Louis. As discussed in *note* 21 above, he commanded the first wagon train to cross what became the Oregon Trail in 1830.

27 A German from St. Louis, Henry Fraeb entered the far western fur trade early. A seasoned veteran, he was usually called "Frapp" by his men. In July 1841, his party met the Fitzpatrick-led party of missionaries and pioneers on the Green River. One of the westbound travelers described Fraeb's motley band as "mostly composed of half breeds, French, and Dutch, and all sorts of people collected together in the mountains, and were a wicked, swearing company of men."

    However, Bidwell is astray in his facts about Fraeb's death. In late August 1841, Fraeb was leading a party of men southeast from a fur-trade fort on the Green River to make meat (buffalo jerky). On a branch of the Yampa River in the valley of the Little Snake, they confronted a large party of Cheyennes, Arapahoes, and Sioux. A pitched battle ensued. Although the exact number of casualties on both sides varies, depending on the informant, it is clear that Fraeb and four of his men perished, while the enemy lost between eight and twenty killed. LeRoy R. Hafen, "Henry Fraeb," in Hafen, ed., *The Mountain Men,* III: 131–139.

28 Fort Hall has been previously identified. See *Journal,* note 17.

29 Fort Vancouver was founded by Chief Trader John McLoughlin as the headquarters for the newly established Department of the Columbia on the north bank of the Columbia River and six miles above its confluence with the Willamette River. It served in that capacity until the headquarters were relocated in 1845 to Fort Victoria on Vancouver Island in the wake of the Oregon Settlement between the U.S. and Great Britain. It was finally abandoned in 1860 by the company. Today it is a historic site. Lamar, *Encyclopedia of the American West,* p. 399. John A. Hussey has authored an excellent study, *Fort Vancouver* (Portland, 1957).

30 Bidwell's memory is faulty here. Thirty-four of the emigrants pushed on to California while only twenty-three headed northwest to Oregon. For a discussion of these numbers, consult Appendix A, *post.*

31 To his narrative, Bidwell supplied this note: "Of the Party leaving us at Soda Springs to go into Oregon I can now, after the lapse of forty-nine years, recall by their names only the following: Mr. Williams and wife; Samuel Kelsey, his wife and five children; Josiah Kelsey and wife; C. W. Flugge; Mr. Carroll; Mr. Fowler; a Methodist Episcopal preacher, whose name I think was also Williams; 'Cheyenne Dawson'; and another called 'Bear Dawson.' Subsequently we heard that the party safely arrived in Oregon, and some of them we saw in California. One (C. W. Flugge) was in time to join a party and come from Oregon to California the same year (1841)." (Cheyenne Dawson did not go to Oregon. He stayed with the California-bound party.)

32 Sagebrush's botanical name is *Artemisia.*

33 John Charles Frémont named the Nevada river and mountain Humboldt in 1845 to honor the great German natural scientist, Alexander von Humboldt, who never saw his namesakes. Frémont recorded: "Both the river and mountain to which I gave his name are conspicuous objects; the river stretching across the Basin to the foot of the Sierra Nevada, and the mountain standing out in greater bulk and length than its neighbors . . . " Mary Lee Spence and Donald Jackson, eds., *The Expeditions of John Charles Frémont* (3 vols., Urbana, Ill., 1970–1984), 2: 22.

34 Christopher (Kit) Carson was with Frémont's 1845 expedition and the river was named in his honor. Joseph R. Walker had first traversed the Walker River in 1833, thus his name was affixed to what he himself had discovered. *Ibid.,* pp. 51–52. Their names were also given to two lakes. *Ibid.,* pp. 53–54.

35 As pointed out in Bidwell's *Journal, note* 25, Joseph R. Walker and two of his party were the first to see the giant sequoias, a fact they reported to Captain Bonneville on their return to rendezvous with him in 1834 after their trek to California.

36 Runaway mission neophytes in the early decades of the nineteenth century fled into the Tulare Lake region. There they came into contact with the resident Indian peoples, the Southern Valley Yokuts. From these strangers the Yokuts "acquired a taste for horseflesh; later they wanted horses to ride. Aided by the apostate neophytes, the Yokuts began making forays against the mission and rancho herds. They raided so successfully that they became known as the 'Horsethief Indians.'" Robert F. Heizer, ed., *California,* Vol. 8, in *Handbook of North American Indians,* ed. by William C. Sturtevant (Washington, D.C., 1978), p. 460.

CHAPTER FOUR

Statement of Historical Facts of California

By Josiah Belden

Dictated in 1878

Biographical sketch

Josiah Belden was born in Upper Middletown, Connecticut, May 4, 1815. He could claim direct descent from one of the state's oldest families. In 1645, his English ancestors, Richard and Josiah Bayldon [Belden], settled in Wethersfield, sinking roots into colonial Connecticut's virgin soil.[1]

Early life for Josiah Belden was less than happy; it was plagued with personal tragedy. When he was four years old, his mother, Abigail McKee, died, and when he was fifteen, his father's death forced him to quit school and to seek his subsistence.

An orphan, he moved to Albany, New York, to live with an uncle. After brief residence there, he went to New York City, finding employment as a dry goods store clerk. A few months later, he returned to Albany, apprenticing himself to Luke F. Newland, a jeweler. In place of formal eduction, Belden sought the security of a trade.

Infected with a desire for travel, on May 4, 1836, he journeyed to New York, then Philadelphia. From there he took passage to Mobile, voyaging on to Liverpool, England; subsequently returning to Philadelphia. Still restless, he "went south to New Orleans" to winter. Moving from there in early 1837, he established himself in mercantile business at Vicksburg, Mississippi; the next year he transferred his commercial activities to Yazoo City. In joint partnership with a Mr. Watton, he opened a general store and cotton exchange emporium.

Dissatisfied with the small returns that came to that endeavor, he sold out to his partner in 1841 and headed upriver for St. Louis. Shortly after his arrival, he met up with two enthusiasts who had caught the California fever, Henry L. Brolaski and David W. Chandler; later they were joined by a fourth, George Shotwell. With them he formed a "mess" for the projected trip overland. After outfitting themselves with the necessary supplies and equipment, the four made for the appointed rendezvous at Sapling Grove.

126

Not long after the Bidwell-Bartleson party's arrival in California, Belden headed first for San Jose to obtain the required passport and then moved on to Monterey, where he found employment with Thomas O. Larkin. He opened a branch store for him in Santa Cruz. A year later, Belden returned to Monterey and clerked for Larkin there. Several years later they became partners in developing mutual real estate holdings in San Francisco.

In the spring of 1844, Belden formed a partnership with William G. Chard. They operated a small shop and boarding house for distressed American seamen who threw themselves on the mercy of Larkin, by then United States Consul in Monterey. Profits were modest, but helpful.

The next year Belden became a citizen of the Republic of Mexico. In consequence of his support of Governor Manuel Micheltorena, he was able to procure a land grant of 21,000 acres in the upper Sacramento River valley near present-day Red Bluff. Dissolving his partnership, he spent the winter of 1845–1846 with his former trail companion, Robert H. Thomes, and possibly his old partner Chard, in the vicinity of his newly acquired domain.

Returning in early spring 1846, Belden found a position with Captain John Paty as his commercial agent. In the fall of that year when Paty closed out his major business affairs in the San Francisco Bay area, Belden was hired by William Heath Davis. In that employment, he journeyed south on firm business to Los Angeles and San Diego. Out of that travel came an appointment as a business partner for Mellus & Howard in San Jose; thus J. Belden & Co. was established.

Broadening his commercial activities, Belden entered into a partnership with Larkin in the early fall of 1847. By Christmas he was a partner in the exploitation of a quicksilver mine on the rancho of Grove Cook near San Jose, practically on the eve of James W. Marshall's gold strike on the American River.

After a brief sojourn in the gold fields in 1848, a wiser Belden returned to San Jose to exploit a more profitable and enduring endeavor as a merchant supplying the needs of the gold seekers. That, coupled with judicious investments in real estate, built his fortune.

In 1850, a year after his marriage to Sarah Margaret Jones, a pioneer of the 1846 emigration, he was elected the first mayor of San Jose. The next year he served a term on the city council.

Versed in the ways of business, he astutely disposed of his store and invested his money in the exploitation of property. As Bancroft attests, "real estate made Belden a capitalist."

Belden, indeed, prospered. His annual income, around $60,000 a year, afforded him leisure and pleasure. The family home, a splendid estate of ten acres near San Jose, landscaped with formal gardens and practical orchards, was built in 1855. He and his wife traveled to Europe in 1859 and on a more extended trip, which included the Middle East, in 1872–1873.

In 1876 Belden served as a delegate to the Republican National Convention in Cincinnati, casting his ballot for Rutherford B. Hayes. Perhaps the experience turned his eyes permanently eastward, for in 1881, he moved his family to New York City. He became a member of the Union League Club and a director of the Erie Railroad. And it was there, on April 23, 1892, that he died.

1 This biographical sketch is based on *Josiah Belden, 1841 California Pioneer: His Memoir and Early Letters,* ed. and with an introduction by Doyce B. Nunis, Jr. (Georgetown, Calif., 1962), pp. 17–20, and *notes* on pp. 29–32.

Historical Statement

I came from Middletown, Ct., lived in Albany from the age of 15 till I was 21, and then went south to New Orleans, spent a winter there, and then went to Mississippi, and was engaged in mercantile business in Vicksburg, and then in Manchester.[1] I sold out there, and went to St. Louis, and after being there a short time, in the spring of 1841, I met with two or three young men there, who told me of an expedition that was being got up to go to California. Being rather fond of that kind of adventure, naturally I agreed with those parties to make up a little mess of our own, four or five of us, procure an outfit at St. Louis, and then proceed to the town of Independence, on the western frontier of Missouri, where this expedition was to be organized, and a company formed for the purpose of proceeding to California. This was the inception of the emigration across the plains. This party opened the road, so to speak, was the beginning. In getting up this expedition, those who joined it had heard some reports about California, but very vague, and they knew but little about it or the means of getting there, and started it as an exploring expedition to find their own way out there, and see what the country was. If it proved attractive, some had an idea of settling there, and others joined it more as a matter of adventure, to see something of Indian life, and indulge in hunting on the plains, and all that kind of thing. For my part, when I was younger, I had read Cooper's novels, and about Astor's expedition to the Columbia River, and that rather excited a desire in my mind to see something of a wild country, of buffalo hunting, and to have some adventures among the Indians.[2] That expedition should have the credit of starting the emigration to California. Those who joined it were really pioneers, for there had been no emigration before; there was nothing known of the road, or how to get there.[3] It was something of a perilous undertaking, and it was the beginning of the whole settlement of this country.

We started from Missouri. Mr. Chandler, Mr. Brolasky, Mr. Shotwell and myself formed the mess from St. Louis. We left that place about the first of May, 1841.[4] We bought a wagon in St. Louis, and the princip[le] things we considered necessary for our outfit, harness, provisions, and some things to trade with the Indians on the road. We went up the Missouri in a steamboat to near Independence. When we got there, we found a number of persons collected from different sections of the country. After being there some days, the company was formed and organized, laid in the necessary provisions, procured an outfit of animals &c. We elected a leader for the company by the name of Bartlettson [Bartleson]. We were all armed, of course.[5]

At Independence, the persons who designed going to California made arrangements with a party of missionaries, who were going to the Columbia River, to the Flathead nation, to travel with them as far as they were going in our direction. They had a man named Fitzpatrick as a sort of leader or guide, who had never been across the continent, but had been a hunter and trapper in the neighborhood of the head waters of the Columbia River.[6] The following were the members of our company: Bartlettson [Bartleson] as Leader, Robt. H. Thomes, now of Tehama, ...Bartlett, Jos. Childs, Major [Robert] Rickman, Josiah Belden, Paul Geddes, Ch͏s Weber of Stockton, Henry Hubert [Huber], John Bidwell of Chico, [Elias] Barnett, [Henry L.] Brolask[i], Ch͏s Hopper, Grove Cook, Benj. Kelsey, Andrew Kelsey, Mrs. [Nancy A.] Kelsey, [George] Henshaw, James McMah[a]n, [Andrew Gwinn] Patt[o]n, Nelson McMah[a]n, Nich. Dawson, V. W. Dawson, [David W.] Chandler, Ambrose Walton, [John L.] Schwartz, [Thomas] Jones, Jas. Littlejohn [Johns], Ch͏s Flugge, [Michael] C. Nye, [James P.] Springer, Pfeiffer [Fifer].[7] There were about the same number of the missionaries, with their servants and guides, making about 60 all together, who started from Independence.[8]

We left about the 10th of May. We had made some rules for our protection against the Indians, setting guard, patrols &c.[9] The company divided into watches for guard, each taking it in turn. There was one woman in our party Mrs. Kelsey; the missionaries had none.[10] We moved along very gradually; a part of the wagons were drawn by oxen, and part by mules.[11] We had riding animals besides. We took as much provision as we could haul and carry, to last us until we should get into the buffalo country, when we expected to supply ourselves by hunting.

We travelled to the Kansas River, and were ferried across, and followed up the Little Blue (I think it was called) to near its headwater, and then struck across the country to the Platte; a prairie country all through there. We followed up the South fork of the Platte, I think, and in fording lost some animals, and we had considerable trouble to get across finally with all our wagons. We reached Ft. Laramie [June 20], and passed on into the Black Hills, and near the Wind River Mountain, and came to Independence Rock on the Sweetwater

Creek [July 5], and when we got into buffalo country, we stopped two or three days and killed buffalo, and jerked the meat, and made packs of that to carry us through. Meantime we were travelling through a country pretty badly infested by the Crow and Blackfeet Indians.

One day one of the party had strayed outside into the country, and a party of Indians came upon him, and robbed him of his gun and ammunition, and after detaining him some time, let him go, and he got onto the trail and joined the company.[12] Soon after, we saw a body of Indians coming up full charge in our rear, as though intending to attack us. They came within several hundred yards. The party stopped, and formed a hollow square with our wagons, and prepared to defend ourselves as well as we could. They halted, and Fitzpatrick, the leader of the missionary party, advanced toward them, and made signs for them to send their Chief for a consultation. They did so, and they had a talk, and they agreed that they would not make any attack upon us, but professed a desire to treat with us, and he made an arrangement with them that we should form a camp there, and a portion of them might come in at night while they were camped a distance off, and then they could treat with us if they wished. A few of them came at night, and smoked the pipe of peace, and said they did not want to fight us. We found them, however, to be a war party of the Cheyenne tribe, about 50 or 60 warriors, fine looking, and they said they were looking for the Pawnees. They were fully armed with bows and arrows and tomahawks, and some few guns. They were the finest looking body of men I ever saw for Indians, quite a formidable looking party. We asked if some of their men had not robbed Dawson of his gun and pistol, and demanded that they should be restored, and they brought them back. They traded a little with us for tobacco and beads, and made no demonstrations of hostility; but we kept a pretty strong guard, and everything passed off peaceably, and we separated from them the next morning.[13]

We went on, following the Sweetwater some distance, and crossing the divide of the Rocky Mountains, and passed on and went down on to Green River, stayed there a day or two, and recruited our animals, and fell in there with a company of trappers under command of a man named Frapp [Fraeb]. They had been sent out by the fur companies from St. Louis. That company of trappers, about 30 or 40, after we left them at Green River, and started on our way west, we afterward learned, left a day or two after we did, and soon after encountered a party of Sioux Indians, and fought with them nearly a day, and had four of their men killed. Frapp [Fraeb] himself among the number, I think. It appeared that we had just missed that party of Indians, and if they had met us, they probably would have whipped us, as the party they encountered were old mountain trappers and Indian fighters, and we had had no experience in that line.[14]

We struck Bear River [August 3] some distance below where the town of Evanston [Wyoming] now is, where the coal mines are, and the railroad passes, and followed the river down. It makes a long bend to the north there, and comes down to Salt Lake. We arrived at Soda Springs, on Bear River and there we separated from the company of missionaries, who were going off towards Snake River or Columbia. There we lost the services of their guide Fitzpatrick. Several of our party who had started to go with us to California also left us there, having decided to go with the missionaries. Fitzpatrick advised us to give up our expedition and go with them to Ft. Hall, one of the Hudson Bay Stations, as there was no road for us to follow, nothing was known of the country, and we had nothing to guide us, and so he advised us to give up the California project. He thought it was doubtful if we ever got there; we might get caught in the snow of the mountains and perish there, and he considered it very hazardous to attempt it. Some four or five of our party withdrew, and went with the missionaries.[15] About thirty-one of us adhered to our original intention, and declined to give up our expedition. As we had attempted to go to California, we determined we would not give it up, but continue the attempt, and do the best we could to get through.[16]

After separating from the missionaries, we followed Bear River down nearly to where it enters Salt Lake, about where Corinnes [Corinne, Utah] is now. We had some knowledge of the Lake from some of the trappers who had been there. We turned off more to the west and went round the northerly end of Salt Lake. There we found a great difficulty in getting water for several days, all the water near the lake being brackish. We had to make it into strong coffee to drink it. We went on, hunting our way along the best we could, amongst the rocks and gullies, and through the sage brush, working along slowly for a number of days, aiming to travel westward as fast as we could, having no other guide than an intention to get west. After travelling several days, passing over a very desert country where there was scarcely any food for our animals, and very rough getting along with our wagons, we finally came to a spot where there was moist ground, some springs, and a little patch of green grass, which we denominated the oasis. We camped there for about a week to recruit our animals. While there we did not know which direction to take, nor how to go, but we had heard before leaving Missouri that there was a river somewhere in that section of the country, which was then called Mary's River, which ran to the westward, and this we thought might be a guide for us in some measure, if we could strike the headwaters of it and follow it west. So while the company were camping there, three of the party who had the best animals started out in a westerly direction, to explore by themselves, and see if they could find any such river, any water running west. After waiting there several days, these men came back, and reported that they had found a small stream of water that seemed to be running westward, and they thought that might perhaps be the headwaters or some branch of the Mary's River that we wished to find.[17] After they returned, we raised camp, and under their direction, as near as we could follow it, we travelled two or three days, I think, and struck this little stream they had spoken of. We followed it down, and found it tended westward, though varying its course, and it proved to be the South fork of Mary's River. We followed it all the way down to the sink of it. Before we struck this river, we found we were so delayed by our wagons that we concluded to abandon them, and we took what things we could and packed them on to our horses and oxen, and what we could not carry, we left with our wagons standing in the plains.

We were then within sight of the Sierra Nevada mountains, which we knew we had to cross. But we could see no appearance of any opening or depression which we might avail of to get across. Then we struck south, until we finally came to what is known as Walker's River. We then followed the west branch of this river, I think, up into the mountains. When we struck that river, however, after following it for some distance and getting into the neighborhood of the mountains, without finding any depression, or any place where it seemed possible to cross, there was some division of opinion among the members of the company. Our provisions had given out before, while we were travelling down Mary's River, and then we commenced killing the cattle we had with us and eating them. At the sink of the Humboldt River, a portion of the company who had the best animals, about nine of them, parted from the others, and said they were going to travel faster, and get in before they became exhausted.[18] The balance went on, and, as I said, got to Walker's River. When we reached there, there was a difference of opinion about whether we should attempt crossing the mountains, or give up the expedition then, and turn back, and try to get back to Ft. Hall. While we were stopping there, one day two others and myself left the party, and went up to some of the higher peaks of the mountains to explore and see if we could find any place where we could cross.[19] We returned and reported that we could see no opening in the mountains, that so far as we could see, the mountains seemed to be rather higher beyond than lower, and there was no appearance of any end or termination of them, and very little chance to get through. There was a vote taken in the company to determine whether we should go on and try to get across the mountains, or turn back and try to reach Ft. Hall. I think we had only one majority for going ahead. Although it looked discouraging on the mountains, my idea was that we should perish in trying to get back to Ft. Hall, and we had better take our chances of getting across the mountains. So we decided to travel on.

The next morning we were packing up to start into the mountains, and in looking back we saw the dust rising on the trail we had travelled the day before, and we waited to see what it was, and presently we saw the nine men who had left us several days before with the idea of going ahead, coming up on our trail, very hungry and forlorn looking. We had a quarter of beef left from the last animal we had killed, and gave them something to eat. They had made a kind of circle, and reached our camp, having struck our trail. We then all went on together.

We worked our way into the mountains with a great deal of difficulty and hardship. The way was very rough, and one day, in winding round the side of a mountain, we lost four of our animals, who missed their footing, and rolled down the mountain. We finally reached the summit with great labor and difficulty, and after getting a little beyond the summit on the other side, we struck a little stream of water that seemed to run westward, and we judged we had got over the divide, and thought that by following the stream as well as we could, it would lead us down the westerly slope of the mountain.

Meantime we had eaten the last of our beef from our cattle, and we were reduced to the necessity of killing our horses and mules, and living on them. We had nothing else of any kind whatever to eat but clear horse or mule meat, without even salt to salt it.

After passing the summit, and striking this stream, we worked our way along down for some distance, occasionally having to leave the track and go on to the ridges, to avoid getting into deep cañons blocked with immense boulders. We got into some of these, and had to go back on to the ridges. We finally succeeded in working down to the north side of the river, and finding difficulty there, got on to the south side of the river. We went a little ways from the river, working down on that side, and passed I suppose the neighborhood of where Sonora is now.

Finally we got out of the mountains, striking the plains probably not far from where Knight's Ferry is now. When we got to the plains, we found no water or grass, it having been a dry season. That little stream we struck in the mountains proved to be what is now known as the Stanislaus River. We got on to the plains just at night, and followed down and camped about ten o'clock without water, and the next morning seeing a belt of timber to the north of us in the plain, we struck for that, our animals being much exhausted for want of water and feed, and it took us about all day to reach the place. We got into the belt of timber, and found a river there, the Stanislaus, the same that we had struck in the mountains. We found in that neighborhood signs of deer; so we agreed to stay there the next day, and go hunting. We did so, and killed several deer, and brought them into camp, and had a feast of fine venison.[20] Then we started to follow the river down, and after going a little way, we met two of our men who had left the party a number of days before in a cañon of the Stanislaus, and had worked their way down on foot ahead of us, and had reached Marsh's ranch at the foot of Mt. Diablo, and had told him of us back in the mountains, and he had furnished him with some Indians and animals and provisions, and fortunately, they just happened to meet us, and gave us the provisions, and we went on to the pass of the San Joaquin and to Marsh's ranch. That was the first settlement we reached in the country, about the 4th of November.[21]

Crossing the valley at that time, we saw immense herds of wild horses and elk running over the plain, and we had no further trouble about provisions. Marsh had got out here through New Mexico, I think, and came up the coast. Several men had been out trapping, and finally worked their way through Mexico, and got into the southern part of the country, and worked their way up the coast, and Marsh was one of them. He was called Dr. Marsh.[22] We stayed there a day or two, and a portion of the company left, and went from there to Sutter's Fort, which had been established a year or so before.[23]

About a dozen of us, after resting a day or so at Marsh's Ranch, started out to go down to the Pueblo San Jose, with directions from Marsh how to find our way there. We came on to that place, crossing what is now Livermore's Ranch, but there was no settlement there then.[24] We proceeded, and stopped one night at Geary's [Joaquin Higuera] ranch, two or three miles south of the mission of San Jose.[25] We excited a good deal of interest as we passed by the mission of San Jose, where there was a mission station, and some native Californians lived around there. . . .

Notes

1 Belden's version here of his youth conflicts with two statements he previously gave on the subject. Shuck, *Sketches,* p. 919; Phelps, *Contemporary Biography,* I: 246, present a more accurate and detailed appraisal which has been utilized in the brief biographical sketch given in the Introduction. Allen Johnson and Dumas Malone, eds. *Dictionary of American Biography (20 vols., New York, 1920–1937),* II: 145, place his birth in Cromwell, Connecticut, failing to note that the community's name had been changed from Upper Middletown.

2 Belden's references are to the books of James Fenimore Cooper and to Washington Irving's *Astoria, or Anecdotes of an Enterprise Beyond the Rocky Mountains* (Philadelphia, 1836).

3 As pointed out in the Introduction, the Bartleson party did have some information to guide them.

4 Belden's three traveling companions were David W. Chandler, Henry L. Brolaski, and George Shotwell. Shotwell never reached California. As John Bidwell relates, he accidentally shot himself, June 13, "while in the act of taking a gun out of the wagon, drew it, with the muzzle towards him in such a manner that it went off and shot him near the heart — he lived about an hour and died in full possession of his senses. His good behavior had secured him the respect and good will of an the company, he had resided some 8 or 9 months on or near the Nodaway River, Platte Purchase, Missouri, prior to his starting on this expedition; but he said his mother lived in Laurel County, Kentucky, and was much opposed to his coming into the West — he was buried in the most decent

manner our circumstances would admit of after which a funeral sermon was preached by Mr. Williams." *Journal,* p. 7 (although on p. 1, Bidwell incorrectly lists the name as James Shotwell). *Williams Narrative,* p. 225, states that the burial took place 8 miles below Ash Creek or Ash Hollow on the south fork of the Platte. Williams gives the date as June 20, but Bidwell's would appear to be the more accurate; affirmed by *John Diary.*

Chandler, having resided in California until 1847, and having been employed by Vioget for a number of those California years, tried Hawaii in an effort to get ahead, but returned to the coast in 1848. He is reported as having died in California. Bancroft, *California,* II: 757; Vioget to Sutter, February 18, 1842. *Six French Letters* [:] *Captain John Augustus Sutter to Jean Jacques Vioget 1842–1843* (Sacramento, 1942), p. 150. Bidwell, *Journal,* p. 1, lists J. W. Chandler.

Brolaski did not tarry long in California. He moved to Monterey in 1842. From there he sailed to Callao, probably residing there for several years. By 1848, he was back in St. Louis, anxious to return west. Infected with gold-fever, he did return in 1849. Bancroft, *California,* II: 731; Hammond, ed., *Larkin Papers,* II: 170; *Missouri Republican, July 7, 1849; Argonauts of California* (New York, 1890), p. 402. Bidwell, *Journal,* p. 1, lists H. S. Brolaske.

5 The party sporadically assembled two miles west of the Kansas River by May 16. On the 18th, rules and regulations for the trek west were adopted. *Ibid.,* p. 2. *John Diary* notes that the company camped at Wakaroatia Creek.

6 Thomas Fitzpatrick, long established as a mountain man, was employed as guide for the Jesuit missionary party. For a roster of this party's membership, consult Appendix A, *post.*

7 Belden's listing of the members of the party is inaccurate. See Appendix A for the full membership. Other than a number of omissions, Belden has three mistakes in his list. There was no Bartlett; perhaps Belden meant William Belty. Likewise, there is no listing of James Littlejohn. This should have been James John, who was nicknamed "Jimmy John." Bidwell, *Echoes,* p. 39. The reference to Pfeiffer is undoubtedly meant to be Augustus Fifer or Pfeifer.

8 For a discussion of the rosters of the parties, see Appendix A.

9 The rules and regulations were not adopted until May 18th. Only once during the trek west were the rules decisively enforced. Bidwell, *Journal,* p. 6, notes under date of June 10, near the south fork of the Platte: "Through the remissness of the sentinels, the guard last night was nearly vacant; and as this was considered dangerous ground on account of the warlike Pawnees, Chiennes [Cheyennes] &c. a Court Martial was called to force those to their duty on guard, who were so negligent & remiss."

10 Belden is mistaken. Bidwell lists five women and an unstated number of children in the party. There were two Mrs. Kelseys: Mrs. Benjamin and Mrs. Samuel Kelsey. In addition, there was the widow, Mrs. Gray (probably a sister of the latter Mrs. Kelsey), and Mrs. Richard Williams and daughter. Miss Williams married Isaac Kelsey on the trail, June 1. Mrs. Gray took Richard Fillan [Phelan, according to the late Dale L. Morgan] (whom Bidwell calls Cocrum, and *John Diary* calls Cockrel) as her husband after he joined the party at Fort Laramie, July 23. The Rev. Williams performed the first marriage and Fr. De Smet, the second. Bidwell, *Journal,,* pp. 4, 12; *Williams Narrative,* pp. 221–222; *John Diary.*

11 Bidwell, *Journal,* p. 2, states that his party had 15 wagons and the missionaries had 4 carts and a small wagon. *Williams Narrative,* p. 220, has 20 wagons in the party. Later, Bidwell, *Narrative,* p. 16, lists the missionary party with 5 or 6 "Red River" carts drawn by two mules each. The Bidwell-Bartleson party's wagons were drawn by mules, some by oxen.

Nicholas Dawson kept a detailed travel chronology of the trek west. See *Dawson Chronology* in Appendix C.

12 This was Nicholas Dawson, later renowned because of this incident as "Cheyenne" Dawson. The encounter took place along the banks of the Platte, June 4th. *Williams Narrative,* pp. 222–223, describes it: "On Friday evening the company had a terrible alarm. One of our hunters who was in the rear, was robbed of all he had by the Indians. They struck him with their ramrods, and he ran from them. Soon a war party of the Sioux Indians appeared in view. We soon collected together in order to battle, to be ready in case of an attack. The Indians stood awhile and looked at us, and probably thinking that 'the better part of valor is discretion,' they soon showed signs of peace. Captain Fitzpatrick then went to them, and talked with them, for he was acquainted with them. They then gave back all that they had taken from the young man, and our men gave them some tobacco, and they smoked the pipe of peace." Also, *Dawson Narrative,* pp. 11–12; *De Smet Letters,* 311–312; Bidwell, *Journal,* p. 4.

13 This incident took place near the Platte. Fitzpatrick and John Grey were able to handle the situation diplomatically. Hafen, *Broken Hand, The Life of Thomas Fitzpatrick,* pp. 176–177.

14 The trapper involved was Henry Fraeb, an old friend and trail companion of Fitzpatrick. Fraeb and his party met up with the company on the Green River, July 23. The incident alluded to by Belden took place a month after the parties split. Fraeb, with several of his companions, was slain in a fight with the Cheyenne and Sioux near the Colorado-Wyoming boundaries at a place later known as Battle Creek. *Williams Narrative,* p. 230; LeRoy R. Hafen, "Fraeb's Last Fight and How Battle Creek Got Its Name," *Colorado Magazine,* VII (1930): 97–101; Nolie Mumey, *The Life of Jim Baker* (Denver, 1931), pp. 22–23. *John Diary* gives the date as the 22nd, noting that the hunter's party consisted of 60 men. The *Dawson Chronology* notes that the party was traveling along the Green River, July 23–25, and on the 24th was encamped.

Charles Flügge, who joined the Oregon splinter party, later deciding to travel south from there to California, reached Sutter's Fort, December 27, 1841. (Bancroft, *California,* III: 741, believes Flügge came by land down from Oregon. The advanced season of the year would make this seem unlikely. Mayhap he came by the coastal bark, the *Columbia.*) Nevertheless, it was he who conveyed the news of Fraeb's death to his former trail companions. He reported that Fraeb and "1 of his men were killed by Chienne [Cheyenne] Indians 2 or 3 days after we had left [them on the trail]." Bidwell, *Journal,* p. 30. This version conflicts with several other reports. See Hafen's article cited above, pp. 97–101.

15 The date of this division, August 11, is given by Bidwell, *Journal,* p. 14; the place, Soda Springs in Idaho. *Dawson Chronology* enters the date as August 10.

Belden's memory here is faulty. Four of the California-bound company traveled to Fort Hall with Fitzpatrick to glean any additional information they could about the route west. About ten days later the four men returned to join the Bidwell-Bartleson party, which had in the meantime traveled some 100 miles toward Salt Lake. They brought information that the route west should be south of that lake, with caution not to go too far south since they would hit an arid wasteland. Caution was also needed so as not to go too far north, for there the party might end up in a maze of rugged canyons. Bidwell, *Echoes,* pp.38–39, 42.

16 Bancroft, *California,* IV: 270, fixes the remaining number at "thirty-two men—with one woman and child, the wife and daughter of Benjamin Kelsey."

17 Bartleson and Charles Hopper were the scouts. According to Bidwell, *Journal,* p. 18, they left the company on August 29, rejoining them September 9, after having located

a branch of St. Mary's River. *Dawson Chronology* records the arrival at a "Good spring" on August 27. His dates indicate the party remained there at least through September 4, moving on the 5th.

18 Bartleson and eight others struck out on their own, October 7, but rejoined the caravan October 16. Bidwell, *Journal,* p. 28.

19 Bidwell records that four or five of the party went scouting on October 16. *Ibid.,* p. 28.

20 Bidwell entered under date of September 23, the fact that while still looking for St. Mary's River, they were able to catch a few trout to supplant a growingly dangerous lack of food. But under date of November 1, only four days march away from their objective, Dr. Marsh's rancho, game was killed along with fowl: 18 deer and antelopes were brought into camp for the half-starved emigres. Writing on this occasion, Bidwell remarked: "My breakfast, this morning, formed a striking contrast with that of yesterday which was the lights [lungs] of a wolf." *Ibid.,* pp. 21, 28.

21 Andrew Kelsey and Thomas Jones had left the party in October 24, to forge ahead. It was they who returned to the company on November 4, with Marsh's gift of supplies. *Ibid.,* pp. 26, 28.

22 Lyman, *John Marsh,* has rendered a tolerable biography. Suffice it to state here that Marsh had journeyed to California in 1836 via the southern route from Santa Fe, arriving in early January. After several years of medical practice in the Los Angeles area, based on his Harvard B.A., he traveled rather extensively in the northern parts of the state. By 1839, he obtained the Los Médanos rancho at the foot of Mt. Diablo. He must be considered as a contributory cause to the 1841 emigration since he wrote a number of letters extolling the virtues of California, urging emigrants to come west. Bidwell, however, was far from impressed with Marsh's hospitality and surroundings. For two views on this matter, Bancroft, *California,* IV: 273–274 and *notes;* Caughey, *California,* p. 213.

23 *Dawson Narrative,* p. 27, states that a number of the party went to the Stanislaus River first, among them Kelsey and Bidwell. Bidwell, *Echoes,* pp. 69–70, later recollects that he visited Don José Amador on his Livermore ranch, while others went south of Marsh's rancho. Bidwell was in San Jose by November 18, because on that date Mariano Vallejo issued him a passport. *John Bidwell Papers,* California State Library.

24 Under date of November 6, Bidwell, *Narrative,* p. 74, and in his *Journal,* p. 29, notes that fifteen of the company started for San Jose to "seek employment." In crossing Livermore Ranch, Belden's San Jose–bound party must have run across the small settlement on that property. Under November 10, Bidwell reports that he visited that ranch, some twenty miles from Marsh's, where he found "5 or 6 Spanish families." *Ibid.,* p. 30. In a subsequent letter, Sutter wrote to Jacob P. Leese, November 8, 1841: ". . . another . . party is close by from Missouri—one of the party arrived here, some of my friends and acquaintances are among them, they are about forty or fifty men of Respectability and Property. They came in the intention to settle here." *John A. Sutter Collection,* California State Library.

25 This was the Palo rancho of Joaquín Higuera. Shuck, *Sketches,* p. 290. Belden, writing to his sister from Monterey, December 21, 1841, makes no mention of this event; rather he implies the party went directly to San Jose where they were arrested.

CHAPTER FIVE

Letter of Josiah Belden to His Sister, Mrs. Eliza M. Bowers

From the Coe Collection, Yale University Library

MONTEREY, CALIFORNIA
DEC. 21, 1841

Dear Sister:

I have at last the pleasure to inform of my arrival in California. We reached here on the 4th of November after being 6 months lacking a week on the way. We were much longer coming from the Rocky Mountains where I wrote you last, than we expected to be owing to our not knowing the way and in fact there were times when we scarcely expected to get here at all or anywhere else and almost made up our minds to starve to death in the mountains. We kept wa[n]dering on over mountains valleys and rivers. Sometimes in one direction and sometimes in another without knowing whether we were right or wrong until we got nearly out of provisions and found winter approaching when we concluded to leave our wagons and take the cattle that drawed some of them to eat. We then packed our things on our horses and pushed along as fast as we could until we at last struck St. Mary's River which we had been directed to follow down to where it emptied into a lake and then we struck into the California mountains. In coming down Mary's River we frequently fell in [with] large parties of Indians and were several times in expectation of being attacked by them but I suppose they saw that we were well prepared for them and thought it best to let us alone. When we got to the mouth of Mary's River we hired two Indians for guides to take us across the mountains but the scoundrels led us into the very worst part of the mountains and then ran away in the night and left us there. We were then in a most discouraging situation. We were in an unknown wilderness enclosed by mountains on every side rising to an immense height and covered with snow. To that there seemed to be no possibility of getting over them and when myself and another climbed to the top of one of them we could see nothing but mountains upon mountains as far as the eye could reach in the direction we wanted to go. We could not turn back as we knew we should starve before we could get back to where there was anything to eat for we were then just eating our last ox and there was no game to be found in the country.

We, however, toiled along slowly up and down the mountains for 22 days when we at last came out onto the plains almost worn down with hunger and fatigue. We had to walk nearly all the way over the mountains and throw away many of our things as our poor horses could hardly scramble up the steep rocky precipices without anything on them. Some of them slipped on the sides of the steep mountains and were pitched down headlong and dashed to pieces among the rocks. We had to kill some of our horses and eat them as we had nothing else to eat except acorns for about 2 weeks. We however worked our way through it and in 5 days after we got out on to the plains of California we came to the house of an American farmer. We rested there two days and then a party of us started for one of the towns 45 miles off. But what was our surprise on arriving there to find ourselves all made prisoners by the government. The law here requires that every foreigner coming into the country shall bring a passport from the country he leaves and as we had no passports to show we were arrested and our arms taken away from us. They put us in the guard house but did not keep us too [long]. [W]e had liberty to go out and in when we chose but were not allowed to leave the town. They kept us so 6 days when they set us at liberty and gave us passports to travel about the country by our getting some Americans who are living here to go security for our good behavior whilst we are in the country. Myself and one more then left there and came to this place. This is a fine country and a most delightful healthy climate. It is hardly ever cold enough here in the winter to make a fire necessary for comfort. I like the country better than the Spanish people who live here for many of them are great rogues as I can testify for they stole 4 horses from myself and my friend at the town where we were arrested. Some of the Spaniards though have treated us very hospitably and the Americans we have found here have treated us very well. Our company have now scattered themselves about the country seeking employment and most of them I believe have gone to work, some in one place and some in another.

I am at present working a little here at my trade but there is not much to do at that and I shall soon have to look out for something to do. I have some prospect of getting employment as clerk in a store but it is uncertain. If I do, I shall probably stay here a year. If not I expect I shall go home in the spring. This place is situated on the Pacific Ocean and there are at present several American vessels here. P.S. I have just made an engagement with Mr. Larkin to go clerk in a store for a year. I do not get much wages this year but if I choose to stay another, I have a chance of doing better. I don't think I shall stay another year unless I see a chance of making a fortune. I hope you will write to me immediately. Send your letter by a private hand if you can hear of any chance. If not, put it in the mail but if you put it in the mail you must pay 25¢ postage. When you put it in the office or else it will not come, direct your letter to the care of Mr. Thomas O. Larkin, Monterey, California . . .

[Envelope addressed to Mrs. Eliza M. Bowers, Upper Middletown, Conn., United States of America. (Postmarked: NEW YORK-Mar. 25).]

[Written along the margin of page one:]

Direct your letter like this — Mr. Josiah Belden, Upper California care of Mr. Henry A. Pierce, Charlestown, Massachusetts and pay postage and he will send it. I have written to Susan and sent the letter by sea so that if this is lost she may get the other.

CHAPTER SIX

A Visit to California in Early Times

By Col. J. B. Chiles, 1878

Biographical Sketch

Joseph B. Chiles was born in Clark County, Kentucky, on July 16, 1810, the youngest child of John H. Chiles and Sarah Ballinger. His father was the descendant of 1638 Virginia colonists who, like so many others, were westering pioneers. By 1830 the entire family was relocated in Missouri, with the exception of young Joseph. He remained in Kentucky to marry a neighbor's daughter, his sweetheart, Polly Ann Stevinson. A year later, they, too, moved to Jackson County, Missouri.

Chiles was ripe for the 1841 trip to California. He helped form the "Chiles Mess," which included his friends and neighbors John Bartleson, Charles Hopper, Michael Nye, and Robert Rickman. Although a widower with four small children (his wife had died in 1837), he was bent on realizing the opportunities California offered. He arranged to leave his children in the care of family.

After the party's arrival, Chiles, accompanied by Hopper, visited Monterey, Sonoma, and other parts of the country. He was able to solicit a promise from General Mariano G. Vallejo for a grant of land for a mill site in present-day Sonoma County. With that in mind, in 1842 he and Hopper returned to Missouri via a variant of the Old Spanish Trail from Los Angeles to New Mexico, then the Santa Fe Trail north to Independence, which was reached on September 9, 1842. Accompanying them were eight other party members who elected to return east.

Chiles made good his plan to return. He led what is known as the "Chiles party" in 1843, but the mill equipment had to be abandoned by a splinter group of his party under the leadership of Joseph R. Walker which had taken the southern route. Undaunted by this setback, in 1844 he received the Rancho Catacula in present-day Napa County, consisting of two leagues, which was patented to him in 1865.

Chiles returned east again in 1847, bringing his own family back with him in

1848, a son and three daughters, with their respective spouses. His family settled in and around Washington in Yolo County.

A fourth and final round trip to Missouri was undertaken in 1853–1854. While visiting his brother, Joel, who lived at Buckner Hill, not far from Independence, he met Margaret Jane Garnhart. A brief courtship ended in marriage on December 25, 1853. The following May she accompanied him west again for California. It proved an easier passage than the other three. Returning to his Napa ranch, Chiles and his bride began to raise a second family.

In the ensuing years, Chiles suffered many financial reverses, mainly because he trusted others. He lost land holdings in Napa and Sacramento valleys, in Oregon and in Modoc County because of it. He was an ardent sympathizer of the Southern cause during the Civil War, as reflected in the name of one of his children, Dixie Virginia, born in 1862. But his greatest delight was his new brood of children. In 1872 he built a house and took up permanent resident in St. Helena. There he died on June 25, 1885. Helen S. Giffen, Trail-Blazing Pioneer: Colonel Joseph Ballinger Chiles *(San Francisco, 1949), affords a solid biography.*

I joined a company of volunteers in 1838 under Colonel Richard Gentry for the Florida [Indian] war. This being a mounted regiment [it] soon sought the place of action. They engaged in but one battle, that being at Lake Okochobee, Dec. [18]38, where their Colonel lost his life. Not long after, the company returned to Missouri. This trip had greatly improved the health of Mr. Chiles, and also created in him a love for adventure. This he communicated to his beloved friend, Mr. William Bladridge, whom he claims to be the best man in the world, and quite a noted millright. After having considerable talk upon the subject of travel and health, Mr. Baldridge proposed the venturesome journey to Cal[ifornia]. Mr. Baldridge had for some time given considerable attention to the subject and had been corresponding with Dr. Marsh, whose descriptive letters of Cal[ifornia] and its climate and resources, had awakened in him a great desire to join him. They at once set about making a company of venture[some] persons to seek the far off shore. After much preparation had been made for journey, Mr. Baldridge was detained on a large contract for building mills, and the company was formed with a man by the name of Battleson [Bartleson] at the head, hence it was called the Battleson [Bartleson] party, which consisted of thirty-one men and one woman and one child.[1] It was considered almost rash for a woman to venture on so perilous a journey, but Mrs. Kelsey said, "Where my husband goes, I can go. I can better endure the hardships of the journey than the anxieties for an absent husband." So she was received in the company and her cheerful nature and kind heart brought many a ray of sunshine through the clouds that gathered round a company [of] so many weary travelers. She bore the fatigues of the journey with so much heroism, patience, and kindness that there still exists a warmth in every heart for the mother and her child that were always forming silver linings for every dark cloud that assailed them. Thus on they traveled seven long and weary months with no guide, no compass, nothing but the sun to direct them. They had learned through Dr. Marsh's letters the latitude of San Francisco Bay, and they thought the sun was sufficient to guide them there. But alas the journey proved longer than they had supposed, and they were tired and hungry long before they reach[ed] that point. They had been subsisting on horseflesh almost entirely and that not of the choicest kind. But little game could be found on that part of the journey and other provision was not known. Imagine the wild delight of so many hungry men, one might say starving men, when they reached the Stanislaus River in whose valley was [where] the deer was very abonndant [abundant], and happy were they to find such a camping place and that evening they brought 26 deer into camp and every man wept that night as they feasted.[2] They camped there a few days to recruit themselves, and then set out to find their old friend Dr. Marsh who lived near Mt. Diablo. In a short time J. B. Chiles, Charles Hopper, Battleson [Bartleson] were enjoying the hospitality of the Dr., whose house consisted of three small rooms, built of sticks and mud; the furniture, which they considered excellent, consisted of two or three benches, and a rude table, and if the weather was foul, a skin was spread upon the ground inside the dwelling and a skin or two for covering, but if the weather was fair, sleeping was always out of doors. Dr. Marsh, although a man of good education, had taken himself an Indian wife and had several children with whom he seemed well pleased. Their living was almost entirely beef which was roasted over a fire out of doors and the hungry travelers thought it excellent fare, as well as did the family. Some of the party, however, had not reached the Dr.'s. They had lost their way and reached San Jose, where they were detained by the government, for not having passports, but only a short time elapsed before Dr. Marsh and his visitors heard of the difficulty and hastened to their relief.[3] They had, however, some little difficulty in proving that a party could pass through such a hostile Indian Country and made their way by land. However, it was settled in a short time by proving that they had gone by land, and their ignorance in regard to a passport [was accepted by the authorities] . . .

Notes

1 If one includes George or James Shotwell, who died on the trail, then Chiles's figures are correct.
2 Bidwell in his Bancroft dictation recalled only thirteen deer as being slain, along with a quantity of birds.
3 This is not accurate. All of the party, with the exception of James John, made it to Marsh's rancho on November 4, 1841. Later fifteen of them headed for San Jose to obtain passports. See Belden's and Bidwell's dictations.

CHAPTER SEVEN

Narrative of Nicholas "Cheyenne" Dawson Overland to California in 1841

Biographical Sketch

Nicholas Dawson was the last of the surviving members of the Bidwell-Bartleson party when he wrote his recollections of that epochal overland journey. He was born at Glasgow in Beaver County, Pennsylvania, on January 22, 1819, the offspring of westering pioneers like so many of his overland companions. As he grew to adulthood, he received a good education. "I went to school a great deal," he wrote, "and very early imbibing a thirst for knowledge, became a great reader. Books of voyage and discovery were my delight, and created in me an overweaning desire to travel . . ." Thus motivated, he left home at age nineteen "with the purpose of spending about six years in seeing the world." Leaving without parental approval, he had saved his money and, to augment his meager funds, sold all his books to his brother. With ten dollars in his pocket, he began his peripatetic adventures.

He headed for Missouri, settling first at Lexington. He then joined the rush to the Platte Purchase, as had young Bidwell. There he built himself a cabin on a piece of land, a squatter like many other neighbors. But finances dictated a reliable source of income. He decided to teach. The first job was not far from present-day St. Joseph, where Antoine Robidoux operated a well-known trading post.

His employment, however, did not last long. Losing his post, he returned to the Platte Purchase and found a buyer for his property. The deal netted him ten dollars. With that in hand, he went to Liberty, then headed north to the Upper Mississippi with the intent of working in the Galena lead mines. But running out of money, he hired himself out as a day laborer. Failing to find a teaching position, he became a farm hand for a month and was able to earn twenty dollars.

In association with two other hired hands, Dawson spent the winter cording wood. Together, the partners built a skiff when spring came and headed down river.

144

When they got to New Madrid, they dissolved their partnership and parted company. Young Dawson pushed on down river to New Orleans, working his way as a hand on a boat loaded with corn for that city's markets. From New Orleans, anxious to visit the Red River, he took a boat for Shrevesport and got as far as Natchitoches, where his money ran out again. Luckily, he got a school job, but he had to abandon it when his employers failed to agree amongst themselves. So he went back to cording wood for his living. His itchy feet, however, longed to resume wandering.

He got lucky again. A stranger came along in a "big canoe," headed for Mansfield, a trip by water "through bayous, lakes and swamps to the high country . . ." The journey proved uneventful but hardly pleasant; they got lost and they "suffered extremely with cold." Arriving at journey's end, Dawson found a teaching position and taught for the ensuing three months. But wanderlust reared its head again, so off he went by boat to Fulton, Arkansas. With funds again running low, he decided to seek a teaching job. Leaving his trunk in Fulton, he headed for Sevier County where he found his steadiest employment. For nine months he taught in a rural country school. There he also met his bride to be, twelve-year-old Margaret Wright. But his gypsy nature reared its head again as the school term neared its end.

As Dawson wrote:

> *. . . I began to take stock; nearly three years had passed by out of the six that I had planned to spend in travel, so I thought I should set out for foreign lands. My plan was to go to Independence, Mo., where I should most likely find a company going to Oregon. I could take in the Rocky Mountains and buffaloes on the way, and go on to the Pacific.*

Taking the stage from Sevier County to Little Rock, he transferred there to a steamer which took him to Van Buren, Arkansas. There he bought his first horse. He then headed for Independence. It is at this point that we pick up his narrative of the 1841 overland trek. That narrative speaks for itself. After reaching California, Dawson remained in the territory almost three years when his wanderlust surfaced again. This time he decided to travel through Mexico to the east coast and take a ship to New Orleans. From there he made his way back to Sevier County to claim his former pupil as his wife in 1848.

But marriage could not deter Dawson from joining in the gold rush. He headed a second time for California, the new Eldorado. By freighting in the mines, he was able to accumulate a sizeable nest egg, some $1,600. With that in hand, he returned east via the Isthmus in 1851 to rejoin his wife. Shortly after, they settled, finally, near Austin, Texas, in 1852. This time Dawson sank his roots.

Although a staunch supporter of the Confederate cause, that support did not deter him from receiving a handsome inheritance from his father. With that legacy, he purchased a farm near Austin. There he died on November 24, 1903. He was survived by four children, nine grandchildren, and three great-grandchildren.

In the twilight of his life, he decided to record the highlights of his travels:

The following narrative was commenced by me on the first of March, 1894 — fifty-three years after the occurrence of the principal events narrated — and was written mostly from memory, but with an anxiety to say only the truth; and if any errors have been made they were unintentional . . . [1]

1 Biographical details and quotations are taken from *Narrative of Nicholas "Cheyenne" Dawson (Overland to California in '41 & '49, and Texas in '52)*, with an introduction by Charles L. Camp (San Francisco, 1933), *passim.*

To California in 1841

I went up through the western part of Arkansas and Missouri to near Independence. Learning here that a company was soon to go to California and Oregon, I stopped with a man by the name of John Bartleson, who was preparing to go. I soon decided to make one of the company, and remained with Bartleson until the crowd should be made up. Some doubt existed as to whether a sufficient number would congregate to make it safe to go, but as the time drew near (May 1st, 1841) men began to drop in until, when we started there were about one hundred.[1]

It was a very mixed crowd. There were heads of families going out first to find a spot to bring their families to, and heads of families taking the families along to share whatever fortune might bring. There were many adventurous youths like myself, and John Bidwell (afterwards governor of California), who wanted nothing but to see and experience. There were gentlemen seeking health, and an English lord, Lord Romain, going out with a half-breed hunter, John Grey, to shoot buffalo. Among the last to come in were some priests, bound for the Flat-head Mission.[2] They had with them a fine pilot, Fitzpatrick. The modes of transportation were as mixed as the crowd. Some had wagons drawn by oxen, others wagons drawn by horses; a few had hacks; and the priests had carts; many were to make the journey on horseback; and a few brought nothing but themselves. I had traded my horse for an old mule and had bought an interest in Bartleson's wagon and team. When this and my share of the provisions was paid for, I had seventy-five cents left — and I had that still when I reached California in November.

The mess to which I belonged was composed of John Bartleson; Charles Hopper, noted as a hunter; Gwynn Patton, a young fellow, a relative of Hopper's; Talbot H. Green, a young man of evident culture and very pleasing address, whose most important possession seemed to be a quantity of lead that he was taking with him; and a young man named Grove Cook, who joined us after we had started, and begged to be allowed to pay his way by driving our wagon, as he could furnish nothing.

The whole crowd rendezvoused, until all was ready, at Sapling Grove, a few miles from West Port (now Kansas City). Bartleson was elected captain, but after the priests and Fitzpatrick came in, Fitzpatrick was given almost complete control. We were advised to take only provisions enough to last till we reached buffalo, but to take plenty of coffee.

On May 12, 1841, we set out, Fitzpatrick in the lead. A little before night, he would gallop on ahead and select a camping place. When the camping place was reached, the wagons were placed in a hollow square, leaving a space between each two for tents and campfires. The horses were grazed outside until night, when they were picketed inside, and a guard kept outside all night.

Before we passed beyond the range of friendly Indians, I made a trade, which, as it brought in what proved to be a very important member of our company, I will tell of. The old mule I had traded my horse for proved very unsatisfactory. When I wanted him to go to water he wanted to go to grass; when I wanted him to go to grass, he wanted water—perhaps enough is told when I say that it was he that taught me to swear. One day we met a gang of Indians. The leader was riding a spirited white pony, which I at once coveted. Riding up alongside the Indian, I drew my forefingers across each other and holloed "swap!" "Swap," grunted the Indian. He jumped from his horse, I from my mule. He took off his saddle, I took off mine. He fastened his saddle upon my old mule, and I girthed mine around the white pony. Then we each sprang into our saddles and rode off. Thus came into my possession, "Monte." This was the only trade I remember ever to have made in which I did not get the worst of the bargain.

Our route soon crossed the Kansas river, and then passed over to the Platte. While we were in the Platte valleys a little incident occurred that gave me a nickname for the rest of the journey: we were now in the country of hostile Indians, and Fitzpatrick had warned us not to stray beyond sight of the wagon train. But one day, curious to see the country that lay beyond a range of hills, I had ventured farther than usual, and coming upon a herd of antelope I, in my eagerness to get a shot at them, had followed them still farther. I was off my mule (I was riding "The Badger," one of our wagon mules) trying to creep near enough for a shot, when I was startled by an Indian whoop. I sprang upon my mule, but he perversely wheeled and ran toward the sound, I pulling desperately at the reins. Finally I got his head in the direction I wanted to go, but no amount of urging could get that mule to hurry, and in an instant I was surrounded by Indians. One galloped by me, thrust a spear along my back, and motioned me to dismount. I did so. They seized my gun and knife, stripped me of my outer clothing, and taking my mule, left me. I hurried after our train, and over taking it, told my story. The alarm spread along the line, and all was confusion. Fitzpatrick galloped back, calling out the horsemen as he came, and was off with them to find the Indians, and, if necessary, give them battle. I was very angry now, and intent on vengeance, so hastily borrowing a horse and gun, I hurried after the party. I came on at full speed and was aiming at the first Indian within range, when I was stopped by some forcible language from Fitzpatrick, and perceived that Fitzpatrick and the Indians were engaged in friendly pow-wow. It had proved to be a band of Cheyennes, friendly but thievish. They camped near us that night, and Fitzpatrick attempted to get back my property. He and I and the Indians sat around in a circle, and for every article to be returned, gifts of blankets, clothes, etc., had to be thrown down, a peace pipe smoked by all and much haranguing done. Fitzpatrick's patience gave out before all was got back, and declaring that I ought to be satisfied to have got off with my life, he refused to intercede further. I chafed under my enforced friendliness, and after that, to distinguish me from another Dawson in the company known as Bear Dawson, I was called Cheyenne Dawson.

We had a great deal of work to do in digging down banks to cross ravines, and fuel becoming scarce we had to resort to buffalo chips. We struck buffalo on the Platte—by the millions it seemed—and we found the meat delicious. Here Lord Romain, going out unaccompanied by John Grey to shoot buffalo, got lost. He did not return at nightfall, nor during the night. The next morning Grey trailed him down and brought him back. The whole country, except spots in the valleys, was covered with sage bushes two or three feet high, through which the wagons forced their way raking and scraping. Horseback riders also had their clothes torn off them.

On the Sweetwater river we began to lay by to kill and barbecue buffalo meat for future supply, but we had delayed too long and soon found them scarce. This resulted in our obtaining a scant supply, and proved in the end our most fatal mistake.

From the Sweetwater, we went on through South Pass to Green river, a tributary of the Colorado of the West. We reached Green river on July 23rd. On this river we met a few trappers and traders with whom we struck up a barter trade, giving store clothes and ammunition for dressed skin, buckskin clothing, moccasins, and ropes. Those trappers were a rough looking set, dressed in their home-made leather clothes, and at a distance resembled Indians. They had contracted many Indian customs, such as eating every time they were invited, without regard to previous meals, and making the squaws do all the camp work, even to saddling their horses.

At Green river a few of our pleasure and health seekers left us to try to get back to civilization—Lord Romain and John Grey, Amos Fry, and a few others.

Our journey from here to Soda Springs, on Bear river, was more difficult—more mountains and fewer valleys. Ours, I presume, were the first wagons to pass over this route. At times we could pass along the mountain sides only by having fastened to the top of our loads ropes to which men clung to keep the load from tipping the wagon over, and we descended steeps by having behind the wagons men clinging to ropes.

At Soda Springs we parted company with the crowd that was going to Oregon, which crowd included Fitzpatrick and the priests. Thirty-one of us, including one woman (Mrs. Benjamin Kelsey) and her child, decided to strike out for California.[3] We knew nothing positive of the route, except that it went west. True, we had some old maps picturing a river called Buenaventura, or St. Mary's river, which, flowing out of Great Salt Lake and pursuing a westerly course emptied into the Pacific; and from this map we had thought that all we should have to do was to find our river and follow it.[4] However, we had been told by trappers that there was no river flowing from the lake, but that there was a river (which they called Ogden's) that had its source west of the lake and flowed west, and that it might take us to California. There was but one man in the mountains that had ever been to California—Joel Walker by name—and he was supposed to be at Fort Hall, on Snake river.[5] So we sent two men to the fort for Walker, and the rest of us were to travel leisurely down Bear river until we reached a beautiful valley which the trappers called Cache, and there await their return.[6]

While we were traveling down Bear river, the "snow incident" related by Gen. Bidwell in an article in the Century Magazine some years ago, occurred. Bidwell and Jimmy Johns had gone off fishing. They did not return, and much anxiety was felt. At midnight the guard reported that they had not come in. Then the camp was aroused, the wagons were corraled, and everything ready, we awaited a daybreak attack—for that was the Indians' time. We were sure that Bidwell and Johns had been killed, and we expected to have to fight for our own lives. Daybreak at last came, but no Indians. Later in the day, we decided to send out parties to search for the bodies of our comrades. I was riding along, looking for Indian signs and gory corpses, when I saw two men running down a mountain. When they came nearer I saw that it was the supposed dead. As soon as Bidwell was within hearing, he triumphantly held up a handkerchief full of something and shouted, "Snow!" Then I spoke forcibly. "Snow! ——! ——! We thought you were dead." They had seen a snow-summitted mountain a short distance, as they thought, ahead of them, and had set out for it. They had traveled all day, reaching it a little before night. They had climbed and climbed until they got so cold that they had to stop and build a fire to keep from freezing. When morning came they had reached the prize, got a handkerchief full of it and hurried back.

As I have said, we intended to await at Cache valley the return of the messengers we had sent for Walker, but we passed Cache valley without recognizing it, and were astonished one day to find our teams and wagons sinking in a mire, while there lay in front of us, apparently, a wide plain. What could it mean? We halted, and holding a consultation, concluded we must be near the Salt Lake. Seeing the timber of Bear river to the left, we set out in that direction, intending to lay by there until the two men should return. We could use the river water, although we found it quite brackish, proving that we were near to the Salt Lake.

The two men came in in a day or two, without Walker, but brought word that we must be careful in searching for Ogden river to avoid falling over into feeders of Snake river, lest we should get into the cañons without grass or water. So we struck out again, heading westward, and, crossing our trail, we reached higher ground and came in sight of the Salt Lake to the left. We now skirted the north end of the lake, sometimes traveling in a valley and again along the the shore of the lake when the mountains jutted down nearer to its shores. In places our wagons would break a crust of salt, like ice in a northern clime. We found water in holes, like wells, but it was all brackish. Finally a wide valley opened out before us, and we struck across it toward the mountains on our right, hoping to find water fit for use. After pushing on until late in the night, our animals fagging from thirst, we halted and went into camp, still without fresh water. The next day, however, we found a beautiful spring of fresh, cold water, and abundant grass. We concluded to rest here for a few days, and send out explorers to hunt for the Ogden. They soon returned, having found the river, but reported the route impracticable for wagons. They thought, however, from appearances, that a wagon route could be found farther to the south. Accordingly we turned southward around the northwest corner of the lake, and found a pass where, by roping them, we took the wagons through. This led us into a valley which afforded good grass and water.

As we neared a beautiful little fresh water lake in the valley, we were astonished to see, coming to meet us, laughing and making gestures of extravagant joy, an old Indian. He signed that he was expecting us; that he had dreamed of our coming. When we camped, he moved his camp near ours, and went from mess to mess, making us welcome, with a countenance full of happiness. The boys began to make him presents of old clothing, pieces of iron, etc. His joy was childish. As each gift was made, he would point a bony finger to the east and slowly revolve his hand to the west, apparently mumbling as he did so a prayer. This was interesting, and the presents came in faster. The boys put the articles on him hind-part-fore, upside down, until they could get no more on, and then he carefully made a pile of his gifts near his camp fire.

Our valley was charming: but the line of mountains ahead of us seemed unbroken by a pass; we had been delayed so much by our wagons and had had to toil so hard to get them this far—we held a consultation that night and decided to abandon our wagons here, make pack saddles, and pack through. This abandonment of the wagons meant much abandonment of property, from deficiency of animals to convey it, so our old Indian received many more gifts. We made pack saddles out of the wagon beds, and tore up the tents for ropes. Bidwell and Kelsey were to miss the wagons most, for their teams were oxen, and an ox is not easy to pack or easy to stay packed. Finally we were ready for our forward climb. We signed to our aged host that the wagons and everything abandoned were his, all his, and left him circumscribing the heavens—the happiest, richest, most religious man I ever saw. Why was he in that valley alone? What was his faith?

There was one thing we had no trouble to pack—our provisions. Though we had been eating very sparingly for several weeks, our last provisions had been consumed just before we reached Salt Lake, and since, we had been subsisting on what game we could kill, and when no game was to be had, an ox out of our train. Now some of us were inwardly rejoicing over leaving the wagons behind, for it meant more beef—poor beef, but a long way better than nothing to eat. On the eighteen or twenty lean oxen that had drawn our wagons, we subsisted until we entered the Sierra Nevada, for there was no more game to be had. When the oxen were gone, we lived on horse and mule meat, and acorns.

Wearily, and with much trouble with our packs, we made our way to the Ogden (since the Humboldt) and down it, without incident worth relating. The country on both sides appeared a desert. The river seemed to be dwindling instead of receiving big tributaries to swell its flood and guide us into the plains of California and on to the Pacific, where our suffering and troubles would end, and where we could eat, eat, eat—and something that had some fat in it. But the route was getting more nearly impassable; and, alas! what meant those big mountains ahead with no opening through them?

One day while we were toiling on, but forebodingly, an Indian wearing a ragged calico shirt came into camp. Thinking that the shirt meant California close to us, we by signs made him understand that we wished him to pilot us. This he agreed to do. Under his guidance we left the river the next morning, and traveled all day in a southeast direction, over a sandy desert. At night we struck a lake on the bank of which was an Indian village. The Indians supplied us with fish, roasted whole, which we gladly ate without criticizing the method of cooking. The next day we passed another lake having a considerable stream emptying into it. There was a plain trail, which we were following, and we hoped it lead to a pass in the mountains that still confronted us on the west.

After fording the stream that flowed into this lake some ten or twelve of us who had no pack animals to look after went ahead on the trail, expecting the others, with the pilot, to follow. Crossing a ridge we came in sight of another lake and went on to it, intending to await there the rest of the crowd. They never came. We concluded they must have gone up the river. In front the mountains jutted up against the lake. We thought we would explore a little, to see if we could find a road leading to the said-to-be pass. Finding no road and no signs of a pass, we decided to bear towards the river, hoping to strike the trail of the rest of the company.

In the meantime Hopper had seen some deer signs; so we camped, and sure enough, Hopper soon killed and brought in a black-tailed deer. We made short work of eating him all up. We also found some baskets of grass seed hidden away by Indians. We confiscated them, poured the seed into the water we had boiled the deer in, and made a delicious soup. While we were devouring the deer, I had noticed Barnett cramming bones into his pocket. I understood this next day when I saw him, as we rode along, gnawing bones.

Traveling on the next day we finally struck the river. On the opposite side was a bunch of Indians preparing to leave in haste. By shaking a white rag, we induced them to remain until we approached, for we had nothing left to eat, and thought they might have something we could barter them out off. Although they were frightened at first, we soon gained their good will, and having smoked the pipe of peace with them, let them know by signs our wishes. They produced their stock of trade—a gallon or two of pinion nuts. After tasting these we agreed to take them all, swapping butcher knives for them. We and the Indians then parted, very good friends, each thinking he had the best of the bargain. We now divided the nuts by measure; and I remember that I cogitated for some time—should I make one bait [bite] of mine, or dribble them out. I decided on the latter course, and dropped them into my pocket; but they were delicious.

We went on, and soon came upon the trail of our comrades. They had the commissary with them (it was now reduced to two oxen), so we traveled faster than they and soon overtook them. When we came up with them they had followed the river into the mountains and thought it could not be followed farther. We sent men on ahead to explore, and they returned and reported that it would be possible to ascend it farther. We clambered then for several days, and crossed the divide and came to streams running west.

By this time, short rations and toil had reduced both man and beast to a very weakened condition. The animals began to drop down. They would be relieved by distributing their loads among others. Occasionally a horse or mule could go no farther, and had to be left behind. Some of the crowd started the practice of knocking these on the head, cutting off flesh and eating it. This soon became general. About the middle of October, we came into Oak timber, with acorns lying on the ground. The first tree we found with acorns under it we camped at, although it was early in the day. We feared we might not find another.

We were now traveling on a descending grade; and one day while we were going down a ridge between two converging streams, we saw ahead high cliffs with a narrow opening between them. We suspicioned a cañon and halted, for we knew that if we were unable when we reached that point to go on, that neither men nor animals would have the strength to climb back up the slope. We sent two men, Bidwell and Jimmy Johns, ahead to explore. While they were gone, the pilot slid out, thus proving his treachery. Bidwell returned alone, and reported that only a bird could go through. Jimmy Johns did not come back, but we learned afterwards that he struck out alone for California, and made it by some Indians finding him and taking him to Sutter's Fort. After Bidwell's return, we parleyed, and decided to camp for the night. Turning off toward one of the streams, we were unable to reach it, so made a camp and carried water up for the animals. The next morning we turned up the smaller stream, trying to find a crossing. After going back some distance, we succeeded in getting across.

By this time our animals were failing so fast that we thought we would dig a hole, put our things in it, cover them over with soil and build a fire over the spot. This mode of secreting furs, and other valuables, is called cacheing. But before we had finished digging our pit, an Indian was discovered watching us, and the cacheing was given up. A day or two after this, someone returning to camp after we had started found our old pilot and some other Indians searching the camp to pick up what was left. Grove Cook, on hearing this, vowed vengeance, and the next morning remained behind, hidden. We had not gone far when we heard the report of a gun. Cook soon overtook us, laughing, and said that at the crack of the gun the old scamp jumped off the ground with a shriek, and the others ran off. The next morning some one saw a big bunch of Indians approaching our camp, from behind a mountain. In great haste we prepared for an attack, but they did not make any.

One day a stark-naked Indian came into camp, and as he was very friendly, we employed him to pilot us. We were now following a trail, and one day a member of the company, named Jones, went on ahead, expecting the rest to follow. But our new pilot left the trail and struck down a mountain, toward a stream to the left, we, of course, following. Jones never came back; and as he was on foot and had no gun, we were anxious as to his fate.[7] We followed the Indian, and he led us along shelves of rock which overhung vast precipices. Here and there great rocks projected over the path and frequently a pack would strike against one of these rocks and over the precipice would go pack and animal, and be lost to us entirely. We all went on foot, leading our animals. Once, I remember, when I was struggling along trying to keep Monte from going over, I looked back and saw Mrs. Kelsey a little way behind me, with her child in her arms, barefooted, I think, and leading her horse — a sight I shall never forget. As we neared the stream and were passing the last projecting rock, old Monte struck the rock and would have gone over had I not braced myself and held him hard.

I had concocted a plan to get some meat. As soon as I got down the edge to the stream I took out my knife, and standing to one side asked each one as he came by whether any animal had gone over. "Yes. 'The Badger' had just gone over." I struck out up the gulch, and soon found "The Badger," struggling and alive. The Badger belonged to Bartleson, and was packed with bed clothes and camp utensils. Others of the party coming up, we lifted the old mule to his feet and removed his pack. He was badly crippled, but made it to camp. Bartleson agreed that we might kill him and eat him. We ate him nearly all that night, for it was the understanding that each should eat all he wanted. Bartleson made us promise to pay for him when we reached California, and I did pay my portion, but doubt if the others ever did. I also remember to have payed Chiles 75 cents for the butcher knives with which we purchased the pinion nuts. Bidwell and Kelsey, however, never charged us anything for their oxen eaten by us.

Well, our pilot deserted us when we reached the stream, I suppose to go back and plunder the animals that had fallen off the bluffs. He was probably a runaway Indian from the missions; most of the Indians on the west side of the Sierra Nevada at this time were of that class. They would make raids on the missions and ranches and drive off horses, which they used mostly as food. At springs on our route we would frequently see quantities of horse bones.

We crossed the stream, and the country beyond was not quite so rough. About this time, I think it was, that Green, whose pack of lead, which he clung to most solicitously, had been growing heavier for his weakened animal, took Grove Cook with him, and going off into some gulch secreted or cached it.

The roads became better, descending all the time. Ahead were still mountains, but apparently with a valley between them and us. We next came into a rolling country, sparsely wooded. The first night in the foothills was passed at a nasty puddle of water, with only a lean coyote as supper for the whole crowd. This meat—the worst I ever ate—with the dirty puddle, caused a general anxiety to get to good water; for a person suffers more from thirst than from hunger. The next morning we were all very thirsty. We were on a prairie, and no signs of water near. To our right, however, apparently three or four miles away, we saw timber, which we hoped lined a watercourse. We set out for it in a devil take-the-hind-most race. I was on foot; for a short time before Green, for whom I had formed a strong friendship, had asked me to let him ride time about with me, as his mule was disabled, and I had agreed, giving him the first bout.

The distance to the timber proved twelve or fifteen miles. Green, on Monte, was out of sight ahead, and I toiled on, weary, thirsty and angry. Watching eagerly,

I saw the foremost pass into the timber, and my spirits sank; they would have stopped if there had been a stream there. I went on, however, and finally I and other poor footmen reached the timber—open postoak timber, such as I have since seen in Texas. We soon came upon the advance party, halted and parleying—no water! I sank exhausted on the ground, and was debating whether I should not just remain where I was and die, when I heard a gun fired, and shortly after another. "That is Hopper," I thought, "and when he fires twice there is certain to be meat;" so spirits and body rose, and, the crowd moving on, I followed.

Only a short distance beyond where the crowd had halted, they came to a bluff, and below it lay a low bottom covered with young, green grass and at its farther sides willows and other sure indications of a water course. Across that bottom I made rapid headway, and plunging down the banks beyond, lay flat down over the water and swallowed it; then after raising my head to rest, would go at it again. Shortly after, Hopper came in with a deer on his mule, and reported another killed and ready to bring in. He said that there were plenty of signs of deer—then there was great rejoicing, and we decided to tarry, kill and eat. Bidwell says there were thirteen deer killed and eaten, and as we remained there only two or three days, there must have been some tall eating. We found, also, plenty of what seemed to be the most delicious grapes I had ever eaten.

As ascertained afterwards, we were now on the Stanislaus river, in the San Joaquin Valley, and in California; but we did not then believe it; for instead of plains and a big ocean, there ahead were big mountains—and we had come to hate mountains. However, if we had to cross them we would do it on full stomachs, so we enjoyed the present hour.

On the day set for our departure from this happy valley, some of the animals belonging to members of our mess could not be found. Kelsey and his party, containing Bidwell among others, went on down the Stanislaus. We found our animals in a day or two, and followed. We crossed the stream, and finding it heading west, we followed it.

We were traveling along, pretty comfortable on the whole, but casting glances of anxiety towards the mountains ahead, when we saw two men approaching transversely to our route. So rare a sight greatly excited our curiosity, and we stopped and waited. As they drew near, someone said, "Why, one of them looks like Jones!" "No, it can't be." But it was Jones, and an Indian, come to find us and pilot us in, if found alive, to Marsh's ranch.

Jones' story was short. After getting lost from us he had struck westward, had killed with a rock a rabbit, and had subsisted on this until found by some Indians who took him to Marsh's ranch. He had straightway put back, with an Indian guide, to find his comrades. Jones had some provisions, too. We all felt like hugging Jones. We didn't; but those provisions! We must see them. So we camped right there and ate them.

The next morning, under the guidance of Jones and the Indian, we left the river we had been following, struck northwest, crossed the San Joaquin river, and camped on the farther side. The next day, November 4, 1841, we reached Marsh's; for by this route we skirted the mountains. Pilots were sent back to find the Kelsey party, and they were brought in a day or two later. Green and Grove Cook hired an Indian pilot and went back and brought in their "lead."[8]

Native California in '41 and '42

So we had reached California—the first truly distinctive American emigrant train to do so. Bonneville had led a company through a few years before, but I think his was a trapping and trading company of which no account was ever published. Joel [Joseph] Walker was with that crowd.[9]

We had expected to find civilization—with big fields, fine houses, churches, schools, etc. Instead, we found houses resembling unburnt brick kilns, with no floors, no chimneys, and with the openings for doors and windows closed by shutters instead of glass. There were no fields or fencing in sight—only a strong lot made of logs, called a corral. Cattle and horses were grazing everywhere; but we soon found that there was nothing to eat but poor beef. The season before had been exceptionally dry, and no crops had been made except at the missions, where they irrigated; and, as many of the missions were on a rapid decline, but little had been raised at them.

Marsh was very kind and asked us what we craved most. We told him something fat. He had a fat hog. This he killed for us, and divided it among the messes. We relished it greatly. He also had a small quantity of seed wheat that he was saving to plant. A part of this he had made into tortillas for us. He told us that if we wished we could sleep in the house. This novel experience some of us tried, but we were much disturbed by fleas, and sick-stomached men crawling over us to get out. They had eaten too much pork...

Notes

1 The number is exaggerated.
2 This was the Jesuit missionary band.
3 The California-bound contingent totaled thirty-four persons.
4 This map probably was provided by John Bidwell's Missouri friend, Elam Brown.
5 Dawson has confused Joseph Reddeford Walker with his brother Joel. The former was the one who had gone overland to California in 1833. However, others had preceded him, among them Jedediah Smith, Peter Skene Ogden, James Ohio Pattie, and the

annual trader caravans from Santa Fe to Los Angeles beginning in 1829.

6 Bartleson was one of the four men who went to Fort Hall in hopes of securing a guide. They failed, but they did receive, as pointed out elsewhere in his book, invaluable information from seasoned transmontane trappers.

7 Jones was accompanied by Andrew Kelsey, and the two, as noted elsewhere, found their way to the San Joaquin Valley ahead of the Bidwell-Bartleson party.

8 Marsh, in his report to the California authorities, makes it clear that the entire company reached his rancho on November 4, 1841. There was one missing party member, however, James John, who made it to Sutter's Fort alone.

9 This is not an accurate statement. Washington Irving published a two-volume work entitled, *The Rocky Mountains; or Scenes, Incidents, and Adventures in the Far West, digested from the Journal of Captain B. L. E. Bonneville, U.S.A, and Illustrated from various other sources* (Philadelphia, 1837). Bonneville sent a party of his men under Joseph R. Walker to California on a fur-hunting expedition in 1833–1834. He did not accompany that party. Joel Walker is the brother of Joseph Reddeford Walker.

CHAPTER EIGHT

Narrative of Charles Hopper, a California Pioneer of 1841

Written for R. T. Montgomery at Napa 1871

Biographical Sketch

Charles Hopper, a native of North Carolina, was an experienced hunter. He returned east in 1842, serving as one of the guides to the Bidwell-Bartleson party returnees. In 1847 he came back to California with his family and settled on a farm near Napa. There he spent the rest of his life, dying in 1880 at the age of eighty-one. Bancroft, California, III: 787.

I set out about the 1st of May, 1841 with a party of 30 men, 1 woman and 1 child, from Jackson County, Mo.[1] Col. John Bartleson was Captain of our Company, but our number was increased to 75 before starting, tho by another party which was bound to Oregon, and which separated from ours at Soda Springs, near Fort Hall. It was commanded by Capt. Fitzpatrick. Of these in our company, I remember only the following persons:

Col. John Bartleson, Col. J[oseph] B. Chiles, John Bidwell (Hon. John Bidwell of Butte Co.), Charles Hopper, Andrew Kelsey (afterwards killed by Indians at Clear Lake), Nathan Jones,[2] Michael Nye, Capt. [Robert] Rickman, [Nelson] McMahan, Benj. Kelsey, C[harles] M. Weber, [Josiah] Welden [Belden], [David W.] Chandler, John McDowell, [Samuel] Green McMahan, [James P.] Springer, Grove Cook, Mrs. Benjamin Kelsey and child.

While encamped near Soda Springs, Mr. Bidwell became excited on beholding snow upon the mountains apparently close to camp and asked, "Can't I go to it and get back this evening?" He was assured he could not, and that the mountains were at a long distance. He pretended that he was going fishing, but started for the mountains to see the snow. He was gone all night and the company made sure he was killed by the Indians. I took his track for the mountains and at last found him. Bidwell came laughing into camp, but he got soundly rebuked by the Captain for being so venturesome and giving trouble to the company when there was no need of it.[3]

We got safely through to Fort Hall. No incident worthy of notice except that a young man shot himself at Ash Hollow in attempting to pull his gun out from a wagon.[4]

The company concluded a day or two after leaving Soda Springs to stop and recruit the animals, and meanwhile sent Capt. Bartleson and myself ahead to the Forks of the Humboldt to select a route. We were gone 12 days, and when we met the company they had started on without us, thinking we had both been killed by the Indians.

We travelled on till we struck the California mountains, as the Sierras were called. Here we got entirely out of provisions and travelled two days without any, when we killed and ate a mule. We lost two or three animals on this side of the Sierra by the Indians, and got into Sacramento Valley about the 15th of October, having been about five months and a half making the trip.[5] Here we met a man who informed us where Dr. Marsh lived, and kept on to his place, which was near Monte Diablo.[6] He bid us welcome, and killed a fine beef and a hog for us. When we had rested and refreshed ourselves, he said the best thing we could do would be to go to the Mission St. Jo [San Jose], and he would send for the Governor to met us there . . .[7]

Notes

1 The rendezvous date was May 10, but the company was not formally organized until May 18 on the banks of the Kansas River. Hopper does not include Shotwell, who died on the journey west.

2 Nathan is an error; this would have to be Thomas Jones.

3 Bidwell's account of this snow incident is entirely different from that offered by Hopper. See Bidwell's 1877 Bancroft dictation.

4 The party as a whole did not travel to Fort Hall. Four party members went there in search of a guide and/or information. George or James Shotwell was the casualty.

5 The party entered the San Joaquin Valley and the date was certainly the end of October at the earliest.

6 The party met an Indian, later a former party member who had made his way independently to Fort Sutter, James John.

7 The purpose was to obtain the required passports to remain in the Mexican province. Marsh sent word to General Mariano Guadalupe Vallejo, commandant general of California. The governor at this time was Juan Bautista Alvarado.

CHAPTER NINE

The Two Diaries of James John

Biographical Sketch

James John was born on April 27, 1809, at Donnelsville, Clark County, Ohio. He was the second child of a family of three surviving children, two boys and one girl. At the age of four, his mother died; he was reared thereafter by his maternal grandparents, the Rev. Peter Smith, M.D., and his wife, Katherine.

He spent his youth in a variety of occupations ranging from deck hand on Mississippi River steamboats, to small-time farmer, teamster, and construction worker. A peripatetic young man, he married about 1838, but became a widower seven months later.

After arriving in California in November 1841, John elected to travel north to Oregon in the summer of 1842. He joined a northbound party of Hudson's Bay Company trappers led by Francis Ermatinger. On reaching Oregon he spent several years in the vicinity of the present town of Gaston where he started two farms on the Tualatin Plains. The first proved unsuccessful, so he sold out to finance a second purchase. During the winter of 1842–1843, he was persuaded by a new acquaintance to relocate to Linnton, a new settlement founded by Mortimer M. McCarven and Peter H. Burnett, destined to be California's first state governor. There he purchased a town lot and built a warehouse, which was subsequently leased by the Hudson's Bay Company for grain storage. Unfortunately, the town was doomed to failure. It was abandoned during the 1848 gold rush.

John, in the meantime, moved across the Willamette River in the winter of 1845–1846. On March 25, 1846, he filed a claim on the present townsite of St. Johns. On October 7, 1852, he platted "St. Johns on the Willamette," the predecessor to the present town of St. Johns.

John never remarried. His was a lonely bachelor life, a lifestyle of his own choosing. He was a very quiet person, mindful of his privacy, but he was a man who was generous by nature, especially to the fairer sex and to young children. The latter is attested to by his will, dated March 14, 1883, which left his entire estate for the benefit of his community's school children. He died at his home on May 27, 1886, at age seventy-seven. A relative in Indianapolis contested his will, but to no avail. It was upheld.[1]

1 Biographical data drawn from David C. Swap, "James John (1809–1886)," typed Ms., Oregon Historical Society. Also, see the *Oregonian* [Portland], May 29, 1886, p. 6 and March 29, 1903, p. 40. For the will contest, see *ibid.*, April 27, 1893, p. 8 and September 11, 1903, p. 10.

Two diaries kept by James John exist. One resides in the Oregon Historical Society, Portland, the other in the Rosenbach Museum and Library, Philadelphia. The OHS manuscript is entirely in the hand of John and gives every appearance of having been written on the overland trail as the Bidwell-Bartleson party progressed west. The writing is bold and large. The Rosenbach manuscript is a curious item. It is in two different hands. Midway through, the diary shifts from an unknown hand to John's. This is clearly established in comparing the two diaries.

The first diary which follows is recorded in a bound booklet, 2¾ inches wide by 6⅛ inches high (6.6 by 15.10 cm). It consists of 79 leaves, written consecutively on succeeding pages, both sides of the paper. It begins with a kind of odd preface in John's hand, which occupies the first page and a third of the following page. The diary itself commences on the third page, and it is in the hand of another person whose identity has not been established. The writing is neat and small and remains so until page 37 (the leaves are not numbered). Here is an obvious new hand, one which is open and scrawly. At the same time spelling becomes a bit erratic from that of the earlier pages. The hand is definitely that of James John. This diary spans the dates May 16 to October 31, 1841. It starts in Westport, Missouri, and ends with John reaching Sutter's Fort on the Sacramento River. Appended to the diary are an additional nine leaves of extracts copied from the journal of John Bidwell for the dates October 20 to November 4 when John was separated from the company. This would indicate that this diary was a later copy and variant on the trail-kept diary, for John could only have copied from Bidwell's manuscript at a later date, possibly at their subsequent reunion at Sutter's Fort. It is herein published for the first time by the kind permission of the Rosenbach Museum and Library.

The diary has been faithfully transcribed as it reads. However, to aid the reader, sentence structure, capitalization, and punctuation have been supplied. Here and there misspelled words are followed by bracketed corrections so as not to confound the reader. Infrequently, words are supplied in brackets to help clarify the diarist's meaning. Misspelled words that would not confuse the reader have been transcribed as in the original.

The second diary records the trip from May 17 to August 20, 1841. Its text on the whole is more detailed than the first diary, though here and there specific details are omitted which are found only in the first diary. For example, when John records the marriage on the trail of Miss Williams to one of the party, in the first diary he provides the first name, Zedidiah Kelsey, while in the second the groom is simply Mr. Kelsey. Because of the greater detail supplied in the second diary one could hypothesize that the second was the one maintained on the trail, while the first was a latter rewrite, comparable to what Bidwell did with his original trail journal. Another telling point is the second diary is entirely in John's hand and, as pointed out before, is in a bold and scrawly hand which would indicate it was written during the actual trip.

This second diary is recorded in a bound booklet which measures 4 by 6 inches. It is in fragile condition. The early part of the diary is quite legible, but as time goes on, no doubt due to physical strains and diet irregularities, the writing becomes fainter and more difficult to decipher. Fortunately, the diary survived and was presented to the Oregon Historical Society. It was at one time in the possession of John Mock (1895), later John Catlin, an Oregon pioneer of 1848. It was from Catlin that George H. Himes obtained the original. He then proceeded to transcribe it and published it in five installments in the St. Johns [Oregon] Review, March 16, 30, April 6, 12, 20, 1906. The copy which is published herein is taken verbatim from the clippings in the Oregon Historical Society. It has been checked against the original manuscript. In doing so, several typographical errors were detected and corrections supplied.

The First James John Diary

May 16, 1841

This day I left Westport for the Oregon teritory in company with one waggon and two men. The one [who?] owned the waggon was by the name Chiles and the other name weaver [Weber] for we were too late to start with the company. They [were] about one week's [travel] ahead of us. We did not overtake them until the 23rd where we found them encamped on the bank of a small river by the name of Blue river. Nothing particular occured excepting we met a few Shawnee until the first of June [when] we arrived on the banks of the Platte river. This night we had a heavy rain and hail storm. A wedding also took place in camp. [*Written in John's handwriting.*]

May 16, 1841. James Johns travels. Left Westport on the 16th of May in company with Mr. Childs [Chiles] who had one waggon and Mr. Weaver [Weber]. Being one week behind the Company we overtook them on the 23rd encamped on the bank of the Blue River. This day we met a band of Pawnee Warriors 16 in number on their way to fight the Kaw Indians. We gave them some tobacco, shook hands and left them. We caught some fine cat fish in the river.

24th. We came to a creek about noon. It being high we encamped till morning, and crossed it about 4 oclock. We caught some more fish. Some of the company saw some Elk. We encamped this night on a small creek.

26th. Left here at 7 oclock. One of the waggons broke down. Met some 30 Pawnees armed with bows, lances & guns, prepared to fight the Kaws. One of the mule teams ran away and broke the waggons. This night we encamped on a small creek.

27th. Left early this morning. The road is is a little broken and the heat oppressing. Encamped at a handsome little creek.

28th. Set out early. Stopped at a beautiful creek about 9 oclock and took breakfast. Started again at ten oclock. Arrived at a creek called Big Blue and camped and killed one Antelope. This and a few Deer and some Turkeys is all that we killed since we started. The heat was oppressive.

29th. Left early this morning. Killed two Antelope. Camped on the banks of the Blue this evening. This stream runs eastward and we go up it. Camped on it again this night.

30th. Stayed here and rested.

31st. Left early. Met five waggons from Fort Laramey [Laramie] on their way to Independence. The traders told us it would be 4 days before we should see Buffaloe. We traded with them for Buffaloe meat and moccasins. They had Buffaloe Robes with them. We were about 4 hundred miles west of Independence travelling this sandy but fertile Plains. Left the Blue this day and camped on the Prairie.

June 1st. Left this. Arrived on the banks of the Platte at two oclock. Here we camped. There came up a cloud with the appearance of light showers. As it arose it grew dark. The thunder roared. The rain and Hail came until the ground was covered with Hail as large a[s] partridge eggs and some as big [as] a pint cup. The rain ceased while in the evening it commenced again and rained the whole night. We had a wedding this night. Mr. Zedidiah Kelsey married Miss Williams by Rev. Joseph Williams. This morning a council was held to regulate the time of starting which was set at [half] past 6 oclock. We did not leave till later this morning on account of being so thoroughly drenched in the rain. The ground is covered with salt here for many miles.

2nd. We stopped at noon this day at the head of Grants [Grand] Island to dry our clothing. Went on about 12 miles up [the] Platte.

3rd. Went about 20 miles. There was another shower and the air was cool.

4th. Today we started early. Travelled briskly until noon when some of our men scattered to hunt Antelope. And one of them, being alone, creeping along to shoot at a Antelope, was surrounded by a band of Shina [Cheyenne]

Indians and robbed of his mule, gun and pistol and they tried to take his clothing off but he tore loose and came up with the company and informed the Captain. Part of the men went back to recover the property. The Indians came meeting them. The teamsters hastened to prepare for battle. Some were panic struck. They saw the Indians, about 30 in number, and [thought] that there were about a thousand. When the Indians came at them [they] were friendly, brought the property and gave it up, smoked the pipe of peace and camped about 50 yards from us this night.

5th. This morning we set out about sunrise. Stopped at 7 oclock for breakfast. We saw six flat boats landed a little below us. We spoke with some of the men. We saw numerous herds of buffaloe on the opposite [side of the river] and we killed two Antelope. There came up a storm in the afternoon. The wind blew very hard and on the opposite side of the River a tremendous hurricane. We saw trees flying on the air and water blown out of the River as high apparently as the clouds. After the storm abated we travelled about one mile and found Hail stones as large as goose eggs. We made a fortunate escape from the severist of the storm. We camped on the bank of the Platte. Just after we spread our tents another Storm of the same kind came on which lasted until night, leaving the ground covered with Hail. It quenched all the fires and left our goods in bad order.

6th. This morning set out early accompanied by twelve Chian [Cheyenne] Indians who traveled with us we supposed for protection from the Pawnees. This day killed 3 elk. The weather was cool till noon when it became warm and rained at night. We camped on the bank of the river. The Indians left us.

7th. Started at 7 oclock. Travelled about 20 miles and camped at a small creek. The Hunters killed 2 Buffaloe this day. The Capt. sent out a small party to kill meat by turns for the company. We had another storm that not much rain.

8th. We killed 4 Buffaloe and some Hares and camped in the evening on the South Fork of the Platte. The Buffaloe are plenty. Saw several Herds this day consisting of some hundreds.

9th. We crossed the river at the same place where we camped last night. The river being about 14 hundred yards wide here took nearly all day to cross it. The bottom is sandy and water like the Missouri. We forded it with 18 loaded waggons and the bed being level the water was about 3 feet deep. We saw about a thousand Buffaloe. Camped opposite to where we did last night.

10th. This day was pleasant. Travelled about 25 miles. Killed one Buffaloe. Was in sight of them all day. The river banks were lined with them. Camped this night on the North Fork of [the] Platte. The Plains here are Sandy while the river has a level plain on each side and a ridge of Sand Hills about 2 miles each side from the river.

11th. We were surprised this morning by a false alarm. The Oxen strayed.

Two men went after them [and] came back running. Their horses running [and] reported that the Indians were driving them off. Twelve of the company set out and saw no Indians and brought the cattle back. Some of the company had sport today killing a buffaloe bull. They had at him more than 20 times before he fell. We came to a dog warren or town. [These are] prairie dogs who burrow in the earth. [They] are not as large as a common cat. Camped on the bank of the Platte. Had a warm day.

12th. Left the North Bank of [the] Platte. This morning we arrived at the Middle fork about noon. Took dinner here. Saw about one Buffaloe today. Camped this night on the bank of the river.

13th. This morning an accident occurred. I was out of camp seeking [the] oxen from the river. I heard the report of a gun and heard a Scream. I went to the camp and saw a man bleeding on the ground. He was taking his gun out of the waggon with the muzzle towards him and it discharged and shot him thru the left side. He lived about an hour and died. We buried him in the sand about a mile from the Camp.[1] The Company appoved a Committee to appoint an administrator for the estate of the deceased and the Capt. was appointed. We had a sermon delivered by Rev. Williams. We left at eleven oclock and went to Ash Creek. There we killed an Elk.

14th. Was rainy. We staid here all day.

15th. We left. River here is wide like the South fork of [the] Platte and hills on each side consisting of sand and rock and narrow plains. Travelled about 15 miles and camped.

16th. This morning left as usual. The day was pleasant. We made a good days drive. Killed some rabbits and Antelope but we have not seen buffaloe for 4 days. We saw some wild horses on the opposite side of the River. The land here is almost entirely destitute of timber, some cedar on the islands and on the Creeks. Saw some wild cherries and currents of a large size. Camped on the bank of the river.

17th. Travelled on. Crossed a creek of excellent water. Saw a large quantity of pine timber along the creeks and Bluffs. Two hunters were sent out yesterday and did not return until 12 oclock last night. Brought in some Buffaloe meat to camp and saw no Indians. We camped on the Bank of the river near the mouth of a large creek in sight of clay mounds called the Chimneys and in sight of a mound which has the appearance of a large mansion.

18th. Started at 6 oclock. The weather fine and the air pure. Travelled about 25 miles and camped about 2 miles from the Chimney [Rock]. We killed two Antelope and one deer.

19th. We left camp early. The air was cool, a wind high. We killed two Mountain sheep and three Elk, one Antelope. Camped near a deep ravine of water nearly surrounded by high bluffs called the Scotch [Scotts] Bluffs which have a splendid appearance. We left it 6 oclock. Took dinner on Horse Creek. This a cold rainy day and disagreeable for travelling. Camped at night on the bank of the Platte about sixty miles from Laramey [Laramie].

21st. Set out as usual. The day is windy from the appearance of the timber. I should judge that it was always windy here. The Hills are sandy, in some places rocky, some have the appearance of plaster of paris. We see few Buffaloe here but plenty of meat in camp. Saw plenty small game and we enjoy good health excepting two or three persons who have been complaining for a few days, me being one. Camped on the Platte.

22nd. Arrived at Fort Laramy [Lamarie] at 10 oclock. This fort is situated on the north side of the river called Laramey's [Laramie's] Fork. We crossed it here. [There] was another fort building about a mile from this place. Its proprietor's name is Lupton.[2] We camped this night in sight of both Forts and rested all next day. The Forts are situated on the North side of the river in a pleasant site and are built of Doughbies [adobes] or clay. We can see some of the black hills from this place which are 50 miles distant. The River here is narrow and clear and current fetid.

24th. We left the Forts and went 10 miles and camped at a warm Spring in a valley surrounded by Hills with some scattering [of] pines growing on them.

25th. We left the camp at 7 oclock. We have made about 20 miles over hills called the Black hills and thru valleys plenty [with] game and saw some small roots like turnips and good to eat and wild currants and cherries. Two men from the fort over took us and were going to the mountains with us. Two of our Company left us at Fort Laramey [Laramie].[3] We saw a number of buffalo but killed none. Camped in a valley of excellent grass and water. The grass is like the blue grass of the States.

26th. Started at h[alf] past six. Took dinner on a Creek and in the afternoon myself and two others went out to hunt buffalo. We killed one and wounded another. We packed our horses and set out for camp the waggons having gone in a different route to what we expected and travelled till midnight before we overtook them. Camped on the North fork of [the] Platte. Have seen some grizzly bear here but we did not shot any.

27th. Left early. Travelling like 4 or 5 [miles] and camped on a muddy creek. But few springs in this country. Killed one buffalo and some small game.

28th. Started early. Took dinner on the bank of a creek of good water and good grass. Near there is a large cliff as white as snow, a little harder than common chalk and some of the earth is composed of a substance, supposed by the Company to be plaster of Paris. Left this and after a hard half days drive camped on a creek near a spring of good water. We killed one buffalo and [saw] some grey bears but did not kill them.

29th. Started late being hindered by the cattle straying. Took dinner on a small creek, travelling over the black hills and valleys. There are different kinds of stone here, some limestone, sandstone, granite, red stone, plaster of paris, white and red sand in some places. They present a beautiful appearance. Camped this night on the Platte about 20 miles from the main ridge of the Rocky Mountains in sight of the high Mountains.

30th. Left camp at 7. Haulted on the bank of the river. Had a pleasant day. Made good speed. Camped on the bank. Killed two buffalo cows and 2 bulls. The river here is about 200 yards wide.

July 1st. Crossed the river about a mile from our last camp. Difficult crossing river since current swift. All got over safely except a mule was drowned and one waggon upset but not much lost. Camped about 2 miles up the river.

2nd. Left early. Travelled along the bank of the river. Killed 2 buffalo. The country is broken and sandy. On the south side of this river is a chain of high hills covered with fine timber, but on the north side is barren, nothing in sight.

3rd. Travelled until two. Camped. Killed one buffalo and two deer. Man named Belden lost his horse yesterday while hunting, indeed, [he was] hunt[ing] buffalo and returned but could not find the place. Went back this day and found the place but the horse was gone.

4th. Started off. The day was warm. The road was rough. [Travelled] 16 miles and camped at an excellent Spring, about 1 days travel from Sweet water. The country is Hilly, rocky and sandy. Plenty Buffalo, bear and wolves. Killed 3 Buffalo.

5th. Left early and after a hard drive came to Sweet water and camped. Killed some buffalo. A band came near running over the waggons but we shot and turned them away. We have seen scarcely any timber today but a sandy plain destitute of vegitation and some Rocky Cliffs. Our encampment this night is near a mountain called the Independence Rock which stands by itself. It is about 150 feet high, solid granite and is a monument on which is recorded the names of all those who pass that way.

6th. Started at the usual hour travelling up [the] Sweet water valley. Passed by the curiosity in the mountain called cut rock having a gap about 60 feet wide not less than 250 feet high thru which passes the Sweet water creek. We camped this evening on the Sweet water creek which extends nearly the whole length of the valley.

7th. This day was warm and rough. Saw plenty Buffalo, killed 4. Camped on sweet water near a high cliff.

8th. This day was cool. Made good speed. Saw a great many Buffalo. Killed 3 and two Antelope. Camped on sweet water.

9th. Started as usual. The road is sandy and hard travelling. In sight of high Mountains covered with snow. Saw thousands of Buffalos. Killed 16. Camped on sweet water.

10th. This morning was cold and the wind blew hard. Unpleasant travelling. Camped on sweet water this afternoon. Found a great many gooseberries and currants here.

11th. Remained at the same place to secure a supply of meat for the remainder of the journey, this being the last opportunity as we shall soon be out of the range of buffalo. Killed a Cow and a steer today.

12th. Remained at this same place today. Killed 4 buffalo Cows and some sage Chickens and fish.

13th. Left. Went on our journey over a rocky country. Killed 1 Buffalo. Met two of our men who had been sent by the company to rendezvous on Green river on the sixth of July to made arrangement for an exchange of Oxen for Mules, but they did not see any person not even an Indian. We have seen none since we left Laramey [Laramie] except that now two are with us. Camped this night on sweet water.

14th. Lay by to kill more buffalo. Had a heavy frost. Killed about ten buffalo today.

15th. Moved about 1 mile and camped till next day. The nights cool and frost nearly every morning. No wood except a few willows on the creek. We are about 8 miles from Wind river Mountains. They have been in sight the last ten days and we have them on our right hand. They are covered with snow.

16th. Travelled about ten miles. Camped at noon on the same creek for the purpose of drying meat and getting good pasture for our Cattle and horses. Killed a number of sage fowls. They are larger than a prairie chicken.

17th. Started at 8 oclock and went up the creek about three miles and camped. I caught some fine fish at this last camp. Killed 6 Buffalo bulls and a number of sage chickens. Buffalo are getting scarce.

18th. We left Sweet water creek this morning at 6 oclock and travelled 17 miles and camped on one of the head branches of the Colorado of the West. Killed 2 Buffalo bulls and an Antelope. The day was pleasant and we have had no rain since we left the north fork of Platte river.

19th. We travelled about 15 miles and camped on a creek of the Big Sandy. Here is good grass and the wild onions grow about 3 feet high. Still in sight of the Mountains we saw on the 9th of this month. Have seen others which are covered with snow.

20th. Travelled hard all day and did not get more than eight miles in a straight line. Killed one antelope. Camped on the Sandy. The valley is still destitute of timber and almost every thing else but sage. The valley is wider in some places than others, thus varying between one to 60 miles.

21st. This morning was pleasant. Travelled all day on big Sandy and camped on it at night.

22nd. Travelled till noon on the same creek and camped. Went about 12 miles.

23rd. Today a man has returned to the camp who left us on the 14th to try and find some trader on the Colorado river to get information respecting the route to California and to get a Pilot. He brought about 60 men with him who came to trade with us.[4] They told us it was impossible to get waggons thru to California, but we could get down on the Columbia without much trouble.

23rd [24th]. Travelled about 10 miles and came to Green on [the] Colorado river, attended by the men who came to us yesterday and a number of Snake Indians. The River here is about 100 yards wide and has some cotton wood and willow on its banks. Here we stayed until the 25th and traded with the Indians and Trappers for horses and buffalo robes. There is frost here nearly every night, but the days are warm and pleasant. The plains are barren and destitute of timber.

25th. We crossed the river and travelled about 6 miles down it and camped. The Indians and trappers came with us. There is no Buffalo nor any thing else to kill except fish.

26th. This morning we left the river and travelled about 12 miles and camped on a stream called Hams fork which empties into Green River. The Indians and some of the trappers camped with us.

27th. We travelled about 12 miles up Hams fork and camped on the bank. Killed 2 antelope and caught some fish. The nights here are cool and sometimes frosty, the valley being surrounded by Mountains which are covered with perpetual Snows.

28th. Travelled about 18 miles up Hams fork and camped on its bank in the afternoon for we frequently camped about 4 oclock. [*Next line and a half illegible.*]

29th. Travelled about 12 miles [*next three and half lines illegible*].

30th. [*Illegible for two lines*] the water is good here and grass excellent on the creek, but the plains are barren and destitute of timber. Left Hams fork and travelled about 15 miles and camped on a small stream called Blacks Fork of [the] Green River. The road was hilly and rough and rocky and we were in sight of a large range of mountains on our left which are covered with perpetual snow. There was a cloud of smoke in sight resembling that of a volcano which we supposed to be grass set on fire by the Indians west of us.

August 1st. We travelled about 12 miles thru rough mountainous country and camped on a small creek which empties into Blacks fork.

2nd. Today we went about 12 miles up the fork of the same branch. Here one of the waggons broke down and we were obliged to camp until morning. The valley here is small, surrounded by high hills and in sight of some mountains on the north and south covered with snow, probably 100 miles off.

3rd. Travelled about 20 miles over high hills and rough places and came to Bear River and camped on its bank. The River here was about 20 yds [yards] wide and had a sandy bottom. No timber on its banks except some willows. Killed one Antelope.

4th. Lay by and [caught] some trout, some 18 inches in length. There are a number of wild geese and other fowls here and Antelope.

5th. Travelled about 18 miles down Bear River. Caught some trout and killed a antelope and some wild geese.

6th. Travelled 21 miles on the banks of Bear River. There is high hills and Mountains on each side of the river. We caught a number of fine trout and other fish. Killed a porcupine and some Antelope.

7th. Left the river this morning and came to it at twelve. Nooned there and left it again on account of the hills next [to] the river. Came to it at night and camped on its bank.

8th. Did not leave camp until twelve. Travelled about 12 miles and camped on a small branch of pure spring water about a mile from the river. We caught a great number of fish, trout and chubs.

9th. Travelled 16 miles on the bank of the river except in the afternoon we left the river and returned to it at night and camped. Killed two Antelope and caught a number of fine fish.

10th. Travelled about 10 miles and came to Soda Springs on Bear River. There are a number of Springs here which constantly bubble and forment throwing off gass and some spouting the water to a considerable distance and roar like a steamboat. Others form mounds around themselves by a sediment of calcaceous rock. There are high Mountains on each side of the river here.

11th. We went about 4 miles and then the company divided, 4 Carts and 4 Waggons for Oregon and 8 Waggons for California, myself going with the latter Company. We travelled about 14 miles further and camped on the bank of the River. The Indians that were with us joined the Oregon Company. The most of them in that company were from Missouri.

13th. The river here runs thru a deep channel of black rock which has the appearance of being melted by volcanic eruptions and not by Earthquakes. Travelled about ten miles and camped on the banks of the river.

14th. This evening we passed by a boiling hot Spring, constantly smoking and strongly impregnated with soda. Travelled about 15 miles over hills and Mountains and camped on a small brook about 4 miles from the river.

15th. Travelled about 8 miles in a direct line since the way was rough, hilly and winding. Camped on a small branch about 3 miles from Bear River. Killed very little game the past few days, only a few Antelope and fish. The Mountain cherries and currants are ripe at this time and various other kinds of fruit of good flavors.

16th. Travelled about ten miles and camped on Bear River near a place called Cash [Cache] valley.

17th. Travelled about 25 miles and camped in Cash Valley on the river bank two miles below the falls of Bear river [w]here it runs thru a cut in the Mountains which is narrow and nearly perpendicular and about 300 feet high.

18th. This morning we came to a deep muddy creek which we could not cross without going nearly half a days journey up it and we have travelled about 5 miles. Crossed it and camped on the other bank. There are a number of hot Salt springs on the banks of this creek, some are nicely boiling.

19th. Travelled about 16 miles in a round about direction and came back to the river thru a dry, salt plain and found no water till we returned to the river.

20th. Lay by and sent seven men ahead to search for the Salt Lake as our Pilot left us and went with the Oregon Company.[5]

21st. Travelled about 12 miles and came to a large Salt Spring where we camped. There was no timber here except a few willows, Salt bushes and Stormwood and Pine on the tops of the mountains.[6] Game is scarce. We have killed nothing for a few days except a few antelope and some fishes.

22nd. Stayed in camp on account of Oxen straying. We found them towards evening. The men who went to Fort Hall, 4 in number, returned today. They obtained some provisions but could get no Pilot. The governor of the fort informed them that it was about 7 hundred miles to Fort Van Couver [Vancouver] on the Columbia river.[7]

23rd. Travelled about 20 miles. Passed a number of Salt Springs. Some difficulty in finding fresh water. Camped at night at a small spring where we did not get half enough water for the animals. We were near the Salt Lake and frequently travelled over plains covered with salts which is good for use.

24th. This morning we were detained by the Oxen straying. Did not find them till about 10 oclock. Travelled about 10 miles and camped near a number of Salt Springs not far from the Lake. These springs are deep. One of our horses would have drowned had we not saved them in time. There are also extensive plains here which border on the Lake.

25th. Did not travel.

26th. Travelled until ten at night and found no water and camped without it or grass west about 35 miles.

27th. Started early and travelled about 6 miles. Came to plenty water and grass. Here we remained several days. Some Snake Indians camped near us and came and traded some berries for Powder & bullets. The Captain and another man named Charles Hopers [Hopper] left camp on the 30th for the purpose of finding Marys River. There is neither rain nor dew here this season of the year. We have had no rain since we left the Platte river.

September 5th. Left the camp that we came to on the 27th of August and went about 6 miles and camped in a Cedar grove near a Spring of water and in sight of the Plain which borders on the Salt Lake. Captain Bartleson and Mr. Hopper has not yet returned.

[Note. Here the handwriting changes, as does the spelling. Beginning with the next entry to the end, the diary is in John's hand.]

6th. We traveled about 10 miles today in a south west direction and we killed a rabbit and an antelope, game being scarce. Here we we were compelled to kill Oxen.

[7th.] On the 7th we traveled 6 miles and encamped at the foot of a mountain near a small brook. Killed one antelope today. This night was cold and windy. There were some Shoshanen [Shoshone] Indians encamped hear us. One of them agreed to pilot us [to] Marys river for 6 lbs of powder and 100 balls.

8th. This morning was cold and windy. Part of the company were in favor of remaining at camp and six waggons stayed at camp and two went on and expected to meet the next day.

9th. We traveled perhaps 12 miles today and met with the two waggons that left us yesterday and also the two men that left us to search for Marys river. They discovered a small branch which they thought to be some of the headwaters of Marys river. We camped all together this evening with our two Indian guides.

10th. This morning the Indians were dismissed and we gave them some powder and leads and balls which appeared to satisfy them for their service. We traveled about 14 miles today and encamped near the foot of a mountain with neither water water nor grass for our animals.[8]

11th. This morning we started early. Traveled about 14 [?] miles to the south west and found water and grass. Here we camped for the night.

12th. This morning left 2 waggons belonging to B[enjamin] Kelsey, their oxen being worn down by fatigue. They were compelled to leave their waggons and pack their baggage on horses and mules. We traveled about 10 miles today south west and camped at an excellent spring near a large plain covered with salt, partly surrounded by high mountains.

13th. Today we traveled about 15 miles on a south course, leaving large salt plains our left and light mountains to the right and camped at a spring of good water this evening.

14th. We started early this morning. Passed a number of good springs. Took dinner at one of them. We traveled on the border of the salt plain until night. The same plain that we traveled on yesterday, leaving it to the left and the mountains to the right. These plains border on the salt lake. In the evening we left the salt plain, turned our course to the west, crosed crosed the mountain through a gap and could find no water. We traveled until ten oclock at night and could find no water and was obliged to camp without water or grass.

15th. This morning we left the camp at daylight. Traveled 4 miles in the gap of another mountain and found a little water but not half enough to water the animals. Pased the mountain [and] traveled through a plain about 8 miles and came to water and grass at the foot of a large mountain. Here we encamped.

16th. Today we lay at camp and made pack saddles and packed up our goods [and] chattles for we left the ballance of the waggons here, 4 in number, for we cannot get them through to California.

17th. By morning we left the ballance of the waggons and some packed their goods on oxen. The oxen being not used to such sport run away and strewed the goods over the plain which caused some sport and a little trouble. Here we gave a great many things to the Indians not being able to take them along. One old Indian in particular appeared to be very thankful for every thing he received if any one gave him a present. He would hold it up between him and the sun and say over [it] a long preamble. This evening we traveled over a mountain and traveled until 10 oclock at night. Found no water nor grass. Traveled perhaps about 30 miles today.

18th. Left camp early this morning and came to water and grass about 10 oclock. Here we encamped. The Indians saw us and ran in every direction but when they saw that we were friendly with them, they came back and some of them made signs that a company had been here and killed some of them. We supposed it to have been Walker with a company of trapers about 6 years ago.

19th. This day we did not travel in consequence of Bidwell loosing his oxen on the night of the 17th. He left the camp alone and on the 19th inst. returned and brought his cattle with him. We killed a wolf and antelope today and an ox for beef.

20th. We crosed a high mountain today to our right and traveled about 20 miles. Crosed a handsome velley and camped at the foot of a high mountain near the foot of a high mountain near a small brook of water. Camped by an intermiting spring.

21st. We traveled on a south course today, having a rugged mountain on our right hand and some hot springs at the foot of the mountain. The water in them is boiling hot. It is strongly [ink smear, illegible] substance [ink smear, illegible] taste and appearance. This is found where the water came up from the edge of the streams and small lakes and is white like potash. Where the water dries up the ground is covered with it. We traveled about 12 miles today. Killed on antelope and camped at a small brook near the foot of the mountains.

22nd. This morning we were a little surprised by a band of the natives about the time that we were ready for starting. About 100 of them surrounded us. They were well armed with bow and arrows, guns and lances and knives. They tried to get into our corell [corral] and mix in with us under pretence of trading with us, but we beckned [beckoned] them to shove off which made them look very angry. They stood all in a line close along side of our camp with their weapons in their hands ready for battle while part of our men kept them off and the ballance loaded the pack animals. The Indians followed us nearly all day and some of them camped near us all night. We traveled near 15 miles today keeping the same mountain [on] our right hand that we traveled along side of yesterday and camped at the foot of it on a stream that run from the mountain.

23rd. This morning the Indians all left us. We traveled westward [and] crosed the mountain on our right. Traveled about 20 miles today and camped on the bank of a small creek, the head of the south branch of Marys river. Here we caught a few small trout.

24th. We traveled down the stream today about 24 miles and camped on its bank. We killed an ox this evening for beef.

25th. Today we traveled about 16 miles down the creek through a deep valley with high cliffs on each side. We found the banks dry today for about 8 miles and camped on its bank this evening.

26th. This morning we came to the east branch of the river and traveled down the river about 18 miles and camped near its bank on the north side. No timber here except willows.

27th. Today we traveled about 25 miles down Marys river through a deep valley with clifts of rock on each side some times perpendicular for some hundred feet through which the river runs in a southwest course. We camped on the bank of the river this evening where the valley widens a little. We killed an ox this evening for beef.

28th. We followed the river about 26 miles today in a northwest course and encamped its banks. The valley is wide here and the mountain not high. We see plenty of Indian signs today and where they have made fish traps along the river and fresh signs at their camps but have not seen any since we came to this river until this evening. A few of the Root digers [diggers] came to us this evening. They are poor and nearly naked and barefooted.

29th. Traveled about 20 miles today in a west course and camped on the bank of the river.

30th. We traveled about 14 miles today in northwest course and camped on the bank of the river.

Oct[ober] 1st. Today we traveled about 22 miles to the northwest and camped on the bank of the river in the evening.

2nd. This day we traveled about 20 miles westward and camped on the bank of the river in the evening. We saw a good many natives today, perhaps 200. They were friendly and some of them came and traded with with us at night. They told us that two days travel would take us to the mouth of this river where it forms lakes which have no outlet.

3rd. We traveled about 12 miles today, a southwest course over sandhills and plains of loose sand which made hard traveling. We camped on the bank of the river this evening and killed a beef and a few ducks.

4th. To[day] we traveled about 23 miles in a southwest course and camped on the bank of the river. The valley is wide here with mountains on each side of the river and and a high range of mountains west of us running north and south.

5th. Today we only came about 3 miles and camped on the bank of the river. Our animals are growing poor and even the grass is getting scarce here. There is no grass in these mountain valleys except on the lowest banks of the stream .and this river has high banks in general.

6th. This day we did not travel but stayed at camp and killed an ox for beef.

7th. Traveled about 22 miles today through deep dust which was both disagreeable and fatiguing. Captain Bartleson and nine others went ahead and left the Company today for California for having the tough animals, being all mules, they thought they could leave us behind and have the first site [sight] of the beautiful plains of California. Our animals are giving out. Left one horse and mule today and threw away some havy [heavy] bagage [baggage]. We camped tonight at a small Lake near the first Lake that the river emties [empties] into.

8th. We traveled but about 4 miles today for we hired an Indian to guide who told us that we would have to camp here or get to no other watering place today.

9th. Our guide made signs to us that we must start early or we could not get to water so we made an early start. Crosed the outlet of the first Lake and traveled about 30 miles in a south course and came to another small Lake. Here we camped. There are a great many Indians at these Lakes. They appear to be friendly. One of the company lost a mule yesterday and the Indian found it and brought him to us today. We hired an Indian to guide us across the California mountains. We understood by his signs that we could over 3 days from the time we should get to the foot of it.

10th. We traveled about 17 miles today and camped on the bank of the middle Lake for there are three Lakes which drain Marys river. There are a great many kind of fowls here.

11th. We traveled about 20 miles today, a south course in the mountains, and came to a stream which some supposed to be the head waters of the Sacrimenta [Sacramento] but it seemed to run the [w]rong course. Here we encamped for the night and killed a beef. This stream is about 40 yds wide here and affords good clear water and some timber known by the name of Balm of Gilead, and a pine here and there.

12th. Today we only traveled 4 miles for our Indian guide told us that we could not get water without a hard day travel and we camped on the bank of the creek. We lay on last night 4 miles above this river. [It] runs eastward.

13th. Today we traveled about 25 miles in a southwest course. Crosed the creek that we camped on the last two nights at the foot of a high mountain where we encamped this evening.

14th. This day we traveled about 20 miles in a southwest course. Crosed two high ridges and camped near the California mountains.

15th. Traveled about 10 miles in a south course today up the creek and encamped at the foot of the California mountains. The mountains here are partly covered with fine timber.

16th. Today we did not travel but lay by to rest our animals. The men that left us on the 7th of this month came to us this morning following our trail. They followed the stream that we thought to be the Sacrimenta [Sacramento] to its mouth where it empties into a Lake having no outlet. They said that they had suffered much for want of food, allowacing [allowing] themselves on[ly] one meal a day. Our Indian pilot left us last night and left us in a bad condition here. We are nearly surrounded by high mountains on all sides. We see no prospect of getting over the mountains. They are very high and the top covered [with] snow and we have but 3 more cattle to live on and they are poor and consequently we have to live on small allowance or starve.

17th. This morning we set out to try to get over the mountains. We traveled up a deep valley on a southwest course and through thick forests of timber, over high ridges and small streams of pure water rushing down the mountain, roaring and foaming over the rocks. These forests and fine streams of water have to us a beautiful appearance after traveling so long through an allmost entire Desert. We seen some Indians today and traded with them for some venison. We traveled about 16 miles today and camped in the mountain on a small brook that ran from the snow peaks. There are thick forests of pines near our camp of which has a bark resembling beach which is smoothe and white. The wood is very heavy and full of pitch. The air is geting cool as we assend the mountain.

18th. Today we crosed the main ridge of the mountains of California in the morning about 10 oclock and descended a deep and narrow rocky valley on the west side of it, covered with tall trees of pine, hemlock, cedar and fir, some of them a little over 200 feet high and camped in the same valley on the bank of a small stream which we followed from the top of the mountain.

19th. We traveled hard all day and did not get more than 10 miles on account of the way being so rough, rocky and bushy with forests of timber, the largest that I have ever seen, some perhaps 300 feet high. We were obliged to camp this evening on a site of the mountain where there is scarely any grass for the animals.

20th. This morning finding ourselves blocked up in this valley of the creek and surrounded on all sides by high mountains and rock, we thought it best that 2 or 3 men should go ahead on foot and look out for the way to get through. Accordingly 3 men set out on foot and went down the creek. 2 ventured on back a while after they had started but with some dificulty for having to go down so steep [a] place near the near the creek that was so dificult that I had my doubts about geting back again, but a short distance from this place I met two of the men returning to camp. They told me they thought it possible and I went on but did not meet the other man. His name was Hoper [Hopper]. He returned some other way and told them that the way was not pasable and they had to turn back a few miles and leave the valley, but [they] did not leave that day on account of my being absent. I went on down the creek a few miles and waited for the company until night, but no one came here. I camped by the side of a frightful looking precipice. My gun fired accidentally as I lit from my horse this evening and the muzzle was so close to my head that the powder burned my ear and frightened the horse so that [he] jumped and knocked my gun into the creek, but I lost no time in geting it dry again.

21st. This morning I started down the creek but finding the valley inaccessible, the creek runing through a cragged place of rock below, I was obliged to try to get out on one side or the other so I tryed to get out on the north side that I might either return to the camp or strike the Companys trail, but finding it impossible to get out on the north, I went out on the south side and crosed a high spur of the mountain and returned to the creek in the evening where I encamped on its banks. By this time I became hungry having nothing to eat since I left the Company but a few bunches of grapes which I found on the bank of the creek. Here I found plenty of rushes for my horse to eat and eat some myself.

22nd. This morning I started down the creek but finding the valley impasable, I made an attempt to get out on the north side which I affected with much dificulty and traveled on a northwest course, hoping that I might cross the Companys trail, but seen no sign of them. I traveled about 14 miles today over a high spur of the mountain. Had nothing to eat except a few grass seeds. This evening I camped on the bank of another creek with [which] runing through a valley similar to that I left this morning. Here I saw a number of Indian huts but camped behind some rocks to keep from being discoverd by them.

23rd. This morning I crosed on the bank of last night which took me until noon and until nearly night to get out of the other side on account of the deep valley of rocks which it runs through. I was obliged to slide my horse down some places nearly perpendicular for a 100 ft. I camped this night on the side of the mountain by a small spring of water without any thing to eat except a few small frogs that I picked up this evening. I gave up all hope of seeing the Company and trying to steer my course into Californias plains.

24th. Today I traveled about 30 miles in a northwest course, asscended a mountain that took me until the afternoon and descended it in the evening to a creek. Here I camped and found a few bunches of grapes.

25th. I left the creek this morning, asscended a high mountain on the north side of the creek with some dificulty. This evening I shot at a hawk which had a squirrel in its claws. Did not kill the hawk but made it drop the squirrel. This gave me some relief being nearly all I had to eat since I left the Company. I camped this evening on a small brook where I roasted my squirrel.

26th. This day I asscended a high ridge. Traveled on a west course until evening and camped on a small brook near some Indian huts. Tonight there came a heavy rain and I suffered much from the want of a shelter.

27th. This morning the rain ceased and I started as soon as I could to get a little dryer for the rain wet every thing that I had. This seemed to be the last high mountain that I had to cross. The land seemed to lower on the west. I traveled perhaps about 12 miles today and camped near the foot of the mountain. Found nothing to eat today except a few acorns.

28th. Today I traveled all day amongst the hills which are covered with oak and long leafed pines and now and then a handsome valley. The acorns here are fequently more than 3 inches long. This night I came to some Indian camps about sunset. I thought that I should be safer at their camps than to camp alone near or in sight of them and accordingly made signs that I wished to stay with them. They did not appear willing at first, but I made signs to them that there was a large company coming on in the morning and that I would start early and the company should not interrupt them and they agreed for me to stay. They gave me some acorn bread and a kind of pine seeds to eat and also a kind of soup made of acorns. They did not appear to be hostile but I seemed to be a great curiosity to them. I stayed here until morning uninterrupted but kept a good look out, keeping my gun and pistols near me.

29th. I left here early this morning. Saw an Indian dog which I took to be a wolf and shot it and being verry hungry, took part of it and hung it to my saddle. I had not gone far before I heard the Indians rising the whoop and persuing me. I was in a bad condition to flee before them, my horse so near worn out that he could scarcely raise a trot and myself nearly famished with hunger and havin[g] to pass through a thick growth [of] brush and over rocky ground, but I got through into a clear place before they overtook me. I lit from my horse to prepare for battle for I had a rifle and four horse pistols well charged. They came within about 100 paces. I thought I would try a plan to deceive them. I raised a yell as loud as I could, beckning at the same time toward a thick clump of trees that stood near me. They perhaps thought that the company that I was telling them of last evening were laying here in ambush for they turned about and fled as fast as their legs could carry them and as they ran I changed my voice as much as I could in order to make [them] think several persons present. I counted 12 of them as they ran and watched them until they were out of sight and then led my horse down a small valley of smooth rocks to prevent them from tracking me and went on in peace until I had an opportunity of roasting my dogmeat which [I] did not relish verry well, but being hungry made out to eat it. I traveled about 20 miles today. Camped in hearing of some Indians near a small creek.

30th. Today I was followed by 3 Indians. I pointed my gun at them and becned [beckoned] to them to go back, which they did. This evening I camped on a small creek in the plain. Saw a few deer and killed a badger which was fat and made me a great feast. Came perhaps 15 miles today.

31st. Today I traveled down the creek in a south course and seem plenty of deer. Killed one in the evening which was in good order. Here I camped on the bank of a creek called the Cosameie [Cosumnes]. Tonight my horse left me and I remained here 3 nights. Dried some meat. Could find nothing of my horse but seen signs of horses and cattle and also found a Spanish saddle stirup and saw a small path which crosed the creek and led in a north direction.

4th. This morning I hid my saddle and such things as I could not carry and took with me my sadlebag, pistols and some dried meat. I hid my gun barrel also for I broke the stalk [stock] off it the night I camped here for when I shot the buck it was about to run and being in a hurry creased him in the neck. He fell but when I approached him, he raised and made battle with me and having nothing else in in my hand, I pelted him over the head with my gun. I went on down the creek in hope of finding some settlers but found that [it] turned into a flat tula [tule] swamp. I returned and took the path that led across the creek in a north course. Traveled over a plain about 12 miles and came to a lake where I sit down to rest. I saw a Indian on the opposite side of the Lake. They were afraid of me and went back to their camp. I went down the neck of the Lake and saw their chief approaching me cautiously. I becned to him to come to me which he did. He spoke Spanish which I could not under stand. I made signs to him that I wished to go to some settlements. He told me to come to his camp and there would be 2 men there in the evening and they would take me to a house. I stayed here and roasted fish until evening for they were fishing in the Lake with a sein which is near the bank of the Sacrimenta [Sacramento]. About sunset two Indians came on horses and took me and my baggage to Captain Siuter's [Sutter's] house, a distance of 6 miles. Captain Siuter has a fort here made of dobies [adobes] and burned brick, mounted with a few old cannons and guarded by about 29 men, mostly runaway sailors and Canackers or Owihees [Hawaiians] besides a number of pet Indians which he employs for war parties and who built his fort and farm. He keeps also a harem of Canacker [Hawiian] women. This place is called New Helvetia. He has a farm attached to it of perhaps 150 acres in cultivation and also a great number of cattle and horses and mules. This place is situated about two miles from the Sacrimenta [Sacramento] river and about the same distance from the mouth of a small river called the American fork of the Sacrimenta.

[Note. Here John's diary ends. It is then followed by "Extract from Bidwell's journal from the 20th of Oct[ober] to the 4th of Nov[ember]." This is the only known surviving text of the original journal kept by Bidwell on the trek west. Sentence structure and punctuation have been supplied.]

Extract From John Bidwell Journal

Oct[ober] 20th. This morning we sent out men in diferent directions to see if there was any means of extricating ourselves from this place without going back. Some proceeded down the creek and others climbed the mountain. They returned and reported that it was impossible to go down the creek. Capt. Bartleson being impatient left the Company. 8 men went with him but was obliged to wait all day and rest his animals before he could return, while the ballance of the company went on up the mountain directly north or towards the sky about 4 miles and here they camped and found grass and water. Killed an ox.

21st. Our rout was tolerable today but not verry good. We travled about 10 miles and camped. Bartleson overtook us. We could see no termination of the mountains.

22nd. Today we descended towards a creek and had a tolerable road. The timber getting larger and taller. Travled 19 miles today and camped a mile from the small creek. Here we killed the last ox and the only one. Here saw some oak and some thought it was live oak. Indians came to camp this evening.

23. Meat grew scarce in camp. Having only 3 days scanty provision, it became necessary to use all means in our power to kill game which was scarce. 5 of our horses gave out today. We camped near the creek.

24th. This morning we hired 2 Indians as guides but they led us into a dificult place and left us perhaps to pick up the horses we left behind. We crosed the creek today and camped on the south side of it. Travled 6 miles today.

25th. Travled 6 miles today and found it impossible to proceed. Went back about 2 miles and dug a hole in the earth to hide such things that we could not travel with but found the indians watching us. We camped here and found white oak timber.

26th. Went a south course today about 3 miles and camped and threw away every thing that we could spare to lighten the packs.

27th. Commenced raining this morning and rained until noon. We travled about 4 miles today. Some were in favor of killing all their horses and hauling on foot. They were afraid that winter had set in for the mountains were coverd with snow the night before. Some Indians still followed after us, the same that led us into this place to pick up horses and other things that we left behind. A man by the name of Cook shot one of them.

28th. Today the travling was rough. Some horses were killed by falling down the ridge of the mountain. They killed some of their horses to eat for the provision has run out. Travled about 9 miles today and camped.

29th. This morning 2 horses were missing. We supposed that the Indians had taken them for we saw many of them near and found bones of horses in many places.[9] Travled about 9 miles today. By this time many were without horses.

30th. This morning we set out early and about 10 oclock we discovered that we were getting into the plains of California which had a beautiful appearance. We travled until night but found neither grass nor water for the season had been so dry that the fire had burned up all the grass, but we saw signs of elk and wild cattle, bears and other game.

31st. We set out this morning. Came to a stream which we had not followed in the mountains. We found it to be a branch of the St. Joaquin river. The valley of this river has been burned and the young grass sprung up. We came to the main river today and saw numerous herds of elk and wild cattle and other animals, some of which we killed. This was lucky for we were starving.

Nov[ember] 1st. We didnot leave today but lay bye. Killed and feasted on deer and elk and antelope. The land here is fertile and large oaks near the river.

2nd. Today part of the company went about 6 miles and the ballance stayed at camp to save meat and give their animals rest. Here we found great quantities of grass which were good and to our surprize Jones, one of the 2 men who left the Company on the night of the 23rd of last month to hunt has returned to camp. Him and his partner, Andrew Kelsey, had come into the plains 4 days before the Company. They found an Indian who piloted them to the settlement to the house of a man by the name of Marsh and now Jones had returned to met [meet] the Company and brought some sugar and flour with him. Some Indians came with him. They said there had been no rain there for 18 months and no wheat raised.

3rd. This morning the foremost of the company waited until the ballance came up and all started about noon for Marshes house. Travled about 16 miles. Reached the St. Joaquin and crosed it.

4th. Travled about 25 miles today. Saw numerous herds of elks and came to Mr. Marshes house.

Notes to the First James John Diary

1 This was George [James?] Shotwell. He was buried by the Rev. Joseph Williams.
2 This was Fort Lupton, only recently constructed by John Lupton, a former U.S. Army officer turned trader.
3 George Simpson and Elisha Stone turned back at Fort Laramie. One of the unnamed two men was Richard Phelan, whom John calls Cockrel, a fur trader, who subsequently married the widow, Mrs. Gray.
4 This was a fur brigade under the leadership of Henry Fraeb. In the fall of 1840, Fraeb and Joseph R. Walker had visited southern California. There they traded with Abel Stearns, a longtime Yankee settler and shopkeeper in Los Angeles. Stearns purchased 417 pounds of beaver for $1,147. In exchange, Fraeb and Walker received in payment supplies, including beans, coffee, soap, sugar, tobacco, and some *aguardiente* (California brandy), along with 100 mares, priced at $2 each, 17 mules at $12 a head, and 2 stallions at $10 each. Business Accounts, Stearns Papers, Box 73, Huntington Library, San Marino. As to the number in Fraeb's party, John's diary is the only source that provides a figure. Hafen, "Henry Fraeb," in Hafen, ed., *The Mountain Men*, III: 136–137.
5 The pilot had been Thomas Fitzpatrick, famed Mountain Man.
6 The use of the word "Stormwood" in this sentence most likely refers to the German word *Krummholz* (elfinwood in English), which means a forest of twisted and stunted trees on the top of a mountain, buffeted by heavy winds and jet propelled ice crystals in winter.
7 Richard Grant was in command of Fort Hall, which belonged at the time to the Hudson's Bay Company.
8 Beginning with this entry, John repeats a word now and then in his diary. These repetitions are transcribed as in the original manuscript.
9 The Indians west of the Sierras had developed a fondness for horse flesh and raided California ranchos to obtain it.

The Second James John Diary

I left Westport [now included in the boundaries of Kansas City, Mo.] on the 16th day of May, 1841, for California. Stayed this night four miles east of the Saplin [Sapling] Grove.

May 17—Stayed this night about 11 miles from the Wakarootia creek, and crossed it at 12 o'clock on the 18th. This night we encamped at a creek by the name of the above mentioned that we crossed yesterday. Here we met with some difficulty. One of our oxen strayed and we did not get them until ten o'clock in the morning.

May 19—This night we camped at a spring 20 miles from the Canzes [Kansas] river.

May 20—This morning we set out for the crossing place. We had not gone far before we [met] two of the company coming back to meet us. They told us that the rest of the company had gone on ahead. They helped us to push on and we got to the river at three o'clock, and got all our bagage and waggon animals, etc., across the river at sunset. The indians were very active in helping us across. They floated the baggage over in buffaloe hides, swimming and pushing them before them.

May 21—This morning we set out to overtake the company. We had not gone far before five of the company came riding up and told us that the company was two days ahead of us. They stayed until we got up with them, which happened on the 23d. This day we met 14 Pawnee Indian Warriors armed and equipped for battle. They shook hands with us and appeared to be friendly. One of the men gave them some tobacco which pleased them very much. We went on and encamped on a large creek called Blue. There we overtook the company who were waiting there for us. Here we caught some fine fish and stayed until morning.

May 24—This day we arrived at another creek about one o'clock; it being very high, we were obliged to camp there until morning.

May 25—We crossed the creek at 7 o'clock this morning. Here we caught some fish and some of the company seen a gang of elk. We encamped this night on a small creek.

May 26—We left here at 7 o'clock. One of the waggons broke down. Today we seen about 30 Pawnee Indians today. They were very friendly and were well armed with bows, lances and guns, prepared to meet the Caws [Kaws]. One of the mule teams run away and broke the hounds of their wagon. This night we encamped at a small creek.

May 27—Left here early this morning. The route is a little broken today and the heat oppressive. Camped this night at a handsome little creek about 15 miles from the place where stayed last night.

May 28—Set out this morning early. Stopped and took breakfast at a beautiful creek of pure water at 9 o'clock. Left there at 10 o'clock and arrived at a creek called the Big Blue. There we encamped this day. One of the men killed one antelope. The heat was oppressive today. We have killed one antelope and a few deer and turkeys since we started for California and that is about all we have killed.

May 29—Started early this morning. Killed two antelope. Encamped on the banks of the Blue this evening. for we are traveling on the banks of that stream. It rises eastward and we are going west. Encamped on same stream this night.

May 30—Started early this morning at 7 o'clock. Killed one deer and antelope today. Stayed this night on the banks of the Blue.

May 31—Started early this morning at 7 o'clock. Met 5 waggons going from Fort Laramer [Laramie] to Independence. They said it would be 4 days before we would get to any buffalo. They were loaded with peltry, buffalo hides, etc. We traded with them for some buffalo meat and moccasins. We are about 4 hundred miles west of Independence, traveling through sandy but fertile plains.

We are still traveling on the Blue. Left the Blue this morning and encamped on the prairie.

1841 — June 1 — Left here. Encamped on the banks of the Platte at two o'clock. Here we encamped. There came up a small cloud, with the appearance of a light shower of rain. As it arose it grew darker. The thunder roared, the rain and hail came until the ground was covered with hail as large as partridge eggs, and some four times as large. The rain ceased a little while in the evening, but commenced again and rained nearly the whole night. The guards had a bad night for standing. All the baggage and every thing the rain could get at was in a dreadful condition in the morning; but as bad as the weather was there was a wedding in the camp this night — Mr. Kelsey to Miss Williams by Rev. Mr. Joseph Williams.

June 2 — This morning a council was held for the purpose of regulating the time of starting, which was agreed on to be at 30 minutes after six o'clock in the morning; but we did not early this morning on account of being so well drenched with rain and hail. The animals need no salt here. The ground is covered with salt for [in] many places. We stopped today at noon near the head of Grand Island to dry our clothing. Went on about 12 miles and camped on the banks of the Platte.

June 3 — This day went about 20 miles. Encamped on the Platte. There was another shower of rain today, and the air was cool.

June 4 — Today we started early. Traveled briskly along the banks of the Platte until in the afternoon, when some of our men scattered out from the Company to hunt antelope. One of them being alone, slipping along to get a shot at an antelope, was surrounded by a band of Shina [Cheyenne] Indians and robbed of his mule, gun and pistol. They tried to get his clothing off him, but he tore loose from them. He came up with the Company and informed the captain of the circumstance. Immediately part of the Company were sent back to recover the property. The Indians came, meeting them. The teamsters hastened to put their wagons in order battle. Some were panic struck. They saw the Indians coming, 30 in number, — appeared to them to be an army of thousands. When, lo! 30 Indians came and brought the property and restored it to the Company. They were very friendly. They came to our camp, shook hands and smoked the pipe of peace and encamped about 50 yards from us this night.

June 5 — This morning we set out before sunrise. Stopped at 7 o'clock for breakfast. We seen six flat bottom boats land a little below us on the river. Some of their crews came to us and informed us that they were from Fort Laramie, and that we were about 400 miles from that place. We seen numerous herds of buffalo today on the opposite side of the river from us, and have killed two antelopes today. There came a tremendous hail and rain storm this afternoon. The wind blew very hard where we were, and on the opposite side of the river it blew tremendous. We saw trees flying in the air and water blowing up out of the river as high apparently as the clouds. After the storm had abated somewhat we travelled about a mile farther and found hail stones as large as geese eggs. We made a very lucky escape not to be in the midst of it, but there were some large hail where we were. We went on and encamped again on the banks of the Platte. We had not more than got our tent spread before another storm of the same kind came on and lasted until night, leaving the ground covered with hail. It drowned out all the fires in the camp, and wet the most of our baggage, and left us in an unpleasant situation.

June 6th — This morning we set out early, accompanied by 12 Indians, who encamped with us. They were of the Chian [Cheyenne] nation; they travelled and encamped with us perhaps for protection from the Pawnees. This day we killed 3 elk. The weather was cool until twelve o'clock; then it turned warm, and rained at night. We encamped this night on the banks of the Platte. The Indians left today.

June 7th — Started at 7 o'clock this morning. Travelled almost 20 miles today and encamped on the banks of a small creek. The hunters killed two buffaloes today. The captain sends out a small party of men every day by turn for the purpose of killing meat for the company. We had another storm of rain and wind this evening, but not very much rain.

June 8th — This day we killed some four buffaloes and a few rabbits and encamped in the evening on the south fork of the Platte river. The buffaloes are very plenty here. We have seen several herds today consisting of perhaps some hundreds.

June 9th — Today we crossed the river at the same place that we encamped at last evening. The river being wide we occupied nearly the whole day in crossing. It is about 14 hundred yards wide here and has a sandy bed. The water is of the same culler [color] as that of the Missourie. We have seen, I believe, a thousand buffaloes today. We have killed 2 of them today. We forded the river with our loaded wagons, which were 19 in number. The bottom is so level that the water is about three feet deep nearly all the way across. We encamped this night on the opposite side to where we lay last night.

June 10th — This day was pleasant. We travelled about 25 miles today; killed but one buffalo, but was in sight of them all day. The river banks were lined with them. We can kill as many as we want. We encamped this evening on the banks of the south fork of the Platte. The plains here are sandy. The river has a level plain on each side; next to the plains there is on each side a ridge of sand hills.

June 11th — This morning we were a little surprised. The oxen strayed away from the camp. Two of the men went after them and saw four or five Indians driving them off. They came back running their horses and told the news. Twelve of the Company immediately set out to rescue the cattle. When the Indians seen us coming they left the cattle and fled, and we got them all safe to the camp again. We left the camp at 7 o'clock this morning. One of the men acted very imprudent. He was riding by the side of a clump of willows near the place where he seen the Indians driving away the oxen. He, being enraged at them, fired at the Indians, but they could not be found. Some of the company had a little sport today in killing a buffalo bull. They shot him 20 times or upwards before he fell. There is a great many prairie dogs here. They burrow in the ground and are about the size of a common house cat. This evening we encamped on the bank of the Platte. This day has been a warm day.

June 12th—Left the south fork of the Platte this morning and arrived at the north fork of the Platte about noon. Took dinner here. Seen no buffaloes today except one. Encamped this night on the bank of the north fork of the Platte.

June 13th—This morning a bad accident happened [to] one of our men. I was out of the camp helping to keep the oxen from straying away (for we have to let them feed on grass and watch them to keep the Indians from driving them away), and while I was there I heard a gun fire in the camp and heard some man scream. I went to the camp, saw one of our men lay bleeding on the ground. He had shot himself with his gun. He was pulling his gun from his wagon by the muzzle and the lock caught something and fired and shot him through the left side. He lived about an hour and died. We buried him in the sand on a hill about a half of a mile from the camp.[1] The company appointed a committee of five men to appoint an administrator for the estate of the deceased, which they did. The captain was appointed. We had a sermon delivered on the occasion by the Rev. Mr. Williams. We left there at 11 o'clock and went to Ash Creek. There we encamped and killed an elk.

June 14th—This being a rainy day we did not leave here until the [next day].

15th—This morning we left here. The air has been cold for three days. The name of the creek we camped at last night is Ash Creek. Killed one deer there. The river here is wide, like the south fork, and has hills on each side consisting of sand and rock, and narrow plains next the water. We encamped this night about 15 miles farther up the river.

June 16th—This morning we left the camp at the usual hour. The day was pleasant. We made a good day's drive. Killed some rabbits and three antelopes, but have not seen a buffalo for 4 days. We seen some wild horses on the opposite side of the river today. The land here is almost entirely destitute of timber. There is some cedar along the creeks and on the islands, a few ash trees, some mountain cherries and currants of the largest size I have ever seen. We encamped this evening on the banks of the Platte.

June 17th—We left the camp this morning at 7 o'clock. Crossed a creek of excellent water at 9 o'clock. Seen a considerable quantity of pine timber today, along the creeks and bluffs. Two of the hunters went out yesterday and did not return until 12 o'clock last night. They brought in some buffaloe meat with them, and had seen no Indians. We encamped on the bank of the river near the mouth of a large creek in sight of a rock or clay peak called the Chimney [Chimney Rock], and in sight of a large clay mount which has the appearance of a large mansion house [Courthouse Rock.]

June 18th — This morning we started at six o'clock. The weather is fine and the air pure. We traveled about 25 miles today and encamped about two miles from the Chimney or clay peak. It is a sharp peak of clay mingled with rock. We have killed no buffaloes today, but have [seen] 2 of them, and killed two antelopes and one deer.

June 19th — This morning we left camp at the 30 minutes past six o'clock. The air is cool today and the wind blows hard. We have killed two mountain sheep and 3 elk today and one antelope. We encamped this evening near a deep ravine of water nearly surrounded by high bluffs which have a splendid appearance.

June 20 — We left here this morning at six o'clock. Took dinner on the banks of Horse creek. This is a cold, windy, disagreeable day for traveling. This night we encamped on the banks of the Platte about thirty miles from F. Laramy [Fort Laramie].

June 21 — This morning we set out at the usual hour. The day pleasant except it is very windy, for one would judge from the shortness of the timber that it is always the case here. The hills are sandy and in some places rocky. Some have the appearance of chalk, consisting of a substance resembling plaster paris. We see but few buffaloes here, but have plenty of meat in the camp yet. There is plenty of small game. We enjoy good health, excepting two or three persons, who have been complaining for a few days, myself for one. We have killed no game today, but one antelope. We encamped this evening on the banks of the Platte.

June 22d — This day we arrived at Fort Laramy at 10 o'clock. The fort is on the north side of the river Laramy's fork, which we had to cross. It runs into the Platte half a mile from the fort. There is another fort building about half a mile from it. Its proprietor's name is Lupton. The new fort is on the banks of the Platte. We have encamped this night in sight of both forts.

June 23d — We lay this day where camped last evening, in sight of both forts. Fort Laramee is situated on the north side of Laramey fork on the bank of the river. It has a pleasant site. It is built of a kind of brick made of clay not burned. They are 8 inches wide and 16 inches long. The fort is not finished at this time. The wall is 16 inches wide on the top and at the bottom it is 3 feet, and 160 feet by 120 feet square. When finished it will be plastered with lime and white washed all around outside. The other fort is about one mile from it, on the main fork of the Platte river. It is called Fort John, and will be built in the same way.[2] We can see some of the Black Hills from these forts which are 50 miles distant. I visited thse forts today, but cannot give a full description of them as they are not finished. The river here is narrow and the water low.

June 24 — This day we left the forts and went about 16 miles by way of the road, but only 8 miles across the hills. We encamped in a deep valley and concluded to stay here until morning, for there is no water after we leave here for 20 miles. Near this encampment there is a large spring of clear water. It runs out of the side of the hill. The stream is large enough for an overshot mill. The valley is surrounded by high hills of limestone, with some scattering cedar and pine growing on them. We have seen no Indians lately except about 20 Soos [Sioux] at the fort. The men at the forts are nearly all French and Spanish. Some of them have squaws for their wives which they buy of the parents of the same.

June 25 — We left the camp and warm spring this morning at 7 o'clock. We travelled about 20 miles today over high hills and through deep valleys, but there is plenty of game here and good water and a kind of a mountain turnip. They are about as large as hen's eggs and are tender and good eating; also there is currants and mountain cherries. We were overtaken today by two men and a squaw from the fort. They are going to the mountains with us. Two of our men left us at the forts, but their place is filled by these men, and a squaw thrown in.[3] We saw a good number of buffaloes today, but have not killed any of them. We encamped in a valley. There is plenty of good water here and excellent grass for the cattle and horses and mules. The grass is equal to timothy grass, if not better. It is of different kinds in the valley. It resembles blue grass of the States. It grows tall here and thin on hills and plains and short [and thick in the valleys].

June 26 — This morning we started at 3 minutes past six o'clock. Took dinner on the bank of a creek of good water and grass. In the afternoon myself and two others went out to hunt buffaloes. We killed one and wounded another. We packed our horses and set out for the place where [we] expected to find the wagons, but they had went a different way and encamped on the Platte on the main branch. We travelled until 12 o'clock at night before we reached the camp. There are some gray bears [grizzlies] there which are monsters. Large, but we have killed none of them yet. Some more hunters killed a buffalo today.

June 27 — We left the Platte early this morning. Travelled until 4 o'clock in the afternoon. Encamped on the bank af a creek of muddy water. There is but few springs in this country. The ground is so sandy that the water sinks. We killed one buffaloe today and some small game.

June 28 — We started early this morning. Took dinner on the banks of a creek of good water, and as beautiful grass as I have ever seen. The grass is generally good in the valleys, but on the hills and plains it appears to be dried up. Near our dining place is a large cleft of rocks as white as snow. The rocks are a little harder than common chalk, and some of the earth is composed of this substance, which is the genuine plaster paris, or believed to be by most of the company. We left here and after a hard half day's drive camped on a creek near a spring of excellent water. We killed one buffaloe today. Seen some gray dears [bears], but did not kill them.

June 29 — Did not start early this morning on account of some of the cattle straying away. We took dinner on a small creek. We are now traveling through the Black Hills, over high hills and through deep valleys. The hills are composed of different kinds of substances, some of granite, and some of fine sand, and some of a substance resembling chalk, and some of plaster paris and red stone and clay, also red sand in some places. They have a beautiful appearance. We encamped this evening on the bank of the north fork of the Platte river, about 200 miles from the main ridge of the Rocky Mountains. We are now in sight of some high mountains.

June 30th — Left the camp at six o'clock this morning. Took [dinner] on the bank of that river. The day was pleasant. We made a good day's travel. Encamped on the bank of the Platte. Killed five buffaloe cows today and two bulls. The river is about 200 yards wide here.

July 1, 1841 — This day we crossed the north fork of the Platte river about a mile from where we encamped last evening. We had some difficulty in crossing as the ford was deep and the water ran very swift. We got over safe, all excepting two teams — one drowned, a mule, and the other turned over the wagon, but did not lose much. We encamped on the north side of the river this night, about two miles from where we stayed last night.

July 2d — Left the camp early this morning and traveled on the banks of the river. Killed 2 buffaloes. The country is sandy here and broken on the south side of the river. There is a range of high hills or mountains covered with pine trees, but on the north side there is barren sand hills and plains. We encamped on the bank of the river this evening.

July 3d — This day we traveled until about two o'clock and encamped for the night. Killed one buffaloe and two deer today. One of the men by the name of Belder [Belden] lost his horse yesterday when he was hunting buffaloe. He hitched his horse and could not find the place again. Himself and another man went back this morning, but the horse was gone. They found the place where the horse was hitched, but no horse.

July 4th — Started this morning at six o'clock. The day is warm and the road ruff. We traveled about 15 miles and encamped at an excellent spring of water. We are about a day's travel from a stream called Sweetwater. The country here is hilly, abounding in sand hills and sand rocks and mountains. There is plenty of buffaloes and grizly [grizzly]bears and wolves. Killed 3 buffaloes today.

July 5th — This morning we left the camp at the usual hour, and after a hard day's drive came to a creek called Sweetwater. There we encamped for the night. Killed some buffaloes today, and seen a good number of them. A band had liken to have run over some of the waggons, but we shot some of them and the others fled. We have seen no timber scarcely today, but a sandy plain nearly destitute of vegitation with now and then a cleft of rocks. Our encampment this night is near a rock called the independent [Independence] rock. It is a rock about 130 feet high of sollid [solid] granite.

July 6th — We left the Independent Rock this morning at the usual hour of starting. We are now in a valley that will lead us over the mountains. Nothing happened today worthy of notice excepting we seen some curiosity in the rocks along each side of the creek. There are mountains of granite rocks. The creek runs through a gap in a sollid rock which is not less than 250 feet high on each side and about 50 feet wide at the narrowest place. It is nearly perpendicular on one side and on the other it is shelvey [shelving] over. We encamped this evening on the banks of the Sweetwater creek which extends the whole length of this valley.

July 7th — This day was warm and the way rough. Nothing happened worth notice. We seen plenty of buffaloes and killed four. We encamped this night on the bank of the creek near a high cleft of rocks.

July 8th — This day was cool and the valley more level than it was yesterday. We made a good day's travel and seen a great number of buffaloes. Killed 3 and 2 antelopes. Encamped this evening on the bank of the Sweetwater Creek.

July 9th — This day we started at the usual hour. The route is sandy and hard travelling. We are now in sight of some high mountains which are covered with snow. We seen thousands of buffaloes today and killed 16 of them. We encamped this evening on the bank of creek.

July 10th — This morning was cold and the wind blew hard, which made it disagreeable traveling. Nothing happened worthy of notice today. We encamped on the bank of the creek this afternoon. There are a great many currants and gooseberries here.

July 11th — We stopped at the place we encamped at yesterday for the purpose of laying in a supply of meat for the ballance of the our journey for the old hunters say there is not buffaloes in the mountains and on the other side. We had poor success in killing buffaloes today. We have killed nothing but a cow and a steer, but their meet [meat] is of an excellent quality.

July 12 — We stayed at the same place today that we encamped on the 10th until 13th and dried buffalo meat. Today we killed four buffaloe cows and some turkey and [caught] some fish.

July 13th — This morning we left the encampment and traveled over some rocky country. Killed one buffaloe. We met two of our men about 10 o'clock that had been sent by the company on the 6th of July to the rendezvous on Green river to make some arrangements for [the] company in exchanging the oxteams for mules, etc.; but they found no person there, not even an Indian on the whole route. We have not seen an Indian, except two, that are with us, since we left the Laramee fort. We encamped this evening on the banks of the same creek last mentioned.

July 14th — This day we lay here for the purpose of killing and laying in more meat. We had a hard frost here this morning. We have killed a fine chance of buffaloe today. I do not know the number: perhaps about 8 or 9.

July 15th — This day we moved about 8 miles and camped until next day on Sweetwater creek. The nights are cool here and there is frost nearly every morning. There is no timber here except a few willows along the creek. We are at this time about 8 miles from what is called Wind river mountains. They are in sight of us and are covered with snow. We have seen them for the last 10 days. We leave them to the right hand.

July 16th — This day we moved about ten miles farther up the creek and encamped about noon for the purpose of drying meat and getting good range for our cattle and horses. We killed a good number of fowl which they call sage cocks. They are larger than a common domestic chicken.

July 17th — This morning I caught some good fish at the camp. We left the camp at 8 o'cock and moved about three miles farther up the creek. We have killed 3 buffaloe bulls today and a number of sage chickens. Buffaloes are getting scarce here. Nothing but bulls. There is no cows here.

July 18th — We left Sweetwater creek this morning at 6 o'clock and traveled about 17 miles and encamped on one of the head branches of the Coloradoe of the west. We have killed 2 buffaloe today and one antelope. The day was pleasant and we have had no rain since we left the north fork of the Platte river.

July 19th — This day we traveled about 15 miles and encamped on the bank of a creek called Big Sandy. There is good grass and the wild unions [onions] grow nearly 3 ft. high. We are still in sight of some mountains that we seen on the ninth day of this month and others that are covered with snow.

July 20th — Today we traveled hard all day, and did not get more than 7 or 8 miles on a straight line. Killed no game today except one antelope. We encamped on the bank of Big Sandy this evening. The valley is still destitute of timber and almost every thing else but sage. The valley is wider in some places than others, varying from one to 60 miles in width.

July 21st — This morning was pleasant and we traveled all day on the banks of Big Sandy, the same creek that we encamped on last evening and encamped on it this evening.

July 22d — Today we traveled about 12 miles and encamped at noon on the bank of Big Sandy. Here we stayed until the 23d. Today a man has returned to the camp who was sent out on the 14th to try to find some trader on Coloradoe river in order to get information respecting the route to California and get a pilot. He brought about 60 men with him who came to trade with us. They informed us that it was impossible for waggons to get to California, but they could get down on the Columbia without much trouble.

July 23d—This day we traveled about 10 miles and arrived at Green or Coloradoe river, attended by the men that came to us yesterday and a number of Snake Indians. The river here is about 100 yards wide and has a little timber on its banks, such as cottonwood and willow. Here we stayed until the 25th and traded with the Indians and trappers for packhorses, robes, etc. There is frost here nearly every night, but the days are warm and pleasant. The plains around here are barren and destitute of timber.

July 25th—Today we crossed the river and traveled about six miles down it and camped on its bank. The Snake Indians and trappers camped with us. There is no buffaloe here nor any other kind of game that we can kill except fish. We caught some good fish called chubs. The river is clear at this place and the water is very pure.

July 26th—This morning we left the river and went about 12 miles and encamped on the bank of a stream called Ham's Fork. It em[p]ties into Green River or Coloradoe. The Indians and some of the trappers camped with us this evening.

July 27th—Today we travelled about twelve miles up Ham's Fork and encamped on its banks for the night. Killed two antelope and caught some fish today. The nights are cool and sometimes frosty, the valley being surrounded by mountains that are covered with perpetual snow which has a tendency to cool the air at night.

July 28th—Today we travelled up Ham's Fork about 15 miles and encamped in the afternoon on its banks, for we frequently travel until the afternoon and lay bye until the next day. We caught some good fish here this afternoon. I caught 23 silver myself and one trout.

July 29th—Nothing happened today worthy of notice. We traveled about 10 or twelve miles farther up the creek and encamped on its banks in the afternoon.

July 30th—Today we traveled about 10 miles farther up the creek and encamped for the ballance of the day, for the pilot thought, as we had to leave the creek, we probably could not get to any more water this afternoon, therefore we encamped on its bank. The water is very good here and the grass is excellent in the creek bottom but the planes [plains] and mountains are barren and destitute of timber as far as we can see.

July 31st—We left Ham's Fork this morning and traveled about 15 miles and encamped on the bank of a small stream called Black's Fork of Green River. The way we traveled today was hilly, rough and rocky, and we were in sight of a large range of high mountains on our left which are covered with perpetual snow. There is a large smoke in sight and west of the encampment resembling that of a volcano, which we suppose to be grass set on fire by the Indians.

1841, August 1 — Today we traveled about 12 miles through a rough mountainous country and encamped on the bank of a small creek that enters into Black Fork.

August 2d — This day we went about 12 miles up one fork of the same branch that we encamped on last night. Here one of the waggons broke down and we were obliged to camp until morning and mend it. We are in a small valley this evening, surrounded by high hills and mountains, and in sight of mountains on the right and left or north and south that are covered with snow, some of which are, perhaps, more than one hundred miles off.

August 3d — We traveled about 20 miles today over high hills and rough places and arrived at Bear river and encamped on its bank. The river is about 50 yards wide here and has a sandy bottom and no timber on its banks excepting small willows. Killed one antelope today.

August 4th — Today we did not move from the camp, but lay by and caught a good number of trout, some of which were 18 inches in length. There is a great number wild geese here and other fowls, and antelopes.

August 5th — We traveled about 18 miles today down the bank of Bear River. We caught some trout, and killed a antelope and some wild geese. They are very plenty here.

August 6th — We traveled 21 miles today on the bank of Bear River. There is high hills and mountains on each side of the river. We caught a good number of fine trout, and other fish today and killed one Porquepine [porcupine] and some antelope.

August 7th — This morning we left the river and came to it again at twelve o'clock. Nooned at it and left it again on account of being closed in by high hills on each side. We came to it at night and encamped on its bank.

August 8th — We did not leave the camp today until twelve o'clock. We traveled about 10 miles and encamped on the bank of a small branch of pure spring water about a mile from the river. We have caught a great number of fish today, trout and chubs.

August 9th — Today we traveled about 15 miles on the bank of the river except in the afternoon we left the river and returned to it again in the evening and encamped on its bank. Killed two antelope today and caught a number of fine fish.

August 10th — We traveled about 10 miles today and arrived at the Soda springs on the banks of Bear river. There is a great number of these springs which are constantly bub[b]ling and throwing off gass. Some spout water to a considerable distance and roar like a steamboat. Others form mounds which are round. The water boils out of the middle and forms them by the sediment running down the side. There are high mountains here on each side of the river.

August 11th — Today we traveled about 4 miles and the company became divided; 4 carts and 4 waggons for Oregon, and 9 waggons for California, myself for one. We traveled about 14 miles farther and encamped on the bank of the river. The river here runs through a deep channel of black rock having the appearance of being melted at some future [previous] time.

August 12th — Today we traveled but 4 miles and encamped on the bank of the river. The Indians that were with us are gone with the Oregon Company. The most of them [that company] are missionaries.

August 13th — Today we traveled about 10 miles and encamped for the ballance for the balance of the day on the bank of the river.

August 14th — This morning we passed by a hot spring near the encampment. It is constantly boiling and smoking and is strongly impregnated with soda. We traveled about 15 miles today over hills and mountains and encamped on a small brook about 4 miles from the river.

August 15 — Today we did not travel far, perhaps not more than 8 miles on a straight line, but the way was rough and winding and hilly. We encamped on a small branch about three miles from the river, that is, from Bear River. We killed very little game for a few days, except a few antelope and fishing. The mountain cherries and kerrants [currants] are ripe at this time and other fruit of various kinds of a good flavor.

August 16th — Today we traveled about 20 miles and encamped in Cash valley on the banks of Bear River, two miles below the falls of that River. Here the river runs throught a deep cut in the mountain which is narrow and nearly perpendicular and about 300 feet high.

August 18 — This forenoon we came to a muddy, deep creek which we could not cross without going nearly a half day's journey up it, and consequently we traveled about 5 miles today and came down on opposite bank and camped. There is a large number of hot salt springs on the bank of this creek. Some of them are nearly as hot as boiling water.

August 19th — We traveled about 16 miles today in a roundabout direction. Left the river and had to return to it again in case of having no water. Traveled through a dry, salt plain and could find no water until we returned to the river.

August 20th — Today we did not travel, but lay by at camp for the purpose of sending men on ahead to search for the Salt lake as we have no pilot, for he went the Oregon route.

[Note. — This diary thus ends, with the exception of the following:]

NOTES LEFT OUT.

On the 23d of July seven men left the company and started back to the States. Their names were John Gray, Henry Peyton, ——— Jones, James Baker, ——— Romane, ——— Frye and ——— Rogers. Baker did not go back, but stopped with the trappers.[5]

On the 27th of July there was a wedding in the camp. Mr. Cockrel to Mrs. Gray, by the Rev. Mr. Smith [De Smet], Catholic priest.

On the evening of the 12th of August two men went up on a mountain to hunt for snow. The distance deceived [them.] Night overtook the[m]. They did not return until noon the next day.

July 14.   Dawson
       To butcherknife $1.00
 "   " Mr. Williams
       To 3 hooks   .12
 "   " Isaiah Kelsey
       To 2 skeins of thread   .50

Notes to the Second James John Diary

1 See *note* 1, p. 182, *ante.*
2 See *note* 2, p. 182, *ante.*
3 See *note* 3, p. 182, *ante.*
4 See *note* 4, p. 182, *ante.*
5 Gray is usually spelled Grey; Romane is usually spelled Romaine.

CHAPTER TEN

The Recollection of Nancy Kelsey

Biographical Sketch

Nancy A. Kelsey, the first white woman to reach California overland, was the daughter of hearty pioneers. She was born in Barren County, Kentucky, August 1, 1823. Three years later, her parents moved to Jackson County, Missouri. There she grew to adolescence. When barely sixteen she married Benjamin Kelsey. She and her newborn daughter, Ann, six months old, accompanied him west in the Bidwell-Bartleson party.

Mrs. Kelsey's life after reaching California continued to be that of a pioneer. After settling down in Napa Valley, the family traveled overland to the vicinity of Oregon City with the Joseph Gale party in 1843. The trip was plagued by Indian thefts and threats. Accompanying them were V. W. "Bear" Dawson and Andrew Kelsey, fellow 1841 emigrant travelers. The family returned to Napa Valley in 1844, driving a herd of cattle, to start up a ranch. Their return passage was plagued by hostile Indian encounters. In 1845 at Sutter's Fort, a second daughter, Mary, was born. A third would follow in 1851, Nancy.

Mrs. Kelsey was a witness to the Bear Flag Revolt and the capture of Sonoma in 1846. Reputedly, she provided the cloth and helped make the Bear Flag. After the Mexican War, her husband went into partnership with Mariano G. Vallejo to build and operate a sawmill, an enterprise cut short by the gold discovery. Benjamin Kelsey decided to join the rush. It proved highly lucrative. At Kelsey's Diggings in present-day El Dorado County, he amassed $10,000 in two days' mining. He found, ironically, that he could make more providing miners with sheep than panning for gold. On one venture alone he netted $16,000. With his profit, he and his brother took up land in Clear Lake Valley, acquiring it from Salvador Vallejo, a title which was later rejected by the U.S. Land Commission.

After Andrew's death at the hand of Indians in December 1849, ranching operations ended at what would later be called Kelseyville in honor of Andrew. The Kelseys decided to move to Humboldt County in 1850 to start a new life. Unfortunately, the relocation proved less profitable than expected, but they did assist in founding the towns of Eureka and Arcata.

Undaunted, they returned to Sonoma. In 1851 Oregon beckoned again, so they moved north once more, residing there until the late 1850s, the date of departure being uncertain. Subsequently, Benjamin's precarious health dictated travel to a warmer climate as a likely panacea, so travel they did, first to Mexico in 1859, then to Texas in 1861. These travels were marred by perilous harassment by unfriendly Indians. In one encounter, Mary, Mrs. Kelsey's second daughter, age thirteen, was scalped, but survived the ordeal. But death claimed her five years later while the family was living in Fresno. Finally, the family returned to California, their traveling days at an end.

For a period of time the Kelseys resided first at Lompoc, then Fresno, then Inyo County, and finally in Los Angeles. With the death of her husband in February 1888, Mrs. Kelsey settled down in the shadow of the Cuyama Mountains where she lived out her final years in a remote mountain cabin. Sadly, she developed face cancer. There was nothing medical science could do. But she gamely carried on as the local practical nurse, for her knowledge of herbs and midwifery were legendary among the rural folk to whom she ministered. When she died in 1896, she was laid to rest at the head of Cottonwood Canyon in her beloved mountains. Later, two young children were buried on either side of her, one a grandchild.

In her recollection, she pronounced her own epitaph:

> I have enjoyed riches and suffered the pangs of poverty. I have seen U. S. Grant when he was little known. I have baked bread for Fremont and talked with Kit Carson. I have run from bear and killed most other smaller game. There, I've touched slightly on prominent incidents of my past life, and you will have to be satisfied with that for the present.[1]

1 Biographical data drawn from Mrs. Kelsey's recollection; L. S. Drapeau, "Nancy Kelsey's Two Last Wishes," *The Grizzly Bear* (May 1948): pp., 4, 18; and from sources used in the Biographical Sketches for Andrew and Benjamin Kelsey, where further details can be found.

The memoir which follows was taken down by an admiring neighbor, Addison Powell, who like Mrs. Kelsey, resided at the time in the Cuyama Mountains. It was first published in the San Francisco Examiner, *February 5, 1893, p. 19, cls. 6–7, and has been reprinted twice in* The Grizzly Bear, *February 1915 and February 1937, and again in the* Oakland Tribune, *September 27, 1925, p. 5, cl. 5.*

I was born in Barren county, Ky., in 1823. My parents took me to Jackson county, Mo., in 1826. I was married to Benjamin Kelsey when I was very young, and started overland with him in May, 1841, long before the gold [rush] days. Fitzpatrick was our pilot, and we had a priest with us who was bound for the northwest coast to teach the Flathead Indians.[1] A boy by the name of John Bidwell was in our party. I understand he has grown to be a great man and ran for President.[2] There were others who made themselves known afterwards—Captain Webber [Weber], who founded Stockton and grew so rich, was one. Then there were Colonel Barleson [Bartleson], Colonel Richmond [Rickman], Captain Joe Childes [Chiles], Josiah Belden and Charley Hoffer [Hopper]. We numbered thirty-three all told and I was the only woman.[3] I had a baby to take care of, too.

Our first mishap was on the Platte river, where a young man named Dawson was captured by the Indians and stripped of his clothing. They let him go, and then they followed him so that without his knowledge he acted as their guide to our camp. The redskins surrounded our camp and remained all night, but when daylight showed them our strength they went away.

We left our wagons this side of Salt Lake and finished our journey on horseback and drove our cattle. I carried my baby in front of me on the horse. At one place the Indians surrounded us, armed with bows and arrows, but my husband leveled his gun at the chief and made him order his Indians out of arrow range.

We crossed the Sierra Nevadas at the head waters of the San Joaquin river. On the first of August, 1841, we camped on the summit. It was my eighteenth birthday.[4] We had a difficult time to find a way down the mountain. At one time I was left alone for nearly a day, and as I was afraid of the Indians, I sat all the while with my baby in my lap on the back of my horse, which was a fine racing animal. It seemed to me while I was there alone the moaning of the wind through the pines was the loneliest sound I ever heard.

One old man gave out, and we had to threaten to shoot him before he would attempt to descend the mountains. At one place four pack animals fell over a bluff, and they went so far that we never attempted to recover the packs. We were then out of provisions, having killed and eaten all our cattle. I walked barefooted until my feet were blistered. We lived on roasted acorns for two days.

My husband came very near dying with cramps, and it was suggested to leave him, but I said I never would do that. We ate a horse and remained over till the next day, then he was able to travel. We found plenty of game on the San Joaquin plains, which we killed for meat.

My husband's brother and a man named Jones had strayed from the company while in the mountains, and we supposed they were dead, but my husband, when hunting, discovered their tracks and reported that they were surely alive.[5] At one place I was so weak I could hardly stand, and I lay on the ground while Mr. Kelsey went out and killed a deer. We were then near Dr. Marsh's ranch, which was close to what is now Martinez. Mr. Jones, one of the supposed dead men, and one of Dr. Marsh's Indians rode into camp and brought with them some farina for me. We arrived at Dr. Marsh's on the 4th of October [November] 1841, more than fifty years ago.

In December we went up with Sutter in a leaky row boat to his fort. We were fifteen days making the trip. The boat was manned by Indians, and Sutter instructed them to swim to the shore with me and my child if the boat should capsize. We arrived at the fort on Christmas Day, where I met Joel Walker, who had just arrived with his wife and children—I had been in California five months. . . .[6]

Notes

1 As already pointed out, Fr. Pierre Jean De Smet was traveling with the two other Jesuit priests, accompanied by three Jesuit lay brothers, bound to the Flathead nation. Thomas Fitzpatrick was employed by them as their guide.

2 Bidwell ran on the Prohibitionist ticket for president in 1892.

3 The Bidwell-Bartleson party numbered thirty-four in all. See Appendix A for the other women who headed for Oregon.

4 The Bidwell-Bartleson party certainly did not cross the Sierra Nevadas in August. They probably reached the divide on October 18 and started their torturous descent to the San Joaquin Valley down the Stanislaus Canyon/River, reaching the valley floor on October 30. Consult Bidwell's *Journal*.

5 The two men were Andrew Kelsey and Thomas Jones.

6 It is obvious that Mrs. Kelsey is in error here. She had not been in California five months; at best, she had been in California by October 1841, thus this should read three months at most. But the point: Mrs. Kelsey wanted to make sure that she was the first American woman to reach California by overland travel. And she was.

CHAPTER ELEVEN

An 1856 Letter
by James P. Springer

Biographical Sketch

James Peter Springer was a native of Kentucky. He was born in Washington County on October 27, 1812. After his graduation from college, he developed a passion for travel and adventure. This led him to commence the exploration of the Far West. Thus motivated, he joined the Bidwell-Bartleson party. After visiting various California localities, he returned east in 1842 with the Chiles-Thomes group of former overland travelers. On reaching Missouri, "he published and circulated many pamphlets and articles concerning [California] . . . this El Dorado of his dreams. . . . His zeal and enthusiasm caused many to emigrate. . . ." Springer reputedly undertook overland trips several times in promoting immigration to California. Having married in 1845, in 1852 he returned again to California with his family and took up residence at Saratoga, Santa Clara County. He served in the 1859 state legislature "honestly and faithfully," and died at McCartysville on June 3, 1861, leaving "a widow and one daughter to mourn the loss of a kind husband and loving father." Bancroft, California, V: p. 731; History of Santa Clara County, California . . . (San Francisco, 1881), p. 741; San Francisco Bulletin, June 11, 1861. p. 3, cl. 2.

To the Editor of the San Jose *Tribune*,
July 23, 1856, p. 2, cl. 4.
McCartysville, July 16, 1856.

Ed. Tribune: Seeing in the daily *Chronicle* of June 12th, an article headed "THE PIONEERS OF CALIFORNIA," giving an imperfect list of the persons composing the first overland party to California, I sit down to give you a correct list, as far as can be done at the present time, from memory. I have in Missouri a written journal, giving in detail the travel, incidents, &c., &c., of each day, from the time the party left Independence, in May, 1841, till the return of a portion of the same party in September, 1842.

This journal contains the name, age, birth-place, residence and occupation of each member of the party, the course and distance of each day's travel, the name given to each camp, as also the views of this writer in relation to the *then present condition* and future prospects of this country.

I have long thought of sending for and donating that journal to the "Pioneer Society of California," but must now, in consequence of my straitened circumstances, forego that pleasure, unless the Society would feel willing to make a small appropriation.

The party numbered thirty-two men, one woman and one child, as follows:

Barnett, Elias	Kelsey, Benj.
*Bartleson, Capt. John‡	Kelsey, Nancy
Belden, Josiah	Kelsey, Ann
Belty, William	Kelsey, Andrew‡
Bidwell, John	Nye, Michael
*Brolaski, Henry	McMahon, Greene
Chandler, D. W.‡	McMahon, Nelson
*Childs, Joseph B.	*McDowell, John‡
Cook, Grove C.‡	*Patton, Gwinn‡
Dawson, Nicholas	Rowland, John‡
Dawson, James‡	*Rickman, Robert
Greene, Talbot H.	*Springer, Jas. P.
Henshaw, George‡	Swartz, John‡
*Hopper, Charles	Tomes, R. W.
Huber, Henry	*Walton, Ambrose
John, James	*Walton, Major‡
Jones, Thomas	Weber, C. M.

Those marked with a star (*) returned to Missouri in 1842, by the way of Tejon Pass, Mary's River, Fort Hall, Green River, and Santa Fe, N.M.

Those marked thus ‡, are not now living.

Want of time prevents my giving any of the incidents of the journey, but I may do so at some other time.

Respectfully, your ob't serv't,

JAS. P. SPRINGER

[Note: The roster misspells Chiles and Thomes. Also, the route of the 1842 returnees to Missouri was via Tejon; then arching northward, they crossed the Colorado, then southeast to cross the desert, finally reaching Santa Fe. However, it seems improbable

that they followed St. Mary's River (the Humboldt) and then went on to Fort Hall in present-day southern Idaho. More likely, Chiles learned from George C. Yount about the Old Spanish Trail and that was the route actually taken. Giffen, Trail-Blazing Pioneer: Colonel Joseph Ballinger Chiles *(San Francisco, 1969), pp. 32–33. Regrettably, Springer's journal has yet to be discovered, if it survives at all.]*

CHAPTER TWELVE

The Recollection of Robert H. Thomes

Biographical Sketch

Robert Hasty Thomes was born in Cumberland County, Maine, June 16, 1817. He was a direct descendent of Mayflower pilgrims. In 1839 he journeyed to Missouri and readily joined the Bidwell-Bartleson party. After his arrival in 1841, he worked as a carpenter and builder in San Francisco, 1841–1842. He then moved to Monterey and entered into a partnership with Albert G. Toomes, who came overland with the Workman-Rowland party, also in 1841. The firm of Thomes & Toomes appears frequently in the papers of Thomas O. Larkin. They were carpenter-builders.

Thomes became a naturalized citizen in 1844 and shortly after received a five-league land grant, the Rancho Los Saucos, in what is now Tehama County. He received a patent for 22,212 acres on October 14, 1857. He lived a quiet and productive life with only a brief interval in gold mining on the Feather River and became a wealthy rancher and a "highly respected and influential citizen" in his county. He died at his ranch on March 26, 1878. The father of nine children, four sons and five daughters, at his death he was survived by one son and four of his daughters.[1]

1 Bancroft, *California*, V: 746; Cowan, *Ranchos of California*, No. 584, p. 96; *Tehama County, California* . . . (San Francisco, 1880), pp. 12, 109.

This brief recollection, dictated by Thomes to his friend, Albert G. Toomes, first appeared in the San Francisco Evening Bulletin, *June 27, 1868, p. 2, cl. 3, and reprinted in Oscar T. Schuck, comp.,* The California Scrap-Book: A Repository of Useful Information and Select Reading *(San Francisco, 1869), pp. 181–184.*

I sat down with my old partner Thomes a few days ago and got talking of old times in California, and all that sort of thing. It occurred to us to make a list of our ancient companions in the hard journey we made from Independence a long twenty-seven years ago, and, Sandy, our hairs are getting gray, and we often remember those blessed old *bailies* and *merianders* of gay Monterey. I claim that we were the first regular emigrants who ever started from the States to California, as those who arrived in the country before us, dropped in by mere chance, as old trappers, whalemen, and sailors from the islands and Boston ships. Our party was divided into two companies, who left Independence on the 6th of May, 1841, and we got into California on the 10th November of the same year. The first company was headed by Robert H. Thomes, who crossed over by way of Salt Lake, and the second was headed by William Workman, who went by the way of Santa Fé and the middle route to Los Angeles; and both got into the country at nearly the same time.[1]

We were all armed with rifles, and mounted on horseback, and had literally to smell our way every day of that long, hard journey of 176 days; but we arrived all safe and hearty, and nearly every one of the immigrants mentioned have either died in the State or still reside here.[2] But I never want to cross those hard deserts and big mountains again, except on the railroad, and you bet I shall run over to old Pike on the 4th of July, 1870-car, or mayhap on those of 1869, as I hate salt-water sailing. I have mentioned in subjoined lists those of many "foreigners," then so called, who lived in California before my time, but several have escaped me, as I have never seen a proper list of the names of the first immigration. You know, when Thomes and self got our ranchos up here from Micheltereno and Jimena, this place was out of the world, and league farms to be had for the asking, but it is quite different now. The Indians, once so numerous, are all gone, and the rail cars will soon rush by our doors, and land is worth $20 per acre.[3] That house we built in Monterey for Governor Jimena in 1845 was one of the best jobs we ever did in our lives, for the old gentleman not only paid us well, but got us our farms without any of the trouble others had.[4] Here is the list of our old friends: —

Pioneer Companies by the Overland route of the Mary's, Ogden or Humboldt River, in 1841. — In company No. 1 — Robert H. Thomes, now of Tehama; Mr. Bartlett, Joseph Childs, Maj. Rickman, Talbot H. Greene, Josiah Belden of San Jose; Charles Webber of Stockton; Henry Hubert, John Bidwell of Chico; Charles Flugge, Mr. Barnet, Mr. Brolasky, Charles Hopper, Grove Cook, Benjamin Kelsey, Andrew Kelsey, Mr. Kelsey, all of Sonoma; Mr. Henshaw, James McMahon, Nelson McMahon, Mr. Patten, Mr. Dawson and brother, Mr. Chandler, Michael Nye, Mr. Walton, Mr. Swartz, Mr. Jones, James Littlejohn.[5]

In company No. 2, of 1841. — William Workman, John Roland and Benito D. Wilson of Los Angeles, Albert G. Toomes of Tehama, William Knight, William Gordon, William Moore, Isaac Given, Frank Given, Mr. Pickman, Frederick Bachelor, Mr. Teabo, Frenchman, Wade Hampton, Dr. Meade, Dr. Gamble, Hiram Taylor, Mr. Lindsay, Col. McClure.[6]

There were three or four others in these two companies whose names I have now forgotten, and many on the list are still living in the State. We suffered great hardships, and got into very tight pinches for food and water, but we made up for it when we got among the fat beef and venison of California. . . .

Notes

1 The dates are incorrect. The party set out on May 16 and reached Marsh's rancho on November 4, 1841. Thomes was not the party's leader, rather it was John Bartleson. The William Workman–John Rowland party was the second overland band of pioneers to reach California. That party left Abiquiu, New Mexico, the first week of September and arrived at Rancho Cucamonga in present-day Los Angeles County sometime in November or early December. Albert G. Toomes, in his dictation for H. H. Bancroft, "Overland Pioneer of 1841," gives the date of arrival as November 10, while another member testified to December 12 as the correct date. "Findings of Judge Spencer," p. 2, Beattie Papers, Box 5, File 42, Huntington Library, and H[enry] D. Barrows, "Don David W. Alexander," *Annual Publication Historical Society of Southern California*, IV, Pt. I (1897): 43. The party numbered twenty-three with two families, and it traveled the "Old Spanish Trail." Bancroft, *California*, IV: 227, holds that the party "arrived at San Gabriel early in November," as does De Mofras. Marguerite E. Wilbur, ed., *Duflot de Mofras' Travels* (2 vols., Santa Ana, 1938), I: 186.
2 Not all the Bidwell-Bartleson party emigrants remained in California.
3 Thomes received the Rancho Los Saucos, situated at Tehama, in Tehama County, from Governor Manuel Micheltorena in 1844. The five-league ranch, some 22,212 acres, was patented to him October 14, 1857. Albert G. Toomes received the five-league Rancho Rio de los Molinos, situated at Vina, Tehama County, also in 1844. He received his patent for 17,892 acres April 3, 1858. Cowan, *Ranchos of California*, No. 255, p. 49; No. 584, p. 96.
4 The reference to "Governor Jimena" is misleading. Manuel Jimeno Casarin, a native of Mexico, came to California in 1828. He held a number of political positions, including secretary of state under Governor Juan Bautista Alvarado, 1839–1842. On more than one occasion he was acting governor during Alvarado's reputed illnesses. Bancroft, *California*, IV: 294–295, 692.
5 Some of the names are in error: Bartlett is probably Bartleson; Childs, Chiles; Greene, Green; Webber, Weber; Hubert, Huber; Flügge went to Oregon first, then came south to California later; Barnet, Barnett; Brolasky, Brolaski; McMahon is spelled McMahan and Patten, Patton; the Dawsons were not brothers; there were two Waltons; Swartz is more likely Schwartz; and James Littlejohn is James John. There were only two Kelseys in the Bidwell-Bartleson party, Andrew and Benjamin. A third Kelsey, Isaac (Zedidiah), went with the Oregon-bound party, but later came south to reside in California. The list omits six names and that of Mrs. Nancy Kelsey and her infant daughter.
6 Roland should read Rowland.

CHAPTER THIRTEEN

Extracts From Three Letters by Pierre Jean De Smet to His Superior

Biographical Sketch

Born in Dendermonde (Termonde), Belgium, January 30, 1801, Pierre Jean De Smet immigrated to the United States in 1821 and entered a Jesuit novitiate near the city of Baltimore, Maryland. Two years later he was transferred to a newly opened novitiate in Florissant, Missouri, which subsequently laid the foundation for the Missouri Province of the Society of Jesus. Ordained to the priesthood in 1828, for the ensuing eleven years Father De Smet carried on his priestly duties both in the United States and Europe. His travels in Europe centered on efforts to obtain support for the Jesuits and their work in what was considered at the time a missionary field, the United States.

In 1838 he began a lifetime career as a missionary to the Indians of the Plains and the Pacific Northwest. He began by founding the mission of St. Joseph near present-day Council Bluffs, Iowa. Two years later he made his first trip overland to the Pacific Northwest. Returning to St. Louis, aided and abetted by his superiors, Father De Smet formed a missionary brigade with the intention of opening a mission among the Flathead Indians. Accompanying him west in 1841 to effect that objective were two fellow Jesuit priests, Fathers Nicholas Point and Gregori Mengarini, as well as three lay brothers. To guide their party, Thomas F. Fitzpatrick was hired. It was in the wake of this missionary band that the Bidwell-Bartleson party traveled as far as Soda Springs, which was reached on August 6, 1841. There the California-bound contingent headed south, while the missionary party pushed into the Bitter-root Valley south of present-day Missoula, Montana. There in September 1841, the Jesuits founded St. Mary's Mission. Later additional mission stations were established: St. Ignatius, which served the Kalispels, St. Paul's near Fort Coville, located in present-day northeastern Washington state, and Sacred Heart, located among the Coeur d'Alenes in northern Idaho. The Jesuits' work was highly successful.

Father De Smet earned the trust of the Indian tribes of the area, including the Blackfeet and Sioux. Known as "Blackrobe" among the Indians, he served as a peacemaker on more than one occasion. Notable among his efforts was the role he played in the treaty council of Fort Laramie, 1851, the ending of the "Mormon War" in 1857–1858, and the "Yakima War" in 1858–1859. In 1868 he negotiated a temporary peace with Chief Sitting Bull that cooled for a time Sioux hostility.

Throughout his long years of labor in the mission field, Father De Smet traveled extensively in the United State and Europe ever in search of additional financial support to sustain the Jesuits' missionary activities and to recruit additional missionaries for service in the Far West. Death claimed him in St. Louis, May 23, 1873, at the age of seventy-two.[1]

1 Malone and Johnson, eds., *Dictionary of American Biography,* 5: 255–256 and *Webster's American Biographies,* ed. by Charles Van Doren and Robert McHenry (Springfield, Mass., 1974), p. 273. John Upton Terrell has published a popular treatment in his *Black Robe: A Biography of Pierre-Jean De Smet—Missionary, Explorer and Pioneer* (Garden City, N.Y., 1964).

The three letters which follow have been extracted from Reuben G. Thwaites, ed., Early Western Travels, 1746–1848 *(32 vols., Reprint ed., New York, 1966), XXVII: 189–198, 213–223, 234–248.*

Letter I: Banks of the Platte River, June 2, 1841

Behold us at last on our way towards the long wished for "Rocky Mountains," already inured to the fatigues of the journey and full of the brightest hopes. It is now afternoon and we are sitting on the banks of a river, which, it is said, has not its equal in the world. The Indians call it Nebraska or Big Horn; the Canadians give it the name of la Platte and Irving designates it as the most wonderful and useless of rivers.[1] The sequel will show that it deserves these various affixes. It was to enjoy the freshness and beauty of its scenery that we travelled more than twenty miles this morning, without breaking our fast, through a wilderness without a single rivulet to water our jaded horses, who must therefore rest where they are till tomorrow. I am far from regretting the delay as it will give me an opportunity of commencing a letter which, I know, will interest you.

Like all works of God, our humble beginnings have not been unattended with trials: our journey had even well nigh been indefinitely postponed by the unexpected non-arrival of two caravans on which we had confidently relied; one of two hunters, for the American Fur Company; the other an exploring expedition belonging to the United States, at the head of which we expected to see the celebrated M. Nicolet.[2] Happily God inspired two estimable travellers of whom more hereafter, and afterwards sixty others, to take the same route as ourselves, some for health, others for science, or pleasure; but the greater number to seek their fortune in the too highly boasted land of California. This caravan formed an extraordinary mixture of different nations, every country of Europe having in it a representative, my own little band of eleven persons hailing from eight.

The difficulties of setting out once overcome, many others followed in succession. We had need of provisions, firearms, implements of every kind, waggons, guides, a good hunter, an experienced captain, — in a word, whatever becomes necessary when one has to traverse a desert of eight hundred leagues, and expects nothing but formidable obstacles to surmount, and thieving, and sometimes murderous, enemies to combat, — and swamps, ravines and rivers to cross, and mountains to climb, whose craggy and precipitous sides suddenly arrest our progress, compelling us to drag our beasts of burden up their steep ascents. These things are not done without toil and money, but thanks to the generous charity of our friends in Philadelphia, Cincinnati, Kentucky, St. Louis and New Orleans, which place I visited in person and which is always at the head of the others when there is a question of relieving the necessities of the poor, or showing compassion and munificence to any who may be in need of assistance, we were enabled by the resources thence supplied, and by a portion of the funds allowed by the Lyons Association in behalf of the Indian Missions, to undertake this long journey. . . .

After due deliberation, the fellow-laborers allotted me were five in number, namely two Fathers, Rev. Mr. Point of La Vendee, as zealous and courageous for the salvation of souls . . . ; Rev. Mr. Mengarini, recently from Rome, specially selected by the Father General himself, for this mission, on account of his age, his virtues, his great facility for languages and his knowledge of medicine and music; and three lay-brothers, two Belgians, Claessens and Huet, and one German, of whom the first is a blacksmith, the second a carpenter, and the third a tinner, or a sort of *factotum;* all three industrious, devoted to the Missions and full of good will. They had long ardently desired to be employed on these missions and I thank God that had the choice been left to myself, I could have made none better. . . .[3]

In seven days from my departure from St. Louis, namely, on the 30th of April, I arrived at Westport, a frontier town on the West of the United States. It took us seven days, on board a steamboat, to perform this journey of 900 miles, no unfair average of the time required to travel such a distance on the Missouri, at the breaking up of the winter, when, though the ice is melted, the water is still so low, the sand banks so close together and the snags so numerous that boats cannot make greater headway. . . . We landed on the right bank of the river, and took refuge in an abandoned little cabin, where a poor Indian woman had died a few days before, and in this retreat, so like to that which once merited the preference of the Saviour and for which was thenceforth to be substituted only the shelter of a tent in the wilderness, we took up our abode until the 10th May—occupied as well we might be in supplying the wants created by the burning of our baggage waggon on board the steamboat, the sickness of one of our horses which we were compelled to leave after us, and the loss of another that escaped from us at the moment of landing.

We started, then, from Westport, on the 10th of May, and after having passed by the lands of the Shawnees and Delawares, where we saw nothing remarkable but the college of the Methodists, built, it is easy to divine for what, where the soil is richest; we arrived after five day's march on the banks of the Kanzas river, where we found those of our companions, who had travelled by water, with a part of our baggage.[4] Two of the relatives of the grand chief had come twenty miles from that place to meet us, one of whom helped our horses to pass the river in safety, by swimming before them, and the other announced our arrival to the principal men of the tribe who waited for us on the opposite bank. Our baggage, waggons and men crossed in a pirogue, which, at a distance, looked like one of those gondolas that glide through the streets of Venice. As soon as the Kanzas understood that we were going to encamp on the banks of the Soldier's River, which is only six miles from the village, they galloped rapidly away from our Caravan, disappearing in a cloud of dust, so that we had scarcely pitched our tents when the great Chief presented himself with six of his bravest warriors, to bid us welcome.[5] After having made me sit down on a mat spread on the ground, he, with much solemnity, took from his pocket a Portfolio containing the honorable titles that gave him a right to our friendship and placed them in my hands. I read them, and having, with the tact of a man accustomed to the etiquette of savage life, furnished him the means of smoking the Calumet, he made us accept for our guard the two braves who had come to meet us. Both were armed like warriors, one carrying a lance and a buckler, and the other a bow and arrows, with a naked sword and a collar made of the claws of four bears which he had killed with his own hand. These two braves remained faithful at their post during the three days and three nights that we had to wait the coming up of the stragglers of the caravan. A small present which we made them at our departure, secured us their friendship.

On the 19th we continued our journey to the number of seventy souls, fifty of whom were capable of managing the rifle—a force more than sufficient to undertake with prudence the long march we had to make. Whilst the rest of our company inclined to the West, Father Point, a young Englishman and myself turned to the left, to visit the nearest village of our hosts. . . .[6]

Letter II: On the Sweetwater River, July 14, 1841

Already two long months have elapsed since we began our journey; but we are at length in sight of those dear mountains that have so long been the object of our desires. They are called Rocky, because they are almost entirely formed of granite and silex, or flint stone. The length, position, and elevation of this truly wonderful chain of mountains, have induced geographers to give to it the appellation of the "back-bone of the western hemisphere." Traversing almost the whole of North America, from north to south, containing the sources of some of the largest streams of the world, this chain has for its branches, towards the west, "the spur of the Cordilleras," which divide the Empire of Mexico, and towards the east the less known but not less wonderful mountains of the Wind River, where are found the sources of the large streams that empty themselves into the Pacific and Atlantic Oceans. The Black Hills and the table lands called Prairie hills, which separate the sources of the upper Missouri from those of the Mississippi, the Ozark and the Masserne ridges may all be considered as so many collateral chains of the Rocky Mountains.

According to trigonometrical calculations, and observations, made by means of the barometer, Mr. Boneville, in his Memoirs, asserts that the summits of some of these mountains are 25,000 feet high.[1] This height would appear much exaggerated, if we consulted only the testimony of the eyes, but it is well known that the mountains which are found in immense plains, are not unlike ships seen on the ocean; they appear much less elevated than they are in reality. Whatever may be the height of these colossal mountains, it was at their base that we hoped to meet our dear neophytes. But a messenger we had sent to acquaint them with our arrival, has just returned, and informed us that the Indians who lay encamped there, about a fortnight ago, went in a southerly direction to hunt the buffalo. We know not whether those Indians were Flat Heads or belong to another nation, and it is to obtain the information on this subject, that we are going to despatch a second messenger. In the mean time, I shall continue my journal. The numerous notes, which, on account of our slow progress, we have been enabled to take on the spot, will warrant that exactness of description, which is the more desirable, as it is a quality frequently wanting in the accounts given of these distant regions. Not to exceed the bounds of a lengthy letter, I shall say but little concerning perspectives, flowers, birds, animals, Indians, and adventures.

With the exception of the mounds which run parallel to each other on both sides of the Platte river, and after passing under the Black Hills, disappear at the base of the Rocky Mountains, the whole plain which we traversed for 1500 miles after we had left Westport, might be called the Prairie Ocean. In fact, nearly the whole of this territory is of an undulating form, and the undulations resemble the billows of the sea when agitated by the storm. On the tops of some of these elevations we have seen shells and petrifactions, such are found on several mountains in Europe. No doubt, some impartial geologists may discover here, as they have done elsewhere, incontestible proofs of the deluge. A petrified fragment which I have in my possession, seems to contain a number of these shells.

In proportion as one removes from the banks of the Missouri or penetrates into the Western regions, the forests lose much in height, density and depth, in consequence of the scarcity of water. Soon after, only the rivers are lined with narrow skirts of wood, in which are seldom seen any lofty creeks. In the neighborhood of creeks and rivulets we generally find willow bushes, and where there is no water it would be vain to look for anything but grass, and even this grass is only found in the fertile plains that lie between Westport and the Platte river.

This intimate connexion between rivers and forests is so striking to the eye, that our beasts of burden had not journeyed more than eight days through this desert, when we saw them in some manner exult and double their pace at the sight of the trees that appeared at a distance. This was chiefly observable when the day's journey had been rather long. This scarcity of wood in the western region, so much at variance with what is seen in other parts of North America, proceeds from two principal causes. In the plains on this side of Platte river, from the custom which the Indians who live here have adopted, to fire their prairies towards the end of autumn, in order to have better pasture at the return of spring; but in the Far West, where the Indians do not follow this practice, (because they fear to drive away the animals that are necessary for their subsistence, or to expose themselves to be discovered by the strolling parties of their enemies,) it proceeds from the nature of the soil, which being a mixture of sand and light earth, is everywhere so very barren that with the exception of the absynth that covers the plains, and the gloomy verdure that shades the mountains, vegetation is confined to the vicinity of rivers,—a circumstance which renders a journey through the Far West extremely long and tedious.[2]

At considerable distances, chiefly between the Kants [Kansas] and the Platte rivers, are found blocks of granite of different sizes and colors. The reddish is the most common. In some of the stony parts of the Black Hills are also seen numberless quantities of small pebbles of all shades. I have seen some that were united into solid masses. If these were well polished they would present the appearance of fine mosaics. The columns of the House of Representatives in Washington are deemed very handsome, and are made of similar concretions.

On the feast of St. Peter a remarkable occurrence took place. We discovered an equally curious quarry, which, at first, we took for white marble, but we soon found it something more valuable. Astonished at the facility with which we could fashion this kind of stone into any shape, most of the travellers made calumets of it. I had several made myself, with the intention of offering them as presents to the Indians, so that for the space of forty-eight hours our camp was filled with lapidaries. But the greater number of these calumets could not withstand the action of the fire, and broke. It was alabaster.

The first rock which we saw, and which truly deserves the name, was the famous Rock Independence. It is of the same nature as the Rocky Mountains. At first I was led to believe that it had received this pompous name from its isolated situation and the solidity of its basis; but I was afterwards told that it was called so because the first travellers who thought of giving it a name, arrived at it on the very day when the people of the United States celebrate the anniversary of their emancipation from Great Britain. We reached this spot on the day that immediately succeeds this celebration. We had in our company a young Englishman, as jealous of the honor of his nation as the Americans; hence we had a double reason not to cry hurra for Independence. Still, on the following day, lest it might be said that we passed this lofty monument of the desert with indifference, we cut our names on the south side of the rock, under initials (I. H. S.) which we would wish to see engraved on every spot.[3] On account of all these names, and of the dates that accompany them, as well as of the hieroglyphics of Indian warriors, I have surnamed this Rock "the Great Record of the Desert." I shall add a few remarks about the mounds that are seen in the vicinity of the Platte river. The most remarkable of all, at least that which is best known to the generality of travellers, is the mound to which they have given the name of "chimney." It is called so on account of its extraordinary form; but instead of applying to it an appellation which is rather unworthy this wonder of nature, just because it bears some resemblance to the object after which it is named, it would have been more proper to call it "the inverted funnel," as there is no object which it resembles more. Its whole height, including the base, body and column, is scarce less than four or five hundred feet; the column or chimney is only about one hundred and thirty feet high, so that there is nothing striking in the loftiness of its dimensions.But what excites our astonishment, is the manner in which this remnant of a mountain, composed of sand and clay, has been so shaped, and how it has for such a length of time preserved this form, in spite of the winds that are so violent in these parts. It is true that this mound, and all those that are found near it, is composed of a successive number of horizontal and perpendicular strata, and has about the middle a zone or belt, consisting of a vein of petrified clay. If from these two facts it would be inferred that at a certain height the substance of which the horizontal and perpendicular strata are formed, is susceptible of being hardened so as to approach the nature of stone, then we might perhaps

account in some manner for the wonderful formation of this curious orna-
ment. Yet the main difficulty would still remain, and we would at last be compelled to have recourse to the system of occult qualities. The existence of the
chimney is therefore a problem, and if any scientific person should wish to
solve it, I would advise him to repair to this monument without delay, as a
cleft which is seen at the top, and which in all probability will soon extend
to the base, threatens to leave nothing of it but the remembrance of its existence.[4]

The chimney is not the only remarkable mound to be met with in this vast
solitude. There are many others of various forms. One is called "the House,"
another "the Castle," a third "the Fort," &c. And, in fact, if a traveller was not
convinced that he journeys through a desert, where no other dwellings exist
but the tents put up at night and removed in the morning, he would be induced
to believe them so many ancient fortresses or Gothic castles and with a little
imagination, based upon some historical knowledge, he might think himself
transported amid the ancient mansions of Knight errantry. On one side are
seen large ditches, and high walls; on the other, avenues, gardens and orchards;
farther on, parks, ponds, and lofty trees. Sometimes the fancy presents a castle
of the middle ages, and even conjures up the lord of the manor; but instead
of all these magnificent remains of antiquity, we find only barren mounds on
all sides, filled with cliffs formed by the falling of the waters, and serving as
dens to an infinite number of rattle snakes and other venomous reptiles.

After the Missouri, which in the Far West is what the Mississippi is in the
North, the finest rivers are the Kanzas, the Platte, and the Eau Sucree.[5] The
first of these falls into the Missouri, and receives the waters of a great number
of tributary streams. Of these tributaries we counted as many as eighteen before
we reached the Platte. Hence we may infer that the country abounds in springs,
and that the soil is compact and covered with verdure. The reverse may be
said of the neighborhood of the Platte, where springs and verdure are seldom
seen. Even on the mounds that run parallel to its banks, the waters that fall
from the clouds, upon a sandy and porous soil, run down into the vallies. But
the prairies that receive the overflowing waters of the river are extremely fertile, and appear beautiful in spring, being enamelled with a great variety of
flowers. The sight of the river itself is still more pleasing; though in spite of
all its beauties, it has, like the most remarkable of its mounds, received a vulgar
name. This proceeds from the custom which some travellers have of applying
to objects the names of things with which they are well acquainted. They have
called it *Platte* or Flat river, on account of its width and shallowness; the former
often extending six thousand feet, whilst its depth is but from three to five
feet, and sometimes less. This want of proportion destroys its utility. Canoes
cannot be used to ascend it, and if barges sometimes come down from Fort
La Ramee to the mouth, it is because they are so constructed that they may

be converted into sledges and pushed on by the hands of men. The author of Astoria has properly defined it "the most magnificent and most useless of rivers."[6] Abstraction made of its defects, nothing can be more pleasing than the perspective which it presents to the eye; though besides the prairie flowers and the ranunculus, its banks bear only the eglantine and the wild vine; for on account of the fires made in the autumn the lofty vegetation is entirely confined to the islands that stud its surface. These islands are so numerous that they have the appearance of a labyrinth of groves floating on the waters. Their extraordinary position gives an air of youth and beauty to the whole scene. If to this be added the undulations of the river, the waving of the verdure, the alternations of light and shade, the succession of these islands varying in form and beauty, and the purity of the atmosphere, some idea may be formed of the pleasing sensations which the traveller experiences on beholding a scene that seems to have started into existence fresh from the hands of the creator. Fine weather is common in this temperate climate. However, it happens sometimes, though but seldom, that the clouds floating with great rapidity open currents of air so violent, as suddenly to chill the atmosphere and produce the most destructive hail storms. I have seen some hailstones of the size of an egg. It is dangerous to be abroad during these storms. A Sheyenne Indian was lately struck by a hailstone, and remained senseless for an hour. Once as the storm was raging near us, we witnessed a sublime sight. A spiral abyss seemed to be suddenly formed in the air. The clouds followed each other into it with such velocity, that they attracted all objects around them, whilst such clouds as were too large and too far distant to feel its influence turned in an opposite direction. The noise we heard in the air was like that of a tempest. On beholding the conflict we fancied that all the winds had been let loose from the four points of the compass. It is very probable that if it had approached much nearer, the whole caravan would have made an ascension into the clouds, but the Power that confines the sea to its boundaries and said — "Hitherto shalt thou come," watched over our preservation. The spiral column moved majestically towards the North, and alighted on the surface of the Platte. Then, another scene was exhibited to our view. The waters, agitated by its powerful action, began to turn round with frightful noise, and were suddenly drawn up to the clouds in a spiral form. The column appeared to measure a mile in height; and such was the violence of the winds which came down in a perpendicular direction, that in the twinkling of an eye the trees were torn and uprooted, and their boughs scattered in every direction. But what is violent does not last. After a few minutes, the frightful visitation ceased. The column, not being able to sustain the weight at its base was dissolved almost as quickly as it had been formed. Soon after the sun re-appeared: all was calm and we pursued our journey. In proportion as we proceeded towards the sources of this wonderful river, the shades of vegetation became more gloomy, and the brows of the mountains more cragged. Every thing seemed to wear the aspect, not of decay, but of age, or rather of venerable antiquity. . . .

Letter III: Fort Hall, August 16, 1841

. . . It was at Fort Hall that we took our final leave of the American Colony, with which we had, till then, pursued the same route. It was previously to this, while we were yet at Green river, that those who came to that wild region, merely for information or pleasure, had turned back, with some fewer illusions than when they started out upon the journey. They were five or six in number.[1] Among them was a young Englishman, who had been our mess-mate from St. Louis. In taking leave of us, this young man, who was in many respects estimable, assured us that, if providence should ever again throw us together, the meeting would give him the highest satisfaction, and that he would always be happy to do us all the service in his power. He was of a good English family, and like most of his countrymen, fond of travel: he had already seen the four quarters of the globe. . . . He cherished so many prejudices, however, against the Catholic religion, that, despite all our good wishes, we were of no service to him in the most essential relation. We recommended him to our friends. I have treasured up one of his beautiful reflections: "We must travel in the desert to witness the watchful care of Providence over the wants of man."[2]

They who had started, purely with the design of seeking their fortune in California, and were pursuing their enterprise with the constancy which is characteristic of Americans, had left us, but a few days before our arrival at the fort, in the vicinity of the boiling springs which empty into Bear river. There now remained with us but a few of the party, who had come to the fort in order to revictual. Among the latter were the leader of the Colony and a reputed deacon of the Methodist sect.[3] Both were of a peaceable disposition, and manifested for us the highest regard; but the former, like so many others, being very indifferent as to religious matters, held as a maxim, "that it was best to have no religion, or else to adopt that of the country in which we live". . . .The minister was of the same opinion, but yet he wished some religion, it being well understood that his was the best. . . .

I had daily conversations with some one of the caravan, and frequently with several. And although Americans are slow to change their creed, we had the consolation to relieve our travelling companions of a heavy load of prejudice against our holy religion. They parted from us, exhibiting signs of respect and veneration; nay, even of preference for Catholicity. These controversies so completely engrossed my mind, my heart and my senses, that I arrived almost unconsciously on the banks of Snake river. Here a great danger and a profitable lesson awaited us; but before speaking of the adventures of our journey, I shall conclude what remains to be related of the country we traversed.

We halted with our narrative upon the shore of the Sweet-water. This stream is one of the most beautiful tributaries of the Platte. It owes its name, indeed, to the purity of its waters. It is distinguished from its fellow tributaries by the numerous wanderings of its current—a proof that the fan of its bed is but slight. But suddenly changing its course, we see or rather hear it rushing impetuously through a long cleft in a chain of mountains. These mountains, which harmonize well with the torrent, exhibit the most picturesque scenes; travellers have named this spot the Devil's Entrance.[4] In my opinion, they should have rather called it Heaven's Avenue, for if it resembles hell on account of the frightful disorder which frowns around it, it is still a mere passage, and it should rather be compared to the way of heaven on account of the scene to which it leads. Imagine, in short, two rows of rocks, rising perpendicularly to a wonderful height, and, at the foot of these shapeless walls, a winding bed, broken, encumbered with trunks of trees, with rubbish, and with timber of all dimensions; while, in the midst of this chaos of obstacles, the roaring waves force a passage, now rushing with fury, then swelling with majesty, and anon spreading with gentleness, according as they find in their course a wider or more straitened passage. Above these moving and noisy scenes, the eye discerns masses of shadow, here relieved by a glance of day, there deepening in their gloom by the foliage of a cedar or pine, till finally, as the sight travels through the long vista of lofty galleries, it is greeted by a distant perspective of such mild beauty, that a sentiment of placid happiness steals upon the mind. Such is the spectacle we admired at the distance of nine or ten miles from the Rock Independence, on the morning of 6th July. . . .

Hence we directed our course more and more towards the heights of the Far West, ascending, some times clambering, until we reached the summit, from which we discovered another world.[5] On the 7th of July we were in sight of the immense Oregon Territory. I will not presume to add to the many pompous descriptions which have been given of the spectacle now before us. I shall say nothing either of the height, the number, or the variety of those peaks, covered with eternal snows, which rear their heads, with menacing aspect, to the heavens. Nor will I speak of the many streams descending from them and changing their course, with unexpected suddenness; nor of the extreme rarification of the air with the consequent effect upon objects susceptible of contraction, at so great an elevation. All this is common; but to the glory of the Lord, I must commemorate the imperious necessity I experienced, of tracing his holy name upon a rock, which towered pre-eminent amid the grandeur around. May that ever adorable name be to travellers a monument of our gratitude, and a pledge of salvation. Henceforth we descended towards the Pacific—first, by following, then by crossing the Little and the Great Sandy Rivers.[6] In the vicinity of the latter, as the Captain had mistaken one road for another, the caravan wandered for three days at random. I, myself, on a fine evening, strayed from the rest. I thought myself entirely lost; how was I to act? I did what every sincere believer would have done in the same circumstances, I prayed; and then urging on my horse, I travelled several miles, when it struck me that it would be prudent to retrace my steps. I did so instantly, and it was fortunate, for the caravan was far behind. I found it encamped; still ignorant however of its position, and on a soil so arid that our jaded beasts were necessitated to fast for the night. Days follow, but resemble not each other; two days subsequently, we were surrounded with abundance, filled with joy, all once more united, and on the banks of a river not less celebrated among the hunters of the west, than the shores of the Platte. This river loses itself not far below, in clefts of rocks said to be no less than two hundred miles in extent, among which there are countless swarms of beavers, although the trapper has never ventured to hunt them, on account of the extreme peril of the enterprise. At a certain period of the year, both trappers and Indians flock to this spot, for the purpose of bartering all kinds of merchandise. It was here, but eight years ago, the wagons that first undertook to cross the Rocky Mountains, found the Pillars of Hercules, and it was here too that we found the messenger of the Flat Heads.[7] This river is the Rio Colorado of the West.[8] . . . We rested two days upon its banks, with the company of Captain F., who had just returned from California.[9] What they told us concerning that distant country dissipated many illusions, and caused some of our companions, who travelled for amusement, to return.[10]

On the 26th of July we seriously thought of continuing our journey. To a company like ours, it was not an easy matter. The remembrance of the expedition of Bonneville was still fresh in the minds of all; but our object was not the same; we had no articles but such as were necessary.—They could be transported conveniently only by wagons. We placed all our confidence in God. We soon crossed the river, and our equipage was seen coming in all directions, over vallies and mountains. We were compelled to clear a passage, some times in the middle of a ravine, some times on the declivity of a rock, and frequently through bushes. We travelled in this manner for ten days, to reach Bear river, which flows through a wide and beautiful valley, surrounded by lofty mountains and often intersected by inaccessible rocks. We continued our march through it during eight successive days. The river resembles in its course the form of a horse shoe, and falls into the great Salt lake, which has no communication with the sea. On our way, we met several families of Soshonees or Snake Indians, and Soshocos or Uprooters. They speak the same language, and are both friends to the whites. The only difference we could observe between them, was that the latter were by far the poorer. . . .

Some places on the Bear river exhibit great natural curiosities. A square plain of a few acres in extent presents an even surface of fuller's earth of pure whiteness, like that of marble, and resembling a field covered with dazzling snow. Situated near this plain are a great many springs, differing in size and temperature. Several of them have a slight taste of soda, and the temperature of these, is cold. The others are of a milk warm temperature, and must be wholesome; perhaps they are not inferior to the celebrated waters of the Spa, or of the lime springs in Belgium. I am inclined to believe so, though I am not firm in the opinion; at all events, they are surrounded by the mountains over which our wagons found it so difficult to pass. I therefore invite neither sick nor sound to test them. In the same locality there is a hole in the ground, out of which air and water escape alternately. The earth for some distance around resounds like an immense vault, and is apt to frighten the solitary traveller as he passes along.

It was here that we left Bear River. On the 14th of August our wagons having proceeded ten hours without intermission, arrived at the outlet of a defile which seemed to us the end of the world. On our right and left were frightful mountains; in our rear a road which we were by no means tempted to retrace; in front a passage through which rushed a torrent; but so small that the torrent itself seemed with difficulty, to force its way.[11] Our beasts of burthen were, for the first time, exhausted. Murmurs arose against the captain, who, however, was imperturbable, and as he never shrunk from difficulties, advanced to reconnoitre the ground.[12] In a few moments he made us a sign to approach; one hour after we had surmounted every obstacle, for we had traversed the highest chain of the Rocky Mountains and were nearly in sight of Fort Hall. . . .

Notes

Letter I

1 The allusion is to Washington Irving's *Astoria or Anecdotes of an Enterprise Beyond the Rocky Mountains* (2 vols., Philadelphia, 1836). A like description is also found in John Treat Irving, Jr.'s *Indian Sketches Taken During an Expedition to the Pawnee Tribes* [1833], ed. by John F. McDermott (Norman, 1955), p. 54, which was first published in Philadelphia, 1835.

2 Jean Nicolas Nicollet (1786–1843) was known to De Smet since they traveled together in exploring the Missouri River in 1839, accompanied by John Charles Frémont. Nicollet had planned another expedition, as alluded to by De Smet, but was detained in Washington, D.C. The explorer, famed for his expeditions to the Arkansas and Red rivers and for detailing the source of the Mississippi, was never able to resume his western travels. Howard R. Lamar, ed., *The Reader's Encyclopedia of the American West* (New York, 1977), pp. 843–844.

3 Father Nicholas Point (1799–1868) labored in the Idaho-Montana mission field from

1841 to 1846. In 1847 he was posted to Quebec and died there at age sixty-nine. Father Gregory Mengarini (1811 to 1884) served in the Rocky Mountain missions from 1841–1850, when St. Mary's was abandoned. He was then sent to the newly founded Jesuit college in Santa Clara, California. He spent the rest of his life at that institution. Brother William Claessens (b. 1812) continued to work among the Flathead Indians until the twilight of his life. Because of failing health, he was sent to Santa Clara College to rest. There he died on October 11, 1891. Brother Charles Huet worked with Fr. Point in founding the Coeur d'Alene mission. When he died at his post in 1868, age sixty-two, he was buried in the mission church of the Sacred Heart, one he helped to build. Brother Joseph Specht never left the Flatheads. His life of service ended in 1884 at age seventy-five; at the time, he was Montana's oldest white inhabitant.

It should be pointed out that Fr. De Smet is mistaken on one biographical detail. Fr. Point was born in Rocroy in the Ardennes; he was not a Vendean native. Biographical data drawn from Gilbert J. Garragan, *The Jesuits of the Middle United States* (3 vols., New York, 1938), II: *passim.*

4 Rev. Thomas Johnson of the Methodist church, Missouri Conference, founded a mission school for the Shawnee, conducted by him and his wife, aided by the Rev. William Johnson and wife. In 1839 it was relocated about two miles southeast of Westport and was maintained until 1862. Thwaites, ed., *Early Western Travels,* XXVII: 196–197n.

5 "Soldier's Creek, a northern tributary of the Kansas, entering the latter just below Topeka, near the Kansas River fording place." *Ibid.,* p. 197n.

6 The Englishman's name was Romaine. Bidwell, *Journal,* p. 2.

Letter II

1 Captain Benjamin L. E. Bonneville's western exploits have been chronicled by Washington Irving in the *The Adventures of . . . ,* ed. by Edgeley W. Todd (Norman, 1961). However, it should be noted that the highest peak in the entire Cordilleran system within the United States does not exceed 14,000 feet.

2 De Smet's "Absynth" actually should be absinth or wormwood, which is the European species of the American sagebrush (*Artemisia tridentata*).

3 The initials I.H.S. form a monogram for Jesus, derived from the Greek spelling.

4 De Smet is describing Chimney Rock.

5 Eau Sucree is the Sweetwater River.

6 The allusion is to Washington Irving's *Astoria or Anecdotes of an Enterprise Beyond the Rocky Mountains* (2 vols., Philadelphia, 1836), ed. by Edgeley W. Todd (Norman, 1964). Although De Smet's quote is a paraphrase, it comes close to the language Irving used on page 154 (ed. version). La Ramee is, of course, Laramie.

Letter III

1 Actually, only two of the Bidwell-Bartleson party elected to pull out and return after hearing the adverse comments from the trapper-traders: Henry Peyton and a "Jones." Bidwell, *Journal,* p. 8.

2 This was Romaine. *Ibid.,* pp. 2, 8.

3 The unnamed men were John Bartleson and the Rev. Joseph Williams.

4 Devil's Gate in Wyoming.

5 The ascent of South Pass is so gradual that one needs measuring instruments to gauge it correctly.

6 The Little Sandy later became "the beginning of Sublette's Cut Off, sometimes called the 'Dry Drive,' because of scarcity of water on the route. This crossed directly to Bear

River, without passing southward by Fort Bridger. Such would seem to have been the route taken by De Smet's company. The regular trail went down the Big Sandy, forded Green River near its forks, and proceeded across to the site of Fort Bridger, founded two years later [1843]." Thwaites, *Early Western Travels,* XXVII: 242n.

7   The reference is to Captain Bonneville's large fur-trade expedition mounted in 1832. His caravan numbered one hundred men, twenty wagons, plus horses, mules, oxen, and cows. It departed Fort Osage, Missouri, May 1. This overland party took the first wagons through South Pass on July 24, 1832, which "proved the feasibility of this route for future emigration." Edgeley W. Todd, "Benjamin L. E. Bonneville," in Hafen, ed., *The Mountain Men,* V: 49–58, for a compact history of his three-year trading venture.

8   The Rio Colorado of the West was actually the Green River.

9   Henry Fraeb and Joseph R. Walker, in partnership, took a fur brigade to southern California in the fall of 1840. In Los Angeles they sold 417 pounds of beaver to Yankee storekeeper Abel Stearns for $1,147. In exchange the were received needed supplies, including beans, coffee, soap, sugar, tobacco, and *aguardiente* (California brandy), as well as 100 mares priced at $2 a head, 17 miles at $12 each, and 2 stallions at $10 each. They returned east and by July 1841 were on the Green River. Accounts, Abel Stearns Papers, Box 73, Huntington Library; Hafen, "Henry Fraeb," in Hafen, ed., *The Mountain Men,* III: 136–137.

10   The following decided not to go any further: Amos E. Frye, Rogers, and Romaine, the pleasure seekers. In addition the trappers James Baker, John Gray, William Mast, and Piga (a Frenchmen) joined the hunting party or else struck out on their own in the mountains to hunt. Bidwell, *Journal,* p. 8.

11   "This was the route by which the trail crossed the waters of the Colorado to those of the Lewis, a difficult mountain path in Bannock County, Idaho. . . ." Thwaites, *Early Western Travels,* XXVII: 248n.

12   As pointed out elsewhere, Thomas Fitzpatrick was captain of the De Smet missionary party. Bidwell, *Journal,* p. 2.

CHAPTER FOURTEEN

Narrative of the Rockies

By Father Gregory Mengarini

Biographical Sketch

Father Gregory Mengarini, S.J., was Roman by birth. Born on July 21, 1811, in the Eternal City, he entered the Society of Jesus and was ordained to the priesthood at age twenty-nine. In 1840 he immigrated to the United States in answer to the call of Fr. De Smet for missionaries to labor among the Indians of the Rocky Mountains. He spent the years 1841–1850 with the Rocky Mountain tribes, first at St. Mary's Mission. He continued to work among the Flathead Indians until posted in 1851 to the newly opened Santa Clara College in California. The rest of his life was spent at that institution, where he served as professor, vice president, and treasurer. Two years before his death, on September 23, 1886, he dictated his recollections to a confere. Two years after his passing, a few copies of his memoirs were printed and circulated among his fellow Jesuits. The original was published a second time in the Woodstock Letters: A Record of Current Events and Historical Notes Connected with the Colleges and Missions of the Society of Jesus in North and South America, *published by Woodstock College for private circulation, XVII (1888): 298–309; XVIII (1889) 25–43, 142–152. It was subsequently reprinted several more times as pointed out in the Introduction.*

Now when I am old, and life's shortening steps hurry me towards the tomb, I am asked to stop a while and tell the story of the birth, infancy and premature death of the earliest of the Rocky Mountain missions. This labor, for such it is to me, is a labor of love; and my heart is overjoyed that its last feeble throbbings may thus be consecrated to the same sacred cause to which it consecrated the strength of its prime. But memory no longer is for me the placid stream preserving ever a calm and even flow; it is rather a mountain torrent, now full to overflowing and now completely dry, and, even in its fullness, broken by many a rock and rapid. I shall therefore tell things plainly and simply as they now come back to me, and should anyone think that I narrate events too minute and unimportant, let him remember that they are to be valued, not by their real worth, but by the interest which they have for the heart of an old man.

_____

At Westport, [Missouri], our journey by land began. Forty-five years [1841] ago! It seems a long time now to look back through the dim vista of nearly half a century, and glance again at our little caravan when it first started across the plains. Fr. [Pierre Jean] DeSmet had engaged the services of a captain for the party, a man named [Thomas] Fitzpatrick, as well as those of an Iroquois hunter named John Grey, besides those of six Canadian mule-drivers.[1] An Englishman named Roman accompanied us.[2] Seeing that we were well provided with guides, several German and American families started at the same time and followed our tracks.[3]

We had already been several days on our journey and had reached the Kansas River, when, casting our eyes towards it, we saw a waterspout twirling swiftly along its surface.[4] Presently the trees on the river-bank swayed violently from side to side, numbers of them were torn from their roots, and a great mist, spreading rapidly over the river, discharged itself in a fall of hail. We dismounted until the shower was over, and then started forward again on our weary march. We had not gone far when Fr. [Nicholas] Point saw, partially embedded in the soil, something that seemed to be a beautiful piece of quartz, oval in shape and about the size of a goose egg. He hastened to pick it up, and found to his and our astonishment that it was a hail-stone.

So the sun rose and the sun set, and the end of our journey was still over a thousand miles away. Sometimes John Grey would say to me in the morning, "Father, do you see that speck in the distance. Today we must reach there." "Then our day's travel will be short," I would answer. "We shall see," he would say laughingly. And the hours of the morning would pass and we would be already journeying long under a scorching afternoon's sun before that speck would assume appreciable magnitude and distinctness of form; and the last rays of the setting sun would often show us, still some miles distant, the welcome grove where we were to find water and rest.

At night we kept guard by turns, Fr. Point and myself among the number; the only exceptions made being in favor of Capt. Fitzpatrick and Fr. DeSmet. One morning about an hour after sunrise, the discharge of a gun startled us. The report was followed by the prolonged moaning of one in pain. All hastened to the spot whence the cries proceeded, and, weltering in his blood, we found an American named Shotwell. The poor fellow had incautiously taken his gun by the muzzle to draw it from his wagon, the piece was accidentally discharged, the bullet pierced his liver, and in two hours he was dead. We could offer him no consolation for we found him insensible and he remained in that condition until death put an end to his agony. We buried him there on the prairies and mournfully continued our journey westward.[5]

Sometimes we fell in with bands of Sioux and Cheyennes but though importune in asking us for various articles, they did us no harm. To lose the road and be in want of water had become such an ordinary matter as to be daily expected. But why speak of road when no such thing existed. Plains on all sides! Plains at morning; plains at noon; plains at night! And this, day after day. The want of water was sometimes so great that we were forced to boil putrid yellow water, which we found collected in some hollow, and strive to quell the pangs of thirst at the price of others equally great. But while water was scarce game was often abundant. Prairie-cocks, prairie-hens, prairie-chickens, antelopes, supplied us with food. At times we saw the distant hills covered with what seemed to be clumps of stunted trees, but if even a gentle wind happened to blow towards that quarter, the trees would move up the sides of the hills and disappear; they were immense herds of buffaloes.

Thus time wore on until upon reaching Rock Independence, it became necessary for us to cross the Platte River.[6] It was about a mile wide, full of islands, and had a strong current. John Grey went in search of a ford and came back saying that he had found one. He immediately started ahead, and the wagoners started to follow. But as people generally do, some thought that they could find a better way for themselves and so scattered after entering the river, thus leaving it uncertain, for those that came last, what way the guide had taken. A wagon had just entered the stream when I reached the bank, and I determined to follow it. All went well for some time, and we were nearing the other bank when suddenly I beheld the wagon upset, and at the same moment I felt the earth slipping from beneath my horse's feet. I clung to the neck of the animal, if not gracefully, at least firmly; for, as I could not swim, I held on to life the more vigorously. The current was strong, but my horse was a good swimmer and in a few minutes both of us were landed on the bank. I turned to look at the wagon and saw it abandoned and floating down the stream. No lives were lost, but a man whom we called "the Major" had been in imminent danger. I retired quite a distance from the others, hung up my clothes to dry and, comfortable once more, I betook myself to camp.

Slowly we toiled on while May, June and July scorched our pathway. At length, separation from the emigrants became necessary; they took the road towards Oregon and California, we kept more to Fort Hall. . . .[7]

Notes

1 Bidwell's *Journal*, p. 2, states there were only five Canadian mule drivers in the Jesuit party. John Grey (sometimes Gray) was half Iroquois; his Indian name was Ignace

Hatchiorauquasha. He entered the fur trade in the employ of the North West Company sometime around 1818 for he was apparently with Donald Mackenzie's Snake Country brigade that year, the year in which he discovered Gray's Hole not far from Pierre's Hole (named for his fur-trapping associate.) His name was given to Grey's River and Gray's Lake, as well as some other natural features in the present states of Idaho and Wyoming. Later, when his firm merged with the Hudson's Bay Company, he worked for them for a short time before the arrival of American trappers in 1826. In 1836 he settled in Missouri on a site which soon developed into Kansas City. He continued active in the fur trade until around 1848 when he met his death at the hands of a neighbor. Merle Wells, "Ignace Hatchiorauquasha (John Grey)," in Hafen, ed., *Mountain Men,* VII: 161–175.

Also in the Jesuit party was James Baker, another fur man. Born in Belleville, Illinois, December 19, 1818, he began his career in the west in 1838, which marked his debut as a fur trapper. In the twilight of the fur trade, he took a native wife and lived for a time among the Shoshone. Deft at Indian languages, he served the U.S. Army as a guide and interpreter. By 1858 he returned to the life of a white man, rushing for gold in the 1859 Colorado gold rush, which became his home. In 1873 he sold out his property and took up land on the Little Snake River on the Colorado-Wyoming border where he lived out the rest of his long life. He died on May 15, 1898, and was buried near his home not far from Savery, Wyoming. Nolie Mumey, "James Baker," in Hafen, ed., *Mountain Men,* III: 39–53.

2 Romaine, apparently an English nobleman.

3 The Bidwell-Bartleson party.

4 This was a tornado.

5 The Rev. Williams buried Shotwell, who died on June 13, 1841.

6 Mengarini has his geography confused. Independence Rock is on the banks of the Sweetwater River, a tributary of the North Platte, in present-day Wyoming. The crossing referred to here is apparently near Grand Island in the vicinity of Kearney, Nebraska.

7 The separation took place at Soda Springs, Idaho, August 6, 1841.

CHAPTER FIFTEEN

Historical Notes

by Father Nicholas Point

Biographical Sketch

The eldest of several children, Nicholas Point was born near Rocroy in the Ardennes, April 10, 1799. On June 28, 1819, he entered the Society of Jesus at St. Achuel College several miles from Amiens. On completing his studies there, he took his novitiate at Montrouge. Ill health forced him to suspend his religious preparation for a period of time during which he returned to his family. With health restored, he resumed his novitiate at Montrouge, taking his vows on March 9, 1827. He then returned to St. Achuel to complete his theological studies. This in turn lead to his ordination to the priesthood on March 30, 1831.

Already spotted by his order as a college teacher, he was sent to Frieburg, Switzerland for a year, then to San Sebastián, Spain, as vice-rector of the College of St. Roch. When the Jesuits were obliged to leave Spain in 1834, he returned to his homeland, France. It was there that he was recruited for service in the United States.

Sailing from France on August 15, he finally reached New York on December 15, 1835. It took him six months to make the trip west to Kentucky, where he was posted to teach at St. Mary's College, located ten miles outside Lebanon. He remained there until February 1837, when he was sent to Grand Coteau, Louisiana, to head a new college being founded there, ten miles southeast of Opelousas. St. Charles College opened on January 5, 1838. Two years later he was sent to St. Louis. It was there he was selected in 1841 to join Father De Smet's missionary band to the Flathead Indians.

He labored in the Idaho-Montana mission field from 1841 to 1846. As an amateur artist, he recorded the overland trek from Westport to Soda Springs in his sketches. He continued to record his encounters with Indians amongst whom he ministered, leaving an invaluable ethnological record. On May 19, 1847, due to his precarious health, he was sent to Canada and took up residence at Sandwich, now Windsor, Ontario, to rest. There he remained until 1849 when he was retired at Sault-au-

Recollect, near Montreal. Finally, in 1865, he moved to Quebec, where he died on July 4, 1868. He was so esteemed that his remains were interred in the crypt of Quebec's cathedral.

It was at Sault-au-Recollect that Fr. Point began writing his "Recollections of the Rocky Mountains," first published in the Woodstock Letters, *XI (1882): 298–312. This was reprinted in* Wilderness Kingdom, Indian Life in the Rocky Mountains: 1840–1847. Journals & Paintings of Nicolas Point, S.J., *translated and edited by Joseph P. Donnelly, S.J. (New York, 1967), pp. 11–18. The latter also published for the first time Point's "Historical Notes," pp. 19–39.[1]*

The extract which follows is taken from the latter and is herein reprinted by the permission of Loyola University Press, Chicago, which retains the copyright.

Notes

1 Biographical details of Point's life are provided on pp. 1–9.

On May 10, we left Westport, taking with us all the supplies for our dear mission in five two-wheeled carts driven by two Canadians who were excellent wagoners, and three of our brothers, still novices at that difficult art. The three priests rode horseback.[1] On quitting Westport, which is separated from the river by a stretch of woods about two or three miles wide, we saw before us what the inhabitants of the region call the Great Prairie. What a beautiful perspective for a missionary! But especially for me, who for twenty years have seen nothing but the walls of a college. At the sight of the azure distances, so pleasing to the eye, I thought I could perceive what is most attractive about the beautiful ideal of the apostolic life. The verdure of the earth and the thousands upon thousands of small spring flowers helped support the illusion.

From the very first day onward we saw Indians. The first encampment on the great plains always has something memorable about it. What we noted particularly about this one was that it coincided with the feast of one of our most celebrated missionaries, Blessed Francis de Geronimo.[2] In the following days— after having passed through the territory of the Shawnee,[3] and the Delaware, where the only noteworthy thing we saw was a Methodist college, which, for reasons easily understandable, had been erected in the midst of the best Indian territory—we arrived at the right bank of the Kansas River.[4] There we found two men who had transported part of our baggage by water, and two relatives of the great chief of the Kansa, who had come to meet us. While one of them aided the pack animals in crossing the river by swimming ahead of them, the other announced our arrival to the first of the tribes awaiting us on the other side. As soon as they learned that we would camp at a spot only six miles from their village, they left, full gallop, and disappeared in a cloud of dust. Scarcely had our shelter been erected, when the chief of the area, accompanied by six ranking warriors, came to pay his respects.

First of all, he had us seat ourselves on a mat which he spread out on the grass and then, drawing forth a large portfolio with great solemnity, he handed Father De Smet a document, signed by the President of the United States, which recommended his tribe to the good will of the whites. The calumet was not forgotten, nor, on our part, a present for the occasion, which earned for us the honor of having placed at our disposal the two warriors who had visited us at Westport. These two braves, one armed with lance and shield and the other with bow and sword, stood watch before our door during the three days we had to spend waiting for the stragglers.

Only on May 18 the American element assembled. The most remarkable traveler among them was Colonel Bartleson, whom the Americans had made their leader in their search for fortune in the much-vaunted territory of California. This man, already somewhat advanced in years, calm in temperament but enterprising in character, was kind to us during the whole trip. His maxim in religious matters was that one should either have no religion at all or adhere to the religion of those with whom it was necessary to live. This was hardly our attitude toward religion. Nevertheless, through the maintenance of mutual respect, the most perfect concord reigned between him and us right up to the end. The rest of the travelers were a composite of all ages, languages and denominations. Some were traveling in pursuit of purely material interests, others for pleasure, and still others, of the age of the prodigal son, only to relieve their families of their unfortunate presence. Although their views differed, as we have just seen, all agreed on one point, namely, that they must try not to perish on the journey. This kind of agreement facilitated the establishment of good discipline.

In these immense solitudes it was necessary to have an experienced guide. The choice fell not on the colonel, who had never crossed the mountains, but on the captain Father De Smet had engaged.[5] He was a courageous Irishman, known to most of the Indian tribes as Tête Blanche (White Head). He had spent fully two thirds of his life crossing the plains.

The missionaries and their party were regarded as the first body of the vanguard. Each day the captain gave the signal to rise and to depart, ordered the march and the stops, chose the spot in which to camp, and maintained discipline. Whenever possible, camp was pitched on the wooded bank of some river so that there would be no lack either of drinking water or of wood for cooking. First, the captain would mark a spot for our tent; then the vehicles would be arranged one beside the other in a circle or in a square, more or less regular according to the nature of the terrain, but always in such a manner as to provide the pack animals a secure enclosure for the night. For added security, everyone picketed his own animals at a sufficiently great distance from the others, and on tethers long enough to permit them, without doing injury to themselves, to supplement by grazing what they had been fed in the evening. From the moment when the camp retired until the break of day, all the travelers, including the priests, stood watch according to roster, in order to guard against a surprise attack. Our little army of seventy persons, of whom more than fifty were able to bear arms, would, with a little prudence, be more than adequate for the long journey before us.

On May 19, while the rest of the party continued toward the West, Father De Smet and Father Point bore off to the left to visit the big village of the Kansa. . . .

The terrain between Westport and the Platte is one of endless undulations which bear a perfect resemblance to those of the sea when it is agitated by a storm. We found, on the summits of some of them, shells and petrified remains such as are found on some of the mountains of Europe. I have no doubt that sincere geologists would find there, as elsewhere, certain indications of the Deluge. A fragment of stone which I have saved seems to contain some.

As we left Missouri behind and penetrated farther west, the trees became less tall and more sparse and the forests less extensive, because of the smaller amount of water which nourished them. On the banks of rivers there was only a thin fringe of timber growth and rarely anything resembling a full-grown forest. In the vicinity of streams there were only willow thickets. And where water was lacking, one searched in vain for anything except grass. This connection between trees and water was so obvious that our pack animals, after only a week on the plains, would, especially after a long march, become excited and double their speed at the sight of trees in the distance.

After two or three days we observed two Indians to our left. One was draped in an American flag and the other had a scalp attached to his horse's bridle. What we beheld boded nothing good for the fate of our [recent] hosts. But when the captain inquired about the results of their expedition, they informed us that they had not even seen the Kansas and that they were very hungry. We gave them, and about fifteen others who had followed them, something to eat and to smoke. They ate, but they did not smoke and, contrary to the custom of other Indians, who, after one meal, wait for another, they took their leave with an air which seemed to indicate that they were not satisfied. The abruptness of this departure, the rejected calumet, the poor success of their expedition, the proximity of their tribe, their well-known inclination for easy pillage, all combined to convince us that these Indians might attempt something, if not against our persons, then at least against our supplies. But, thanks be to God, our fears were groundless. After their departure, not one returned.

During the first days of June we found ourselves on the banks of a river which, it is said, does not have an equal anywhere in the world. The Indians called it the Nebraska or the River of the Deer. The French *voyageurs* called it the Platte, and Father De Smet, in his first description of the Rocky Mountains, called it "the most marvelous and useful of rivers."

Next to the Missouri, which is for the West what the Mississippi is for the North and South, the most beautiful rivers of this area are the Kansas, the Platte, the Sweetwater, and the Green. The first, which empties directly into the Missouri, is quite remarkable for the large number of its great tributaries. Between the Kansas and the Platte we counted eighteen tributaries, which presupposed a large number of springs and, consequently, a very compact soil. The contrary is true in the vicinity of the Platte. Even on the buttes, which run parallel to the low shore for some distance, there are neither springs nor woods, since the soil, practically all sand, is so porous that water runs to the lower level of the valleys almost as soon as it falls. Hence the neighboring plains are very fertile and especially beautiful in the spring because of the great variety of flowers which grow there. By picking fifteen of each variety, I was able, on the eve of the Feast of the Sacred Heart, to fill an entire basket to honor this great day. The most common of the flowers is the *epinette des prairies*, a small five-petal flower of yellow color.[6] The plains on which they bloom, when seen from a distance, seem to have no green at all; all is a yellow-gold, similar to the color of the narcissus in northern France. Beside *la Cheminee*, the *pricleper* [prickly pear?] together with the *turnsol*, is dominant.[7]

The prettiest of them is the *Cactus Americana*, which had already been domesticated in European flower beds. I never saw anything as pure and vivid as the bloom of this charming flower. All shades of rose and green decorate the exterior of the blossom, which, like that of the lily, widens at the top. The flower, surrounded by a great many thorns, is only two inches from the earth and grows naturally only in the desert. Thus it, more than the rose, could be the symbol of the pleasures of this world. The most elegant flower is something like the European campanula, but surpasses it by the gracefulness of its form and the delicacy of its colors, which vary from pure white to dark blue. The noblest of them, found only on the mountains, is the "Needle of Adam." Its stem is about three feet high. Halfway up the stem begins a pyramid of blossoms matted closely together, shaded lightly with red, and narrowing to a point at the top. Its base is protected by a kind of tough, long and sharp leaf. From the roots can be made soap, often called Mexican soap, and, in times of emergency, this root might also serve as food.

We saw three other remarkable flower varieties, so rare that, even in America, their names were not generally known. The first one, whose bronze leaves are arranged something like the capital of a Corinthian column, we named the *Corinthienne*. The second, something of a straw color, which, because of the arrangement of its stem and branches reminded one of the dream which caused Joseph to be hated by his brothers, we named the Josephine. The third, which had around a yellow disk, shaded in black and red, seven or eight stems of blossoms, each one of which might have been a beautiful flower in itself, was named *la dominicale,* not only because it appeared to us to be the mistress of all the flowers found in the area, but also because it was first found on a Sunday.

The sight of the Platte, always beautiful, is sometimes admirable. In spite of its beauty, the river bore a very common name because the poor *voyageurs,* unable to think of a comparison for something of which they were ignorant, named objects for the first thing which came to mind. This did not prevent such names from being very apt in certain instances. Thus, the river which the Indians called the Nebraska was named the Platte by the French because of its width. In some places it is as much as six thousand feet wide. It is, however, no more than six feet deep and in some places only a foot. Once the deceptive character of the river is recognized, it can be said that there is nothing more gracious or more varied than the perspective it presents, at any rate toward midstream. But aside from prairie flowers, one saw on its banks only a stubble of forest and a few small bushes. Larger vegetation has sought refuge from the autumn fires on the islands which dot the river.

In spite of repeated warnings from the captain, a young man of the party chose to go hunting for buffalo. He fell into the hands of a party of Indians who began by appropriating his gun and horse and ended by responding violently to his remonstrances. Very angry and chagrined by his misadventure, he returned to the camp and gave the cry of alarm.[8] It was toward evening. The campsite had already been chosen and the horses unsaddled when the cry reached our ears. In an instant the horses were rebridled, resaddled, remounted, and ranged in a battle line. It was the colonel who had ordered this maneuver. Women and children were placed between two lines of wagons. The men who were able to bear arms were drawn up on the right and on the left. In the distance one could see various detachments of Indians assembling. The young man wanted to pounce upon the robbers without delay, killing everyone and smashing everything if his property was not returned. Already he had charged with raised gun and at such speed that he failed to notice that his hat blew off. Fortunately, he was pursued by our captain, a man of good sense as well as of spirit, who had a great deal of experience behind him. By great good fortune, he was readily recognized by the Indians because of his white hair. And very soon there was no question of fighting, but only of friendship, provided restitution was made. Our young man learned that, even with the Indians, calm reason accomplishes more than force or anger. These Indians were Cheyenne in search of adventure.[9] They were reputed to be the bravest Indians on the plains. When they camped about twenty paces from us, we

The Overland
Trail Drawings
of Nicholas Point, S.J.

Passage of a muddy ravine (sometime in May, date unknown). (Courtesy Jesuit Missouri Province Archives, St. Louis, hereinafter cited JMPA)

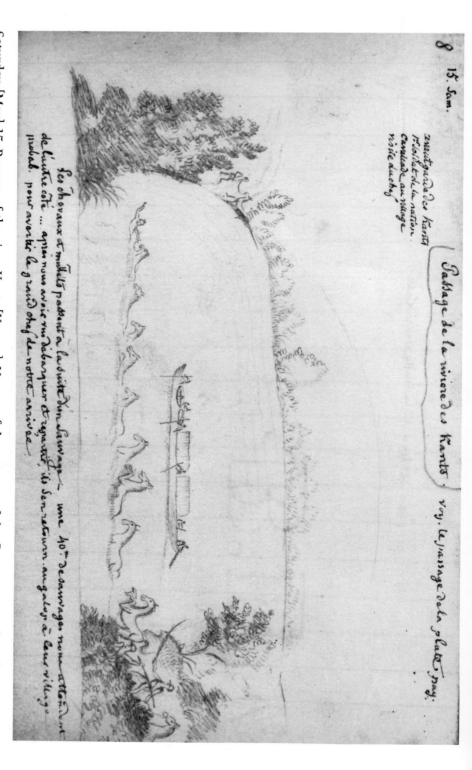

Saturday, [May] 15. Passage of the river Kants [Kansas]. Voyage of the passage of the flat country side. Advance guard at the Kants / first soldier of [the Indian] nation / cavalcade to the [Indian] village / visit to the chief. The horses and mules pass through following an Indian. Approximately 40 Indians are waiting for us on the other side. After having seen us get off the boat and continue on, they turned around and fled to their village on horseback probably to warn the chief of our arrival. (Courtesy JMPA)

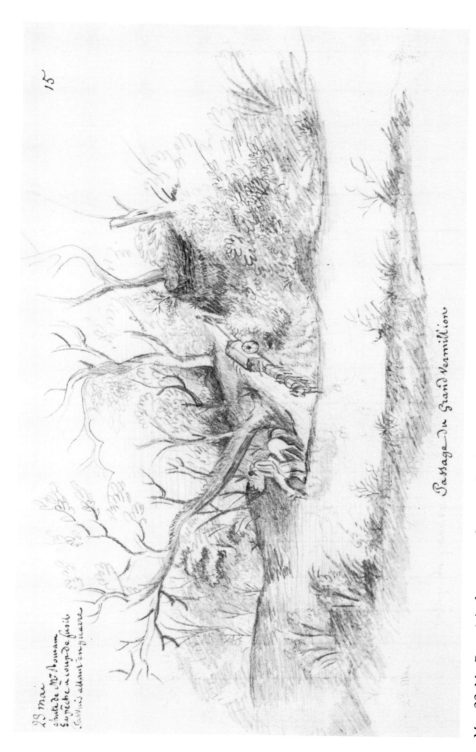

Passage Du Grand Vermillion

May 23. Mr. Romain's descent to the river / Fishing with a gun / Pawnes [Pawnees] going to war. Passage of the Big Red [Vermillion River]. *(Drawing No. 5 from the Pierre Jean De Smet Papers, Washington State University Libraries, Pullman, hereinafter cited WSUL)*

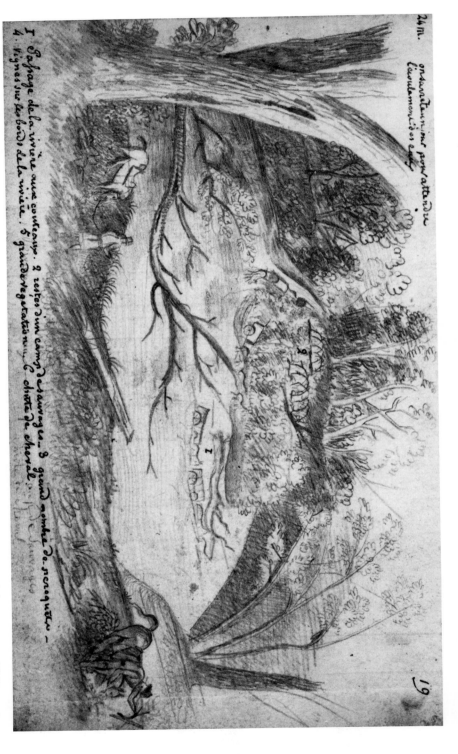

May 24. We always stop and wait for the water level to go down. 1) Landscape of the River of the Knives. 2) Remains of an Indian camp. 3) Large number of parrots [meaning colored birds]. 4) Vineyards on the river's edges. 5) Large vegetation. 6) Horse's chute. (Courtesy JMPA)

Island Camp. June 3. Wagon stuck in the mud. Isabelle, Lagrande, and Marguerite [names of the three horses pulling the wagon]. [Below] Buffalo head. (*Drawing No. 7. Courtesy WSUL*)

New species of iris. June 10. View from mountain range which overlaps the first 2 branches of the plate [Platte River]. Prairie dogs / keel-like part of a ridge / wild geese / Buffalo remains / new species of iris. (*Drawing No. 10. Courtesy WSUL*)

Native family wanting to follow us everywhere. [Actually, they did. They joined the company at Fort Laramie on June 24 and traveled with them as far as Green River.] (*Drawing No. 15. Courtesy WSUL*)

June 28. Black Lady, the Highest of the Black Hills. (*Drawing No. 14. Courtesy WSUL*)

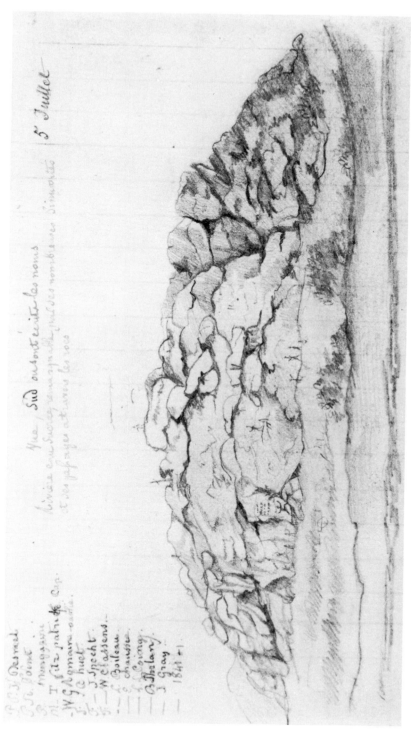

[The list of names on the upper left reads:] P P J De Smet [the P is for Pater = Father], P N Point, P [G] Mengarini [the three Jesuit priests], M [Mr.] T Fitzpatrick Cap[tain], W G Romaine — forgot [an Englishman], F [the F is for Frater = Brother] F C Neut, F J Specht, F W Classens [Claessens] [the Jesuit brothers], L Boileau, F Chaussie, L L Coing [or Coiong?] [the Jesuit teamsters], R Phelan, J Grey — 1841. July 5. South view where names are written. [This was Independence Rock.] Sweet Water River [is] remarkable, not very winding, and passage through the rocks. (*Drawing No. 18, Courtesy WSUL*)

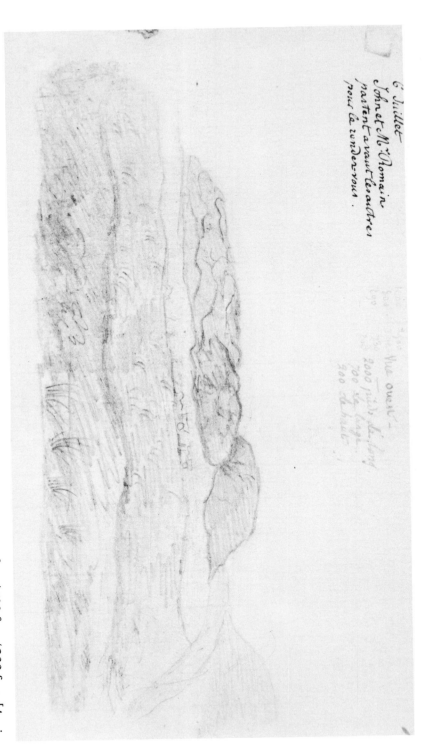

6 Juillet
Le Sketch. M.ᵣ Romain
partent avant le autres
pour la rendezvous.

Vue Ouest
2000 pieds de long
700 de large
200 de haut

July 6. John [Grey] and Mr. Romain[e] leave for a meeting with others. West view / 2000 feet / 700 feet / 200 feet. [Again this is Independence Rock. Grey and Romaine set out in their wagon to see if they could rendezvous with trappers on the Green River. They returned without success on July 13. See Bidwell Journal entries for these two dates.] (*Drawing No. 19. Courtesy WSUL*)

A camp kitchen. [Observe the iron kettle on tripod and the long-handled skillet used to fry food over an open fire. *(Drawing No. 19. Courtesy WSUL)*

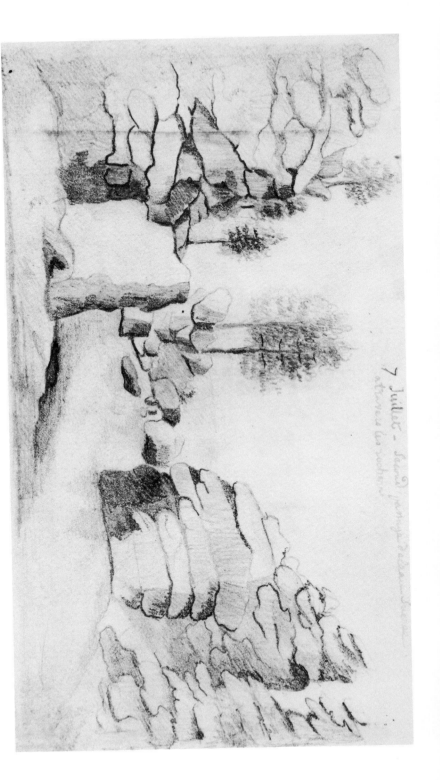

July 7. Second passage of the Sweet Water through the rocks. (*Courtesy JMPA*)

Third view of the plate [Platte River]. Number 4. Sweet Water July 14. [This was the Sweetwater, not the Platte.] (*Drawing No. 22. Courtesy WSUL*).

July 31. Thom kills two wild goats at the same time. He brings them back another one on his shoulders. [Thom should probably read John, referring to John Grey, who was the hunter for the missionary band.] (*Drawing No. 24, Courtesy WSUL*).

thought only of exchanging tokens of confidence. Lances were planted in the ground; shields were hung on them, and the braves divided into several groups. They conversed, listened, and asked questions, laughed and smoked the calumet in our honor. . . . The chief was invited to eat with us, but, in the evening, at our request, he consigned his men to their camp. The next day and for several days after, until we reached the river, they followed us.

You kill a certain number of buffalo, skin them, arrange the skins in the form of a canoe by stretching it over poles, and then seal the openings with the tallow of the animals. You load into this vessel as much as you wish and then, by using a pole or even by getting into the water yourself, you propel it toward the other bank.

This time we came off with less trouble than usual, for our guides had discovered a means of crossing. But it required the most extreme caution, especially with the cattle, which were more difficult to drive than the horses. While the driver lashed away at the beasts from his seat, others, on horseback or wading on foot on either side of the wagon, shouted and whipped them, to keep the vehicle in motion as well as to prevent it from being turned aside. For greater security a number of ropes were tied to the top of the wagon and held taut by men placed at some distance in the river to help preserve equilibrium. The water and the cattle roared, the horses neighed, the men shouted in an earsplitting fashion. I have never heard such an uproar. Nevertheless, strange as it may seem, the crossing was made almost without mishap.

The most sorely inconvenienced members of the expedition were the poor dogs. How they ran to and fro on the bank! How piteously they yelped! Most of them remained on the first bank all night, not daring to swim across. Finally, the example of the more daring ones prompted the others to venture into the treacherous element and with great effort they all had the good fortune to be able to rejoin the camp. What courage can be inspired by the love of the fatherland!

Of all the many knolls to be found in the vicinity of the Platte, the most interesting one was commonly called The Chimney. After this one came The Castle, The Fortress, and so on. They are all, however, much more beautiful from a distance than close at hand.

Everyone has heard of the rattlesnakes and mosquitoes which have been mentioned so frequently in accounts by the first missionaries in America. I will, therefore, mention them only to thank God publicly for the protection he gave us from the former and for the patience he gave us to endure the latter. On the feast of St. Francis Regis, the wagoners, without once leaving the trail, killed a dozen rattlesnakes with their whips.[10] The menacing heads of these reptiles, and their rattling tails always warn one of their hostile intentions. Next to the more destructive winged insects, the small, inoffensive ant is very common. At almost every step, one found anthills of several feet in diameter constructed, not of grain, as in our European fields and gardens, but out of small pebbles. This observation would seem to necessitate a modification of that opinion which holds that ants exercise foresight in storing food and in constructing their dwellings. The grain, which ants collect in Europe, could well serve to feed them during the winter. But does it really serve that purpose as directly as the other? This seems to me scarcely probable, especially since provisions of another nature can be found in their individual cells. At any rate, the wonderful instinct with which God has endowed them for the continual preservation of their species is admirable. Why are these hills composed of tiny globules, and why are the globules arranged in little mounds? Why are the mounds given a specific inclination, and why is the entry always made on the side opposite to the prevailing wind? All of these things point to some kind of wisdom in these tiny heads. . . .

I do not know how the prairie dog got its name. In shape, size, color, agility, and timidity, it resembles a squirrel more than a dog. Some think it to be a kind of marmot. Each single family of prairie dogs has its own burrow. On the prairies, families are so very numerous that they form villages. These villages differ from those of the beaver in that, instead of being on a stream's bank, they are located as far from water as possible. It is said that the prairie dog feeds only on grass roots and drinks dew. A tradition of travelers in the West, which borders somewhat on the fantastic, has it that the prairie dogs sometimes leave their burrows en masse to form a general assembly. When a prairie dog hears or sees something hostile, it scampers into its burrow and from there gives forth a piercing cry which is repeated from burrow to burrow, putting the entire colony on the alert. Since it is naturally very curious, however, in a few minutes it pokes its nose out of its hole. The hunter chooses that moment to shoot it. This requires a great deal of skill, for the small animal, endowed with great agility and piercing sight, ordinarily does not expose more than the top of its head.

What is said about the strength of the beaver's four small teeth is very true. I have seen trees, more than two feet in diameter, cut in two by these apparently feeble instruments. I do not know if what is said in addition to this is true. Some hold that before felling the trees which are to serve in the construction of their dams they examine, among the trees suitable to this purpose, those which lean toward the spot on which they are to be used. If none of the trees offers this advantage, they wait until a good wind comes to their assistance and, while the wind is bending the tree, set to work and soon have the tree toppling.

There is a kind of frog which differs essentially from those we see in Europe, in that it has a tail and lives in arid places which are stony and hot. I have heard it called a salamander.

On June 28 we left Fort Laramie to continue westward. Before us lay the Black Hills.[11] As we advanced, the shade of the vegetation became increasingly somber, the form of the hills much more rugged, the face of the mountains more towering. The general impression was one not of decay but of age or, rather, of the most venerable antiquity.

The most remarkable landmark in this beautiful solitude is Independence Rock, so-called, not, as would seem to be the case, because of its isolation and the extraordinary strength of its position, but because the Americans who named · it arrived in its vicinity on the day on which their separation from Great Britain is celebrated. It is probable that, having thus named the rock, they inscribed their names on it, together with their birthdates. Hence its nickname, "The Great Register of the Wilderness." We ourselves arrived on the morrow of a similar day, that is, on July 5. According to custom, each one of us wrote down his name [on the rock], following the Name one pronounces only with a reverent inclination.

At the foot of this colossus runs the small, peaceful river called the Sweetwater. It is distinguished by its limpidity and its numerous twists, an indication of the evenness of its bed. But higher up, near its source, its aspect is altogether different. There one sees it leaping or, rather, one hears it rushing through a long crevice filled with rocky fragments—a blackish mass and a horrifying sound, which have earned for it the name "Devil's Door." It could have been given a more cheerful name, for if its precipitous passage suggests Hell by the horrors it conceals, it resembles the path of Heaven by the shades of rose and blue it displays from a distance. It was impossible to rest one's gaze on it without thinking of happiness.

Buffalo are so plentiful in the area that a single member of the party killed eleven of them within a few hours, satisfying himself with bringing back only the tongues.

Two long months had passed since our entry into the wilderness, but at last we were arriving, if not at the end of our journey and of the greatest perils, at least at the Rocky Mountains to which our most ardent prayers had so long transported us. A celebration was held in camp in honor of these mountains. Why are they called rocky? Because they are composed of granite and flint. Some travelers have given them the more pompous name of "Backbone of the World" because they are the principal chain which divides the North American continent lengthwise. This great chain is buttressed on the west by the Cordilleras and on the east by the Wind River Range. It was toward mid-July that we crossed the highest ridge of the latter. Behind us we had the tributaries of the Missouri; before us lay the rivers that empty into the Pacific. What a magnificent view! But who could describe the majesty of the wilderness as we then saw it? At this sight, a single need filled our souls, that of exclaiming like the King Prophet, "From the rising of the sun until its setting the name of the Lord is admirable." And we carved into the bark of a cedar which overlooked all this majesty the ever-adorable name at which every knee in Heaven, on earth, and in Hell bends. May this blessed name be for those who pass after us a sign of hope and salvation!

Descending from these heights, we first followed, and then crossed, Little Sandy Creek and Big Sandy Creek. For three days our column floundered through the sands. There was neither good pasturage for the animals nor game to be shot for the men. We thought about the eleven buffalo tongues at the Sweetwater River.

By July 21 we were on the banks of the Green River. All about us was luxuriantly green; we reveled in the abundance. It was there that, nine years earlier, Captain Bonneville had reached the point beyond which he could not proceed.[12] It was there that we met the vanguard of the Flatheads and also a party of French Canadians returning from California. In response to the question, "What news?," the latter painted a picture so little encouraging that many of our party thought only of taking advantage of the opportunity to turn back.[13]

To the great satisfaction of those who were in need of rest, we remained on this spot for two days. We were able to say Mass, and all who were Catholic assisted most piously. On the day on which our parting took place, two persons who had frequented our bivouac, our hunter and a young Englishman, both came to bid us good-by. The Englishman was a Protestant, but not withstanding his religious principles, he promised that if Providence should ever bring us together again, he would be happy to show us his gratitude for the services we had rendered him. I have retained this beautiful reflection of his: that one must travel in the wilderness to learn how attentive Providence is to the needs of man. What became of him? I learned that he was able to pass safely through the danger of the return journey, but that his companion, without having had time to repent, was killed by an Indian woman who was an enemy of his family.[14]

As for the travelers returning from California, many acknowledged that they had more than one duty to fulfill, and all promised to fulfill them—but next year. Unfortunately for most of them next year never came. Two weeks had not passed before they were attacked and killed, some by Sioux, others by Arapahoes and Cheyennes. Among them was the greatest blasphemer of the party. Their leader had been one of the first to fall, struck by a stray bullet. He had made his fortune and had anticipated spending his remaining years resting from his adventures. In all matters one should profit by favorable opportunities.

Meanwhile our column was winding its way through a labyrinth of mountains. Once, when we had traveled from sunrise to sunset only to end up in a blind alley, we had to retrace our steps, surrounded by Indians seeking to kill and plunder. On August 10, after a long march across an open plain, we arrived, by skirting Bear River, at the most beautiful campsite that we had seen. Limpid springs, refreshing fruits, game in great abundance, the most varied and picturesque views, all seemed to invite travelers to make this their winter quarters. There were some who thought seriously of doing this, but not all deemed it advisable. Since the small size of the group would not make a safe stay here possible, the march was resumed through a narrow pass which opened out into a plain stretching as far as eye could see.

It was there that the missionaries left the rest of the group, turning off to the right, while the Americans bore off to the left. We had lived together for three months amidst the same perils and were as of one fatherland. Farewells were sad. Many prejudices had disappeared during the journey. But, since most of them seemed firmly attached to error, there seemed little hope that we should see each other in the true fatherland.

Notes

1 As noted elsewhere, the three Jesuit priests were De Smet, Mengarini, and Point. The three Jesuit brothers were Claessens, Huet, and Sprecht.

2 An Italian Jesuit, St. Francis de Geronimo (1642–1716) spent most of his life in Naples. His feast day is May 11.

3 The Shawnee had originally been persuaded by the Spanish, when they ruled the Louisiana Territory, to move to Missouri in 1793. About 1825 they moved to the present state of Kansas. Frederick F. Hodge, *Handbook of North American Indians* (2 vols., Washington, D.C., 1907–1910), II: 538.

4 The reference is probably to present-day Shawnee Mission, Kansas.

5 Thomas Fitzpatrick was also known as Broken Hand due to a deformity. Born in 1799, he died in 1854 after an adventure-filled life in the Far West. He entered the fur trade in 1823. With its decline, he became a guide and served in 1836 as guide to Marcus Whitman for a portion of his journey west. He ended his career as an U.S. Indian agent. LeRoy R. Hafen, *Broken Hand: The Life of Thomas Fitzpatrick* (Denver, 1973), provides a detailed biography.

6 *Epinette des prairies* is the wild rose.

7 The French word *turnsol* means a sunflower.

8 This was Nicholas "Cheyenne" Dawson.

9 The Cheyenne probably originated in the state of Minnesota. They were a plains tribe of Algonquins. Hodge, *Handbook of North American Indians,* I: 250.

10 May 16 is the feast of St. John Francis Regis.

11 This was Fort Laramie, which is near the site of the present city of Laramie in Wyoming.

12 The reference here is to Captain Benjamin L. E. Bonneville (1796–1878) who was an officer in the U.S. Army who turned to exploration and the fur trade. Between 1832–1835 the latter two pursuits were his primary occupation. His exploits were first celebrated by Washington Irving in his biography, *The Adventures of Captain Bonneville,* published in 1837. An edited version was prepared by Edgeley W. Todd in 1961.

13 This was the fur-trading party lead by Henry Fraeb.

14 The Englishman was named Romaine. When he decided to part company, he was joined by Amos E. Frye and a man named Rogers. As to which of these Fr. Point is referring to is unclear. The inference is that he was accompanied east by an unnamed Indian. This was John Grey, since his death is accurately described by Fr. Point. (See *note* 1, p. 223, *ante.*)

CHAPTER SIXTEEN

Narrative of a Tour from the State of Indiana to the Oregon Territory in the Years 1841–2

by Joseph Williams

Biographical Sketch

The Rev. Joseph Williams was born in Cumberland County, Pennsylvania, a year after the American Revolution began. He was raised in Virginia, so he tell us. As to his clerical training, little is known other than he was an ordained Methodist minister. In 1841 he decided to trek to Oregon to see for himself the activities of the Protestant missionaries in that far-off land. He set out from his home in Napoleon, Riley County, Indiana, and made his way to Westport. There he learned of the Bidwell-Bartleson party, who were already on the trail headed west. He caught up with the party and joined that company for the trip to Soda Springs. When the company split into the California-bound and Oregon-bound contingents, he traveled with the latter.

After visiting the Protestant missionary stations, Williams started his return overland trip in the summer of 1842. By June 16 he was at Fort Hall. He left there on June 28 in company with a few others and reached Bridger's Fort on the Green River by July 3. From there he struck south to Rubedeau's [Robidoux's] Fort and left that establishment with the proprietor on July 27 headed for New Mexico. By August 20 the Rio Grande River was reached. By September 16 he arrived at Bent's Fort, traveling the Santa Fe Trail. He reached his Indiana home at ten o'clock at night on an unstated subsequent date. As to his last years, nothing has been found so far. However, in 1843 he had his narrative of his travels published and noted that he was then sixty-six years old. That would date his birth in the year 1777 and would mean he made his overland journey west at the age of sixty-four, making him the oldest member of the Bidwell-Bartleson party.[1]

The extract which follows is reproduced from the reprint edition of Williams's Narrative . . . (New York, 1921), pp. 29–45.

1 Data drawn from Williams's narrative of his trip.

I rode over, the next morning, to Westport, and finding the company were all gone, and no possibility of overtaking them, with much pain of mind I gave up going any farther, and knew not what to do. I then rode across the Shawnee mission, three miles from Westport, across the Missouri line, and there I met brother Greene, presiding elder, who told me the company, about four days previous, was eight miles ahead of me, on the Caw River. I said within myself, surely the Lord is opening my way to go on. I began to get ready to go on, but could not get half prepared. Bought some powder and lead, and some provision and a gun, but was disappointed in getting my gun. My feelings were much harrowed up with the brethren trying to discourage me, and keep me from going to the Mountains. One of the preachers told me it was almost presumptuous for so old a man as I to attempt such a hazardous journey, and added, that he had awful feelings for me through the last night; and he said, so had some of the rest. Mr. Greene said there was a *possibility* of my returning, but not a probability.

I started out on Saturday, with brother Johnson, a missionary, and two Indian chiefs of the Caw tribe. We reached, that night, Wakloosa Creek, and camped under the trees. Brother Johnson cooked supper, and we had cakes and coffee. We laid down to sleep; the thunder and lightning could be heard and seen, and the wind began to blow. I was somewhat alarmed, for fear of the trees falling on us. The rain soon began, and the wind ceased. Then I soon fell asleep, and rested well and comfortably. I arose next morning happy; bless the Lord, O my soul; praise him who takes care of us in the desert!

This day we traveled through extensive rolling prairies, with some few skirts of timber. We rode forty-five miles that day, and reached brother Johnson's mission. Brother and sister Johnson furnished me with provision, and every thing that I needed, and offered to do any thing that they could for me. Brother Johnson has died since, and I doubt not, has gone to heaven to reap his reward. I shall never forget their kindness to me. Next morning I started, in company with Mr. Brensill. When we came to the Caw River, the Indians said we could cross it. We entered in, and the water ran over our horses' backs, and I got my provisions wet. We inquired of the Indians, and they told us the company was ahead about four days' journey, and they gave me directions and how to find their trail. I rode about seven miles. I was then alone, about 9 o'clock; and being about to pass through the territory occupied by the Pawnee tribe, I thought of what they told me about being robbed or killed, and put my whip to my horse. Passing through a small thicket of woods, I saw a pishamore lying near the trail, and lit down to get it, when I saw that there was an Indian's pack, that I concluded was laid there to decoy me. I then sprang upon my horse, gave him the whip, and rode till dark. This day traveled about forty miles, and came to a willow thicket; tied my horse with a long rope, laid down, and slept till next morning, nothing breaking the silence of the night but a few bull-frogs. I arose and returned to the road, and saw some fresh horse tracks that had been made during the night, I supposed by the Indians, who had been following me. The Caws (or Kauzas) told me that the Pawnees were a bad nation, and that they had a battle with them; that they had their women and children hid in a thicket, whom they (the Pawnees) slaughtered in a barbarous manner. I can hardly describe my feelings as I was traveling alone, up Caw (or Kauzas) River. Pursuing my journey that day, I tried to give myself up to the Lord. I could scarcely follow the wagon tracks, the ground was so hard in the prairie. I had almost concluded, at last, to turn back, and got down on my knees, and asked the Lord whether I should do so or not. These words came to my mind: "The Lord shall be with thee, and no hand shall harm thee." I then renewed my resolution to go on in the name of the Lord, believing that all would be well, and that I should, in the end, return safely home. I went cheerfully for some time; but was occasionally perplexed with doubts. About an hour before sunset, I got down off my horse, and prayed again. God renewed the promise, and I got up and started on refreshed in spirit, and with renewed courage, thinking all would be well; and instead of sleeping in the prairie, I got to an encampment where there was fire, and plenty of wood, and good water, and I praised God with all my heart. I roasted my meat, sweetened some water, and, with my biscuits, made a hearty supper; laid down by my fire, and slept well and comfortably till morning. A little dog that the company had left, kept around the camp, barking and howling.

Next morning I arose quite happy in my soul, and said, "My God hath preserved me hitherto, and now God has answered my prayer." I then ate my breakfast and started, happy in my soul. I crossed the Vermillion Creek, and arose on the rolling prairie. I shouted some hours over these beautiful plains. No fear nor trouble came near me, for God had given me so many glorious promises, that I could not doubt or fear for a moment. Not an Indian appeared that day. About 4 o'clock in the afternoon, I saw the company about four miles ahead, but soon lost sight of them again; and coming to the place where the company had stopped to eat dinner, I alighted, and let my horse feed awhile. At this place, as the company afterwards told me, about two hundred Indians had been seen only an hour before. They had sometimes hung on the rear of the company, and had made some show of attacking those who lingered behind the main body. Awhile before, they had robbed four men of all they had, stripped them naked, and left them in the open prairies to perish before they could get to the white settlements. The company said it was ninety-nine chances to one that I escaped the hands of the Indians, for they had seen all along where I had come. Surely a wise God controlled the heathens, and protected me; for as I came along the day before, I found a piece of a buffalo robe in the trail, which I thought some of the company had dropped, but after I had put it on my saddle, I saw on the other side of the road a skin bag, full of something, which I then knew was an Indian bag. I then rode on as fast as I could till evening, when I took up my lodging. O how good the Lord is; let all the world with me praise him. Praise him, O my soul; for I trusted in him, and he has preserved me. How good it is to converse with the Lord. The company seemed glad that I had made my escape. The company consisted of about fifty. The greater part were bound for California; a few only for Oregon. There was about twenty wagons belonging to the expedition, drawn by oxen. One of the company was a Catholic priest, a Mr. de Smidt [Smet], who was extremely kind to me, and invited me to come and eat supper with him that night, and next morning brought me some venison. He appeared to be a very fine man. I was invited to sing by a woman, and then to pray. I did so.

MAY 27th. We marched on through plains. 28th. Saw two antelopes, the first I ever saw of those animals. We traveled three hundred miles up the Caw River from Westport, on the west line of the Missouri, all the way through prairies, which seem almost to have no end. On Sunday, 30th, I had a thought of trying to preach to the company. There were some as wicked people among them as I ever saw in all my life. There was some reluctance shown by the captain of the company; others wanted me to preach to them. Part of this Sabbath day was a happy time to me. My soul was drawn out to God, for he was with me, though in the midst of an ignorant and hard-hearted people. The men killed several antelopes, and saw some elks. On Monday, the 31st, we left the Blue (or Blue Earth) River, a fork of Caw River, and traveled over to the Platte River. We passed the Pawnee towns the next day, about six miles to the north of us. We then turned more to the southwest, and camped on Platte River that night. We had two Methodists in company with us. Col. Bartleson had been a Methodist, but is now a backslider. Our leader, Fitzpatrick, is a wicked, worldly man, and is much opposed to missionaries going among the Indians. He has some intelligence, but is deistical in his principles. At 2 o'clock, commenced a most tremendous bad storm, with wind, which blew down most of the tents, accompanied with rain and lightning and thunder almost all night. I slept but little, the ground being all covered with water. That night, dreadful oaths were heard all over the camp ground. O the wickedness of the wicked.

On this night I was called upon to marry a couple of young people belonging to our company, without law or license, for we were a long way from the United States. Perhaps this was the first marriage in all these plains, among white people.[1]

Next morning we continued up the Platte River. This river is said to be about sixteen hundred miles long, and is here about one-fourth of a mile wide, and very muddy. The Indians call it Elk River. lt empties into the Missouri, a few miles below Council Bluff. The Caw River is said to be about seven hundred miles long. It empties into the Missouri River, at the west line of the state of Missouri. On Thursday, we traveled through the most level plains I ever saw in my life. Here is such a scenery of beauty as is seldom witnessed. The Platte plains are lower than the the banks. There are bluffs all along here, for four or five miles. The next day there came on a tremendous storm of rain, wind, and thunder, which lasted about an hour and a half. We traveled up the river, and encamped all night where wood was very scarce, and hard to be got, and we made our fires of some willow bushes. On Friday evening the company had a terrible alarm. One of our hunters, who was in the rear, was robbed of all he had by the Indians. They struck him with their ram-rods, and he ran from them. Soon a war party of the Sioux Indians appeared in view. We soon collected together in order of battle, to be ready in case of an attack. The Indians stood awhile and looked at us, and probably thinking that "the better part of valor is discretion," they soon showed signs of peace. Captain Fitzpatrick then went to them, and talked with them, for he was acquainted with them. They then gave back all that they had taken from the young man, and our men gave them some tobacco, and they smoked the pipe of peace.

The next morning we continued up this river, along smooth banks, without any timber. That afternoon we had a very severe hail storm, accompanied with thunder; one Indian was knocked down with a hail stone, about as large as a goose egg. We soon discovered a water spout, which came down into the river. When it struck the river it made a great foam, and then passed off in a dreadful tornado. The next day we saw six flat-bottomed boats coming down, loaded with buffalo robes and skins. The poor fellows in the boats looked very dirty and ragged. We now began to see plenty of buffalo signs; all the way previous, game had been scarce. Here we had not very good water to drink, having to use the muddy water of the Platte River. On Sunday, we staid where we had tolerably good water. Companies of Indians still came into our camp to trade with us. The bluffs here are getting larger and higher and wider from the river. These plains are covered all over with buffalo bones and skulls. I long to get out of these plains to where we can get plenty of good water and wood. I am still weary of hearing so much swearing by the wicked white men. On Monday night, we had another hard storm of rain, hail, and thunder. These beautiful bluffs look, in some places, like magnificent buildings.

JUNE 1st. We had storms all the time. Sunday, 7th. Our hunters killed an elk, for the first time. On Wednesday, they killed three buffaloes. The Indians still continued to travel with us. This night we were threatened with another thunder storm, but it passed off without much rain. Our hunters killed some more buffaloes, and we then had plenty of meat. It is thought that the Platte plains here are several feet below the surface of the water. The river banks are very low, but never overflow. Some small cedars grow on the top of the bluffs. The bluffs get larger and higher as we ascend the river. Monday morning we began to make ready to cross the south fork of Platte River. This fork is about one-fourth of a mile wide, with sandy bottom; some places the wagons nearly swam. We got across with some difficulty, but not much danger. There were seven or eight buffaloes seen coming up with our oxen; our hunters shot one of them. Some more were seen with the other oxen. They seemed to form an attachment to each other. Thursday, we traveled up the north side of the south fork. Here we saw thousands of buffalo, all along the plains. Our hunters shot down one bull; they thought it unnecessary to kill any more. Here we saw packs of wolves, which followed them. This morning there was a great alarm given that the Indians had driven off some of the oxen, and our men went in pursuit of them, and brought them back. One man said he saw an Indian, and shot at him, but some did not believe him. All this time, I had to stand guard every fourth night. The Indians still come to trade with us. Here we have nothing to make our fires but buffalo manure. This morning a large buffalo bull came near us, when we were marching along and seemed regardless of the bullets; but after fifteen or twenty were shot at him, he fell. We started across to the north fork, about two miles to the northwest, and then traveled about twenty miles up the river; staid there on Saturday night. Here an awful circumstance took place: A young man by the name of Shotwell, shot himself accidentally, and died in about two hours afterwards. I was called upon, by his comrades, to preach his funeral, which I did. The death of this young man caused some seriousness in his comrades for a few days. On Sunday evening, we went up the river about eight miles, to the mouth of Ash Creek, and staid there one day and two nights. We then traveled up through the bluffs and bald hills, the weather still cold and windy. Nothing grows here but some willow bushes on the banks. The plains are poor and broken. Many curious shapes and forms may be seen among the bluffs. Some abrupt elevations look like houses, with steeples to them. One we saw sixteen or eighteen miles ahead of us, which resembled a house with the chimney in the middle of it; or like a funnel, with the small end uppermost, and covering about two acres of ground. The chimney part is about one hundred feet high, and about thirty feet square. We passed an old fort below the mouth of the Larrimee River; and crossing that river, we went up to a new fort that they were building, called Fort Johns.[2] Here is a mixture of people; some white, some half breeds, some French. Here is plenty of talk about their damnation, but none about their salvation; and I thought of the words of David, "Woe is me that I sojourn in Mesech, that I dwelt in the tents of Kedar." Here we came in sight of the Black Hills. We have now buffalo meat in abundance, which they cut up in slices, and dry in the sun. I never experienced colder weather for the time of year, now late in June. The people here appear healthier than at any other place in the country. The white people have Indian women for their wives. There are two Forts here, about one mile apart, and another about one hundred and fifty miles south.[3] I tried to preach twice to these people, but with little effect. Some of them said they had not heard preaching for twelve years.

Leaving the Fort, we soon entered the Black Hills. Traveling up the Larrimee River, we had plenty of good wood and water, and felt ourselves much refreshed, thanks be to God. I am now getting well used to eating buffalo meat.

JULY 1st. We crossed the north fork with difficulty, and in the passage had a mule drowned. Buffaloes and bears are very plenty, and our hunters shot them down all around, so that we had good fat meat in abundance. All this country is still very poor and the timber small — cotton wood and willow. Few Indians to be seen; some mixed breeds are with Mr. de Smidt, going on to the Columbia River to the Catholic mission. Here grow a great many wild shrubs, with wild sage and grease-wood, resembling young pine, with which the bald hills are covered. It is seldom eaten by any kind of animal. Here we have the Black Hills upon our left. The third day of the month, we left the Platte and went on to the Sweet[water] River, a branch of the Platte, which heads up in the mountains. We are now supposed to be in north latitude 41°. The streams of water are very good. I notice here large quantities of something like glauber salts. It looks like white frost. This country is thought to be extremely healthy.

JULY 4th. Came in sight of the Big Horn (or Wind River) Mountain. The next day we passed the Red Bluffs, and at night reached the Independence Rock, on Sweet River, at which a company celebrated the 4th of July, 1838. Next night (Sunday) I proposed having prayers; several of the wicked class came up. Near this, we passed a place where the whole river runs through a narrow channel, or sluice in the rocks. This night we have the sound of the violin, but not much dancing. "Woe unto the wicked; for they shall have their reward." Our company is mostly composed of Universalists and deists. Here is an almost solid rock, like a mountain, on the right side of Sweet River. Buffaloes and antelopes are very plenty in this region. Driving through dry, rough plains, we try to get to the creeks to obtain grazing for our animals. We are now in the neighborhood of the Crow nation of Indians, who are peaceable. We have this morning again come in sight of the Wind River Mountain. Its summit is still spotted with snow.

JULY 10th. At night we were cold. I could not keep warm, although I had a buffalo robe to cover me. It is said here, that the ground is sometimes frozen in August an inch deep. Today we traveled over some high, bald hills; dined on good fat buffalo, that our hunters had just killed. We went over on Sweet River, and dried our meat for the remaining part of our journey, where we expected not to find any more game. We are still in sight of the big Wind Mountain; for it may be seen at the distance of seventy or eighty miles. For hundreds of miles we have to pass over barren ground. I went out with the hunters to bring in meat to dry, and we soon killed a buffalo, which Mr. Jones and myself loaded our animals with, and started back to camp, I acting as pilot. We struck too high on the creek, and such places for rocks and hills and cliffs I never traveled over before. We arrived home just after dark. The next day we came in sight of the Sweet River Mountain. Its peaks were tolerably well whitened with snow. There are some white bears in these mountains, but we have not killed any yet. There are also some white wolves, about as white as sheep. They are a dull, sleepy looking animal, and very surly; not very mindful of any thing, nor much afraid. They are about the size of a common wolf. 16th, July. We are engaged in drying our meat for crossing the mountains. This morning we had a very great frost, and some ice. We are still in sight of the Sweet River Mountain.

Today, we lay by for the arrival of the Snake Indians to come and trade for our articles, and a man was sent to tell them to come. Today, Col. Bartleson gave some of our deists a down-setting, which pleased me very well. We moved about three miles up the river, to get better grazing ground for our animals. This river is very beautiful; clear, running water, fine springs all along; no timber, soil poor and barren. Sunday, 18th. We lodged on Little Sandy Creek, a beautiful stream. 19th. We stand on Big Sandy Creek. These two creeks run into Green River, a branch of the Colorado River.

We have now just crossed the ridge between the Green River and the Missouri. All these mountains that we have been traveling through, are spurs of the Rocky Mountains, whose peaks are covered with eternal snow. Although the mountains are spotted with snow, yet the plains are very hot and sultry. Today, we saw some white, grizzly bears, and killed some mountain sheep, the horns of which are as thick as a man's leg, and about two feet long; but they have no wool upon them, and are not much larger than our common sheep. Friday, 23rd. We lay on Green River bottom, where we fell in with Mr. Frap, who was on a hunting expedition. This man, with nine or ten of his company, was afterwards killed in a skirmish with the Sioux Indians. His company was mostly composed of half breeds, French, and Dutch, and all sorts of people collected together in the mountains, and were a wicked, swearing company of men. Here sugar sold for $1.50 per pound; powder and lead from $1.50 to $2.50 per pound. While here, a wedding took place in our company, between Mr. Richard Fillan [Phelan] and a Mrs. Gray, who had left her husband in Missouri. They were married by Mr. de Smidt, the Catholic priest. Six of our company left us and returned to the United States. Leaving Mr. Frap's [Frapp] company, we continued our journey down Green River. On Sabbath we have nothing but swearing, fishing, etc. Here I gave myself up to God, determined to serve him better than ever. 27th. We encamped on Black's fork. We are now among the Snake nation and Flat Head Indians. These latter are like other Indians, but their heads have been clamped up in a box while infants. We traveled about ten miles a day, much impeded by the thickets of sage and grease-wood. Here we find the little prairie dogs. They are about the size of the fox squirrel, and of a brownish color. They are in shape like a little dog with short tails. Here we also find other small animals, about the size of the ground squirrel. They all live, as it were, in towns, burrowed in the ground. These little animals appear to visit one another, from the appearance of their paths from one burrow to another. Their houses are covered up; and when they see travelers, they run to their holes. The sage hen is found here also. They are somewhat less than the turkey hen, and are supposed to live on the sage leaves. They are not very good to eat.

JULY 28th On Ham's fork of Green River. One of our wagons broke down today. 30th. We traveled across the barren hills towards Bear River. This was a hot, sultry day; yet we could see snow on the Eutaw Mountains, on the head waters of the Colorado River. Next night we lay on Black's fork. August 1st. At night I tried to preach to the deists and swearers. Some of them seemed angry, but I thought I cleared my conscience. Next day we traveled through hills and bad roads till we came to Bear River, which runs into Big Salt Lake. Here we rested, and waited for the Snake Indians to come and trade with us. The Bear River bottoms are beautiful to look at, but not rich, and have no timber. On each side of the river are high, naked bluffs, in some places like small mountains; and in the valleys, large springs of beautiful cold water abound. Farther on, we found tolerably good lands, and beautiful small creeks, having good mill sites. Some few pines are growing along these bluffs. This day I felt weak from living on dry buffalo meat, without bread. Sunday, 8th. We rested. The employment is still fishing and hunting, and such swearing I never heard in my life before. God will surely punish these swearers. Still we find large beautiful streams coming down from the mountains, whose sides are covered with pine trees. Fish are plenty in all these streams. A fine settlement might be formed along this river. We next came to the soda springs. These springs seem to boil like a pot of water; but there is no heat in them, except one, that is just on the, bank of the river, which is built in the form of a crawfish hole, about three feet high, formed a sediment thrown up by the water, which spouts about three feet high every quarter of a minute. There is an air hole near it that makes a noise like a steamboat, but not so loud. This water is something similar to the artificial soda water. Some of these springs are situated in the bottom of the river, and occasion an ebullition on the surface. This water is somewhat purgative, and is thought by some to possess medical qualities, which may hereafter make it a place of great resort by invalids and others. This place looks as if it might once have been a great volcano. There is something like lava that has been thrown out of a hole, and lies some inches thick on the ground. Around it is a fine country of rich land, good fresh water, healthy, and a very mild climate. Some of the sediment is of a red color, and the stones have the appearance of pumice.

Here our hunters killed a pelican, as white as snow, and its legs and feet like those of a goose. Its bill is about eighteen inches long, and it has a pouch under its jaw that will hold about three pints. The pelican is about six feet long, its tail short, the flesh coarse, and not very good to eat. This day we parted with some of our company. They went down the Bear River in order to go to California. There was some division and strife among us about going; some who set out for California changed their minds to go to the Columbia. Those who went to California, (as I afterwards learned) were much perplexed about getting through, as they had no regular guide; and were forced to kill some of their animals, to save themselves from perishing with hunger. They passed the Big Salt Lake. At this Lake, abundance of salt is made by evaporation in the sun.

Notes

1 Williams married Miss Williams to Zedidiah Kelsey. This was the first such emigrant marriage on the plains.
2 The old fort was the remains of Fort William, founded in 1834. Fort John, not Johns, was an early name for Fort Laramie. Hafen, ed., *The Mountain Men,* I: 143; II: 291.
3 Lancaster P. Lupton built an adobe-walled fort in 1840–1841 on the right bank of the North Platte, about three-fourths of a mile north of the mouth of Laramie Fork. Williams in referring to "another fort one hundred and fifty miles south" of Fort Laramie is referring to a string of forts on the South Platte. There in 1836, Lupton built Fort Lupton and within three years had three rival trading posts, Forts St. Vrain, Vasquez, and Jackson. LeRoy R. Hafen, "Early Fur Trade Forts on the South Platte," *Mississippi Valley Historical Review,* XII (1925): 334.

The 1841 Caravan: A Census Summary

Company Rosters

The Missionary Party and Associates
   Thomas Fitzpatrick, Captain
   Jesuit Fathers: Pierre Jean De Smet, Nicholas Point, Gregory Mengarini
   Jesuit Brothers: William Claessens, Charles Huet, Joseph Specht
   Teamsters: L. Boileau, E. Chaussie, L. L. Coing (or Coviong)
   Trappers: Jim Baker, John Grey, William Mast, Piga (a Frenchman)
   Pleasure Seekers: Amos E. Frye , ——— Rogers,
                  W. G. Romaine (an Englishman)
   Lone Traveler: Reverend Joseph Williams (Protestant minister)

The Bidwell-Bartleson Party
   Those who arrived in California:
      John Bartleson
      Elias Barnett
      Josiah Belden
      William Belty
      John Bidwell
      Henry L. Brolaski
      David W. Chandler
      Joseph B. Chîles
      Grove C. Cook
      Nicholas Dawson
      V. W. Dawson
      Paul Geddes, alias Talbot H. Green
      George Henshaw
      Charles Hopper
      Henry Huber

James John
Thomas Jones
Andrew Kelsey
Benjamin Kelsey
Mrs. Nancy A. Kelsey, and her young daughter
John McDowell
Nelson McMahan
Samuel Green McMahan
Michael C. Nye
Andrew Gwinn Patton
Robert Rickman
John Roland
John L. Schwartz
James P. Springer
Robert H. Thomes
Ambrose Walton
Major Walton
Charles M. Weber

Those who went to Oregon:
——— Carroll
Augustus Fifer [Pfeiffer]
Richard Phelan (sometimes Fillan) and wife (Mrs. Gray)
    and her child by former marriage
William Fowler [Towler]
Charles W. Flügge
David F. Hill
J. M. Jones
Samuel Kelsey, wife and five children
Zedidiah (sometimes Isaac) Kelsey and wife
    (daughter of Richard Williams)
Samuel Kelsey, wife and five children
Edward Rogers
James Ross
Richard Williams and wife

Those who left the company prior to the division at Soda Springs:
——— Jones
Henry Peyton
George Shotwell, deceased
George Simpson
Elisha Stone

Commentary

The number of members of this caravan has been subject to disputation. Bidwell (*Journal*, pp. 1–2) declares there were 64 men in addition to women and children. In later recollections, he gives various figures (ranging from 64 as the total complement to declaring that the missionary party had some 17–18 men, in addition to his own group). (*Echoes*, pp. 22, 37–38.)

Dawson Narrative (p. 9) presents the figure at 100. Father De Smet (*Letters*, I: 280), under date of May 19, 1841, fixes the number at 70, carefully noting that 50 of the company could manage a rifle, which implies grown men. It should be noted that Father De Smet's estimate would exclude the seven men who joined the company several days later. This would raise his figure to 77. Charles Hopper claimed there were 76. (C[ampbell] C. Menefee, *Historical and Descriptive Sketch Book of Napa, Sonoma, Lake and Mendocino . . .* [Napa City, Calif.], 1873, p. 149.) Reverend Joseph Williams, the last person to join the west-bound party on May 26, presents the figure of 50. (*Williams Narrative*, p. 219.) Bancroft (*California*, IV: 268) states that at the beginning there were 48 men and 15 women and children in the Bidwell-Bartleson party, 63 emigrants in all, while there were 14 members in the Jesuit band, a total complement of 77, which squares with De Smet's tally.

John W. Caughey and Norris Hundley, Jr., *California, History of a Remarkable State* (4th ed., Englewood Cliffs, N.J., 1982), p. 90, and Robert G. Cleland, *From Wilderness to Empire* (New York, 1944), p. 179, agree on the number 69 for the Bidwell outbound party. Andrew F. Rolle, *California, A History* (4th ed., Arlington Heights, Ill., 1987), p. 139, states the "company consisted of forty-seven emigrants, three trappers, a group of Catholic missionaries, their wagon freighters, a lone Methodist minister, and various adventurers. Fifteen women and children were in the party." Warren A. Beck and David A. Williams, *California, A History of the Golden State* (Garden City, N.Y., 1971), p. 109, merely records "some sixty persons." Ralph J. Roske, *Everyman's Eden, A History of California* (New York, 1968), p. 197, sets the number at 48 men and 15 women and children, a total of 63, while Walton Bean and James J. Rawls, *California, An Interpretive History* (5th ed., New York, 1988), p. 64, agree with Caughey, Hundley, and Cleland on a party of 69 members, as does the latest state history, Richard B. Rice, *et al., The Elusive Eden, A New History of California* (New York, 1988), p. 142. So much for recent basic histories of California and their respective estimates.

The missionary party's complement seems to be rather accurately established. Bidwell (*Journal*, pp. 1–2) specifically notes that the group consisted of 11 members. He includes in that number Thomas Fitzpatrick, the three Jesuit priests, John Grey (Bidwell uses Gray), Romaine, and five teamsters. He then lists, separately, three trappers, Baker, Piga, and William Mast, and the pleasure seekers, A. E. Frye and Rogers, along with the Rev. Joseph Williams, bound on a visit to Oregon. In a latter recollection, written in 1889, he listed the party as composed of Fitzpatrick, the three Jesuit priests, "and ten or eleven French Canadians," in addition to John Grey, Baker, and "a young Englishman named Romaine." (Bidwell, *California*, pp. 15–16.)

Thus, from Bidwell's 1841 accounting, based on his *Journal,* in the missionary party, taking his roster as an accurate measure of that party's number, there were 17. *De Smet Letters*, I: 276, 278, sheds little light on the census problem. Father Mengarini, writing many years later, mentions "a man named Fitzpatrick, as well as . . . an Iroquois hunter John Grey, besides those of six Canadian muledrivers. An Englishman named Roman accompanied us. Seeing that we were well provided with guides, several German and American families started at the same time and followed our tracks." He makes no mention of the three Jesuit brothers, apparently counting them among the muleteers. (Albert J. Partoll, ed., "Mengarini's Narrative of the Rockes," *Frontier and Midland,* XVIII [1939]: 193–203, 258–266; reprinted in *Sources of Northwest History No. 25* [Missoula, Mont., n.d.], and in *Prontier Omnibus,* edited by John W. Hakola [Missoula and Helena, Mont., 1962], pp. 139–160).

The first doubt cast on Bidwell's reported census is that he omits listing the Jesuit brothers: William Claessens, Charles Huet, and Joseph Specht. De Smet (*Letters,* I: 300–301) names these brothers. Another source, a sketch by Father Point that depicts the party's encampment at Independence Rock, July 5, 1841 (which is published in this study), records that the three Jesuit priests and three brothers inscribed their names on the famous landmark. In addition, he lists the following as well: R. G. Romaine, L. Boileau, E. Chaussie, L. L. Coviong (or Coing), R. Phelan, and J. Grey. This is the only record which provides the name of the three teamsters, who along with the three lay brothers, drove the missionary wagon and two-wheel carts. In addition, this drawing, executed on the spot by Father Point, has R. Phelan as a member of the overland party. Yet Bidwell in his *Journal,* entry dated July 30, which recorded Phelan's (Bidwell incorrectly calls him Cocrum) marriage to Mrs. Gray, a widow, states he joined the party at Fort Laramie. This was certainly the case, as proved by the contemporary Point drawing. Based on this drawing, the missionary company totaled 17 at the outset. This corroborates Bidwell's figure of 17.

Another Point drawing produces a puzzle. Again, it is published herein. He sketched "Thom" killing two goats and bringing them to camp on his shoulders. This is the only appearance of this name. The hunter for the party was John Grey (whom Bidwell calls Gray), a fact mentioned on a number of occasions. Could it be that the good father meant "John?" This is a surmise. Therefore, "Thom" will not be added to the missionary roster.

Another question posed is the name Rogers. In the roster of the Bidwell-

Bartleson party, Edward Rogers is listed as belonging to that group. Yet, Bidwell lists the name of Rogers as also among the missionary party. It can be assumed that there were two men of that name in the beginning caravan.

Of the missionary party, at least six left the company before it reached Soda Springs. William Mast took his leave while the travelers were at Fort Laramie, June 22. George Simpson, a member of the Bidwell-Bartleson party, joined him. When Henry Fraeb's trapper party was encountered on the Green River, July 23, Jim Baker (mayhap Piga?) cast his lot with them when they departed on July 25, while "John Gray [Grey], Peyton [a Bidwell-Bartleson party member], Frye, Rogers, Jones [a Bidwell-Bartleson party member], and Romaine, started to return to the United States." (Bidwell, *Journal,* pp. 8, 11.) In his later memoirs (*California,* p. 25), Bidwell merely lists Rogers (spelling it Rodgers) and Amos E. Frye as turning back, although he notes that Peyton, one of his own party, joined them. It is a fair assumption to conclude that Jones was one of the emigrant party who had a change of heart. *Williams Narrative* (p. 231) records merely the fact that six members left the company on the Green River in late July. Father De Smet (*Letters,* I: 295) says that five or six turned back along with Romaine. *Dawson Narrative* (p. 14) lists only Frye, Grey, Romaine, and "a few others" as departing the company.

It would appear from Bidwell's *Journal* that the missionary party was diminished prior to the Soda Springs split between the company by the loss of Baker, Frye, Grey, Mast, Piga (?), Rogers, and Romaine, thus reducing their original number from 17 to ten, while the emigrant company lost four, Jones, Peyton, Simpson, and Stone, as well as one death, Shotwell, a total of five.

Of the Bidwell-Bartleson party, it is safe to observe that those members who are listed in the California-bound roster were in the company from the outset and arrived in California at John Marsh's ranch, November 4, 1841. Bidwell in his *Journal,* under date of August 11 (p. 14.), notes 32 men, one woman and child, a total of 34, headed for California. This is confirmed by Nicholas Dawson and in the roster of emigrants given to the California authorities by Marsh, wherein he reported the arrival of 31 men, one woman and child, coupled with the independent arrival of the missing member, James John, who made it to Sutter's Fort on his own. (Bidwell, *Echoes,* p. 75; *Dawson MS,* Bancroft Library.)

The California arrivals, other than James John, were duly recorded by Marsh in a letter, written in Spanish, to Antonio Suñol, sub-prefect at San Jose, November 5, 1841. (*Vallejo Collection,* X: 300. See Appendix C for translation.) The enumeration has a few variations in the spelling of names or initials, which crop up in any attempt to present an accurate census of the Bidwell-Bartleson party. For example, Marsh spells Weber, Waver. Otherwise, it is correct except for the Spanishization of names. Another well-known roster of the first California overland emigrant company was published in the Sacramento *Transcript,*

May 21, 1850, as copied from the San Franciso *Journal of Commerce,* date unknown. This census has a number of name variants: Barnet-Barnett; Brolaskey-Brolaski; W. W. Dawson-V. W. Dawson; McDowl-McDowell; McMahon-McMahan; Rolland-Roland; Swartz-Schwartz; Jacob B. Springer-James P. Springer; Thoms-Thomes; and Webber-Weber. Of all the names, the one most difficult to pin down is John L. Schwartz; variants are De Swart, Swart, or Schwart.

That group of the Bidwell-Bartleson party which elected to go to Oregon, when the missionary party headed north to Fort Hall from Soda Springs, is more difficult to appraise with certainty. Accepting Bidwell's roster as presented in his *Journal* (p. 1) and substantiated to some extent in his 1889 recollections (*California,* p. 26, *note*), the listing presented above seems to be accurate, with these possible exceptions.

There is an area of doubt over the entry of two names, Jones and Rogers. Bidwell (*Journal,* p. 1) lists three separate entries for the name Jones: Thomas Jones, J. M. Jones, and simply Jones. Of the Joneses, we are sure that Thomas Jones reached California. (Bancroft, *California,* IV: 695; Marsh to Suñol, November 5, 1841, *Vallejo Collection,* X: 300.) As to J. M. Jones and plain Mr. Jones, doubts arise. On July 25, Bidwell recorded (*Journal,* p. 11) that a "Jones" elected to return to the United States with Frye, Grey, Peyton, Rogers, and Romaine. No other entries elucidate which Jones this was. It can only be assumed that one of the two Joneses elected to return east while the other continued on to Oregon, this being J. M. Jones. *John Diary* lists a Jones as returning as well, but no initials are given.

The same plight plagues the entry for the name Rogers. Bidwell (*Journal,* pp. 1–2) lists Edward Rogers in the Bidwell-Bartleson party and a Rogers in the missionary company who was on a "pleasure excursion." Under entry of July 25 on the Green River, Bidwell enters the name of Rogers as returning with Frye, Grey, Jones, Peyton, and Romaine to St. Louis. *John Diary* concurs with these names. From this, it would appear that Edward Rogers cast his fortunes with the Oregon-bound party, while the pleasure-seeking Rogers returned east. In his 1889 account (*California,* p. 25), Bidwell lists a "Rodgers" as returning east.

In Bidwell's original roster (*Journal,* p. 1), there is no listing for a Mrs. Gray, a widow with child. On July 30, Mrs. Gray, a sister of one of the Mrs. Kelseys, was married by Father De Smet to Richard Phelan (sometimes Fillan, whom Bidwell calls Cocrum, and John in his diary calls Cockrel). Bidwell described him as a man with one eye, who joined the party at Fort Laramie. (*Journal,* p. 4.) The Phelans opted for Oregon after their marriage. The couple followed the lead of Mrs. Phelan's sister, Mrs. Samuel Kelsey, and accompanied that family after the split at Soda Springs. (The best treatments of the Kelseys to date is given in two articles written by Mrs. Eugene F. Fountain, published in the Blue Lake [California] *Advocate,* June 13, 30, 1957. Copies sent to this writer by Mrs. Fountain of Arcata, California.)

In his later recollections (*California,* p. 26, *note*), Bidwell records that Richard Williams and wife; Samuel Kelsey, wife and five children; Isaac (Zedidiah) Kelsey and wife, daughter of Richard Williams, who was married on the trail on June 1 by Rev. Joseph Williams (*Williams Narrative,* pp. 221–222; Bidwell, *Journal,* p. 4); C. W. Flügge; Fowler; Williams, the Methodist minister; "Cheyenne" Dawson and "Bear" Dawson headed for Oregon. The last two listings are in conflict with the roster of California emigrant arrivals and must be discounted. The two Dawsons were not related. Both came to California with Bidwell. (*Dawson Narrative,* pp. 12, 43; Marsh to Suñol, November 5, 1841, *Vallejo Collection,* X: 300.) The list presented above would seem to be accurate for the Oregon-bound emigrant party. This would place the number in that roster of at least 14, which leaves unaccounted some nine names.

However, in tabulating the census for the 1841 caravan, three other problems need to be clarified, in particular for the Bidwell-Bartleson party. Since Bancroft (*California,* IV: 268) indicates that there were 15 women and children, this figure must be examined. There were five women in the company, this is certain: Mrs. Benjamin (Nancy A.) Kelsey, Mrs. Samuel Kelsey, Mrs. Richard Williams, Mrs. Gray (who married Phelan), and Miss Williams (who married Zedidiah Kelsey, according to the *John Diary,* but who is called Isaac by Bidwell).

The statements of the number of children in the emigrant train, from the records consulted, totals only seven. These were: the child of Mrs. Gray, the child of Mrs. Benjamin Kelsey, the five children of Mrs. Samuel Kelsey. The family of Richard Williams, other than the daughter who married Isaac Kelsey, as to number is nowhere indicated. It could be assumed that since the Williamses had a daughter of marriageable age, there may have been younger siblings. Excluding Miss Williams from the category of children, this would definitely fix the number of seven children that is verifiable. Adding the five women in the party, the total figure would be 12. If Bancroft's figure of 15 women and children is correct, this would imply that the Williams family had three other offspring. But there are no supporting data for such a probability.

A third problem is the entry made by Bidwell at Fort Laramie. There, on June 22, he recorded the fact that two men had joined them, along with an Indian woman, to travel with the company to the Green River. (*Journal,* p. 8.) He later states that a man named Cocrum joined the party at Fort Laramie. John in his diary seconds this, though he calls the man Cockrel. Actually, as noted previously, this was Richard Phelan. Based on the Point drawing, which was sketched at Independence Rock, July 5, it distinctly lists "R. Phelan" as having been a member of the party who inscribed his name on that notable trail landmark. Thus, it may well be that there was a Cocrum or Cockrel who joined the party at Fort Laramie. Yet, it is clear that the reference to this man by Bidwell and John is to Richard Phelan, for both record his marriage to the widow Mrs. Gray using the name each gave him, Cocrum and Cockrel.

One thing is clear. At Fort Laramie the overland caravan was joined by an Indian family, husband, wife, and two children. This is graphically attested to by another of Point's on-the-trail drawings (which is published herein). As for the second man, this was Richard Phelan. However, it appears that the Indian family left the company at the Green River and thus can be discounted as prospective Oregon-bound emigrants.

As to the members of the Bidwell-Bartleson party who decided to return east prior to Soda Springs where the company split, the number can be fixed at four. Elisha Stone was the first to give up the trip, returning on June 5 with a band of American Fur Company trappers. George Simpson elected to withdraw at Fort Laramie, June 22. Jones and Henry Peyton made their decision on July 25 on the Green River, joining the departing missionary party members, Baker, Frye, Grey, Mast, Piga (?), Rogers, and Romaine. (Bidwell, *Journal,* pp. 5, 8, 11.) The *Daily Missouri Republican,* September 28, 1841, reported that nine or ten had returned.

Lastly one of the Bidwell-Bartleson party became a casualty. George (sometimes James) Shotwell accidentally shot himself on June 13. Mortally wounded, he lingered for about two hours, died, and was buried by the Rev. Williams. (Bidwell, *Journal,* p. 7; Mengarini, "Narrative," in *Frontier Omnibus,* p. 141.)

Accepting the lists and exceptions as presented above, these conclusion can be reached:

First. The original Bidwell-Bartleson company definitely consisted of 61 persons, with the probability of at least three additional children in the Williams family, which is undocumented.

Second. The California-bound contingent is accurately fixed at the number 34, while the Oregon-bound emigrees totaled at least 23, with the possibility of the questionable Williams family's three children.

Third. Four of the Bidwell-Bartleson party returned east and a fifth died. But a new recruit was gained at Fort Laramie when Richard Phelan joined the emigrant party.

Fourth. The missionary party had a beginning complement of 17 persons, losing seven members before they reached Soda Springs.

Fifth. The Oregon emigrant party numbered at least 23. They were: Carroll, August Fifer [Pfeiffer], Richard Phelan and wife (Mrs. Gray) and her child; William Fowler [Towler], Charles W. Flügge, David F. Hill, J. M. Jones, Zedidiah (Isaac) Kelsey and wife (daughter of Richard Williams), Samuel Kelsey, wife and five children, William P. Overton, Edward Rogers, James Ross, and Richard Williams and wife. Accompanying them was a lone traveler, Rev. Joseph Williams.

In respect to this roster, H. E. Tobie, "From the Missouri to the Columbia," pp. 152–154, does not include in his list Fifer or Jones. He lists the Samuel Kelsey children as six and infers there was probably a Williams child. By doing so, he comes to the conclusion that the Oregon contingent totaled 24 or 25 (the latter includes Piga) as based on the testimony of Mrs. Narcissa Whitman. The more correct number would appear to be 23.

Accepting these conclusions, if we omit the possibility of the Williams family having three unlisted or unrecorded children, a supposition predicated *only* on Bancroft's statement that there were 15 women and children, then the original westbound caravan had a complement of 79 souls. En route to Soda Springs, four emigrants changed their minds, one was killed, and seven of the missionary party opted out for sundry reasons, leaving a total of 67 in all. One must add the new recruit, Richard Phelan, who joined the emigrants at Fort Laramie. Thus, when Soda Springs was reached on August 11, 1841, Bidwell simply records (*Journal,* p. 14) that 32 men, one woman and child, headed southwest for California, the rest were bound north for Fort Hall. This contingent would include the ten-member missionary band and 23 emigrants making for Oregon.

It should be noted that in a later recollection Bidwell used the figure 69 (*Echoes,* pp. 22, 37–38), which finds currency in a number of contemporary state histories. That number must be questioned since at the time of the breakup of the pioneer overland travelers in southern Idaho there were only 56 original recruits left. However, at the outset of the trek westward, discounting the 17 member missionary contingent, subsequently reduced to ten, the total number of pioneers numbered only 61 and was reduced to 56 (plus the one new recruit, Phelan) when they went their separate ways, one group striking for California, the other for Oregon.

Biographical Sketches of Members of the 1841 Overland Party

Since complete biographical data is elusive for many of the Bidwell-Bartleson party, what follows is at best a compromise. For some sketches, there is very detailed information; for others, details are either scarce or very spotty at best.

However, a number of party members can be rather quickly dismissed, since some left California to return east as early as 1842. Among these returnees were John Bartleson, Joseph B. Chiles, George Henshaw, Charles Hopper, John McDowell, Nelson McMahan, Andrew G. Patton, Robert Rickman, James P. Springer, and Ambrose Walton. Of these ten, three returned to reside in California at a later date: Chiles, Hopper, and Springer. They are included among the biographies.

The basis of all the biographical sketches that follow are rooted in Hubert H. Bancroft's "Pioneer Register," which is found at the end of volumes II–V in his seven-volume *History of California,* hereinafter noted as Bancroft, *PR,* with appropriate volume and page or pages. Additional sources, where used to supply data, are cited as occasion warrants.

Elias Barnett was born in Prestonburg, Floyd County, Kentucky, in 1805. In his early manhood he traveled in Virginia, Ohio, Illinois, Indiana, and Tennessee, finally settling in Jackson County, Missouri, in 1831. He later remarked, concerning the 1841 overland trip, about the near-starvation that faced the company: "I was so near starved that the coyote did taste good, but hang me if I could make the horse or mule taste well; it was too bitter." After his California arrival, Barnett spent the winter at Sutter's Fort and in the spring of 1842 spent several weeks with George C. Yount on his Rancho Caymus in the Napa Valley. He then moved to the vicinity of present-day Healdsburg and commenced building an adobe house. He subsequently worked for Yount in 1843 before settling in Pope Valley. There in 1844 he married the widow of William Pope. Recruited by Sutter, he was one of the Americans who supported Governor Manuel Micheltorena, but to no avail. In 1846 he was an active participant in the short-lived Bear Flag Revolt and enlisted under John C. Frémont's command as a volunteer. In that capacity, he made the difficult march to Los Angeles, starting out in September 1846, reaching the southland town in March 1847. After the war, he was discharged from the California Battalion, Company E, and returned to his Pope Valley ranch in Napa County, where he spent the rest of his life. Bancroft states that he died "shortly before [18]50," but this date would appear inaccurate since he was referred to as a resident of Pope Valley in an 1873 county history. In fact, he died on February 8, 1880. Bancroft, *PR*, II: 711; C[harles] A. Menefee, *Historical and Descriptive Sketch Book of Napa, Sonoma, Lake and Mendocino . . .* (Napa City, 1873), pp. 171–172; Biographical Information File, California State Library, Sacramento.

John Bartleson returned to Missouri in 1842. He died there in Washington Township, Jackson County, October 7, 1848, age sixty-one years, eleven months, twenty-two days. Thus he was born on October 15 or 16, 1786. Missouri County Records, Sutro Library, San Francisco.

Josiah Belden's biographical sketch appears in the introduction to his Bancroft dictation reprinted in this volume (Chapter Four).

William Belty, a German emigrant from Missouri, does not leave much of a biographical trail. Reputedly, he returned east and died there, but a man of the same name was a volunteer in the California Battalion, Company A. In addition, the name appears in Thomas Oliver Larkin's account books at Monterey in 1847–1848. According to one informant, Henry J. Dally, Belty was killed when he fell from his horse in the mines in 1849. Dally helped bury him. Bancroft, *PR*, II: 716.

John Bidwell has been biographically treated in the Introduction, at least up to 1841. Two months after his arrival in California, he entered the employ of John A. Sutter. He was posted to Bodega Bay to oversee the transfer of all Russian property, including Fort Ross, which Sutter had only recently purchased. Having successfully completed that task, he returned to Sutter's Fort. His next assignment was the management of Sutter's Hock Farm. In early 1845 he was made bookkeeper and general manager. In 1845 he received two land grants. The first was the Rancho Colus in Colusa County, two leagues. This property he later sold for $2,000 to Charles D. Semple, who received a patent for 8,876 acres in 1869. The other grant was the Rancho Ulpinos in Solano County at Rio Vista. He also disposed of the latter, for his heart had early been captured by the lovely countryside sprawling along Chico Creek in present-day Butte County.

On the eve of the Mexican War, Bidwell evidenced an interest in the welfare of the local Indians, a concern that continued until his death, one equally shared by his devoted wife, Annie Kennedy. He was also responsible for laying out the town of Suttersville for his employer. With the Mexican War, interest in that new community waned, but was revived with peace in 1848. At the same time, the gold discovery accelerated the prospect of California statehood. To that end, Bidwell was elected a delegate from the Sacramento district in 1849 to attend what evolved into a state constitutional convention. Parallel with these events, Bidwell took advantage of the gold discovery, profiting not only from mining but also from operating a trading post in the northern mines. His name was fixed to an important strike, Bidwell's Bar, located on the middle fork of the Feather River, twelve miles north of Oroville.

His new wealth made possible the acquisition of the Rancho Chico, a splendid property that he added to his other land holdings in the vicinity of what was later named Butte County. His 22,000-acre ranch became the proto-type of modern agricultural development, for Bidwell was interested in experiments with fruit and olive trees in particular, as well as new crops. His ranch became a model for others to emulate.

In addition to his abiding commitment to agricultural advances, Bidwell was much the political animal. In 1844 he had become a naturalized Mexican citizen and, along with Sutter, was a staunch supporter of the embattled governor, Manuel Micheltorena. That attachment, however, did not deter him from drawing up a declaration of independence from Mexico in 1846, and his enlistment as a lieutenant in John C. Frémont's California Battalion during the Mexican War.

After statehood, he continued to be politically active. This led to his being appointed to the rank of brigadier general in the state militia by Governor Leland Stanford in 1861, a title he used consistently thereafter. He served in a variety of political posts: state senator, U.S. congressman for one term; three vain ef-forts at seeking the governorship; and a vain run for the presidency of the United States on the Prohibition ticket in 1892.

On the personal side, Bidwell married his beloved Annie on April 16, 1868. It was a happy but childless marriage. He died on April 4, 1900, in the fullness of life. His widow carried on and became well known in her own right for her many philanthropic, humanitarian, and suffrage activities. In death, Bidwell was honored by having his portrait hung in the State Capitol.

Rockwell D. Hunt has rendered a solid biography in John Bidwell, *Prince of California Pioneers* (Caldwell, Idaho, 1942), from which the above data have been drawn.

Henry Lyons Brolaski (sometimes Brolaskey) settled at Monterey in 1842 but not long after sailed for Callao, Peru. From that city, he wrote to Larkin and Talbot H. Green in 1844. That same year, he succeeded to his brother's Peruvian business and operated it until 1847. By 1848 he was back in St. Louis, eager to return to California, where he planned to build a sawmill. Apparently nothing came of his plans, for it is reported that he was still living in Missouri as late as 1870. Nothing more is known. Bancroft, *PR*, II: 731.

Miecislaus Haiman, *Polish Pioneers in California* (Chicago, 1940), p. 38, opines that Brolaski returned to California during the gold rush. He finds a H. S. Broloski listed as a member of the Haviland Mining Company of New Orleans in *Argonauts of California* (New York, 1890), p. 402, and believes this to be Brolaski, the first Polish-American to reach California.

David W. Chandler sailed for Honolulu not long after his arrival in California. There he resided until 1848, when he returned to San Francisco. However, all trace of him disappears after November of that year, though "he is said to have died in Cal." Bancroft, *PR*, II: 757. Another source states he died in San Francisco. *History of Yuba County, California* . . . (Oakland, 1879), p. 29, a like fact repeated in *History of Monterey County, California* . . . (San Francisco, 1881), p. 41. However, the San Francisco *Alta California,* March 5, 1862, p. 1, cl. 2, reports the following: "FROZEN TO DEATH—The body of David Chandler was found on the 2nd inst., near the Old Empire saw mill, on Oregon hill, Yuba county, where he had frozen to death, about five weeks since. The deceased left the Indiana ranch, on the evening of 27th of January, intending to go to Dr. Cannon's saw mill, near the Milch ranch, where he had been employed as engineer, since which time he had not been heard from." Whether this David Chandler was David W. Chandler remains to be proven.

Joseph B. Chiles's biographical sketch appears with his recollection for Bancroft (Chapter Six).

Grove C. Cook, apparently a native of Kentucky, had wanderlust for several years after reaching California. In 1843 he was residing in the Monterey area, for his name appears in Larkin's accounts. He became a naturalized citizen in 1844, and the year following was working on a distillery at Sutter's Fort. During the summer of 1845, Sutter's Fort was visited by a party of Walla Walla Indians under Chief Yellow Serpent and his son, Elijah. They came seeking cattle. In order to pay for them, they commenced to round up wild horses. Among the animals corralled by the Indians were several with brands on them, one belonging to Cook. Sutter tried to sort the matter out, but before a solution could be reached, Cook and Elijah had an angry confrontation; Cook shot and killed him. As Bancroft opines, "According to white witnesses present, the Indian was the aggressor; though it would be more reasonable to suppose, in the absence of witnesses, and the safety with which an Indian might be killed under the circumstances, that Elijah was deliberately murdered by Cook." The following December, Cook was married by Sutter to Rebecca Kelsey, "who presently had some reason to regret it." In 1846 Cook moved to Yerba Buena, then settled in the vicinity of San Jose. With the Mexican War, he had some slight involvement in military action and was a member of the 1846–1847 San Jose council or junta. By 1849 he was a man of considerable wealth, but consequently lost it. He died in Santa Cruz in 1853. Bancroft summed his life up in these words: "He is described as a man whose wit and generosity went far to counterbalance some less desirable qualities." Bancroft, *PR*, II: 765; *California*, V: 300–301.

Nicholas Dawson won the nickname of "Cheyenne" because of his well-reported encounter with a band of those Indians en route to California, so aptly described in Bidwell's *Journal*. Bancroft also records other nicknames, "'Bear,' 'Berry,' and 'Birny,'" but does not list any source for them. Since Dawson in his later published memoirs does not mention a brother, at least not a V. W. Dawson, it can be assumed more correctly that they were not brothers. Apparently he kept a store in Santa Cruz in 1843 "but closed it and went away . . ." For a fuller biographical sketch, see the introduction to Chapter Seven. Bancroft, *PR*, II: 777.

V. W. Dawson is a hard man to pin down. Bancroft in his "Pioneer Register" has him confused with Nicholas "Cheyenne" Dawson. He implies that they were probably brothers, but there is no solid evidence to support that assumption. Bancroft calls him James, "Cheyenne," John, and "Long John" Dawson. Marsh records his name as V. W. Dawson, which corresponds with Bidwell's roster of the Bidwell-Bartleson party. One piece of data appears to be solid: he drowned in the Columbia River sometime before 1850. Bancroft, *PR*, II: 776; Sacramento *Transcript*, May 21, 1850; Bidwell, *Journal*, p. 1.

Talbot H. Green, whose real name was Paul Geddes, was born in Lewisburg, Pennsylvania, August 10, 1810. His Scotch ancestors had settled in the colony at the beginning of the eighteenth century, and the family established for itself an honorable reputation. In early manhood he married nineteen-year-old Henrietta Fredrick on August 21, 1832. They had four children; a son and daughter lived to survive their father.

As he later revealed to his longtime friend Thomas O. Larkin, Green had withdrawn a sizeable amount of money from the bank and promptly was robbed of it while under the influence of heavy drink. A local bank asked him to serve as courier for $105,000; in doing so, he removed $8,000 to pay his debts and then, abandoning wife and children, headed west. While on a steamboat going up the Mississippi to St. Louis, he tended a dying Englishman; when the Englishman died, Geddes adopted his name, Talbot H. Green.

After his arrival in California, Green was employed as a clerk and agent for Larkin at Monterey and quickly gained his employer's full confidence and trust. By 1846 Green had an enviable reputation as a solid businessman and was noted for his generosity to widows and orphans. He was appointed collector of the port of Monterey by the U.S. military authorities, serving from 1846–1847.

After the conclusion of the Mexican War, he decided to relocate in San Francisco in light of its importance as the port of entry for eager gold seekers. In 1849 he became a partner in the firm of Mellus, Howard & Company, which became the city's largest business firm. His financial success continued unabated.

Affluent and prominent in the city, he married, on October 25, 1849, the widow Mrs. Sarah Montgomery, nee Armstrong, at the home of Grove Cook in San Jose. They had one son, born in 1851. At the same time, Green was elected to San Francisco's first city council in 1849 and decided to run for the office of mayor in 1851. That decision proved his undoing. He was exposed, by whom is still debatable, as a bank embezzler, named Paul Geddes, a married man with four children! He elected to return east, supposedly to clear his name, sailing on April 15, 1851, leaving wife and son behind.

Actually, Geddes decide to hide out in Tennessee. There he remained in obscurity until 1856, with occasional trips, including one to Havana. In the meantime, through correspondence with Larkin, he was able to tap his California assets, which he had left for the care of his California wife and son. In 1854, Sarah divorced him and was happily remarried in 1855.

Finally, in 1856, Geddes visited his aged parents, wife, and two surviving children in Lewisburg. As a result of that visit, he and his wife moved, in 1857, to Texas, where he lost a considerable amount of money in land speculation. Little more is known, other than the fact he was serving as the clerk to the secretary of the U.S. Senate from 1876 to 1878, paid at least one visit to California, in 1876 (and perhaps others; the record is unclear), and apparently elected to return permanently to his boyhood hometown, Lewisburg, sometime after 1878. There he was forgiven for his youthful bank folly, and there he died, on July 2, 1889, survived by his first wife and two children.

Biographical data have been drawn from John A. Hussey, "New Light Upon Talbot H. Green as Revealed by His Own Letters and Other Sources," *California Historical Society Quarterly,* XVIII (1939): 32–63.

George Henshaw returned east in 1842. Nothing more is known. Bancroft, *PR,* III: 781.

Henry Huber was granted in 1845 eight leagues of the Rancho Honcut in the vicinity of Honcut in Yuba County. However, that claim was rejected by the U.S. Land Commission in 1853. He later purchased some San Francisco lots, 1847–1848, and made that city his permanent California home. He reputedly became the proprietor of a "well known liquor-store" in that city and was still in that business as late as 1885. Bancroft, *PR*, III: 788; Cowan, *Ranchos of California*, p. 40, No. 193. In Frank Soulé, *et al., The Annals of California . . .* (New York, 1885), p. 822, his name is given as Francis Henry Huber.

James John has been profiled in the introduction to his diaries (Chapter Nine).

Thomas Jones did not leave many footprints in California. He was settled in San Jose by 1845 and applied for land in that town in 1846. Nothing more is known. Bancroft, *PR*, IV: 695. He is listed as dead in the *History of Yuba County, California . . .*, p. 29, published in 1879.

Andrew Kelsey was one of four brothers, Benjamin, David, and Samuel being the other three. According to Bidwell's *Journal,* the Kelseys came from Arkansas. Benjamin and Samuel, with their families, along with Andrew, joined the 1841 overland trek to California. At Soda Springs, Samuel decided to go on to Oregon, while the other two brothers headed for California. Little is known of Andrew's activities. In 1843, the same year brother David and family trekked overland to Oregon, Andrew accompanied Benjamin and his family north to Oregon. In 1844 all the Kelseys decided to relocate to California, so the Kelsey party headed south. That same year it appears that Andrew served in a company of foreigners who supported Governor Manuel Micheltorena, but to no avail. Like Benjamin and Samuel, he was an active participant in the Bear Flag Revolt.

In 1847 Andrew and Benjamin obtained some horses and cattle from Salvador Vallejo and pioneered the opening of Clear Lake Valley in what is now Lake County. It would appear that both brothers were extremely cruel to the local Indians, natives who had a long hostility to Californios, a hostility not without cause. With the gold rush, many of the local Indians were impressed into labor by the Kelseys in an effort to exploit a mining claim held by Andrew and Benjamin. Having struck it rich at Kelsey's Diggings, or Kelsey's Bar, located on the North Fork of the American River, Andrew and Benjamin resumed their ranching operations.

To further that prospect, Andrew entered into partnership with Charles Stone. They built an adobe at what was later named Kelseyville west of Kelsey Creek. Andrew was destined for a violent end. The story goes as follows:

> In the fall of 1849, when Stone and Kelsey were away with the vaqueros, attending to their cattle one day . . . [an Indian] squaw poured water into their guns. The next morning some of the Indians made a charge on the house. Kelsey was killed

outright with an arrow shot through the window. Stone escaped upstairs and on the Indians rushing up after him, jumped out of an upper window, ran to the creek and hid in a clump of willows. . . . An old Indian found him and killed him with a blow of a rock on the head.

A more graphic and perhaps inaccurate account of the killing of Kelsey and Stone has been provided by an Indian informant, but since he was not an eyewitness to the event, one must approach that account with caution.

Another account of their deaths, from an Anglo point of view, also must be looked upon with caution. It reads:

> They [Kelsey and Stone] cultivated the friendship of a large tribe of Indians in the Clear Lake Valley or basin, employed some of them, and paid them well for their services as *vaqueros* in herding cattle and breaking wild horses to the saddle. They ate at the same table after their employers were done, and had ample food; but one morning in the early spring of 1850, while their employers were seated at the table, eating their breakfast, two Indians, one named Prieto and the other George, treacherously murdered Kelsey and Stone by shooting them with the rifles they had secretly got possession of. . . .

In the 1860s when a town was established not far from the adobe that Kelsey and his partner had built, it was named Kelseyville in his honor, as was Kelsey Creek. Bancroft, *PR*, III: 697–698; Aurelius O. Carpenter and Percy H. Millbery, *History of Mendocino and Lake Counties* (Los Angeles, 1910), pp. 125 *et seq.*; Max Radin, ed., "The Stone and Kelsey 'Massacre' on the Shores of Clear Lake in 1849: The Indian Viewpoint," by William Ralganal Benson, *California Historical Society Quarterly*, XI (September 1932): 266–271; "Sherman Was There: The Recollections of Major Edwin A. Sherman," *ibid.*, XXIV (March 1945): 51; Erwin G. Gudde, *California Place Names* (2nd rev. ed., Berkeley and Los Angeles, 1969), p. 162 and his *California Gold Camps* (Berkeley and Los Angeles), 1975), ed. by Elizabeth K. Gudde, p. 184.

Benjamin Kelsey was one of the four Kelsey brothers. Accompanied by his young wife, Nancy, and baby daughter, brothers Andrew and Samuel, the latter with his wife and five children, he joined the 1841 overland emigrant train. At Soda Springs, Samuel and his family decided to opt for Oregon, while Benjamin and Andrew elected to push on to California. After their arrival, the brothers headed for Sutter's Fort, but little is known of their activities during 1842. In May 1843 they decided to head for Oregon to join brother Samuel, who, incidentally, was heading south with his family in the Hastings' party, but turned back when he met his brothers. The Kelseys were members of an emigrant train led by Joseph Gale. In the meantime, that same year, David traveled overland with his family to join the Kelsey clan. (Bancroft is mistaken on one surmise: David was a brother, not the father of the Kelseys mentioned.)

The Oregon sojourn lasted only until 1844, when the Kelseys and their respective families decided to settle in California. Benjamin, wife, and daughter; David, wife, and three daughters and mayhap a son; Samuel, wife, and five children; and bachelor Andrew took the trail south. Aptly, this pioneer band has been named the Kelsey party.

David settled with his family at French Creek but died in Stockton in 1845, the victim of smallpox. The rest of the Kelseys settled in the vicinity of Napa Valley. Benjamin and Andrew made their living as hunters with occasional employment at New Helvetia. As Bancroft writes, "They were rough men, often in trouble with the authorities."

The three surviving Kelsey brothers were active participants in the Bear Flag Revolt, and tradition has it that Nancy Kelsey, Benjamin's wife, made the original Bear Flag. During the Mexican War the Kelseys resided at the fort in Sonoma. This led to a joint partnership between Benjamin and Mariano G. Vallejo and the building of a sawmill on Sonoma Creek.

In 1847 Andrew and Benjamin obtained some cattle and horses from Salvador Vallejo and commenced ranching activities in Clear Lake Valley, though Benjamin did not reside there as did Andrew. With the discovery of gold, the brothers, along with Samuel, went to what is today El Dorado County and at Kelsey, later named in their honor, made a remarkable strike at Kelsey's Diggings. Reputedly in two days they amassed some $10,000 in gold. By 1849 a large camp mushroomed around the site. It had six hotels, twelve stores, twenty-four saloons and gambling houses, as well as a polyglot population. Today, Kelsey "is only a hamlet of a few dozen inhabitants, with one store, a post office, and a few scattered homesteads and farms, but with many memories vivid with the music and color of other days. James W. Marshall, the discoverer of gold at Coloma, spent his last years in Kelsey and died [t]here."

After the heyday of the gold rush, Benjamin took his wife and family, now two daughters, one born at Sutter's Fort in 1845, to Humboldt County in 1850 to pioneer that area. They helped start two towns, Arcata and Eureka. But prosper they did not. So they returned briefly to Napa Valley before relocating to Oregon, where they lived until 1855. By 1859 they were traveling, first in Mexico, then Texas for Benjamin's health. A third daughter had been born to the couple in the meantime. One of their brood on this trip, at age thirteen, was scalped by marauding Indians but survived the ordeal, dying in Fresno five years later.

In 1861 the family headed west again for California, driving a small herd of cattle. They took up resident in Lompoc, later Fresno, then came back to southern California for life in Los Angeles. There Benjamin died in 1888, survived by his widow and two daughters. Bancroft, *PR,* III: 698; Mrs. Eugene Fountain, "The Four Kelsey Brothers," *Sonoma County Historical Society Journal,* II

(June 1964): 13; III (March 1964): 5–8; III (June 1965): 7–8; III (September 1965): 8–9; Henry Mauldin, "Kelsey Family," Oakland *Tribune,* September 9, 1956, *Knave,* cls. 2–3; September 16, 1965, *Knave,* cls. 3–5; September 23, 1956, *Knave,* cl. 2; William N. Abeloe, ed., *Historic Spots in California* (3rd rev. ed., Stanford, 1966), p. 86; Tom Gregory, *History of Solano and Napa Counties* (Los Angeles, 1912), pp. 728–729.

Sadly, there is no further record of Samuel Kelsey and his family. However, Benjamin's daughter Nancy, born on Valentine's Day in 1851, married John W. Clanton in Inyo County and lived to her ninety-seventh year, dying on May 28, 1958. Sacramento *Bee,* February 22, 1941, p. 20, cl. 2; May 31, 1948, p. 13, cl. 2.

Mrs. Nancy A. Kelsey is described in the introduction to her recollections (Chapter Ten).

John McDowell returned east to Missouri in 1841. Nothing more is known. Bancroft, *PR, IV:* 723. The 1879 *History of Yuba County . . . ,* p. 29, lists him as dead.

Nelson McMahan (variant McMahon) was a first cousin of Samuel Green McMahan. He either returned east or went to Oregon. Bancroft opines, "I think he did not return to Cal., though he is mentioned also as one of the Clyman party of '45." Bancroft, *PR, IV:* 725; *California, IV:* 270, 275, 573. Ellen L. Wood, "Samuel Green McMahan Member of the Bidwell Party and Owner of Bartlett Springs," *California Historical Society Quarterly,* XXIII (December 1944): 298, *note* 5, provides a correction to Bancroft, who stated Nelson was a brother of Samuel. The 1879 *History of Yuba County . . . ,* p. 29, states he returned to Missouri.

Samuel Green McMahan (sometimes spelled McMahon) was born in June 1819 in Cooper County, Missouri, on the family farm located three miles south of the town of Arrow Rock. After his arrival in California, he spent the winter of 1841–1842 at Sutter's Fort. From the fall of 1842 to the spring of 1843 he was employed by John R. Wolfskill on Putah Creek, then part of Wolfskill's rancho. In May 1843 Samuel elected to try his luck in Oregon, joining the party formed under the leadership of Joseph Gale, some forty-two men and 1,250 head of cattle. But Oregon proved not to his liking.

On June 8, 1845, in association with James Clyman, Samuel led a return party of thirty-nine men, a woman, and three children southward from Oregon, the so-called McMahan-Clyman party. By July 30 Samuel was in Monterey, where he resided for a short time. While in residence there, he was badly mauled by a female grizzly bear but luckily survived the attack.

He briefly served in John C. Frémont's California Battalion during the Mexican

War but, not yet recovered from his bear wounds, saw little in the way of action. At this time he purchased 160 acres on Putah Creek in present-day Solano County from his former employer, John Wolfskill. In 1859 he purchased from him an additional 1,367 acres. Like his neighbors, he became a prosperous wheat farmer.

On March 7, 1860, he married the widow Lavenia Ellen Yount and became stepfather to her four children by her first husband, John Yount, a nephew of George C. Yount. Not long after he acquired Bartlett Springs, whose waters were believed to contain health-giving properties. There he suffered a stroke in the fall of 1884, lingering for several weeks before expiring on November 21 at Dixon. He was buried in the Sacramento City Cemetery. Wood, "Samuel Green McMahan," pp. 289–399; San Francisco *Call,* November 25, 1884, p. 1, cl. 2; p. 8, cl. 5.

Michael C. Nye became a naturalized citizen in 1844. As a result of his service to the *Californio* cause against Governor Manuel Micheltorena, he was granted the four-league Rancho Willy, situated at Marysville in Yuba County. However, his claim was rejected as fraudulent by the U.S. Land Commission. In June 1847 he married a widow, Mrs. Harriet Pike, of the ill-famed Donner party. They resided in Marysville but later moved to Oregon. There Mrs. Nye died in 1870. It is quite clear that he remarried and resided at the time of his death in Prineville, Cook County, Oregon. His funeral was held on July 14, 1906. He was the last surviving member of the Bidwell-Bartleson party. On the record of his funeral his age is given as eighty-five, and he was survived by his widow. He was buried in the local cemetery, Lot A6 A-U, Section A. Bancroft, *PR,* IV: 757; Cowan, *Ranchos of California,* No. 663, p. 107; Record of Funeral, No. 17, courtesy Evelyn Adams, Deputy County Clerk, Prineville, Oregon.

Andrew Gwinn Patton elected to return to Missouri in 1842. Nothing more is known. Bancroft, *PR,* IV: 769. The 1879 *History of Yuba County . . . ,* p. 29, lists him as dead.

Robert Rickman also returned to Missouri in 1842. Nothing more is known. Bancroft, *PR,* V: 695. He is listed as dead in the 1879 *History of Yuba County . . . ,* p. 29.

John Roland was another party member who returned east in 1842. Bancroft, *PR* V: 702.

John L. Schwartz, sometimes Swart, Schwart, or De Swart, according to Bidwell's roster, was of German descent. In 1844–1845, with John A. Sutter, he was granted the three-league Rancho Nueva Flandria in Yolo County, a claim that was later rejected. On the property he established a fishing station and constructed a boat, which permitted travel on the Sacramento River and in the delta. Thus he is frequently mentioned in the records at Sutter's Fort. He died sometime between June 1 and 24, 1852, for he is so listed under the name of "J. L. De Schwartz," age fifty-five, a native of Germany, in the Sacramento *Union,* June 26, 1852, p. 2, cl. 5.

James Peter Springer has been profiled in the introduction to his 1856 letter to the editor of the San Jose *Tribune* (Chapter Eleven).

Robert Hasty Thomes's sketch precedes his recollection (Chapter Twelve).

Ambrose Walton decided to return east in 1842. Nothing more is known. Bancroft, *PR,* V: 766.

Major Walton is something of a puzzle. Bancroft states that he, too, returned east in 1842 but hedges by pointing out that "acc[ording] to some sketches, was drowned in the Sac [ramento] Riv[iver]." An 1850 roster lists him as having drowned. If he returned east in 1842, he may have come back to California with the 1843 Joseph B. Chiles party. However, there is disagreement in respect to the latter possibility. Bancroft, *PR,* V: 766; *California,* IV: 393 *note;* Sacramento *Transcript,* May 21, 1850, p. 2, cl. 2.

Charles M. Weber was born February 16, 1814, in Steinwenden, Germany. He received an excellent education but due to health reason turned his energies and talents to business pursuits. When a favorite uncle immigrated to the United States in 1836, Weber and a cousin decided to follow. Sailing from Le Harve, France, October 3, 1836, the two travelers reached New Orleans later that winter. In the intervening years, illness plagued him as he visited Texas, later Illinois, to see his uncle.

In the spring of 1841 he took a steamboat up the Mississippi to St. Louis in search of a dried climate for reasons of health. His timing was perfect; he joined the Bidwell-Bartleson party headed for California. He was able to catch up with the company on May 23 at the Big Vermillion River in eastern Kansas.

After reaching California, Weber made his way to Sutter's Fort and was employed there for a period of time. He is credited with planting the first garden in California, an interest that became a lifelong passion. In 1842 he settled in San Jose, where he entered into a partnership with a longtime resident, William Gulnac. They operated a store, a blacksmithy, and a flour mill, "the first powered by water in San Jose." Soon they were in the bakery business, making sea bread and crackers for the maritime trade. Later they started a salt works, a cobbler shop, and a hotel. In July 1843, the partnership was terminated; Weber bought out Gulnac's interest.

Since Gulnac was a naturalized citizen, Weber used their friendship to obtain a dummy land grant. In 1844 Gulnac received the eleven-league Rancho Campo de los Franceses in San Joaquin County, including the town of Tuleburg, now known as Stockton. In the meantime, Weber became naturalized so the title could be placed in his name. Weber received the patent for 48,747 acres. He founded and named the present city of Stockton in 1846.

Weber quickly became one of early American California's most prosperous citizens. On November 29, 1850, after conversion to the Roman Catholic Church, he married Helen Murphy. They had three children, two sons and a daughter. The family lived in a magnificent house that Weber bought for his bride. Theirs was a happy marriage until late in life.

Weber died in Stockton on May 4, 1881, age sixty-eight, from pneumonia. Bancroft recorded this judgment:

> Weber was an intelligent, energetic, and honorable man of business; generous in his many gifts to his town and to his friends; but in later life eccentric to the verge of insanity, morbidly sensitive, avoiding his fellow-men. There is nothing apparent in his record, that of a successful man, who was neither the author nor victim of any great wrongs.

Mayhap he was suffering from Alzheimer's disease, a condition not yet medically diagnosed. George P. Hammond and Dale L. Morgan, *Charles M. Weber: Pioneer of San Joaquin and Founder of Stockton, California* (Berkeley, 1966), pp. 1–27; Bancroft, *PR,* V: 770.

Miscellaneous Documents

Nicholas Dawson's Trail Chronology
of the 1841 Overland Journey

A list of encampments and supposed distance travelled by the California Company under the command of Capt. John Bartleson.

May	Camps	Distance
We 12	McLeans Branch	10
Th 13	Elm Grove	8
Fr 14	do do	00
Sa 15	Double [illegible]	20
S 16	Prairie branch	25
Mo 17	Kansas river	15
Tu 18	do do	10
We 19	Stormy Creek	12
Th 20	Kansas village	10
Fr 21	Mark Shooters	10
Sa 22	Willow Grove	12
S 23	Little Vermillion	8
Mo 24	Great Vermillion	12
Tu 25	[illegible]	20
We 26	Missionary Creek	20
Th 27	Blue River	23
Fr 28	do do	25
Sa 29	do do	25
S 30	do do	20
Mo 31	do do	25

[June]

Tu 1	Platte River	15
We 2	do do	15
Th 3	do do	20
Fr 4	Platte R[iver]	15
Sa 5	do do	18
S 6	South Fork	20
Mo 7	do do	15
Tu 8	do do	20
We 9	do do	00
Th 10	do do	20
Fr 11	do do	12
Sa 12	North Fork	18
S 13	Shotwells Camp	8
No 14	N[orth] Fork	00
Tu 15	do do	15
We 16	do do	20
Th 17	do do	20
Fr 18	do do	18
Sa 19	Mountain Spring	20
S 20	N[orth] Fork	20
Mo 21	do do	25
Tu 22	Laramie Fork	5
We 23	do do	16
Th 24	Big Spring	14
Fr 25	Sage Creek	18
Sa 26	N[orth] Fork	20
S 27	Muddy Creek	20
Mo 28	Buffalo run	18
Tu 29	N[orth] Fork	18
We 30	do do	20

[July]

Th 1	Cross Platte	10
Fr 2	Platte R[iver]	20
Sa 3	Sulphur Spring	15
S 4	Willow Spring	20
Mo 5	Independence Rock	20
Tu 6	Sweet Water	8
We 7	do do	15
Th 8	do do	20

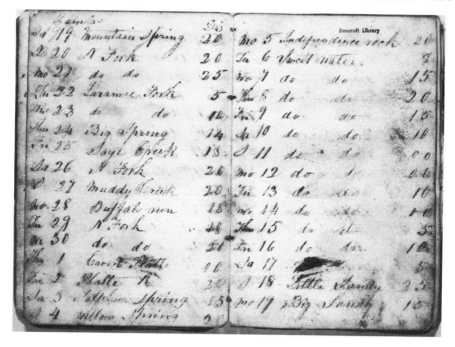

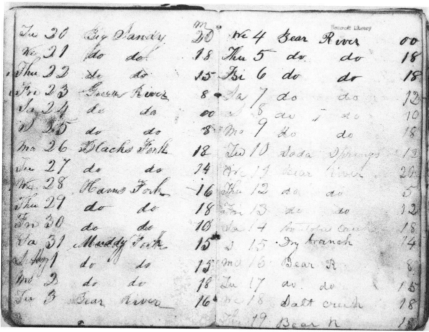

Pages 5–8 of the chronology of the overland trip kept by Nicholas "Cheyenne" Dawson. (*Courtesy Bancroft Library*)

Fr 9	do do	15
Sa 10	do do	10
S 11	do do	00
Mo 12	do do	6
Tu 13	do do	10
We 14	do do	10
Th 15	do do	5
Fr 16	do do	10
Sa 17	[smeared]	5
S 18	Little Sandy	25
Mo 19	Big Sandy	15
Tu 20	Big Sandy	20
We 21	do do	18
Th 22	do do	15
Fr 23	Green River	8
Sa 24	do do	00
S 25	do do	8
Mo 26	Blacks Fort	18
Tu 27	do do	14
We 28	Hams Fork	16
Th 29	do do	18
Fr 30	do do	10
Sa 31	Muddy Fork	15

[August]

S 1	do do	15
Mo 2	do do	18
Tu 3	Bear River	16
We 4	Bear River	00
Th 5	do do	18
Fr 6	do do	18
Sa 7	do do	12
S 8	do do	10
Mo 9	do do	18
Tu 10	Soda Springs	12
We 11	Bear River	20
Th 12	do do	5
Fr 13	do do	12
Sa 14	Antelope Creek	18
S 15	Dry branch	14
Mo 16	Bear R[iver]	8

Tu 17	do do	15
We 18	Salt creek	18
Th 19	Bear R[iver]	18
Fr 20	Bear R[iver]	00
Sa 21	Salt well	15
S 22	do do	00
Mo 23	Sulphur Spring	18
Tu 24	Salt Spring	12
We 25	do do	00
Th 26	Prairie	25
Fr 27	Good Spring	5
Sa 28	do do	00
S 29	do do	00
Mo 30	do do	00
Tu 31	do do	00

[September]

We 1	do do	00
Th 2	do do	00
Fr 3	do do	00
Sa 4	do do	00
S 5	Cedar	7
Mo 6	Antelope branch	9
Tu 7	Birch run	8
We 8	Indian Creek	15
Th 9	[scratched out]	00
Fr 10	[scratched out]	15
Sa 11	Rabbit spring	15
S 12	Mountain spring	12
Mo 13	Salt plains	18
Tu 14	Prairie	25
We 15	Packing camp	15
Th 16	do do	00
Fr 17	Dry Cedar	25
Sa 18	Mountain branch	12
S 19	[scratched out]	20
Mo 20	Clear branch	15
Tu 21	Squaw branch	15
We 22	S[outh] fork of M[ary's River]	18
Th 23	do do	20

Fr 24	Canian camp	15
Sa 25	lay by	00
S 26	Marys R[iver]	20
Mo 27	do do	25
Tu 28	do do	25
We 29	do do	15
Th 30	do do	20

[October]

Fr 1	do do	20
Sa 2	do do	25
S 3	do do	12
Mo 4	do do	25
Tu 5	Marys R[iver]	30
We 6	do do	00
Th 7	Slough	30
Fr 8	Lake	25
Sa 9	Lake	15
S 10	Unknown R[iver]	25
Mo 11	Mountain	15
Tu 12	do do	15
We 13	Canian R[iver]	20
Th 14	do do	20
Fr 15	do do	20
Sa 16	do do	20
S 17	mountain	15
Mo 18	California water	15
Tu 19	do do	15
We 20	Canian [River]	2
Th 21	mountain	15
Fr 22	do do	15
Sa 23	River	5
S 24	mountain	12
Mo 25	do do	8
Tu 26	Rainy camp	5
We 27	mountain	5
Th 28	Badger camp	15
Fr 29	mountain	15
Sa 30	Plains	20

[November]

S 1	Hunting camp	10
Mo 2	do do	00
Tu 3	Camp of Grapes	8
We 4	Pass of River	25
Th 5	John Marsh	25
Fr 6	do do	00
Sa 7	Lost Camp	10
S 8	Fandango	15
Mo 9	Pueblo [San Jose]	15

Nov. 20th went to the Redwoods where I continued making shingles until the 10th of May [1843] when I went to Monterey where I continued keeping store until the 16th of June when I went to Sta [Santa] Cruz when I continued until the 12th of June 1843 keeping store.

This manuscript is in the Brancroft Library and is published herein by permission.

1841 Emigrant Public Meeting

The following excerpt from an anonymous article titled, "California and Oregon," first appeared in the Colonial Magazine, *V (1841): 229–236.*

On the 1st of February, 1841, a public meeting was held in Independence, a frontier town of Missouri, at which fifty-eight persons volunteered to leave that state for Upper California, nineteen of whom will take their families with them. Among other resolutions, the meeting passed the following remarkable ones: —

"Resolved, That our object in going there is that of peace and good will towards the people and government of California, and our principal inducement for emigrating to that country, is, that we believe it, from the best information we have been able to procure, to be more congenial to our interests and enjoyment than that of our present location.

"Further Resolved, That as this company wishes to co-operate with all others that may design to emigrate to California the ensuing spring, it is recommended that all companies and individuals intending to so emigrate, rendezvous at the Sappling [sic] Grove on the old Santa Fé route, about nine miles west of the Missouri State line, against the 10th of May next, in which time and place they request the concurrence of all other companies and individuals.

"Further Resolved, That inasmuch as other companies are expected to join them, the election of the officers to conduct the expedition to be deferred till the general rendezvous.

"Further Resolved, That all persons, either single or having families, shall be provided with a sufficiency of provisions and other necessaries to insure them against want, till they reach the Buffalo region at least, which shall be determined at the general rendezvous.

"Further Resolved, That no person shall be permitted to take any spirituous liquors, except for medical purposes, and this shall be determined by the company at the general rendezvous.

"Further Resolved, That a cannon having been presented to the company and thankfully accepted, Mr. A. Overton be selected to have it properly equipped, and amply supplied with ammunition, at the expense of the company.

"Further Resolved, That Marsh's route is believed to be the best by which to cross the mountains."

This early notice of the planned emigration to California was subsequently picked up by Chambers' Edinburgh Journal, *No. 498 (August 14, 1841): 245, cls. 1 and 2, under the title "Emigration from Missouri to California." The anonymous author commenced by writing:*

That extraordinary spirit of enterprise which animates the Anglo-Saxon race in America, and lately gave them possession of Texas, is now urging them to make a new inroad on the miserably mismanaged territory of the Spanish Americas; and that they will be successful, we have not the smallest doubt. The enterprise, as we learn by a paper in the *Colonial Magazine* for last June, first assumed a determined aspect at a public meeting held on the 1st of February 1841, in Independence, a frontier town of Missouri. At this assemblage fifty-eight persons volunteered to leave Missouri for Upper California, nineteen of whom were to have families with them. The resolutions passed on the occasion were extremely pacific, pointing simply to peaceful emigration to California; but it is evident that a cause of quarrel and political dispossession would not be long wanting, and that a new independent government and nation would be the result. . . .

This opening paragraph was followed by a reprinting of the resolutions as given above in the Colonial Magazine *with one minor difference; the introductory phrase, "Further Resolved," is omitted.*

The article concludes with this pointed paragraph:

As nothing has been heard to the contrary, it may be supposed that this daring band of emigrants, like a swarm from the parent hive, is now on its way through the defiles of the rocky Mountains, and will speedily settle down on the coast of the Pacific, California, to which the enterprise tends, is a large and fertile region on the Pacific, and then Anglicised, will develop immense resources both as respects productiveness and trade. At no distant date it will be the great seat of traffic between Canton and other Asiatic parts, and the United States of America. It will be interesting to watch the manner in which these expectations are realized.

Announcing the Arrival of the Emigrants in California

John Marsh to Señor Don Antonio Suñol

Rancho de Pulpunes
Oct. [*sic*] 5, 1841

Señor Sub-Prefect

Yesterday there arrived at this point thirty-one men and a woman and child from the state of Missouri, with the intention of settling in California, and with this purpose I give information of their arrival.

They ask that your honor will concede them the favor of allowing them to rest for some days from the fatigues of such a long journey, and later they will give notice of their intention to become Mexican citizens in conformity with the law. They are the following:

Robert Rickman	M. Walton
John Bartelson [*sic*]	Ambrose Walton
John Bidwell	G. McMahan
George Henshaw	Nelson McMahan
T. H. Green	John McDowell
Charles Hopper	B. H. Thomas [*sic*]
J. P. Springer	Andrew Kelsey
A. G. Patton	Benjamin Kelsey,
N. Dawson	wife and family
J. Belden	V. W. Dawson
D. W. Chandler	William Belty
John L. Schwart	Thomas Jones
H. L. Brolaski	Henry Hubber [*sic*]
Michael C. Nye	Joseph B. Childs [*sic*]
Elias Barnett	Grove Cook
	James John [added later]
	Charles Waver [*sic*]
	John Roland

Hoping that I have fulfilled my duty, I am with respect
Your servant, John Marsh, who kisses your hands
To Senor Don Antonio Suñol, Sub-Prefect of the jurisdiction of San Jose.
Vallejo Document, X: 300, Bancroft Library. It is erroneously dated October but should read November.

The Commandante-General [Mariano Vallejo] to Don J. Marsh
Office of the Commandante-General

A number of foreigners having arrived in the country from Missouri without legal international documents, and having declared that their coming was in consequence of an invitation that was given them, it comes necessary for you to come to this place [San Jose] for the purpose of giving the required reports and declarations with the greatest possible promptness concerning those individuals and their claims.

November 11, 1841

1841, November 11. The Commandte-General to Don J. Marsh. It is ordered that he present himself at the Commandte's office to give information, since it has been learned that the foreigners came from Missouri were invited by him.

Señor Don J. Marsh

Vallejo Document, X: 335, Bancroft Library.

BOND EXECUTED FOR ALL THE PURPOSES OF THE LAW BY DR. JOHN MARSH, CITIZEN OF THAT PLACE (SAN JOSE), IN FAVOR OF THE INDIVIDUALS OF THE EXPEDITION FROM MISSOURI WHOSE NAMES ARE SEEN IN THIS SAME BOND.

I, the undersigned doctor of medicine and proprietary citizen settled in this jurisdiction declare:

That I constitute myself, freely and spontaneously, surety for the fifteen individuals of the expedition from Missouri, whose names follow:

Robert Rickman
John Bartleson
T. H. Green
A. G. Patten [*sic*]
D. W. Chandler
Michael C. Nye
Elias Barnett
John McDowal [*sic*]
Andrew Kelsey
Benjamin Kelsey
   and family
Joseph B. Childs [*sic*]
Grove Cook
S. J. McMahan [*sic*]
M. Walton

I stand surety for all these, and oblidge myself to present them before the civil or military authorities whenever required. This surety will last until the individuals named become legally interned in the country or evacuate it, according as the governor may dispose. In the meantime I guarantee that their conduct will not be subversive of public order and tranquility; and in case it should not be so, I oblidge myself to place them at the disposition of justice, to do with them as may be best.

John Marsh

Vallejo Documents, X: 340, Bancroft Library.

Two Letters From John Bidwell
and One From Mrs. Bidwell

The following letters written by John Bidwell in 1891 and 1892 and by his wife in 1902 to Nicholas Dawson are published by permission of the Bancroft Library.

Chino, Cal[ifornia]
Dec[ember] 20, 1891

Dear Mr Nicholas Dawson
Austin, Texas

Your very welcome letter of 12th instant is received, and, I assure you, it takes me entirely by surprise. You were very kind indeed to write me. Our party of 1841 are now few and far between. Besides yourself and myself I know of but two others, namely (now living), Michael C. Nye who lives in Oregon, and Josiah Belden who lives in New York City. Belden is very rich — Nye is not rich, but quite well off I think. But I have not seen him for ten years or more. Saw Mr Belden about five years ago. There may be others of our party alive that I do not know of — Do you know of any others? If so please tell me about them for I shall be glad to hear from them. Mrs Benjamin Kelsey, the only woman in our party after our separation at Soda Fountain, was living at Los Angeles in this State about three or four years ago, and may be alive now; but I have not seen her since 1843 — when she and her husband were on their way up this valley (Sacramento) to Oregon.

As to myself I have lived in California (with the exception of two years that I was in Congress, and a few visits East, and a short trip or two to Europe) — now over fifty years.

Please, write me, for I shall be very anxious to hear from you. My business is farming, but we raise a large amount of fruit as well as grain and other products. What may I ask is your occupation? What political party do you belong to? As to myself I am a Prohibitionist — have lost all faith in the old parties — they are corrupt — non-progressive — controlled by the liquor and foreign vote. I believe in progress — that Americans should rule this country — that all the corrupt rings and monopolies must be overthrown — and that woman should be given the ballot.

Yours very sincerely
John Bidwell

San Francisco
Aug[ust] 12, 1892

Dear friend
Nicholas Dawson
Austin, Texas

I have received your kind letter of July 31st—also your photograph, for which please accept my thanks. Herewith please find photograph of myself— Our friend, Josiah Belden, died April 23rd last, age 76 years, 11 months and 19 days. Talbot H. Green (Paul Geddes) died June 30, 1889, at his home in Lewisburg, Pa. aged 79 years. His life was a most remarkable one, but I have not time to write more. I have on my hands letters by the hundred. Of our party of 1841, yourself, M. C. Nye and myself are the only ones living so far as I know. Nye lives in Oregon and his address is, "Michael C. Nye, Prineville, Cook Co., Oregon." But I think I gave you his address in a former letter. Please pardon my haste and believe me

Yours very sincerely
John Bidwell

Unfortunately, Dawson's letters to Bidwell have yet to come to light, that is, if they survive at all. These two letters by Bidwell were presented to the Bancroft Library by Dawson's daughter along with a brief biographical sketch she prepared of her father. Also included in the gift was a letter to Dawson from Mrs. John Bidwell. Extracts of that letter germane to the above two letters follows.

Rancho Chino, Cal[ifornia]
Aug[ust] 30, 1901

Dear Mr Dawson

Your interesting and valued gift of your reminiscences of California and Texas came to hand while I was in the Sierras, not far from Lassen Butte, camping, and would have been acknowledged immediately had I been able to write. . . . Even now I can not write all I wish . . . but I hope to be able to express in some measure at least my heartfelt thanks for your gift as also a deep sense of reverence in reading of the bravery of those early days. . . . . I wish my husband had had the pleasure of seeing them [his memoirs]. . . . The incidents to which you refer regarding my husband have been told me by him, and just as related in your memoirs. . . .

Gratefully yours,
Annie K. Bidwell

Bibliography

MANUSCRIPTS
Bancroft Library, University of California, Berkeley:
　　Adele Ogden, "Trading Vessels on the California Coast, 1786–1848." [Typed Mss.]
　　John Bidwell, "Early California Reminiscences." [1877 dictation for H. H. Bancroft.]
　　Nicholas Dawson Mss.
　　Charles Hopper, "Narrative of Charles Hopper a California Pioneer of 1841 written by R. T. Montgomery at Napa 1871." [1871 dictation for H. H. Bancroft.]
　　Thomas O. Larkin Papers [unpublished Mss.]
　　Alexander Taylor, Scrapbook No. 7 (2 vols.): "Discoverers and Founders of California," 1: 27.
　　Mariano Guadalupe Vallejo Papers ["Documentos para la Historia de California."]
California Historical Society Library, San Francisco:
　　Biography and Obituaries Scrapbooks
California State Library, Sacramento:
　　John Bidwell Papers
　　Biographical Information File
　　John A. Sutter Collection
Henry E. Huntington Library, San Marino:
　　George and Helen Beattie Papers
　　Fort Sutter Papers
　　Dale L. Morgan, "The Mormons and the Far West." [Newspaper Transcripts]
　　Mariano Guadalupe Vallejo Papers
Other Repositories:
　　Diary of James John. Oregon Historical Society, Portland
　　Diary of James John. Rosenbach Museum and Library, Philadelphia

PRINTED PRIMARY SOURCES
Anonymous, "A California Heroine [Recollections of Mrs. Benjamin A. Kelsey]," *The Grizzly Bear Magazine,* XVI (February 1915): 6–7.
Anonymous, "California and Oregon," *Colonial Magazine,* V (1841): 229–236.

Anonymous, "[Western Emigrant Society Resolutions]," *Chambers Journal,* X (August 21, 1841): 245

Belden, Josiah, "The First Overland Emigrant Train to New California," *Touring Topics,* 22 (July 1930): 14–18, 56.

Bidwell, John, *A Journey to California, with Observations about the Country, Climate and the Route to this Country.* . . . [Independence, Liberty, or Weston [?], Missouri], 184[?]. Under the same title, an edition was published by John H. Nash in San Francisco, 1937. Introduction by Herbert I. Priestly.

———, *A Journey to California, 1841. The first emigrant party to California by wagon train. The Journal of John Bidwell.* Introduction by Francis P. Farquhar. Berkeley, 1964. (A facsimilie of the item above, the only known copy in the Bancroft Library, is reproduced in this printing of Bidwell's *Journal.*)

———, "Early California Reminiscences [Dictated to O. B. Parkinson of Stockton, California]," *Out West,* XX (January 1904): 76–78; (February 1904): 182–188; (March 1904): 285–287; (April 1904): 377–379; (May 1904): 467–477; (June 1904): 559–562; XXI (July 1904): 79–80; (August 1904): 198–195. [This version was apparently the one which was republished in C[harles] C. Royce, *John Bidwell: Pioneer, Statesman, Philanthropist* (Chico, California, 1906).]

———, *Echoes of the Past.* Chico, California [c. 1914].

———, *Echoes of the Past.* Edited by Milo M. Quaife. Chicago, 1938. (Coupled with Rev. John Steele's *In Camp and Cabin.*) Reprinted under the same title in New York, 1962.

———, *In California Before the Gold Rush.* Introduction by Lindley Bynum. Los Angeles, 1948.

———, "The First Emigrant Train to California," *The American Progress Magazine,* [n.v.] (May 1910): 5–13. (Reprint of the article listed immediately below.)

———, "The First Emigrant Train to California," *The Century Illustrated Monthly Magazine,* XLI (November 1890): 106–130.

———, *The First Emigrant Train to California.* Introduction by Oscar Lewis. Palo Alto, California, 1966.

———, "Life in California Before the Gold Rush," *The Century Illustrated Monthly Magazine,* XLI (December 1890): 163–183.

———, *Life in California Before the Gold Rush.* Introduction by Oscar Lewis. Palo Alto, California, 1966.

———, "Frémont in the Conquest of California," *The Century Illustrated Monthly Magazine,* XLI (February 1890): 518–525.

Chittenden, Hiram M., and Alfred D. Richardson, eds., *Life, Letters and Travels of Father Pierre-Jean De Smet, S.J., 1801–1872.* 4 vols.; New York, 1905.

[Dawson, Nicholas], *Narrative of Nicholas "Cheyenne" Dawson (Overland to*

California in '41 ¿ '49, and Texas in '51. Introduction by Charles L. Camp. San Francisco, 1933.

De Smet, Pierre Jean, *Life and Sketches: With a Narrative of a Year's Residence Among the Indian Tribes of the Rocky Mountains.* Philadelphia, 1843.

Donnelly, Joseph P., trans. and ed., *Wilderness Kingdom: Indian Life in the Rocky Mountains: 1840–1847. The Journals & Paintings of Nicolas Point, S.J.* New York, 1967.

Ewer, John C., ed., *Adventures of Zenas Leonard, Fur Trapper.* Norman, Oklahoma, 1959.

Farnham, Thomas J., *Travels in California and Scenes in the Pacific Ocean.* New York, 1844. Reprint ed.; Oakland, California, 1947.

———, *Travels in the Great West Prairies. . . .* Poughkeepsie, New York, 1841.

Ferris, Warren A., *Life in the Rocky Mountains.* Edited by LeRoy R. Hafen. Rev. ed.; Denver, 1983.

Frémont, John C., *Report of the Exploring Expedition to the Rocky Mountains in the Year 1842, and to Oregon and North California in the Year 1843–44.* Washington, D.C., 1845.

Hafen, LeRoy R., and Ann W. Hafen, eds., *To the Rockies and Oregon, 1830–1843.* Glendale, California, 1955.

Hammond George P., ed., *The Larkin Papers.* 10 vols.; Berkeley and Los Angeles, 1961–1968.

Heath, Minnie B., "Nancy Kelsey—The First Pioneer Woman to Cross [the] Plains," *The Grizzly Bear Magazine,* XL (February 1937): 3, 7.

Himes, George H., ed., "The Diary of James St. John [James John]," St. John [Oregon] *Review,* March 16, 30; April 6, 13, 20, 27, 1906.

Irving, Jr., John T., *Indian Sketches Taken During an Expedition to the Pawnee Tribes.* Edited by John F. McDermott. Norman, Oklahoma, 1955.

McBride, J. R., "Recollections," *Tulledge's Quarterly,* 3 (1884): 311–320.

Mengarini, Gregory, *Recollections of the Flathead Mission. . . .* Translated and edited by Gloria R. Lothrop. Glendale, California, 1977.

Morgan, Dale L., and Eleanor T. Harris, eds., *The Rocky Mountain Journals of William Marshall Anderson.* San Marino, California, 1967.

New Helvetia Diary. A Record of Events Kept by John A. Sutter and His Clerks. . . . San Francisco, 1939.

Nunis, Jr., Doyce B., ed., *Josiah Belden, 1841 California Overland Pioneer: His Memoir and Early Letters.* Georgetown, California, 1962.

Partoll, Albert J., ed., "Mengarini's Narrative to the Rockies," *Frontier and Midland,* XVIII (1938): 193–202, 258–266. Reprinted in *Sources of Northwest History No. 25.* Missoula, Montana, n.d. Also in *Frontier Omnibus.* Edited by John W. Hakola. Missoula and Helena, Montana, 1962.

Royce, C[harles] C., comp., *Addresses, Reminiscences, etc., of General Bidwell.* Chico,

California, 1907. Includes the first reprinting of Bidwell's *Journal*.

———, *John Bidwell, Pioneer Stateman, Philanthropist, a Biographical Sketch*. Chico, California, 1906.

Shuck, Oscar T., comp., *California Scrap-Book: A Repository of Useful Information*. San Francisco, 1869.

Six French Letters [:] *Captain John Augustus Sutter to Jean Jacques Vioget, 1842–1843*. Sacramento, 1942.

Spence, Mary Lee and Donald Jackson, eds., *The Expeditions of John Charles Frémont*. 3 vols.; Urbana, Illinois, 1970–1984.

The Diary of Johann August Sutter. San Francisco, 1932.

Thwaites, Reuben G., ed., *Early Western Travels, 1748–1846*. 32 vols.; Cleveland, Ohio, 1904–1907. Reprint ed.; New York, 1966.

Wilbur, Marguerite E., ed., *Duflot de Mofras's Travels*. 2 vols.; Santa Ana, California, 1938.

Wilkes, Charles, *Columbia River to the Sacramento*. Oakland, 1948.

———, *Narrative of the U. S. Exploring Expedition*. 5 vols.; Philadelphia, 1844.

Williams, Joseph, *Narrative of a Tour from the State of Indiana to the Oregon Territory in the Years 1841–2*. Cincinnati, 1848. Reprint ed.; New York, 1921. Introduction by James C. Bell, Jr.

SECONDARY SOURCES

Adams, James T., ed., *Dictionary of American History*. Rev. ed., 5 vols.; New York, 1942.

Andrews, Thomas F., "The Controversial Hastings Overland Guide: A Reassessment," *Pacific Historical Review*, XXXVII (1968): 21–34.

Arbuckle, Clyde, "Grove C. Cook," *Westways*, 48 (December 1951): 19.

Argonauts of California. New York, 1890.

Bancroft, Hubert H., *History of California*. 7 vols.; San Francisco, 1884–1890.

Barrows, H. D., "Don David W. Alexander," *Annual Publication of the Historical Society of Southern California*, IV (1897): 43–45.

Burgess, Sherwood, "Lumbering in California," *California Historical Society Quarterly*, XLI (1962): 237–248.

Benjamin, Marcus, *John Bidwell, Pioneer. A Sketch of His Career*. Washington, D.C., 1907.

Caughey, John W., *California*. Rev. ed.; Englewood Cliffs, New Jersey, 1959.

Cleland, Robert G., *A History of California: The American Period*. New York, 1922.

———, *From Wilderness to Empire*. New York, 1944.

———, *This Reckless Breed of Men: The Trappers and Fur Traders of the Southwest*. New York, 1950.

Concise Dictionary of American Biography. New York, 1946.

Cowan, Robert E., and Robert G. Cowan, comps., *A Bibliography of the History* of California. Reprint ed.; Los Angeles, 1933.

Du Four, Clarence C., "The Russian Withdrawal from California," *California Historical Society Quarterly,* XII (1933): 240–278.

Engelhardt, Zephyrin, *Missions and Missionaries of California.* 4 vols.; Santa Barbara, 1908–1915.

Frazer, Robert, *Forts of the West.* Norman, Oklahoma, 1965.

Garragan, Gilbert J., *The Jesuits of the Middle United States.* 3 vols.; New York, 1938.

Geiger, Maynard, *Franciscan Missionaries in Hispanic California, 1769–1848.* San Marino, California, 1969.

Giffen, Helen S., *Trail-Blazing Pioneer: Colonel Joseph Ballinger Chiles.* San Francisco, 1949.

Gudde, Erwin S., *California Place Names.* Rev. ed.; Berkeley and Los Angeles, 1969.

Hafen, LeRoy R., *Broken Hand: The Life Story of Thomas Fitzpatrick, Chief of the Mountain Men.* Reprint ed.; Denver, 1973.

———, "Early Fur Trade Posts on the South Platte." *Mississippi Valley Historical Review,* XII (1925): 334–341.

———, "Fraeb's Last Fight and How Battle Creek Got Its Name," *Colorado Magazine,* XII (1930): 97–101.

———, ed., *The Mountain Men and the Fur Trade of the Far West.* 10 vols.; Glendale, California, 1965–1972.

Hall, Frederic, *The History of San Jose and Surroundings, With Biographical Sketches of Early Settlers.* San Francisco, 1871.

Hammond, George P., and Dale L. Morgan, *Charles M. Weber: Pioneer of San Joaquin and Founder of Stockton, California.* Berkeley, 1966.

Hart, James D., comp., *A Companion to California.* Rev. ed.; Berkeley and Los Angeles, 1987.

Heizer, Robert F., ed., *California,* Vol. 8 in the *Handbook of North American Indians.* Edited by William G. Sturtevant. Washington, D.C., 1978.

Hill, Joseph J., "Antoine Robidoux, Kingpin in the Colorado River Fur Trade, 1824–1844," *Colorado Magazine,* VII (1930): 125–132.

Hunt, Rockwell D., *John Bidwell, Prince of California Pioneers.* Caldwell, Idaho, 1942.

Hussey, John A., *Fort Vancouver.* Portland, Oregon [1957].

———, "New Light Upon Talbot H. Green as Revealed in His Letters and Other Sources," *California Historical Society Quarterly,* XVIII (1939): 32–63.

Irving, Washington, *The Adventures of Captain Bonneville, U.S.A.* Edited by Edgeley W. Todd. Norman, Oklahoma, 1961.

Johnson, Allen, and Dumas Malone, eds., *Dictionary of American Biography.* 20 vols.; New York, 1920–1937.

Lamar, Howard R., ed., *The Reader's Encyclopedia of the American West.* New York, 1977.

Lawrence, Eleanor, "Mexican Trade Between Santa Fe and Los Angeles." *California Historical Society Quarterly,* X (1933): 27–39.

Lyman, George D., *John Marsh, Pioneer.* New York, 1930.

McDermott, John F., "De Smet's Illustrator: Father Nicholas Point," *Nebraska History,* XXXIII (1952): 35–40.

McKittrick, Myrtle M., *Vallejo, Son of California.* Portland, Oregon, 1944.

Menefee, C[ampbell] A., *Historical and Descriptive Sketch Book of Napa, Sonoma, Lake and Mendocino. . . .* Napa City, California, 1878.

Miller, David E., "The First Wagon Train to Cross Utah, 1841," *Utah Historical Quarterly,* XXX (1962): 41–51.

Moody, Ralph, *The Old Trails West.* N.p., 1963.

Morgan, Dale L., *The Humboldt, Highway of the West.* New York, 1943.

———, *Jedediah Smith and the Opening of the West.* Indianapolis and New York, 1953.

Mumey, Nolie, *The Life of Jim Baker.* Denver, 1931.

Munro-Fraser, J. P., *History of Santa Clara County.* San Francisco, 1881.

Nunis, Jr., Doyce B., "The Fur Men: Key to Westward Expansion," *The Historian,* XXIII (1961): 167–190.

———, *The Trials of Isaac Graham.* Los Angeles, 1967.

Paden, Irene D., *The Wake of the Prairie Schooner.* New York, 1943.

Parke-Barnet Galleries, *The Celebrated Collection of Americana Formed by the Late Thomas W. Streeter.* 7 vols., New York, 1966–1969.

Phelps, Alonzo, *Contemporary Biography of California's Representative Men.* 2 vols.; San Francisco, 1881–1882.

Shuck, Oscar T., *Sketches of Leading and Representative Men of San Francisco.* San Francisco, 1875.

Sommervogel, Carlos, ed., *Biblioteque de la Compagnie de Jesus.* 11 vols.; Brussels and Paris, 1890–1912.

Soulé, Frank, *et al., The Annals of San Francisco.* New York, 1854.

Stewart, George R., *The California Trail.* New York, 1962.

Sunder, John E., *Bill Sublette, Mountain Man.* Norman, Oklahoma. 1959.

Swartzlow, Ruby J., "Peter Lassen, Northern California Trail Blazer," *California Historical Society Quarterly,* XVIII (1939): 291–314.

Tehama County, California. . . . San Francisco, 1880.

Terrell, John B., *Black Robe: The Life of Pierre-Jean De Smet.* Garden City, New York, 1964.

Tobie, H. E., "From the Missouri to the Columbia, 1841," *Oregon Historical Quarterly,* XXXVIII (1937): 135–159.

Ulsh, Emile J., "Doctor John Marsh, California Pioneer, 1836–1856," Master's Thesis, University of California, Berkeley, 1934.

Unruh, Jr., John D., *The Plains Across: The Overland Emigrants and the Trans-*

*Mississippi West, 1840–*1860. Urbana, Illinois, 1979.

Wagner, Henry R. and Charles L. Camp, comps., *The Plains & the Rockies: A Bibliography*. . . . . Edited by Robert H. Becker. San Francisco, 1982.

Wallace, William S., *Antoine Robidoux.* Los Angeles, 1953.

Weber, Francis J., comp., *The Penultimate Mission: A Documentary History of the San Rafael Arcangel.* Los Angeles, 1983.

Wilbur, Margurite E., *John Sutter, Rascal and Adventurer.* New York, 1949.

Winther, Oscar O., *The Great Northwest.* 2nd ed., New York, 1950.

NEWSPAPERS

Blue Lake *Advocate,* June 13, 20, 1957.

Napa County *Reporter,* March 23, 1872.

Napa *Register,* March 15, 1872.

New York *Tribune,* April 25, 1892.

Niles Register, August 15, 1840; May 22, September 11, October 16, 1841; January 28, February 11, 1843.

Oakland *Tribune,* September 27, 1925.

Sacramento *Transcript,* May 21, 1850.

Sacramento *Union,* April 25, 1892.

St. Louis *Daily Missouri Republican,* April 20, May 19, September 28, 1841.

St. Louis *Missouri Argus,* June 26, 1840.

St. Louis *Missouri Intellegencer,* October 9, 1830.

San Francisco *Alta California,* February 8, 1849; February 1, 1852; March 28, April 15, 1866.

San Francisco *Call,* April 24, June 19, 1892.

San Francisco *Chronicle,* June 12, 1856.

San Francisco *Evening Bulletin,* June 27, 1868.

San Francisco *Examiner,* February 5, 1893.

San Jose *Tribune,* July 15, 23, 1856.

Index

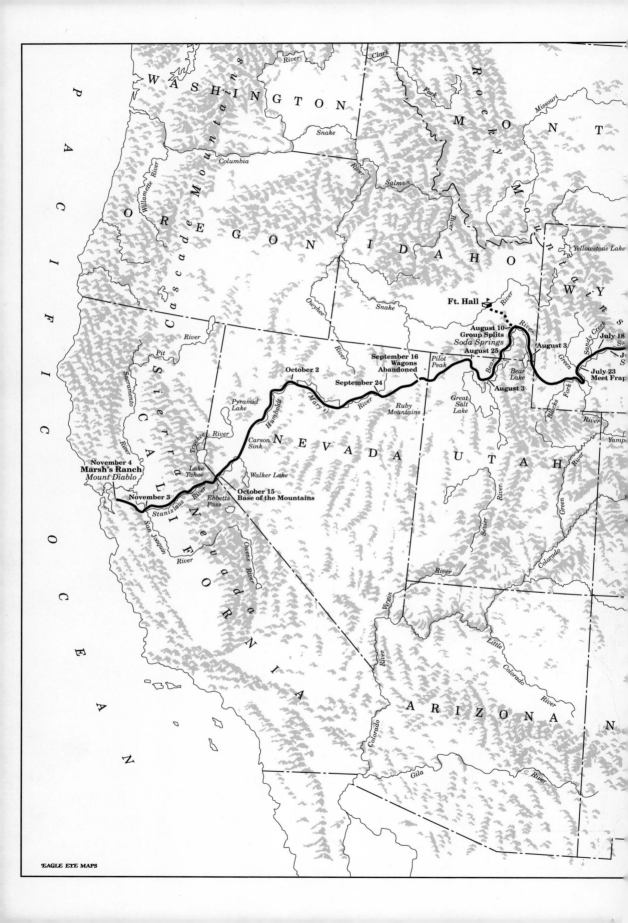